FROM TOURISM ATTRACTIONS TO HERITAGE TOURISM

SECOND EDITION

D1344911

From

Tourist Attractions

to

Heritage Tourism

Second Edition

Pat Yale

Copyright Pat Yale, 1990, 1991, 1997

This Second Edition of From Tourist Attractions to Heritage Tourism is published January, 1998 by ELM Publications, Seaton House, Kings Ripton, Huntingdon PE17-2NJ. Tel. 01487-773238. It is printed by St. Edmundsbury Press of Bury St. Edmunds and bound by Woolnough Bookbinding of Irthlingborough.

British Library Cataloguing in Publication Data
Yale, Pat. 1954 -
   From tourist attractions to heritage tourism.
   1. Tourism   2. Great Britain
   I. Title
   338.479141

   ISBN - 0185450-189-5

ABOUT THE AUTHOR

Pat Yale studied history at Newnham College, Cambridge. Following holiday jobs in Gunnersbury Museum and the Council for Places of Worship and several seasons of archaeological digging, she started work as a travel agent for Thomas Cook Ltd. She then became an agency trainer for American Express Travel. After a period as an associate lecturer in travel and tourism at Soundwell College in Bristol, teaching on the BTEC National Travel and Tourism course, she became a freelance travel writer.

CONTENTS

LIST OF FIGURES

INTRODUCTION

Visitor attractions lie at the heart of the leisure tourism industry; without them there would be little point in anyone travelling and no need for the various accommodation and transport undertakings that make up the industry. However, while many guidebooks and gazetteers describe individual attractions, less has been written about the overall attractions industry. This book attempts to fill that gap and is particularly aimed at teachers and lecturers involved with travel and tourism courses up to degree level. Students may also find it helpful, as may people working in the industry itself and in tourist offices and information centres around the country.

The term 'tourist attractions' covers sites as diverse as national parks and stately homes. For convenience of discussion I have divided them into narrower categories than those usually used by the tourists boards. Even so there is considerable overlap between the chapters. Although I have chosen to treat them as 'miscellaneous historical attractions', many heritage centres could as easily have been considered in the chapters on museums or industrial heritage. Steam railways and canals are clearly part of the industrial heritage. However, I have dealt with them separately because the business of running a preserved railway or canal is very different from that of presenting a disused mill to the public. The chapter on heritage marketing is not an introduction to marketing concepts, a job well done by other excellent books already on the market. Instead it examines specific ways of marketing attractions.

Dealing with the UK's many attractions was job enough, without considering those in the rest of the world as well. However, it would be senseless to discuss theme parks without mentioning the pioneering parks in the USA, or to consider wildlife attractions while excluding the African game parks. In the book I have also tried to show that change is as important a theme in the attractions industry as elsewhere in tourism. Many of the ideas for change in heritage presentation originated outside the UK. So although in general the book focuses on Britain, occasionally it also ventures further afield.

My interest in tourist attractions as an industry rather than just as pleasant places to visit was first sparked by a Neal Ascherson review in *The Observer* which led me to Robert Hewison's *The Heritage Industry*. To this I am indebted for inspiration. I am also grateful to the English, Scottish, Wales and Northern Ireland Tourist Boards for providing many of the statistics from which I have worked. Help has also come from press and information officers too many to name individually. I am immensely grateful to all of them. It goes without saying that errors in interpreting the information they supplied are mine alone. I would also like to thank my publisher, Sheila Ritchie, for her patience as I pieced together this second edition.

The most striking change since the first edition was published in 1991 has been the arrival of the National Lottery which looks set to transform the heritage industry in ways which are only just becoming apparent. With luck, by the time a third edition is mooted, the rules will have been changed to allow lottery funding of revenue as well as capital costs. Britain may then move into the next millennium with a matchless array of visitor attractions.

POST-1997 ELECTION NOTES

The change in government in 1997 occurred too late in the production service for its effects to be considered in the text. However, the new Labour government has indicated that in general it is in favour of free access to museums which could therefore see a brake put on the steady introduction of charges. It has also changed the name of the Department of National Heritage to the Department of Culture, Media and Sport.

A new regional museum premier league should see more money directed towards the most important local collections.

At the time of writing it seemed likely that Loch Lomond would eventually become Scotland's first national park.

CHAPTER 1 :
FROM TOURIST ATTRACTIONS TO HERITAGE TOURISM

Tourism is a boom industry in Great Britain. In 1995 22 million overseas visitors spent £12 million in the UK, while domestic holidaymakers spent a further £12,775 million on tourist activities (excluding day trips) within the country. Figures for both numbers of visitors and their expenditure have risen steadily since the blip caused by the Gulf War in 1991.

Despite the spectacularly hot summer of 1995, the British climate generally has none of the appeal that turned countries round the Mediterranean into holiday paradises. Nor does the UK boast the palm-fringed beaches and warm seas that guarantee the Caribbean its tourist trade. Instead it is unusually dependent on a range of so-called tourist attractions to bring in its visitors; in 1995 the Overseas Visitor Survey showed that 62% of respondents had visited museums, 73% historic properties, 67% churches and cathedrals and 56% gardens open to the public during their stay. In 1995 theBritish Tourist Authority (BTA) estimated that more than 50 million people visited a tourist attraction in Britain, with a total of 392 million visits in all. In the course of those visits over £1,100 million was spent, about half coming from admission charges, the rest from catering, the sale of souvenirs, etc.

WHAT ARE TOURIST ATTRACTIONS?

Tourist attractions could be defined as all those things that draw visitors to particular places, but such a vague definition is effectively meaningless. Instead, in *Marketing for Travel and Tourism* Victor Middleton defines a tourist attraction as 'any designated permanent resource which is controlled and managed for the enjoyment, amusement, entertainment and education of the visiting public'. The British Tourist Authority (BTA) prefers to use the term visitor attraction which it defines as 'a permanently established excursion destination, a primary purpose of which is to allow public access for entertainment, interest or education, rather than being principally a retail outlet or a venue for sporting, theatrical or film performances. It must be open to the public without prior booking for published periods each year, and should be capable of attracting tourists or day visitors as well as local residents.'

However, both definitions raise some questions:

- Not all attractions are *designated*. Historical monuments like Stonehenge may well be, but empty beaches and the sun and sea that draw visitors to many resorts are not. Designation implies enclosure and not all attractions are enclosed.

- Nor are all attractions *permanent*. An event attraction like the Changing of the Guard can be described as regular, but it is not permanent; you can visit London and miss it because of the timing of your visit.

- In an increasingly commercially-minded world most tourist attractions are certainly *controlled and managed*; even Land's End now boasts a theme park. Nevertheless the climate is the main attraction in many parts of the world and certainly can't be managed, although the increasing number of all-weather playgrounds in the UK, like the Center Parcs complexes with their constant 29° Centigrade temperatures, represent an attempt to control and manage even the intrinsically uncontrollable.

- Most sports, shopping and entertainment facilities fit as neatly as Madame Tussaud's and the Tower of London into Middleton's definition of tourist attractions, even though they should more properly be seen as part of the wider leisure industry. In contrast the BTA definition specifically excludes theatres which are important tourist attractions in London and New York.

In *Sightseeing in 1995* the English Tourist Board subdivides tourist attractions into historic properties, museums and galleries, wildlife attractions, gardens, country parks, farms, visitor centres, workplaces, steam railways, leisure parks and 'other' attractions. However, these categories are still very broad; although royal palaces and archaeological sites are certainly both types of historic property, they tend to appeal to different market sectors, as do vineyards and 'edutainment' centres like the Granada Studios Tour which are lumped together as 'other' attractions despite their differences. Narrower subdivisions have therefore been used in this book.

Although there is considerable overlap between the leisure and tourism industries, this book is primarily concerned with those attractions usually thought of as part of the pure tourism industry. In general it treats as true tourist attractions only things likely to persuade someone to travel away from their home town. This excludes local sports centres, shops and entertainment facilities.

CATEGORIES OF TOURIST ATTRACTION

Tourist attractions are often subdivided according to distinguishing features. This can be done in several ways:

- The simplest distinction can be made between *indoor* and *outdoor attractions*. Indoor attractions include historic buildings (castles, palaces, stately homes), museums, art galleries and theatres. Outdoor attractions include zoos, safari parks, parks, gardens, archaeological sites and permanent funfairs like Blackpool Pleasure Beach.

- A further distinction can be made between *man-made* and *natural attractions*. Man-made attractions include buildings like castles and museums but also archaeological sites and permanent funfairs. Natural attractions include beaches, mountains, rivers and other beauty spots. However, very few natural attractions remain completely natural. For example, the East African game parks are clearly 'natural' in origin, but the hotels, tented camps and restaurants that enable people to visit them are obviously man-made (see Chapter 10).

- A third division is between *site* and *event attractions*. Site attractions are all those, whether man-made or natural, indoor or outdoor, that are permanent and fixed to one spot. Event attractions are phenomena that may occur in the same place at a regular time each year but which are only ever temporary and could, at least in theory, move to a different site. Some event attractions draw just as many people as famous site attractions like Blenheim Palace. Examples are the Chelsea Flower Show, the Edinburgh Festival and the Lord Mayor's Show (see Chapter 12).

- The English, Scottish and Northern Ireland Tourist Boards also subdivide attractions into those with *admission charges* and those that are *free* (see Fig.1/1).

- A final distinction is sometimes drawn between *nodal* and *linear attractions*. Nodal attractions are those which form the focus for a staying visit: the Roman Baths Museum in Bath, for example. In contrast linear attractions tend to be visited in a series of touring stops. The Cotswold villages, the wool' churches of East Anglia and theScottish whisky distilleries are good examples.

BRITISH TOURIST ATTRACTIONS IN THE 1990s

In 1995 Britain was estimated to have 5,818 definable tourist attractions, 4,316 of them in England, 955 in Scotland, 342 in Wales and 205 in Northern Ireland.

The highest density of attractions relative to area is in London (248), the South-East (513) and the North-West (296). Relative to population they are most densely concentrated in the West Country (625) and Cumbria (138).

Forty per cent of attractions offer free admission and receive 54% of all visits. Seven per cent receive 57% of all visits (216,580,000 people).

WHAT MAKES A TOURIST ATTRACTION SUCCESSFUL?

However enticing an attraction, it will only achieve large visitor figures if it is also easily accessible and supplied with suitable amenities.

Accessibility

By 1995 the *Social Trends* survey showed that 69% of households in the UK had access to at least one car. Consequently access by road is generally more important for an attraction than access by public transport. overseas visitors also travel to attractions by coach which makes easy road access even more important. Ideally the attraction should be within an hour's drive of a motorway since journey time tends to dictate the catchment area for visitors. Roads in the immediate vicinity of the site must also be able to cope with the traffic generated and there must be adequate parking facilities (see below). When work began on Thorpe Park, Britain's first theme park, the Ready Mixed Concrete (RMC) Group plc paid for a new roundabout to improve access to the site. Advance signposts were also provided to route traffic away from Thorpe village. Free parking was laid on to prevent traffic bottlenecks forming as people queued to pay at the entrance. Today Thorpe Park has parking space for 8,000 cars and 250 coaches.

FIG.1/1: BRITAIN'S TOP TWENTY ATTRACTIONS IN 1995

Free Attractions		Attractions with Entry Charges	
1. Blackpool Pleasure Beach	7,300,000+	1. Alton Towers	2,707,000
2. British Museum, London	5,745,866	2. Madame Tussaud's	2,703,283
3. National Gallery, London	4,469,019	3. Tower of London	2,536,680
4. Strathclyde Country Park	4,150,000	4. Chessington World of Adventures	1,770,000
5. Palace Pier, Brighton	3,800,000	5. Science Museum, London	1,556,368
6. Funland & Laserbowl Trocadero	2,500,000	6. St Paul's Cathedral	1,500,000
7. Eastbourne Pier	2,300,000	7. Natural History Museum, London	1,442,591
8. Westminster Abbey	2,245,000	8. Windsor Castle	1,212,305
9. York Minster /Pleasure Beach, Great Yarmouth /Pleasureland, Southport	2,000,000	9. Blackpool Tower	1,205,000
10. Tate Gallery, London	1,769,662	10. Thorpe Park	1,166,000

(Source: British Tourist Authority)

However, in the 1990s as concern mounted about traffic pollution the National Trust opened Prior Park in Bath to the public without providing parking space. Visitors must walk to the park or use local buses.

Although the ideal site will be within easy reach of the main rail and bus networks, the Land's End theme park shows that a sufficiently appealing and well marketed attraction may be able to succeed when it doesn't match these requirements to the letter. Despite being at the westernmost tip of the UK, with no station and only a poor bus link, it still managed to draw 521,000 visitors in 1995, no doubt benefiting from being in the country's prime domestic tourism county and, perhaps, from a traditional British willingness to travel to leisure destinations. The existence of a hotel at the site also makes it possible for people to stay the night, encouraging visits from further afield.

In the *developed world* few potential attractions are completely cut off. In fact in some areas like parts of the Lake District access is having to be restricted to prevent visitors ruining the very peace and beauty they have come to experience by their sheer numbers. However, in the *developing world*, where the infrastructure frequently leaves much to be desired, otherwise promising sites can be prevented from fulfilling their potential as attractions by access problems. Dinder National Park in Sudan is the most northerly of the great African game parks. Since the plane that connected the park to Khartoum crashed outside its gates the only access has been by a long overland journey on the back of passing trucks. Not surprisingly hardly anyone goes to Dinder while some of Kenya's more accessible parks are overrun with safari vehicles. A similar problem confronts the Sepilok Orang-Utan Sanctuary in Sabah, Malaysia. While the orphaned orang-utans are guaranteed to appeal to visitors, the sanctuary is only accessible after a lengthy bus ride over terrible roads or by air which limits the number of people able to reach it. The provision of transport infrastructure is usually the task of central or local governments, so tourist attractions can be adversely or beneficially affected by decisions made in high places.

Opening Hours

All attractions need to open at times that suit their visitors. Consequently most are open at weekends, but may close on Monday or another week day when lower attendances could be expected. Traditionally most state-owned properties, including the national museums and art galleries, were closed on Sunday mornings. However, most newly-opened attractions treat Sunday as a normal working day.

At attractions where there is no attendant, including many English Heritage properties, visitors may be allowed into the site from dawn to dusk. Most cathedrals are also open from very early in the morning until dusk, as are those churches which are not kept locked.

Where there is an attendant attractions are usually open from 9am to 5pm or 6pm, with shorter opening hours in winter. Only half the attractions in the UK will be open in January, but some, like the large theme parks, open all year round, even on Christmas Day. Depending on the size of the attraction visitors may only be admitted until half an hour or an hour before closing time. The average attraction in England was open for 248 days in 1995; wildlife attractions were open for an average 297 days, 'other' attractions for 275, museums for 251, gardens for 219 and historic properties for 206.

Amenities

A tourist attraction needs many amenities in order to fulfil its potential. Some of these will be provided *on-site* (toilets, lifts, cafes, bookshops, restaurants, etc.) while others will be *off-site* (hotels, signposts, etc.).

The USA has led the way in showing what can be provided to make a visitor's stay enjoyable, and Disneyworld pioneered ideas like short-term camera loans. The UK quickly caught on, and most new tourist developments come equipped with lavatories with access for the disabled, mother and baby rooms, etc. The Thatcherite 'enterprise culture' also encouraged more imaginative attitudes. With most attractions under pressure to pay their way, profit-generating 'extras' like souvenir shops and restaurants became necessities; no museum worth its salt now lacks its cash-generating shop.

Inevitably poorer developing countries often suffer from a lack of amenities to encourage visitors. To return to Dinder, while there is comfortable '*banda*' (thatched hut) accommodation on-site, there is little running water for showers, let alone a shop or restaurant. Shortages of fuel and spare parts also mean there is rarely sufficient transport for visitors to explore the park. Sometimes even food is hard to find. In such circumstances it would be surprising if Dinder ever became more than a 'wishful thinking' attraction.

ON-SITE AMENITIES

Parking

Because so many visitors arrive at tourist attractions by car or coach providing adequate parking space is vitally important. Sometimes it is provided by the owner of the attraction, as at Beamish North of England Open-Air Museum, Thorpe Park and Alton Towers. However, sometimes the local authority provides it to prevent traffic jams forming; Housesteads, the most popular Roman fort on Hadrian's Wall, is owned by the National Trust but Durham County Council provides the car park.

Parking spaces are usually provided free to encourage people to use the official site rather than clogging up side streets. At Housesteads, however, there are 'honesty boxes' for people to pay a small charge. Where visitors might try to park away from official sites, ditches can be dug, low fences erected or boulders placed along the roadside to prevent illicit parking without marring the landscape with garish yellow lines.

Parking sites can be ugly. Ideally they should be screened from view by trees. Alternatively they can be positioned a little way away from the actual attraction. In that case it's sensible to try and make the route from car park to site as interesting as possible.

Since more space is usually needed in high season, it may be possible to lay gravel for parking over a relatively small area and then use adjacent fields in summer to reduce the impact on the scenery. Spaces for coaches need to be marked out, but it's best to let car drivers work out their own space rather than mark each area for the largest car likely to fill it, thereby wasting space for much of the time. At particularly busy sites car-park attendants are employed to direct drivers to empty spaces. Separate entrances and exits may also be needed for safety reasons.

Separate spaces (or car parks) near the entrance should be provided for disabled visitors. Supermarkets increasingly mark out spaces for parents with young children too. Expect tourist attractions to follow in their footsteps.

It would be possible to lose a car in the vast parking lots attached to Disneyworld and other American theme parks. To prevent that happening special tickets leave a space for marking the row and aisle where the car is parked.

Visitor Centres

Several factors ensure that most attractions now have visitor centres providing information to help tourists make more of their visits. Firstly, they are a good way to deal with the UK's unhelpful climate; visitor centres ensure there is somewhere for visitors to go when it rains. Secondly, with increasing pressure to charge for admission to attractions, visitor centres make it possible to levy a charge where previously there was none on the basis that better facilities and therefore value for money are being provided. This is often the case with countryside attractions where charging is particularly difficult; a Visitor Centre not only provides an 'excuse' for a charge but also a way of collecting it. Sometimes merely providing a centre makes it possible to turn a non-site into something interesting; for example, at Kittyhawk in the United States where the Wright Brothers first flew in a heavier-than-air machine in 1903 there would be nothing to draw visitors were it not for the centre.

Different centres offer different types of information. For example, the National Trust for Scotland visitor centre at Glencoe explains the historical background to the massacre associated with the site, while the one at Torridon concentrates on local wildlife. Others are more like glorified shops-cum-restaurants with all the revenue-generating extras brought together under one roof. They may also house essentials like lavatories, information desks, audio-visual displays and rangers' offices.

Sometimes humble buildings can be reused to provide visitor centres. Others are purpose-built. Siting is particularly important. Where it is to act as a ticket office the centre must be conspicuously positioned, preferably within easy reach of the car park. However, in the countryside or at an archaeological site it may be desirable to camouflage the building with trees to limit its impact on the scenery.

Deciding how large it should be may be difficult. Where coach parties are expected the centre will need to be big enough to accommodate sudden rushes of people, although that may mean it looking bleakly empty at other times. Clearly the bigger the building, the more it will cost both to build and operate. Where fewer visitors are expected a mobile centre may be appropriate; although this will not encourage visitors to linger and spend money it will be less obtrusive than a permanent building.

Ideally the centre should be designed so that the interpretive section is separate from the entrance and exit; then it won't become cluttered with people who don't want to read the information provided.

Of an estimated 425 visitor centres in the UK in 1995, 82% have opened since 1980, 204 of them between 1989 and 1995.

Signs and Labels

Within tourist attractions signs perform several different functions. While some sites, like the Captain Cook Birthplace Museum in Middlesborough, are laid out so that the best route round them is obvious, in others there are several possible routes and directional signs are needed. At large sites like Alton Towers or Beamish the signs simply direct people towards the different attractions which can be viewed in any sequence. But in many museums and art galleries the signs indicate the best or most logical sequence for viewing. Temporary signs may be used in zoos to draw attention to recent births, and in museums and art galleries to direct people to new acquisitions or temporary exhibitions.

Other signs are needed to give instructions. Sometimes these will be about safety; many English Heritage sites have signs warning visitors of the dangers of crumbling walls. Emergency exits are now marked with the pictogram of a white figure running on a green background throughout Europe. Signs will also indicate timed events that visitors may want to see; for example, different feeding times at a zoo. They may also point out what is and isn't allowed in the attraction; for example, prohibitions on touching or photographing objects. However, since too many rules can seem off-putting, attractions like the Roman Baths in Bath try to phrase as many of their notices as possible in positive terms... telling visitors what they *can* do rather than what they can't.

Where overseas tourists are expected there should be signs in languages other than English. French, German, Spanish and Italian are the usual choices, but some sites also have signs in Arabic, Japanese and Scandinavian languages. Choice of language should be dictated by research into where visitors are coming from; those within reach of the Channel Ports and Tunnel are most likely to need French and German but on the Pennine Way near Haworth signposts are provided in Japanese for the many Japanese visitors to the Bronte Parsonage.

Unless they are there for safety reasons, signs should be as unobtrusive as possible. Simple arrows are often adequate, and where it's not immediately clear what is needed temporary signs should be used at first. Symbols or pictograms are often as good as written signs and can be understood by overseas visitors as well Some attractions reinforce their identity by adding their logos to all signs.

Labelling is also important at sites which aim to educate as well as entertain. Nowadays shorter messages which people are more likely to read and remember are preferred to lengthy descriptions. Colour and graphics often supplement words. Some attractions provide 'talking' labels as an addition to or even an alternative to written labels; London Zoo has provided 'talking' labels for many years. In the Morpeth Bagpipe Museum in Northumbria visitors can read traditional written labels while listening to taped music through head-sets which react to signals from the different exhibition cases.

Audio-Visual Presentations

Despite presenting certain problems, audio and audio-visual presentations are increasingly popular. In the first place not everyone understands English. The best attractions therefore offer commentaries in more than one language, sometimes by providing alternative sets of headphones, as at the Jorvik Centre and the Oxford Story in Oxford. Elsewhere, presentations are given in different languages either consecutively or at different times. This is less satisfactory because it means visitors must either sit out the commentary in the alternative language or fit in with someone else's schedule.

Where the audio-visual presentaton is a staged affair (as at the Whisky Heritage Centre in Edinburgh or the Guinness Centre in Dublin), visitors may have to wait up to half an hour before being admitted to the auditorium. To get round this snag, some attractions provide commentaries throughout an attraction. Where individual headsets are provided this is relatively problem-free. However, where the commentaries are broadcast it can result in a cacophony of competing sounds reverberating around the exhibition. Other attractions provide short versions of the tour for those in a hurry.

Some attractions provide different commentaries spoken by different commentators for adults and children, presenting the same material at different levels of comprehension.

Stereo tours are now available at 44 English Heritage properties, while the Roman Baths Museum keeps 1300 stereo units on hand. The National Gallery provides CD-Rom recorders with headsets; the user taps in the number appearing beside each painting to hear the relevant commentary, thus obviating the need to walk round the gallery in a fixed sequence.

Guides and Guidebooks

In the UK relatively few tourist attractions employ official guides; in contrast, in Spain most historic properties can only be visited in escorted groups. Where there are guides, as at some National Trust properties, they are often volunteers. Apart from providing information for visitors, guides also serve as custodians, dissuading their charges from touching exhibits or taking flash photographs. In many heritage centres guides dress up in appropriate costumes and act as 'interpreters', often carrying out traditional crafts, cooking or sewing so visitors can watch and ask questions.

Just as labelling should reflect the linguistic mix of the visitors, guiding services need to be available in appropriate languages. The HMS *Victory* provides information in 20 languages, including Korean, Urdu and Mandarin.

Many attractions provide guidebooks to help tourists make the most of their visit. These range from simple sheets of paper costing only pence in many churches to the definitive texts costing upwards of £20 published to accompany temporary exhibitions in the national museums and art galleries. The vast majority of guidebooks fall somewhere in between, costing £1 or £2.

Some attractions offer a range of guidebooks suitable for different ages and languages. Obviously only the largest attractions can afford to publish such a variety; however, it does ensure that few potential customers go away disappointed.

Ideally guidebooks should be pocket-sized, with clear pictures and plans. If they are likely to be used outdoors they should also have as weather-resistant a cover as possible.

Shops

Commercial pressures have ensured that most tourist attractions now include retail outlets. Large sites like theme parks have many different shops, but even archaeological sites in the care of English Heritage sell key-rings and mugs in addition to the more traditional guidebooks and postcards.

What the shops sell is dictated by the number of likely visitors, the length of the average stay (the longer people stay, the more likely they are to purchase a souvenir) and the types of visitor expected. Ideally they will offer a range of goods from things like pens costing less than 50p and aimed at school groups to more expensive designer items for the A/B socio-economic groups. To charge high prices they need to offer an inviting sales environment and employ professional sales-staff. They will also need to sell high quality goods, preferably with a link to the attraction. The expensive pottery at the Wedgwood Visitor Centre sells well because it can draw on the company's reputation for providing quality goods that have stood the test of time.

Ideally attractions have their own *merchandise*, bearing a distinctive advertising logo. However, where few visitors are expected this is unlikely to be economically feasible unless several attractions band together to design their goods, as the Treasure Houses of England group has done (see Chapter 3). The National Trust produces a wide range of goods which can be sold in all its on and off-site shops. However, attractions need not actually own and run all the shops on their premises; open-air museums like Beamish and St. Fagan's lease space to outsiders to sell produce like cheese, pottery or ironmongery which is in keeping with the attraction.

Siting of the shop is vital to achieving maximum returns. Many planners have followed the Disneyworld model where shops are dotted all round the site, with a 'Main Street' of shops right by the entrance in the hope that visitors who didn't buy at first will succumb when they see something again on their way out. In long-established attractions the shops are being moved into more prominent positions; even the Science Museum now has a bookshop and a souvenir shop in its entrance hall.

What has happened in the once-staid Victoria and Albert Museum exemplifies the changed attitude towards retailing even within public sector tourist attractions. A trading company called Victoria and Albert Enterprises now runs two sales outlets within the museum, as well as an outlying shop in the Bethnal Green Museum of Childhood. Rent and service charges are paid to the museum, and profits covenanted back to it. A wide range of items from postcards and posters to jewellery and ceramics are on sale, and the stock is varied to suit temporary exhibitions. Other items on sale are replicas of things on display in the galleries. Sales staff have retail rather than civil service backgrounds, unlike the rest of the museum employees. By 1995 Victoria and Albert Enterprises was generating sales worth £80 million a year.

Refreshments

Since the 19th century attractions have recognised catering as an appropriate way to raise extra money; the three original dining rooms at the Victoria and Albert Museum are now attractions in their own right. These days most attractions offer refreshments, varying from the simple cup of tea and home-made cake at National Trust properties to the choice of cooked meals at major theme parks. The largest attractions offer eating options to suit all tastes; Thorpe Park led the way in offering well-known high street names like Burger King but Alton Towers alone has tea and coffee shops, a pizzeria, a brunch bar and several major restaurants. Old stable blocks and other outhouses attached to historic buildings often make ideal novelty eating places and can be hired out for private parties, banquets, etc.

Few tourist attractions have drinks licences, although the Tate Gallery's restaurant, run by Pret-à-Manger, is licensed. However, theatres are always licensed and rushed drinks in the interval are part of the experience of visiting them.

Lavatories

Most attractions provide separate male and female lavatories. These should be spotlessly clean, continuously supplied with toilet paper and hand-drying facilities, and positioned so they can be found without difficulty, perhaps near the car park. Where the lavatories are outdoors the entrances should be on the most sheltered side and porches provided. They should be light and well-ventilated, easy to clean and as vandal-proof as possible, with pipes and cisterns boxed in so they're hard to reach. There should be more female than male cubicles since women's lavatories are usually used by children as well and queues tend to be longer. Ideally cubicles should contain waste disposal bins and hooks for outdoor coats and bags, especially at outdoor sites where the floor will be muddy on wet days. If an outdoor site will be closed out of season it may be better to provide a mobile lavatory unit which can be removed for maintenance and protected from vandalism in winter. At many stately homes lavatories are housed in outbuildings like adapted stable blocks.

Facilities for the disabled can be provided either within the main male and female lavatories or separately. They should have ramp entrances for wheelchairs, enough space to turn a wheelchair round in and hand-rails. High pedestals, sliding doors and light switches on long leads are also desirable.

A separate 'parent and baby' room with nappy-changing table and waste disposal facilities should also be provided, preferably separately.

Litter Bins

The more popular a tourist attraction is, the more litter bins it will require. In rural areas these should be as unobtrusive as possible; wire mesh bins without linings and plastic dustbins look ugly, whereas bins surrounded by wooden palisades can look almost natural. Where mesh is used it should be narrow enough to stop birds and animals pulling the contents out, and lids should be strong enough to resist wind and rain. Ideally bins should be sited where most people congregate: at car parks and picnic spots, next to benches and near the lavatories.

At sites where entertainment is the lynch-pin novelty bins encourage children to be tidy; at the American Adventure Theme Park at Ilkeston bins are shaped like giant grizzly bears.

However, even where plenty of bins are provided litter will still be dropped and the biggest sites like Alton Towers run regular litter patrol vans through the park to ensure it's kept spotless. In general, people seem to drop less litter at sites with high standards of cleanliness.

Seating

Back in 1949 the Director of the British Museum, suggested providing comfortable lounges with reference copies of museum publications for visitors. But while newly-designed museums like Bristol's Exploratory now provide plenty of seats, one of the most frequent visitor gripes continues to be the lack of places to sit down, especially in some of the older museums; the British Museum alone has two and a half miles of exhibition space and not a lot of places to sit down.

Seating is particularly appreciated at beauty spots where people want to soak up a view. However, it should be designed to blend in with the surroundings, preferably by using natural materials, like local wood. Ideally it should be positioned along the edge of the view so that the seat itself doesn't obtrude into it. The same goes for associated litter bins, telescopes, etc.

Lifts, Escalators and Moving Pavements

In the UK many attractions provide lifts to enable the disabled to reach the higher floors of a building. However, escalators are rare and moving pavements even more uncommon although they have considerable potential as a way of keeping people moving at very crowded sites; a travelator now steers people smoothly past the hugely popular Crown Jewels at the Tower of London. The 'time cars' first introduced at the Jorvik Viking Centre (see Chapter 5) perform much the same function in several British heritage centres.

Special lighting

Floodlighting can make historic properties look lovely at night. While tourists certainly appreciate that, and much floodlighting is of famous castles and cathedrals which are popular with visitors, floodlighting also benefits local residents and is often financed by local authorities. To keep costs down, automatic timers can be used to switch the lights on at dusk and off again at midnight.

Facilities for Coach Drivers

Because so many visitors to attractions arrive by coach site owners often make special arrangements for their drivers to encourage repeat business. There will almost always be a separate area for coach parking, partly for safety reasons. Larger attractions often provide a special rest-room and meal vouchers for drivers. Normally they are free to make use of site facilities as well.

OFF-SITE AMENITIES

Signposts

In 1986 the Department of Transport introduced white on brown pictographic signs to direct people to tourist attractions. Such signs are now common throughout Britain and are erected by local traffic authorities with the attraction owner footing the bill. In 1995 the rules relating to tourist signs were relaxed as part of the government's commitment to minimising bureaucratic regulations. An attraction need no longer be open all year or attract a specific number of visitors to be allowed a sign.

Although there is concern that too many tourist signs could detract from other road signs and that proliferating signs can be environmentally damaging, a wider range of attractions are now allowed to erect signs. Local authorities are allowed to take into consideration things like the need for economic regeneration and the promotion of tourism when deciding whether to give approval. As well as indicating specific castles, theme parks, etc. they also mark out scenic drives, like the Northumbrian Coastal Route, and linked attractions like farm trails. Since 1995 some pubs, hotels and retail complexes have also been allowed to call themselves attractions for the purpose of signing. Where there are too many attractions in one area for them all to be listed individually a generic phrase like 'historic town centre' can be used on the approach road, with specific attractions indicated closer to home. In certain circumstances such signs can also list local services (fuel, toilets, refreshments) that are available to tourists.

The Department of Transport has approved a set of standard symbols, most of them readily recognisable (see Fig 1/2). However, it is possible for an attraction to request a different symbol. So Hampton Court Palace, the Iron Bridge Gorge Museum and Wembley Stadium all have their own individual signs.

Tourist signs serve three purposes. Their primary object is to direct people to their planned destination by the best possible route. However, they are also distinctive enough to attract passers-by and so bring in visitors who might not have known there was anything worth seeing. Finally, they can give a quick identity to a town; Cheltenham is signposted as 'Regency Cheltenham', offering an immediate excuse for a detour.

Property owners can still erect their own directional signs but may need planning approval under the Town and Country Planning (Control of Advertisements) Regulations of 1969. If the sign is on their own land consent is not usually needed.

FIG.1/2: WHITE ON BROWN AND OTHER TOURIST SIGNS

1. Castle.
2. Historic house.
3. Picnic area.
4. Woodland recreation area.
5. National Trust property.
6. Preserved or tourist railway.
7. Site with Roman remains.
8. Water sport activities.
9. Historic church.
10. Wildlife park.
11. Zoo.
12. Farm trail.
13. Cathedral.
14. English Heritage property
15. Museum or art gallery
16. Equestrian event.
17. STB recognised attraction
18. Museum or art gallery.
19. Country park
20. Historic dockyard
21. Air museum.
22. Beach.
23. Scottish National Trust property.
24. ETB recognised attraction.
25. Farm park.
26. Industrial heritage attraction.
27. Watermill.
28. Aquarium.
29. Historic Buildings property.
30. Shire horse centre.
31. Flower garden.
32. Windmill.
33. Bird garden.
34. Prehistoric site or monument.
35. Spa, spring or fountain.
36. Vineyard.
37. Pottery or craft centre.
38. Viewpoint.
39. Nature reserve.
40. Pleasure park.
41. Motor museum.
42. WTB recognised attraction.
43. Butterfly farm.
44. Craft centre or forge.
45. Agricultural museum.
46. Canal-side attraction.

However, all illuminated signs need planning approval. While permission for a permanent sign is being sought, the AA or RAC can provide temporary signs although planning permission is also needed for these. The motoring organisations regularly provide signposting for event attractions which only need short-term directions.

The National Trust and English Heritage, and their regional equivalents, continue to provide their own distinctive signposting: the acorn symbol for the National Trust and the red grid for English Heritage.

Within towns and villages signposts also indicate pedestrian routes from car parks and transport terminals to attractions. These signs incorporate a standard 'walking figure' symbol. Traffic authorities are also encouraged to provide tourist information boards in laybys and car parks. Such boards can include paid-for advertisements for tourist services including attractions.

Hotels

Few British tourist attractions provide accommodation, although Alton Towers now has a themed on-site hotel and there is a hotel within the Land's End complex. Abroad, however, the Disney Corporation routinely incorporates a range of accommodation, from camping grounds to luxury hotels, in its developments.

In places like the East African game parks where the provision of accommodation may be vital to the development of the attraction, the government sometimes helps with funding.

Attraction owners work closely with accommodation providers, stocking their lobbies with marketing materials. They get the extra publicity, while the accommodation owners can offer their clients a better all-round service.

HEALTH AND SAFETY AT TOURIST ATTRACTIONS

Those in charge of tourist attractions owe a 'common duty of care' to visitors under the 1957 Occupiers' Liability Act. This means that they must operate the site in such a way as to minimise risks to the public. They can protect themselves to some extent by putting up warning notices where these are 'reasonable' and don't contravene the 1977 Unfair Contract Terms Act. Conditions for use of the site can also be listed on the back of tickets, again provided they conform to the Unfair Contract Terms Act. Site owners are expected to allow for the fact that children are less careful than adults and so need more protection. Site owners can be sued for negligence, even vicariously when an employee was responsible for the incident. This makes rigorous procedures for selecting and training staff particularly important.

The 1974 Health and Safety at Work Act (reinforced by the 1993 Health and Safety at Work Regulations) also obliges those who control premises and the activities that take place in them to ensure that they are safe for all who attend them: 'it shall be the duty of every employer to conduct his undertaking in such a way as to ensure, so far as is reasonably practical, that persons not in his employment who may be affected thereby are not exposed to risks to their health and safety.' Everyone, from the company director to the humblest worker, has an obligation to look after the health and safety of everyone using the site. To comply with the Act, attractions should have first aid facilities available and should take the precautions against fire suggested by local fire officers.

The Health and Safety at Work Act is enforced by the Health and Safety Executive and its inspectors who suggest improvements, post prohibition notices and prosecute where necessary. The Health and Safety Commission creates codes of practice for individual sections of the industry; these don't have the force of law but are admissible in court if an accident occurs and there have been omissions on the part of the attraction owner. Local authorities also appoint 'factory inspectors' to visit sites and ensure they are being operated safely.

Special sections of the Health and Safety Act deal with the management of zoos, circuses and fairgrounds. Theme parks also have their often code of conduct. Some of the regulations are common sense; at Beamish visitors to the drift mine must wear hard hats, and the coal has been removed to eliminate dangers from dust. However, none of the bread baked in the houses can be sold to the public because cooking arrangments are not thought sufficiently hygienic.

Most UK tourist attractions have good health and safety records, although an incident in 1994 when a man who climbed into the lions' den at London Zoo was mauled attracted banner headlines. In 1994 a child was killed on a ride at the Coney Beach funfair in Porthcawl. Fires did serious damage to Hampton Court Palace in 1986, Uppark in Sussex in 1989 and Windsor Castle in 1992 but despite the structural damage no visitors were hurt in any of these incidents.

ORIGINALITY

While all attractions need to be accessible, with good amenities, other factors can also contribute to success. It helps, for example, to offer something unique. There is only one Big Ben, its silhouette recognisable all round the world. There can hardly be a visitor to London who hasn't heard of it and who doesn't want to see it, without any promotional activity on anyone's part. The same is true of the Taj Mahal, the Pyramids, even of sunset at Ayers Rock. An event attraction like the Oberammergau Passion Play also plays on the appeal of originality, guaranteeing it popularity for the foreseeable future.

FASHION

Fashion is also important. In the 1970s safari parks were extremely popular in Britain; new ones opened, and old ones made record profits. However, as concern about animal rights grew in the 1990s, some, like Windsor Safari Park, actually closed down while others, like Chessington Zoo (now the World of Adventures) and Flamingoland, evolved into leisure parks to suit changing tastes.

In the 1990s farms and visitor centres showed the biggest growth in visitor numbers, perhaps because of their relative novelty value as attractions. Country parks and gardens also attracted increasing numbers of visitors. In contrast, the number of people visiting wildlife attractions continued to fall.

Attractions can also be affected by how fashionable their location is. In the summers of 1993 and 1994 attractions within easy reach of coastal Turkey received record numbers of British visitors as Turkey became the 'in' place to go. In the UK events like the Garden Festivals (see Chapter 12) had a similar result. In 1990 attractions in and around Gateshead and Newcastle saw their visitor numbers swell. In 1992 it was the turn of those in and around Ebbw Vale in South Wales. In 1995 Leeds was being hyped as Britain's 'in' city, a status which should translate into increased visitor figures for local attractions. The Millennium Exhibition at Greenwich should ensure traffic jams in south-east London throughout the year 2000.

However, fashion is notoriously fickle and it's rarely possible to maintain the same throughput of visitors once the initial burst of publicity wears off (see Chapter 12).

THE ATTRACTION PROVIDERS

In the 1970s most UK tourist attractions were looked after by the State through departments like the Ministry of Public Buildings and Works (now English Heritage) or by conservation bodies like the National Trust. Ecclesiastical buildings remained the responsibility of the Church and some stately homes were still in private hands. For many reasons there was only minimal private sector involvement:

- Creating a new attraction can involve enormous capital investment. The pioneering Jorvik Centre had cost £2.7 million when it opened in 1984. When Legoland opened on the site of the old Windsor Safari Park in 1996, its owners, the European company Interlogo, had invested some £85 million in the site. Even if many attractions can recoup their running costs from admission fees, few can recoup capital outlay on this scale.

- A tradition of free admission to parks, museums and cathedrals meant visitors were reluctant to pay to visit attractions.

- Because so few private sector companies had been involved with attractions, those that did want to get involved had little UK experience to draw on. Instead American businesses like Disneyworld had to serve as models. (Some of Disney's teething problems in France stemmed from trying to impose an unadulterated American theme park on a notoriously chauvinistic French culture.)

- The UK climate is also problematic. When it's good people prefer to visit beaches and the countryside where most activities are traditionally free. Conversely outdoor attractions like leisure parks lose visitors in bad weather.

- Traditionally the UK tourist attraction business has also been seasonal, with four-tenths of visits concentrated into July and August, when it's easier to cope with trade spread evenly through the year.

As a result those companies involved in UK tourism preferred to concentrate on hotels, holiday centres, casinos, catering and producing merchandise for tourists.

The Entrepreneurs

In the 1980s change began to take place, driven in part by the government's desire to cut public subsidies. The 'enterprise culture' encouraged entrepreneurs to create new tourist attractions and the boom years of the late 1980s gave an added impetus to the process.

After marrying the daughter of the owner of Alton Towers, a crumbling Pugin building with a funfair in its grounds, John Broome spent the ten years to 1983 turning it into a highly successful theme park. He then bought Battersea Power Station in London, intending to create another theme park (see Chapter Eight) on the banks of the Thames.

Peter de Savary was another high-profile entrepreneur who turned his talents to generating new attractions. By 1990 he owned both Land's End (where he was responsible for the controversial theme park) and John O'Groats, as well as Littlecote House which was originally open to the public as the Land of Littlecote.

Other individuals carved out influential careers in tourism development without actually owning the attractions. For example, Andy Grant of the Grant Leisure Group helped revive London's Royal Opera House, developed a crowd control system for the Tower of London, organised a donations payment system at the Victoria and Albert Museum, redeveloped New York's Coney Island fairground, restored Philadelphia and San Diego Zoos, worked at Granada Studios and finally became head of Zoo Operations Limited for the Zoological Society of London. His ventures have spanned both the public and private sectors, showing how the once clear distinction between the two has gradually blurred.

In the early 1990s the role of the entrepreneurs diminished as recession began to bite and the start-up costs for profitable large attractions continued to rise. Broome sold Alton Towers to the Pearson Group, while his plans to turn the old Battersea Power Station into a theme park quickly floundered; latest plans would see it converted into London's largest cinema. Peter de Savary sold Land's End and John O'Groats, and Littlecote House is now a conference centre. With worries that the market could become saturated with competing attractions and the failure of well-known and long-standing enterprises like Windsor Safari Park, the odds on success began to look far less inviting.

The Companies

Of Britain's 2,491 attractions receiving more than 10,000 visitors in 1995, 59% are privately owned although often by trusts and other non-commercial bodies. The only large public limited companies with a sizeable portfolio of attractions are Granada (Granada Studios Tour, and Camelot and American Adventure Theme Parks), Pearson (Alton Towers, Madame Tussaud's, Chessington World of Adventures and other attractions, (see Chapter 11)) and Vardon Attractions, once a distributor of sports equipment and now owner of the Sea Life Centres, and the London and York Dungeons.

Smaller-scale companies were also involved in multiple tourism developments. The consultancy company Heritage Projects evolved out of the success of the Jorvik Viking Centre (see Chapter 5); apart from creating the Oxford Story and the Canterbury Pilgrim's Way, its designers also developed an 1850s coal mine for 'Into the Black' at the Black Country Museum, another mine for the Rhondda Heritage Park and models for the White Cliffs Experience in Dover.

Philanthropists

Many tourist attractions owe a debt of gratitude to generous individuals who have either given their collections for public benefit or financed buildings for museums, zoos or art galleries. This tradition has continued into the 1990s, with the Sainsbury family funding both a new wing for the National Gallery and for the British Museum (not yet completed). Sir Andrew Lloyd-Webber gave a £1 million donation to create the Open Churches Trust, aimed at allowing churches threatened by vandalism to reopen to the public. A reading of the labels in any museum reveals the generosity of thousands of individuals who give, or loan, treasures for public benefit.

Philanthropists sometimes attach conditions to their donations. For example, the Vaughan Bequest of Turner watercolours can only be put on show in the National Gallery of Scotland during January, while the conditions attached to the Burrell bequest were so stringent that it took 40 years to provide the requisite special gallery in Glasgow. Sir Denis Mahon, owner of a renowned collection of Italian Baroque paintings, has willed them to the National Art Collections Fund for display in British galleries. However, in 1996 he announced that the NACF would be required to withdraw the pictures if the galleries where they were displayed sold any of their exhibits. He is also rumoured to be considering sending the paintings to Italy if admission fees are introduced at the National Gallery.

THE GOVERNMENT AND TOURISM FUNDING

The Development of Tourism Act and Section 4 Funding

The 1969 Development of Tourism Act enabled the English, Scottish and Welsh tourist boards to provide financial help to tourism ventures, including attractions, through Section 4 funding or the Tourism Grants Scheme. By the end of 1988 £21 million of Section 4 funding had generated about £167 million of other investment and created approximately 13,500 new jobs. Section 4 assistance came in the form of grants, loans, and interest relief, as well as advice on marketing and business plans. Amongst the tourist attractions to benefit were the Severn Valley Steam Railway, Flambards Triple Theme Park in Cornwall, the Triforium Gallery at

FIG.1/3: GOVERNMENT FUNDING FOR HERITAGE AND THE ARTS

Department of Culture, Media and Sport:	*English Heritage
	*Historic Royal Palaces Agency
	*National Heritage Memorial Fund
	*Occupied Royal Palaces, State Ceremonials and Other Historic Buildings
	*Churches Conservation Trust
	*Royal Armouries
	*Royal Commission on the Historic Monuments of England
	*Royal Fine Art Commission
	*Royal Parks Executive Agency
	British Museum
	Natural History Museum
	National Museum of Science and Technology
	Imperial War Museum
	National Army Museum, Chelsea
	National Maritime Museum, Greenwich
	Royal Air Force Museum, Hendon
	National Museums and Galleries on Merseyside
	National Gallery
	National Portrait Gallery
	Tate Gallery
	Museums and Galleries Improvement Fund
	Museums and Galleries Commission
Arts Council of England	British Film Institute
Scottish Office	Historic Scotland
	Education and Environment Depts
	Scottish Arts Council
	National Museum of Scotland
	National Gallery of Scotland
	National Library of Scotland
	Scottish Museums Council
	Scottish Film Council
Welsh Office	Arts Council of Wales
	National Museum of Wales
	National Library of Wales
	Council of Museums in Wales
	Contributes to Cadw
Northern Ireland Office	Education (DENI) and Environment Depts
	Arts Council of Northern Ireland
	Ulster Folk & Transport Museum
	Ulster Museum
	Northern Ireland Museums Council

Winchester Cathedral and Nottingham's Tales of Robin Hood exhibition. However, in 1989 Section 4 funding for England was scrapped. (It continues to be available in Scotland and Wales.)

THE NATIONAL HERITAGE MEMORIAL FUND (NHMF)

The National Heritage Memorial Fund is the successor to the National Land Fund set up in 1946 as a memorial to the dead of the two World Wars. The 1979 National Heritage Bill converted the Fund into the NHMF. This had capital of £12.4 million which was to be topped up each year by grants from the Department of the Environment and the Office of Arts and Libraries.

The NHMF has been called a 'fire engine for the heritage' which can step in when there is danger of loss, whether through export, dilapidation or damage. It can give grants to help secure anything regarded as important to the national heritage, including works of art. Sometimes it makes joint purchases with the National Art Collections Fund.

Amongst the beneficiaries of grants have been stately homes (Calke Abbey, Kedleston Hall), churches (Jarrow, Little Stanmore), cathedrals (Ely), museums (Ironbridge Gorge, Museum of London), art galleries (National Gallery, Tate Gallery), gardens (Biddulph Grange), industrial heritage sites (Quarry Bank Mill, Big Pit Mining Museum), ships (SS *Great Britain*) and piers (Clevedon).

In the year to March 1995, the NHMF gave grants totalling £10,448,107; £42,297 went to the *Mary Rose* at Southampton and £17,447 to the church of St Michael and All Angels at Great Witley. In 1996 £1.4 million was awarded to Kew Gardens to turn the old Museum No 1 into an Economic Botany Museum. The NMHF also administers the Heritage Lottery Fund, which awarded £95,662,779 in grants in 1995. Two-thirds of these grants went to ancient monuments, historic buildings and churches, with Clevedon Pier receiving £475,042, Highcliffe Castle receiving £2.65 million and Hogarth's House receiving £100,000.

Government Support for Heritage Attractions

The government provides grants towards the maintenance and running costs of historic properties through a network of separate departments and agencies. In 1992 the Department of National Heritage, now the Department of Culture, Media and Sport (DCMS), took over responsibility for 'heritage' monuments from the Department of Environment. The DNH carries out much of its work via nine public agencies, funded mainly by the government but managed at arm's length (see items marked with asterisk in Fig.1/3).

In 1995 the government provided English Heritage with grants amounting to £126.2 million, the Royal Commission for Historic Monuments with £14 million, the Historic Royal Palaces Agency with £20.5 million and the National Heritage Memorial Fund with £8.7 million. Most of this money can be seen as benefiting tourist attractions.

Historic Scotland is funded by the Scottish Office and Cadw by an executive agency of the Welsh Office.

General Tourism Funding

Although the Conservative governments of the 1980s and '90s were generally hostile to public sector involvement in business, tourism was often seen as a way to regenerate run-down inner city areas while simultaneously providing new jobs and so benefited from specific government initiatives, particularly the Tourism Development Action Programmes. Funding for designated localities was also available through Strategic Development Initiatives, Tourism Action Plans, Urban Development Corporations and the City Challenge Scheme.

Tourism Development Action Programmes (TDAPs)

During the 1980s and early '90s the ETB channelled money through Tourist Development Action Programmes to selected areas thought suitable for intensive development. There were TDAPs in 'heritage' towns (Lancaster, Nottingham, Carlisle and Norwich), seaside resorts (Bridlington, Torbay), rural areas (Exmoor, Kielder, the Forest of Dean, Shropshire, the North Pennines), combined rural and traditional areas (East Kent, the Isle of Wight, Cornwall) and industrial/maritime centres (Bristol, Bradford, Portsmouth, Cleveland, Leicester, Tyne and Wear).

The TDAPs brought together public and private sector brains and funding in short bursts of activity to kick-start tourism projects into action. Their remits extended beyond tourist attractions but these tended to benefit both directly and indirectly.

Unfortunately after the English Tourist Board's funding was cut in 1993, no more TDAPs were created. The last one was wound up in 1995.

Working Partnerships

The 1990s saw some new initiatives to separate the ownership and management of attractions. Seventy-seven of English Heritage's 406 properties are now managed locally through a series of Local Management Agreements although they still belong to English Heritage. Their largest partner is the National Trust with whom they share management of 17 sites, including Stonehenge and Avebury. Other partners include the national parks, local authorities and local preservation trusts. Although Tatton Park in Cheshire is owned by the National Trust its day-to-day finances and administration are handled by Cheshire County Council.

European Funding for Tourism

The European Union provides some funding for tourism in areas of high unemployment. In 1993/4 the European Regional Development Fund (ERDF) provided £53 million for infrastructural projects which benefited the arts; for example, restoring theatres, museums and inner city heritage sites. Former coalmining areas have received funding from the EU's Rechar funds which have helped create some mining museums. The European Social Fund (ESF) also gave £300,000 to Merseyside to help create jobs in the arts for the unemployed.

Northern Ireland

Of 162 attractions surveyed by the Northern Ireland Tourist Board in 1995, 102 were owned by central or local government, 44 by private companies or individuals and 16 by the National Trust. In contrast ETB surveys indicate a far smaller percentage of attractions owned by local authorities or central government,

In Northern Ireland public sector tourist attractions may be eligible for grants from the Department of Economic Development as a result of Part III of the Development of Tourist Traffic Act. Grants to private sector attractions may also be available through the International Fund for Ireland Tourist Amenity Development Scheme. In both cases the NITB advises on the suitability of applications.

Attractions in Northern Ireland have also been able to take advantage of EU grants to help develop tourism in border areas. The European Regional Development Fund (ERDF) has also poured money into the region in an effort to bring peace through prosperity. The award-winning Tower Museum in Derry was one beneficiary of such aid.

THE NATIONAL LOTTERY

In November 1994 the National Lottery was launched, bringing about what may prove to be the single greatest improvement in funding for tourist attractions this century, what Arts Council of England chair Lord Gowrie described as 'a cultural revolution' which will see some of the biggest cities 'transformed in a way not seen since the confident years of Victorian and Edwardian industrial and municipal expansion.'

With an estimated 71% of the population taking part in the weekly draw and sale of scratch cards, the National Lottery is generating larger than anticipated profits for 'good causes' in five designated areas: the arts, sport, national heritage, charities and projects to celebrate the Millennium. In theory profits are meant to be spent 'for the public good' rather than tourism. However, four of the designated areas are closely linked to tourism and if grants continue to follow the pattern set so far, roughly 85% will have a knock-on benefit for tourism.

Although the Lottery will be operated by Camelot plc until 2003, the Secretary of State for National Heritage has responsibility for providing the legal framework and ground rules for the distribution of funds.

Currently 28% of net profits are paid to the National Lottery Distribution Fund. This, in turn, pays equal shares to five grant distributing bodies (see Fig.1/4).

In the first year of operation the Lottery generated £1.2 billion for the good causes and the National Heritage Memorial Fund has now overtaken English Heritage as the biggest dispenser of grants for conservation work.

By mid-1996 the Lottery had raised £2.6 billion, and £1.7 billion had been earmarked for 5,812 awards to 7,000 different projects. The Royal Court Theatre was, for example, awarded a grant of £15,803,505, while Christ Church in Spitalfields received £2,441,500. Not all this money has actually been handed over. In many cases it will be paid in stages as work progresses. Most money had actually been paid out to the Heritage Fund to pay for purchases of objects, buildings and land. The first, highly controversial, grant was given to enable the state to buy the Churchill Archive from his heirs.

FIG.1/4: NATIONAL LOTTERY FUND DISTRIBUTION

Grant Distributing Body	Eligible Projects
The Millennium Commission	Projects to celebrate the Millennium
The National Heritage Memorial Fund	Heritage projects
The Arts Council	Arts projects
The Sports Council	Sports projects
The National Lotteries Charity Board	Other charitable causes

There are several restrictions on eligibility for a grant even within the five designated areas. Grants can make up 50 to 90% of the cost of a capital project, up to £50 million for large projects and £100,000 for local schemes. This means many different bodies competing with each other to raise the 'partnership funds' from alternative sources and has led pessimists to forecast a rash of half-completed building projects. A more serious worry is that a new theatre, however smart, is of little use if money isn't available for day-to-day running costs. There are also fears that the government will use the existence of Lottery funds as an excuse to cut conventional grants to theatres, museums, etc.

In 1996 individuals became eligible to apply for grants. The Heritage Fund can now support 'any worthwhile heritage project with a clear public benefit', making private owners of stately homes eligible for assistance and removing an anomaly whereby grants to improve townscapes could be given to properties owned by trusts or public bodies but not to those owned by individuals.

If all goes well Lottery funds are expected to transform huge swathes of Gateshead, Manchester, Liverpool, Birmingham, Bristol and London over the next ten years.

The Millennium Commission

One-fifth of Lottery profits are earmarked to commemorate the Millennium. A planned 12 landmark projects should culminate with a vast Millennium Exhibition at Greenwich where the world's largest dome is planned.

Projects that will be part-funded by the Millennium Commission and will benefit tourists include the new Tate Gallery at Bankside which will receive £50 million towards start-up costs of £106 million; the new Great Court at the British

Museum which will receive £30 million of the £72 million needed; renewal of Portsmouth Harbour which will receive £40 million of the £86.6 million required; and the Lowry Centre in Salford which is expected to cost £127 million and will receive £15.6 million from the Millennium Commision, and another £41.1 million from the Arts Fund and £7.6 million from the Heritage Fund. However, a planned railway to link the Giant's Causeway with Bushmills whiskey distillery in Northern Ireland had to be dropped because of difficulties in acquiring the land quickly enough.

THE VISITORS

In general attractions aim to pull in as many people as they can. But if too many people want to visit, it can pose a threat to the fabric of the attraction itself and to the safety of its visitors. What's more, huge crowds can detract from the pleasure of a visit. Consequently places like Lindisfarne Castle in Northumberland which regularly attract capacity numbers of visitors sometimes place restrictions on how

FIG.1/5: NUMBER OF VISITORS TO TOURIST ATTRACTIONS IN THE UK, 1995

Type of Attraction	Number	Percentage of Total	Millions
Museums	1497	15	57
Historic Properties	1429	20	79
Wildlife	280	5	21
Country Parks	251	15	59
Art Galleries	232	5	20
Leisure Parks	78	11	41
Other Attractions	2051	29	1150

(Source : ETB/BTA)

many people can be let in at one time. So popular is the British Museum that a notice warns that it sometimes has to close until enough visitors have left to make space for newcomers. Nowadays it's often necessary to buy a ticket for a specific time if you want to visit the popular short-term exhibitions in London's museums and galleries.

Overseas Visitors

In 1995 22 million foreigners visited Britain, with more than 15 million of them coming from Western Europe and 3.25 million from the United States. In all, overseas visitors made up an estimated 18% of visitors to all tourist attractions in 1995, although more than 50% of visitors to 132 attractions come from abroad; at

Tower Bridge 81% of all visitors were from overseas, at the Scotch Whisky Heritage Centre 65% and at Anne Hathaway's Cottage 60%.

The British Tourist Authority has been trying to attract high spending Japanese visitors; in 1995 640,000 Japanese visitors came to the UK. Areas like the Potteries which hope to attract more Japanese tourists have even run Japanese cultural courses to make their visitors feel so welcome they want to come back again.

In 1995 overseas visitors made up 34% of those visiting historic properties, 21% of visitors to museums and art galleries, and 5% of those visiting gardens and wildlife attractions. Overseas visitors made up 20% of those frequenting Scottish attractions and 18% of those in Northern Ireland, although attractions in Northumbria, the North West and the East Midlands record only 7% of visitors as foreign. (With the ending of the IRA ceasefire the number of overseas visitors to Northern Ireland can be expected to fall again.)

To encourage overseas tourists to visit more attractions during their stay the British Tourist Authority sells *British Heritage Pass Cards* which can be brought overseas or in the UK. They cost £25 for seven days, £36 for 15 days or £50 for a month and entitle their holders to free entry at properties owned by the National Trust/National Trust for Scotland, the Historic Houses Association, the Treasure Houses of England group, the Department of the Environment, English Heritage, the Scottish Development Department and Cadw. Members of the American Royal Oak Foundation also receive free admission to National Trust and National Trust for Scotland sites.

In general foreign tourists are high spenders; even in 1977 it was estimated that for every 5p they spent in historic buildings they spent another £17.95 on goods and services elsewhere.

The Domestic Market

The UK itself offers a potential market of roughly 37 million people aged between 16 and 65. Within this market it is, not surprisingly, mainly the young who visit theme parks, while older people make up the majority of visitors to stately homes and castles. Arts attractions tend to be most popular with the higher socio-economic groups, with ballet audiences dominated by women.

Children

In 1994-5 it was estimated that children under 16 made up roughly 32% of all visitors to British attractions, with the proportion varying from 48% at leisure parks to 18% at gardens and workplaces. Ninety-four attractions reported that more than 60% of their visitors were children, including the ARC in York (72%), Eureka! in Halifax (70%), the Exploratory in Bristol (66%) and Techniquest in Cardiff (64%). In Northern Ireland children make up 48% of visitors to wildlife attractions.

Most attractions offer discounts for children under 16. Increasingly those that expect lots of children also offer family tickets, covering two adults and two to four children for one all-inclusive price.

School Parties

A 1987 ETB survey indicated that 5% of all sightseeing visits in England were made by school students. At a typical attraction they made up between 5 and 25% of total visitor numbers. Since children sometimes return to the attraction with their families at a later date, and the same teachers bring groups year after year school visits obviously offer potential for repeat business. Most school visits take place in the summer term and are usually to places within 90 minutes' driving time of the school. Three-quarters of all such visits are organised by primary schools.

School parties are not usually big spenders and can be labour-intensive. They can also be noisy and disturb other visitors, a problem which can be alleviated by publicising the times when children are most likely to be visiting.

Attractions which are keen to encourage school groups often provide picnic areas for packed lunches. Alton Towers also provides picnic hampers and vouchers for set lunches.

Research indicates that visits are increasingly associated with the content of the National Curriculum and teachers particularly value attractions which provide teacher's packs and student guides which relate to the syllabus.

Visits to tourist attractions by school groups rose steadily after the 1944 Education Reform Act was introduced, with education authorities assuming that visits made in school time had to be free. Gradually, however, many schools started to charge for trips. When the 1988 Education Reform Act (ERA) reaffirmed that visits in schooltime should be free, many attractions, including theatres, reported a drop in visits, even though they had expected the more project-orientated GCSE exams to bring an increase.

Research carried out by the Wales Tourist Board in 1993 suggested that school visits had recovered to pre-1989 levels. By 1995 the British Museum was hosting around 250,000 children in school groups, three times the number it had received before the introduction of the National Curriculum. As a result its development plan for the Millennium envisages a new Centre for Education with two 250-seater auditoria and special lunch and cloakroom facilities.

Some attractions, especially those within easy reach of the Channel ports and Tunnel, receive many visits from overseas school groups, bringing the additional problems of language difficulties. Canterbury is particularly popular with Belgian and French groups. In 1995 it was estimated that Canterbury benefited by £6 million from these groups although there were indications that local people were tiring of the disruption caused.

Disabled Visitors

In 1949 the Science Museum in London pioneered the ideas of 'hands-on' exhibitions and braille labelling for the blind. Sadly such innovative thinking has not always been followed up although an increasing number of tourist attractions, particularly museums, now provide lifts, ramps and specially-fitted toilets for the disabled. An estimated 75% of attractions admit wheelchair-users, although only 15% provide tapes for the visually handicapped.

While some alterations to make places accessible to the disabled (installing lifts or stairlifts) are costly, others are not. For example it is simple to reserve the parking bays closest to the entrance by marking them with wheelchair symbols. Wooden ramps can usually be introduced into churches and cathedrals to make them accessible to wheelchairs, although at some stately homes and castles the number and slope of the stairs mean that installing lifts would be essential. Major sites like theme parks can also lend wheelchairs or buggies to visitors who need them. Improving lighting, providing seats and handrails, and publishing large-print leaflets are all relatively simple ways to make life easier for the disabled, who will make up an increasing number of visitors as the population ages.

Steps can be made less treacherous for the visually handicapped by lining them with yellow or white paint so they stand out more. At the Slimbridge and Martin Mere Wildfowl and Wetlands Trust sites braille trails enable the visually handicapped to identify the birds they will hear. Several museums, including the Victoria and Albert, have organised special exhibitions where all the objects on show have been selected for their tactile qualities and can be handled. The Cathedrals Through Touch and Hearing project at Lichfield and Coventry Cathedrals provides wooden scale models of the buildings and their ground plans which the visually handicapped can feel. The project also provides braille guidebooks, cassette commentaries and large print materials.

Some cathedrals, including Durham and Ripon, have installed induction loops which amplify sound and make it easier for people with hearing aids to make out what is being said by a guide or to listen to the music.

It is especially important to the disabled that attractions provide adequate and accurate information so they can assess how easy a visit will be. For example Beamish Museum's information for visitors points out that the steep paths may make a visit tiring for a wheelchair-user, arguably more helpful than claiming the site is generally accessible when only small areas really are. Other attractions like Fort Regent in St. Helier provide colour-coded plans which indicate routes accessible to wheelchairs (Fig.1/6). Unfortunately England uses a different set of symbols to indicate degrees of accessibility to Scotland and Wales.

The 1995 Disability Discrimination Act makes it illegal to discriminate against people with disabilities either in employment or the provision of services. Attractions will need to remove barriers to access over the next ten years. Listed buildings are not automatically exempt, although a small historic property like Anne Hathaway's Cottage without space to install a lift would probably be complying with the law if it provides an audio-visual representation of inaccessible rooms.

More or Less Visitors?

When the English Tourist Board asked attractions how they had increased their visitor numbers in 1995, 37% cited better marketing, while 19% attributed the increase

FIG.1/6: MAKING IT EASY FOR DISABLED VISITORS - FORT REGENT LEISURE CENTRE JERSEY

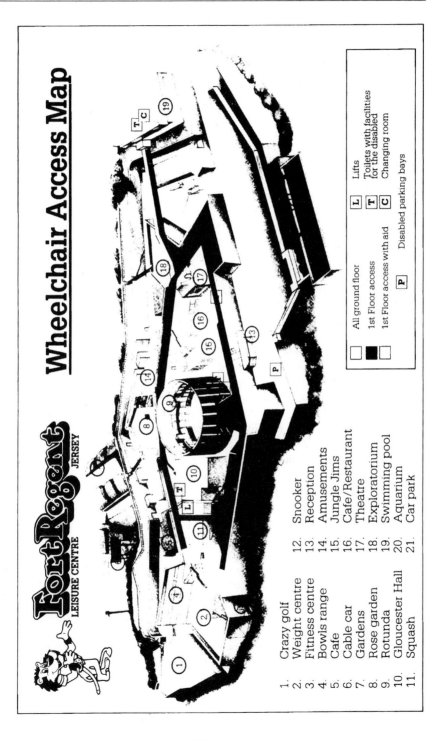

Wheelchair Access Map

Fort Regent
LEISURE CENTRE
JERSEY

1. Crazy golf
2. Weight centre
3. Fitness centre
4. Bowls range
5. Cafe
6. Cable car
7. Gardens
8. Rose garden
9. Rotunda
10. Gloucester Hall
11. Squash
12. Snooker
13. Reception
14. Amusements
15. Jungle Jims
16. Cafe/Restaurant
17. Theatre
18. Exploratorium
19. Swimming pool
20. Aquarium
21. Car park

All ground floor
1st Floor access
1st Floor access with aid

L Lifts
T Toilets with facilities for the disabled
C Changing room
P Disabled parking bays

increase to new facilities. Others said they had been helped by special events/exhibitions, good weather, longer opening hours and more group visits, including those by schools. Reasons given for a drop in visitors included bad weather, less money for advertising, the general economic climate, repairs and renovation, and fewer visitors to the area. Three per cent of attractions in Northern Ireland cited the ceasefire as a reason for increased visitor numbers; Armagh Planetarium alone received 99,923 visitors, a 157% increase on the 1994 figure.

THE EMPLOYEES

Paid Workers

Tourist attractions provide an increasing number and range of jobs, with Britain's 5,818 attractions employing around 85,900 staff. The number has been steadily rising through the 1990s, partly because more attractions have opened than closed and partly because of the emphasis on adding retail and catering outlets.The number of staff at individual attractions often depends on how many visitors are expected; on average three people are employed at attractions expecting up to 10,000 visitors, whereas 200,000 visitors will generate around 85 permanent jobs. The ETB estimates that the average wildlife attraction provides 27 jobs, the average leisure park 167 jobs and the average workplace 9 jobs. Not all these posts are full time or permanent; of 115 jobs at Harewood House in 1995, 40 were full time and permanent, and 75 were full time and seasonal.

In 1995 there were 5,423 people employed in Scottish tourist attractions. Forty-seven per cent of these jobs were full time and permanent, 15% were part time and permanent, 17% were full time and seasonal, and 21% were part time and seasonal.

The number of jobs at individual attractions varies enormously. For example, in 1995 the Imperial War Museum provided 389 full time permanent and 37 part time permanent jobs. Alton Towers had 250 full time permanent posts and 1,000 full time seasonal ones. In contrast the popular Jorvik Viking Centre only needed 27 full time permanent staff to handle more than 600,000 visitors. Where an attraction is expanding, with new restaurants, shops or rides, the number of employees tends to rise accordingly.

Jobs available range from those for which high academic qualifications are essential (for example, as keepers in the national museums and art collections) to more menial jobs serving in on-site shops and restaurants where the fact that the work is at a tourist attraction is more or less incidental. Nevertheless, all jobs which involve contact with the public require sophisticated customer contact skills, and the most successful theme parks demand high standards of dress and behaviour from all their employees.

Modern attractions have provided new types of employment both for designers and for costumed 'interpreters' who have replaced traditional custodians in places like the Museum of the Moving Image in London and Beamish. The former employs staff dressed as Russian revolutionaries who summon people to watch films in an 'agitprop' train; the latter has people in 1920s costumes who talk to visitors at the various sites and demonstrate traditional skills like rug-making and baking, while also looking after the day-to-day maintenance of the individual properties.

Volunteers

Many attractions, particularly churches, cathedrals, National Trust properties and steam railways, also employ volunteers. For example, in 1995 the West Somerset Railway used 400 volunteers; Canterbury Cathedral and Fountains Abbey 350 each; and the Victoria and Albert Museum and York Minster 200 each. However, such large numbers of volunteers were atypical; the average steam railway gets by with 69 volunteers, the average workplace with just 24.

TOURIST ATTRACTIONS AND THE WIDER ENVIRONMENT

Tourist attractions lie at the heart of the tourism industry, providing the reason for people to leave home in the first place. They also exist within the wider environment and have an influence beyond their own walls. In particular they play a vital role in local economies since most visitors spend considerably more than just the cash needed to see the site, in local shops, hotels, restaurants, bars and so on. While expenditure on services and entertainment only makes up 7.1% of what the average tourist spends, this small outlay often provides the justification for the remaining expenditure. The turnover of shops in tourist towns like York and Chester can be as much as 16% higher than in non-tourist destinations like Crawley and Blackburn.

Attractions are also affected by external factors. For example, in 1991 many site owners reported a drop in visitors as overseas visitors reacted to the Gulf War by staying at home; the number of North American visitors alone fell by 22.2%. Many site owners, particularly in the south of England, hope that the opening of the Channel Tunnel will bring more visitors from EU countries, reducing their dependence on the volatile American market. The relatively small number of non-Irish visitors to Northern Irish attractions is an obvious consequence of continuing political problems there. During the short-lived period of peace in the mid-1990s, attractions in the province saw a sharp increase in visitors; revenue raised from the 205 attractions in 1995 was estimated at more than £6 million, a 25% increase on the 1994 total.

The fate of the tourist attractions industry is also closely entwined with the work of British conservation and amenity groups. Although many theme parks, wax exhibitions and heritage attractions are entirely man-made and modern, other UK attractions are the result of the survival of historic buildings and artefacts, works of art and stretches of unspoilt countryside. For that reason conservationists work hand-in-hand with the tourism industry even if they can't be regarded as part of it. In some cases the continued existence of an attraction is solely dependent on the work of the National Trust/National Trust for Scotland or English Heritage and its regional equivalents. Amenity groups like the Georgian Group, Victorian Society and Civic Trust also ensure the survival of the sort of attractive environment in which tourism can flourish, while more of the countryside would rapidly vanish were it not for the efforts of groups like the National Trust, the Countryside Commission and the Wildfowl and Wetlands Trust. Without the National Heritage Memorial Fund and National Art Collections Fund more historical artefacts and works of art would be lost to British museums and art galleries and therefore to UK tourism.

'HERITAGE' TOURISM

If 'enterprise' was the business buzz word of the 1980s, 'heritage' was its touristic equivalent. It first raised its head in the 1970s when the Museums Action Group adopted the title 'National Heritage', the first 'heritage coasts' were designated, and Heritage in Danger and SAVE Britain's Heritage were formed. During European Architectural Heritage in 1975 the first heritage centres were set up. Then the pace hotted up. In 1979 the National Heritage Act renamed the National Land Fund the National Heritage Memorial Fund. In 1983 the Historic Buildings and Monuments Commission for England became English Heritage. In 1986 the Wigan Pier Heritage Centre opened, followed by Edinburgh's Whisky Heritage Centre in 1989. Now every town and village seems to have its heritage trail.

This trend is not restricted to the UK. In 1978 the French Ministry of Culture established a Heritage Directorate and a Commission for the Ethnological Heritage. 1980 was Heritage Year in France, 'heritage awareness' was promoted in schools and there were exhibitions of 19th-century culture. Heritage trails swept France too. During the 1980s and 1990s UNESCO also designated an increasing number of World Heritage Sites (see Chapter 13).

According to the Oxford English Dictionary 'heritage' simply means 'what is or may be inherited'. The current understanding of the word first developed in the United States. In the UK 'heritage' was originally thought of in terms of values, traditions and ideas, rather than in terms of paintings, historic houses, machinery, etc. However, in 1980 a National Heritage Memorial Fund report said that 'the national heritage of this country is remarkably broad and rich. It is simultaneously a representation of the development of aesthetic expression and a testimony to the role played by the nation in world history. The national heritage also includes the natural riches of Britain.., the great scenic areas, the fauna and flora'. In *The Heritage Industry* Robert Hewison claimed that heritage 'means everything, and it means nothing, and yet it has developed into a whole industry'. Clearly the UK tourist industry is very dependent on history but at the same time 'history' and 'museum' are seen as dead words, lacking pizzazz. 'Heritage' sounds less dry, more homely, even more patriotic. Nostalgia has also become important to other areas of business, as if the faster modern life moves, the more people want to look back and cling to their roots. 'Heritage' seems to encapsulate their mood.

So 'heritage tourism' really means little more than tourism centred on what we have inherited, which can mean anything from historic buildings, to art works, to beautiful scenery. In twenty years time it will probably mean Alton Towers and Thorpe Park too.

CHAPTER 2 : THE MUSEUMS

Museums, especially the best known ones like the British Museum and the Louvre, have played an important role in preserving and displaying heritage items over the last two hundred years. As interest in the past has increased in the late 20th century, so more museums have opened; by 1995 there were 1,497 of them in the UK alone. Nor has this growth been restricted to the UK; Japan opened 500 new museums between 1972 and 1987. By 1995 the British museums were receiving more than 57 million visitors a year.

At first museums were mainly seen as educational institutions. However, increasingly they are regarded as places of entertainment, competing for visitors with theme parks, stately homes and safari parks. As a result many have been forced to change, often drastically. In particular they have had to become more market-oriented than hitherto. Even the word 'museum' has sometimes given way to more modern names like 'heritage centre' or 'exploratory'. Actors are used to bring the past to life, videos and slide shows have proliferated and cluttered showcases have been replaced with streamlined displays, owing much to modern shop-window trends. Some of these changes are summarised in Fig.2/2.

WHAT IS A MUSEUM?

According to Dr. Johnson's 1755 dictionary a museum was simply 'a repository of learned curiosities'. In the late 20th century the Oxford Dictionary was more precise about the sort of 'learned curiosities' involved: a museum was a 'building used for storing and exhibition of objects illustrating antiquities, natural history, arts, etc.' In 1969 the Statutes of the International Council of Museums (ICOM) considered the motivation behind a museum; it was 'any permanent institution which conserves and displays, for purposes of study, education and enjoyment, collections of objects of cultural or social significance'. In 1973 the American Association of Museums also included financial considerations and the question of staffing in its definition: 'a museum is...an organised and permanent non-profit institution, essentially educational or aesthetic in purpose, with professional staff, which owns and utilises tangible objects, cares for them and exhibits them to the public on some regular schedule'. The Museums and Galleries Commission currently defines a museum as 'an institution which collects, documents, preserves, exhibits and interprets material evidence and associated information for the public benefit.'

In Great Britain a distinction is usually drawn between museums, which house objects whether from history or the natural sciences, and art galleries which house paintings. In other countries the two are not so clearly separated; the Musée d'Orsay in Paris is mainly devoted to paintings and sculpture and would probably be called an art gallery in England. Paradoxically the decorative arts have always been housed in museums in England too; hence the Victoria and Albert Museum contains one of the world's finest collections of art objects. Museums often contain books and printed documents but differ from libraries in that most of their printed materials are unique and form the raw materials for research. For example, the British

Museum houses the earliest manuscript copy of the old English poem *Beowulf* which forms the basis for the translation copies available in most libraries.

FIG.2/1: THE WORD 'MUSEUM' HAS UNFORTUNATE ASSOCIATIONS IN SOME VISITORS' MINDS.

(Source: David Austin, *The Guardian*, 1989)

In some ways the word 'museum' is a victim of its own long history, bringing to mind images of dusty collections unimaginatively displayed and assembled many years ago (Fig.2/1). Indeed as long ago as 1949 Sir John Fosdyke, then Director of the British Museum, wondered if it wasn't time for a new, less stuffy name which would sound less like a cross between 'mausoleum' and 'Athenaeum'. Consequently some museums now prefer to be called heritage centres.

THE EVOLUTION OF MUSEUMS

The Ancient Greeks used the word 'mouseion' ('seat of the Muses') to refer to a place of philosophical discussion. This passed into Latin and acquired its present spelling while still retaining its original meaning. The first building we know of that was actually called a museum was established by Ptolemy Soter at Alexandria in about 280 BC. It was probably more like the modern idea of a university than a museum.

Excavations at the site of the Chaldean city of Ur in Iraq suggest that as long ago as the 6th century BC monarchs were hoarding collections of objects which even appear to have been labelled, suggesting an outside audience. The Ancient Greeks and Romans didn't have collections of objects that were formally open to the public. However, many shrines and temples held art treasures and curiosities that would have been visible to worshippers. Private individuals also built up collections, and Hadrian's Villa at Tivoli, with its fine statuery, was just one place where ancient relics were carefully preserved. Tivoli even boasted replicas of the Erechtheum caryatids.

After the collapse of the Roman Empire most of the temples disintegrated and their collections were dispersed. Their role as custodians of artistic treasures was eventually picked up by the medieval monasteries which stored ancient manuscripts in their libraries and gold and silver reliquaries in their treasuries. The public were allowed to view particular treasures on saints' feast days although they had no regular access to them.

By the end of the 15th century the Renaissance brought a new emphasis on art and individuals, and private collectors became important again. Kings and queens had continued to gather beautiful and valuable objects throughout the Middle Ages, but now other wealthy individuals also began to collect objects, including paintings. In 1471 Pope Sixtus IV set up a museum of antiquities on Capitoline Hill in Rome. Amongst its exhibits was the famous Etruscan statue of a she-wolf suckling Romulus and Remus, now in the Museo dei Conservatori in Rome. The Medicis of Florence actually called their collection a museum, and in 1582 opened the top floor of the Uffizi Palace to display their pictures to the public. Between 1580 and 1584 the Gonzagas set up the first purpose-built museum at Sabbionetta, near Mantua. In 1523 the Grimani brothers bequeathed their collection to the Venetian Republic to promote learning and honour the state, the first private collectors to make such a donation.

By the late 16th century some Italian museums contained Chinese paintings and bronzes from West Africa alongside items made or collected nearer to home. A trade in works of art (and forged works of art) had also come into existence. Some of the new museums admitted the public without charge; others already levied a fee.

As the prosperity brought by wider trading opportunities spread north, so the focus of museum development gradually shifted towards north-western Europe. Private collectors still led the way and by the mid-17th century Cardinal Mazarin and Jean Baptiste Colbert had already accumulated collections that would form the basis of France's later national museums. However, such collections didn't always survive the death of their owner; in England King Charles I's fine collection of paintings was dispersed after his death in 1653, and when Thomas Howard, twenty-first Earl of Arundel, died his heirs failed to maintain his magnificent collection.

By the mid-17th century the expression 'museum' was sometimes used to describe collections of assorted curiosities. More specialist collections were usually called 'cabinets'. It wasn't until 1656 that any English collection was formally named a museum; a catalogue for the collections of the two Tradescants at Lambeth, popularly called 'Tradescant's Ark', bore the title 'Museum Tradescantianum'. This collection eventually became the Ashmolean Museum, the first English example of a museum built to house a specific collection; it opened to the public in 1683.

In the 17th century private collectors often bequeathed their 'cabinets' to learned societies like the Royal Society of London (1660) which began to take on some of the role of modern national museums. However, there was no real theory of museums (or museology) until Denis Diderot outlined a scheme for a state-run museum service in the ninth volume of his *Encyclopaedia* in 1765. Since 1750 Louis XV had displayed part of his art collection to the public in the Palais du Luxembourg. Now more went on show in the Grande Galerie of the Palais du

Louvre. Following the French Revolution the new government reopened the Grande Galerie as the Musée Central des Arts. However, it wasn't until 1801 that the Louvre was fully open to the public.

Many of Europe's greatest museums started life in the 17th and early 18th centuries. The Prado in Madrid opened in 1787 as a museum of natural science, only to reopen as an art gallery in 1819. Work began on what was to become the Rijksmuseum in Amsterdam in 1808. Tsar Nicholas I opened the Hermitage in St Petersburg in 1852 to display his collection of artworks.

Fig. 2/2: THE CHANGING FACE OF MODERN MUSEUMS

Area	Type of Museum	Change
Name	History	Heritage Centre
	Science	Exploratory
Setting	Folk	Outdoors
Entrance	All	Charges introduced even in public sector
Contents	History/Science/Specialist	More modern and ephemeral items displayed
Contents	All	Increasingly specialised
Presentation	History/Science/Heritage Centre	Employment of costumed interpreters craftworkers and actors
Display	All	Use of audio-visuals (videos, slides, sound recordings)
Display	Science/Natural History	'Hands-on' approach
Visitor comfort	AAAll	More chairs, restaurants, shops
Publications	All	More attractively designed
		Easier to read
		Exhibition catalogues as definitive texts with prices to match
Marketing	All	Increasingly professional
		Distinctive logos
		Links with other local attractions e.g. in heritage trails and brochures
		More advertising

As European colonies spread across the globe so museums spread in their wake. Many important overseas collections also opened to the public between 1750 and 1914. In 1778 the Batavia Society of Arts and Culture in Jakarta (later the Central Museum of Indonesian Culture) opened. In 1812 the Argentine Museum of Natural Science appeared in Buenos Aires. In 1818 and 1824 National Museums opened in Rio de Janeiro and Bogota respectively. In 1858 the Egyptian Museum opened in Cairo, and in 1909 the National Museum of Kenya opened in Nairobi.

By the second half of the 19th century museums had become fashionable and there was a boom in new openings. Almost 100 museums opened in the UK in the 1870s and 1880s, while 50 opened in Germany between 1876 and 1880. These early museums saw themselves as primarily educational and Liverpool museums took the lead in circulating items to schools. As more museums opened and technology offered new opportunities design improved enormously; imaginative curators introduced dioramas to set objects in context. Gas and then electric lighting made longer opening hours possible.

Until the end of the Second World War museums tended to concentrate on the needs of a few well-informed visitors, often researchers. However, the War changed attitudes. Many exhibits were put into storage and the empty buildings allowed curators to improvise with temporary exhibitions. By the time they reopened many curators were ready to experiment with design and to work with specialist conservators. Elitism became unfashionable and the need to encourage a wider audience was recognised.

However, most museums were still state-run and based on the often idiosyncratic collections of private individuals. Some faced considerable problems with shortage of space and lack of funds to make their displays more coherent. Since the 1960s a second boom in museum openings has placed more emphasis on entertainment and profitability. There has also been an upsurge of specialist and often privately-funded exhibitions. In 1993 the Department of National Heritage believed Britain had around 2000 museums, 1600 of them qualifying for help from the Museums and Galleries Commission.

THE BRITISH MUSEUM... DEVELOPING A NATIONAL MUSEUM

Like many long-standing museums the British Museum evolved out of the collections of private individuals, in particular those of Sir Hans Sloane, Sir Robert Bruce Cotton, and Robert and Edward Harley. These were augmented with books from the Royal Library which had been founded by Edward IV in 1471 and later amalgamated with the Royal Society Library and the Arundel collection of manuscripts. In 1753 Parliament passed a bill committing itself to buying the Sloane, Cotton and Harleian Collections and displaying them to the public with money raised from a lottery.

The Board of Trustees considered Buckingham House (now the Palace), the Banqueting House or a brand-new building in Old Palace Yard for their museum but these were all too expensive. Instead a private Act of Parliament enabled them to buy Montagu House in Bloomsbury for £10,000. After another £10,500 had been spent on repairs the collections were moved in during 1755.

From the start the British Museum was short of cash. The £44,000 left from the lottery was invested to produce an annual income of £1,320 but the Principal Librarian could only be paid £200 a year and the Under-Librarians £100 each. Only £79 was left to pay for the maintenance of the building and garden.

By 1758 the Museum had three departments: Manuscripts, Printed Books, and Natural and Artifical Productions. In 1759 the public was granted access under strict controls. Tickets had to be obtained in advance and it took up to three visits to arrange this. Only ten people per hour were admitted, and no more than five could visit in a party. Although the Museum opened late during the summer it was closed at weekends and over most holidays. Nevertheless, from the start it received an average 60 visitors, including some foreigners, every day. A small, dark room was set aside for researchers, staff acted as guides and the first guidebook appeared in 1761.

With so little spare cash for purchases the Museum was dependent on gifts from collectors. These included Egyptian curios, including the first two mummies; and 33,000 mid-17th century tracts donated by George III. In 1772 Parliament made an exceptional grant of £8,410 to allow the Museum to buy Sir William Hamilton's collection of Greek vases.

In some ways the British Museum compared unfavourably with the best continental museums. Although it was still prestigious and continued to acquire important items (including the Rosetta Stone, the Elgin Marbles and the Portland Vase), they were displayed haphazardly and William Cobbett thought the Museum reminiscent of 'the Old Curiosity Shop'.

Within fifty years of opening the British Museum had outgrown its premises. A new gallery was built in 1802 but the Elgin Marbles had to be housed in a makeshift room. Eventually Parliament agreed to provide £157,000 and Sir Robert Smirke drew up plans for adapting Montagu House to its present imposing appearance. However, in 1842 a new Copyright Act meant that the Museum received copies of all new books published which made the problem of space even worse. A new Reading Room was built but the piecemeal development of the Museum eventually resulted in the demolition of Montagu House in 1846. In 1878 all the oil paintings were transferred to the National Gallery and National Portrait Gallery. Then in an effort to make space available and to rationalise the exhibits the natural history collection was moved to a new home in South Kensington in 1880, becoming the British Museum (Natural History), now the Natural History Museum.

Gradually facilities inside the Museum improved. Until 1878 when electric lighting was installed students in the Reading Room occasionally had to be sent home when fog plunged the room into darkness. In 1893 lighting was extended to individual desks. By 1882 the Museum was receiving 767,410 visitors and introduced a restaurant for them. However it took sixty years' acrimonious work before the first definitive printed catalogue to the collections was produced in 1900.

During the First World War the Museum closed and most of its collections were evacuated to Aberystwyth and Malvern. In 1939, items were again moved to bomb-proof shelters in Aberystwyth, while larger items like the Elgin Marbles and Bassae friezes were stored in an Underground tunnel. However, the Museum closed only briefly and Reading Room students were simply advised to bring gas masks with them. In 1940 a bomb hit the King's Library, destroying 150 volumes, and in 1941 a bomb destroyed the Iron Library and another 250,000 volumes. The new Duveen Gallery for the Elgin Marbles was also badly damaged. The collection of provincial newspapers was totally destroyed.

The number of people visiting the Museum increased steadily once restrictions were lifted at the end of the 19th century (Fig.2/3). Opening hours were gradually extended, to Saturday afternoons in 1878, to Saturday mornings in 1881 and to Sunday afternoons in 1896 (although even now the Museum remains closed on Sunday mornings). Cheaper travel brought more overseas visitors, while the spread of higher education and greater interest in subjects like archaeology also helped boost visitor numbers.

In 1963 the British Museum Act changed the way the Museum's Trustees were chosen and removed anachronisms like having to have the Archbishop of Canterbury on the Board. The same Act permitted exhibits to be removed from the buildings, so the ethnography collection was moved to Burlington House in 1967 to form the Museum of Mankind. Most of the official publications had already been found a new home in the Woolwich Arsenal, so what had started out as a catch-all museum was now much more specialised. Items were also loaned to exhibitions in countries as far apart as Sweden and Afghanistan.

FIG.2/3: VISITORS TO THE BRITISH MUSEUM SINCE 1808

Year	Number of Visitors
1808	13,406
1812	27,479
1815	35,074
1817	40,500
1882	767,402
1975	3,000,000
1989	4,250,000
1994	5,896,692
1995	5,745,866

Since the Second World War the British Museum has seen many changes. When the Duveen Gallery for the Elgin Marbles finally opened in 1962 it was the first to be fitted with air filtering equipment to protect the stonework. The second floor now boasts a new gallery for temporary exhibitions. More photographs and electrostatic copies of exhibits are available to researchers, and the Museum's shops sell all sorts of books and merchandise.

Space remains a problem. Although there had been talk of moving the library since 1860, in 1927 88,000 volumes still formed a fire hazard on a basement floor. Between 1951 and 1973 several possible sites for a new British Library were identified. Finally, in 1996 the Library was preparing to move to a new home on a site near St. Pancras station.

As one of the world's oldest and greatest museums the British Museum has the advantage that everyone has heard of it, ensuring that even people with only a passing interest in history will visit it. It was also fortunate in being one of the first museums at a time when foreign administrators and adventurers could still remove property from other countries without penalty. The Benin Bronzes, the Elgin

Marbles, the Codex Sinaiticus, the finds from Ur and the Rosetta Stone are just a few items of worldwide importance which guarantee the Museum visitors, although its right to continued possession of some of these items is now disputed (see Chapter 13).

Although the Museum is perfectly situated, within easy reach of Oxford Street, Trafalgar Square and several underground stations, the building poses several problems. It was designed at a time when public buildings were meant to inspire awe, and the huge steps and pseudo-Greek colonnade fronting it can do just that. Only the sheer volume of visitors now flowing through the doors has removed the somewhat reverential silence which used to greet them. The building itself is listed and cannot be significantly altered which presents problems in terms of modern ideas of museum display. The newer Museum of London, for all its less convenient situation in the Barbican and its less famous exhibits, was at least purpose-designed to meet the needs of modern visitors and those working in it.

A new Japanese Gallery was added to the Museum in 1990, but the biggest changes since the War will only take place once all the books have been removed from the reading stacks in the courtyard surrounding the Round Reading Room. Work will then begin on a new Great Court designed by Sir Norman Foster to ease circulation. A better bookshop and restaurant will be provided together with a new Centre for Education. The Reading Room will become permanently accessible to the public for the first time. The Department of Ethnography will also return to its original home from Burlington House. Of the estimated £72 million cost of redevelopment, the Millennium Commission will provide £30 million. Another £21 million has already been raised, with big donations from the Sainsbury family to pay for a new African Gallery and from.the American Annenbergs for a new Information Centre in the Round.Reading Room.

THE FUNCTIONS OF A MUSEUM

Collecting

A museum's main purpose is often thought of as collecting which is hardly surprising, given that so many of them have evolved out of the collections of private individuals. However seeing museums simply as repositories for what people have chosen to hoard can cause problems.

In the first place a choice must be made between allowing the collection to grow or freezing it as it was acquired. There are still some museums, like the Sir John Soane Museum in London, the Lazaro Galdiano Museum in Madrid and the Phillips Collection in Washington, which are still in much the same state as when their original owners died. However, collections that don't change risk becoming fossilised and old-fashioned; reflecting only the tastes of their original owners, they can also seem idiosyncratic and lacking in coherence.

Nevertheless before a museum opts for a policy of growth it must be clear what it hopes to achieve. A natural history museum can reasonably set out to acquire items that will make it more comprehensive; for example, so that it will have a specimen of a seagull from each area of the world. However, even the Natural History Museum in London now accepts that it is impossible to find an example of every living species; indeed, it has abandoned an active collecting policy altogether. It is more difficult for a museum of decorative arts to do this. In the first place materials from some periods are very hard to find. It is also difficult to decide how many items of, for example Art Nouveau furnishings, constitute a representative collection.

Treating museums simply as collections also leads to other problems. For example, too much zealous gathering of objects can lead to a surplus which can't be displayed and is difficult and expensive to store; in 1988 the House of Commons Public Accounts Committee criticised several national collections for holding too many items which they couldn't display. An emphasis on collecting also tends to lead to museums being judged solely on what they can acquire, whether it is well displayed or not, which puts smaller museums at a disadvantage. It can also lead to the appointment of directors whose greatest asset is an ability to persuade people to part with valued items.

Education

Most museums are more than simple collections, and something of the word's original meaning has lingered in a recognition of their educational role. In 1825 when the Canterbury Historical Society for the Cultivation of Useful Knowledge decided to found a museum it regarded this as 'the most desirable means of diffusing information on various subjects connected with general knowledge'. The Haslemere Museum opened in 1895 with an overtly educational role. When the South Kensington Museum (later the Victoria and Albert and Science Museums) opened in 1857 it was seen as promoting an interest in and knowledge of modern technology.

The part museums could play in education was also recognised abroad, and North America led the way in promoting this aspect of their work; the Museum of Metropolitan Art in New York and the National Gallery in Washington were amongst the first museums in the world to have fully-fledged education departments.

At first most curators thought it was enough just to label items and let the public get on with it. However, increasingly museums are expected to put their possessions into a context and explain the ideas behind them. Few natural history museums simply present collections of stuffed animals any more; instead they attempt to explain complicated ideas like evolution which may need updating as new information becomes available.

In the 1990s most large museums explicitly recognise their educational function, often producing educational packs for teachers and students and setting aside special study rooms. Others have gone one step further; the Science Museum and the Museum of the Moving Image both employ actors to reconstruct scenes from the past for school parties.

Visitors obviously benefit from examining the collections within a museum. However they can also learn from museum publications, loan services, libraries, lectures, exhibitions, photographic services and facsimiles of famous exhibits.

Recently educationalists have made particular use of travelling exhibitions, painting and art classes, and questionnaires. Craftsmen and women have also been brought into museums so people could watch processes they might never otherwise see. 'Hands-on' experiences, with lots of buttons to push and things to do, are also used to bring education to life. The Geffrye Museum, which has a strong educational tradition, even lets children try on some of its costumes.

The line between education and propaganda is inevitably narrow and some museums walk a perilous line between the two. The National Museum of Ireland in Dublin used to devote a room to the life of de Valera, who worked for the revival of the Gaelic language. Most labelling was in untranslated Gaelic, making it of limited use to all but a very few visitors. Opened in 1936, the V.I. Lenin Museum in Moscow was more clearly propagandist since it was built at a time when Soviet Communism supressed all forms of dissent. The award-winning Tower Museum in Derry, Northern Ireland, faces the almost impossible task of presenting the city's troubled history in such a way that it will be seen as 'true' by both sides of the sectarian divide. It attempts to do this by presenting events like the 1689 Siege of Derry in as factual a way as possible and by providing two versions of events like the Home Rule movement seperated by a path, inviting visitors to come to their own conclusions. It's also possible for museums and heritage centres to present times gone by through rose-coloured and not entirely objective spectacles in their efforts to bring them back to life.

Museums also play an important role in providing facilities for research, some of it carried on by museum staff and academics, some by students, some by individuals. This is often 'behind the scenes' work, not visible to the public. Like many museums the Natural History Museum in Kensington houses laboratories, workshops, libraries and study rooms for serious research as well as its four acres of public galleries.

Entertainment

The tendency to treat museums as just another branch of the leisure industry might be thought of as new. However, particularly in the industrial north they were seen as places of distraction and refreshment even in the 19th century. There were even those who saw them as vital in providing something other than drinking for people to do in their spare time. As a result of their evolution some museums contain objects of worldwide cultural and historical importance. Consequently they can be seen as improving the overall quality of life by providing pleasant environments where people can relax surrounded by some of the best the world has to offer.

It can be difficult for museums to balance the competing needs of education and entertainment, and some have succeeded better than others. Deciding which of these functions is the priority can have far-reaching consequences. As long as the national museums see their primary role as educational it is easier to resist pressure to charge for admission. However, once entertainment is regarded as equally important it becomes harder to justify charging people to visit theme parks and stately homes but not museums.

HOW MUSEUMS ARE FUNDED

Museum costs can be divided into three separate areas:
- The capital costs of starting up the museum
- Day to day running costs for staff, electricity, gas, telephones, stationery, fuel, publishing, etc.
- One-off costs of new purchases
    Funding comes from a wide variety of sources.

The Department of Culture, Media and Sport

Many British museums include the word 'national' in their title: for example, the National Motor Museum at Beaulieu. However, there are also true 'national museums' directly funded by the Department of Culture, Media and Sport on behalf of the government. These are:
- British Museum
- Natural History Museum
- Victoria & Albert Museum/National Museum of Art and Design (including Theatre Museum; Bethnal Green Museum of Childhood; Wellington Museum)
- National Museum of Science and Technology /Science Museum; (including National Railway Museum, York; National Museum of Photography, Film and Television, Bradford)
- Imperial War Museum
- National Army Museum, Chelsea
- National Maritime Museum, Greenwich
- Royal Air Force Museum, Hendon
- Royal Armouries/National Museum of Arms and Armour
- National Museums and Galleries on Merseyside
- National Museums of Scotland
- National Museum of Wales, Cardiff (including St. Fagan's)
- Ulster Folk and Transport Museum
- Ulster Museum

The 1983 National Heritage Act established boards of trustees, with funding from central government, for all national museums. Some of the British Museums' trustees are still appointed by academic bodies like the Royal Society, the British Academy and the Society of Antiquaries, but the V&A's trustees are appointed by the Prime Minister and are often selected as much for business acumen as academic credentials; in 1996 the trustees included Maurice Saatchi, Lord Armstrong and Professor Christopher Frayling. Trustees are responsible for the finances of the national museums and develop policies for them. Increasingly they also undertake fund-raising activities to supplement government grants.

In 1985, Liverpool Museum, the Walker Art Gallery and the Maritime Museum became the National Museums and Galleries of Merseyside. This was intended to help improve the care and conservation of their exhibits and the acquisition of new ones, improve public access to the collections, improve their displays and programmes of events and help in the programme to regenerate Merseyside and north-west England.

In 1988 the national museums took over the freeholds of their buildings from the government's Property Services Agency which had previously looked after them.

The Department of Culture, Media and Sport also gives grants direct to several non-national museums: the Horniman Museum, the Geffrye Museum, the Sir John Soane Museum, the Museum of London and the Manchester Museum of Science and Technology. It also gives grants to the Museums and Galleries Commission (MGC) to fund England's seven Area Museum Councils.

University Museums

Through its financing of the universities, the Department of Education funds around 300 university museums and galleries. It also directly finances 18 collections in 12 universities. These include:

- Ashmolean Museum, Oxford
- Fitzwilliam Museum, Cambridge
- Barber Institute of Fine Arts, Birmingham
- Courtauld Institute, London
- Sainsbury Centre for the Visual Arts, University of East Anglia

The Scottish Office funds a further three university museums and the Department of Education for Northern Ireland another one.

Other Government Departments

The Ministry of Health provides support for around 50 hospital museums, while the Home Office funds several police and prison museums. The London Transport Museum is supported by the Department of Transport via London Regional Transport. The Ministry of Defence also funds an estimated 219 military museums.

Local Authority Museums

The 1845 Museums Act permitted local authorities in areas with populations of more than 10,000 to spend money from the rates on creating and administering museums. The 1850 Libraries Act also allowed them to collect artistic and scientific objects and books. The 1964 Libraries and Museums Act confirmed these rights, without obliging local authorities to set up museums. In 1993/4 local authorities gave grants totalling about £150 million to around 800 local museums and galleries.

Some local authorities run their museums as public services and don't charge for admittance. However, with pressure on them to economise, museums make easy targets and most now levy charges.

Municipal museums usually have governing bodies which appoint a Director to look after the day-to-day running of the museum and to liaise between staff and the governors.

Independent Museums

Most of the new museums created in the late 20th century are independently run. Some operate as commercial concerns, while others, like Beamish, are non-profit-making charities. Some, like the Ironbridge Gorge Museum complex, have huge administrations; others, like Sally Lunn's House in Bath, have a tiny staff and very little administration at all. Independent museums can sometimes obtain financial assistance from local authorities and other sources; for example, in 1990 the Wolfson Foundation and the government both contributed to a new £12 million Museums and Galleries Improvement Fund which could make grants to independent museums as well as those in the public sector.

The Association of Independent Museums (AIM) looks after the interests of an estimated 1500 independent museums and helps them pool their expertise through seminars, a newsletter, etc. It also publishes Guidelines on subjects like employment law and audio-visual presentation to help its members. The Museums and Galleries Commission also runs a registration scheme for 1600 independent museums which meet a set of fixed criteria. In 1993/4 it estimated that these museums had a turnover of £287 million, 23% of it earned.

Funding Difficulties

The national museums used to be funded entirely from central government which provided one grant for running costs and another for purchases. The British Museum was strapped for cash from the day it opened, and for many museums the problems have worsened as their buildings have aged and became more expensive to run. The rising price of art and antiquities has also made it increasingly difficult for them to make new purchases.

In the late 1980s and the 1990s, government-funded museums have seen their grant-in-aid frozen or falling in value. In 1988 the Commons Public Accounts Committee warned that they were becoming unable to care for their exhibits, pointing to a backlog of conservation work at the Victorian and Albert Museum and in the British Library. In 1996 the V&A's grant was cut by 3% from £31.5 million to £30.6 million, with a further cut to take effect in 1997. The immediate result was that admission charges of £5 a head were introduced. The Science Museum faced similar cuts, causing Director Neil Cossons to comment on the paradox of a situation in which the Museum had 'enjoyed extraordinary success in its continual pursuit of financial support for capital investment (only to face) the threat of reduced funding for running costs and ongoing maintenance.'

However, the grant to the National Heritage Memorial Fund has been raised to make it easier for it to help museums purchase items that might otherwise go overseas.

Local authority museums are often funded from the council tax and are prime targets for cuts when economies are called for. Even university museums are under financial pressure as cutbacks in overall university funding affect their ability to pay for them.

Faced with such problems museums can economise in several ways:

- They can cut costs by closing for one day a week or closing early.
- They can close entire galleries, or close them on a rotational basis to save staff costs.
- They can make staff redundant.
- They can sell some of their collections.

Alternatively, they can introduce or raise admission charges, or try and raise more money by selling publications and merchandise, charging for temporary exhibitions or renting out their premises for private functions. Almost all museums now have shops and restaurants; indeed much of the ground floor of the British Museum is devoted to fund-raising activities.

THE ENTRANCE FEE DEBATE

It used to be generally accepted that independent museums would charge for admission, but that the national museums and art galleries would not. However, even in the 18th century some people wanted to charge for admission to the British Museum. They were always overruled, and the 1845 Museum Act specifically authorised local authorities to subsidise free entrance to museums from the rates.

In 1972 the Museums and Galleries Admissions Charges Act made it possible for national museums to introduce charges. When the Conservatives returned to power in 1979 their policy of reducing public expenditure meant the question of charges rose up the agenda.

Since the National Maritime Museum in Greenwich introduced charges in 1984, more and more museums have followed suit. In 1987 the Natural History Museum, a long-time family favourite, introduced compulsory charges, claiming it would safeguard jobs and prevent the closure of exhibitions. The Science Museum quickly did likewise.

In general, it seems that admissions to museums fall by around 40% after charges are brought in. A short-term decline in visitor numbers won't necessarily be permanent; by 1990 visitor numbers at the National Maritime Museum had returned to their former levels. However, visitors to the V&A never returned to the level at 1985 after voluntary charges were introduced . Those most easily deterred from visiting by charges are the less well-off, those who live some distance from the museums and casual visitors. The better-off and tourists are relatively unaffected; for a tourist the admission fee represents a small part of their total holiday expenditure and they are unlikely to throw up a once-in-a-lifetime chance to visit just because they must pay to do so.

A few museums hold out against charges. Some, including Southampton Museum and Bangor Museum and Art Gallery, have even abolished existing charges.

Opponents of charges highlight the discrepancy between the 5,745,866 people visiting the free British Museum and the 1,556,368 visiting the Science Museum, the UK's most popular museum with an entrance fee. Julian Spalding, director of Glasgow's museums, points out that Parisians don't visit the Louvre which has an admission charge: 'It appeals to one-off visitors and the better off...who then benefit from the subsidies (while) the ordinary people lose out.'

FIG.2/4: TO CHARGE OR NOT TO CHARGE?

(Source: *The Guardian*)

In 1985 the Victoria and Albert Museum introduced a controversial scheme for 'voluntary' entrance charges. The Museum had been closing on Fridays to economise and had also had to abandon its Circulating Exhibitions Department which loaned objects to provincial museums. Its parlous state was highlighted in 1986 when poor maintenance resulted in water flooding a basement and damaging items being stored for the planned Theatre Museum. In the scheme's first year attendances fell by 40% and only 55% of visitors actually paid; £400,000 was raised through fees, but the cost of collection (installing and manning turnstiles, printing tickets, etc.) might have been as high as £100,000. It has been estimated that the £14 per head cost of subsidising visits to the Museum actually rose to £24 as a result of the reduced number of arrivals.

By 1996 the voluntary donations system was raising around £1 million a year, with the average visitor donating £1, much less than the suggested £4.50. The annual income had also started to fall (Fig.2/5), perhaps because visitors were even less willing to pay for entry if they also had to pay for admission to temporary exhibitions.

Faced with a £1 million cut in its annual grant, the V&A finally made voluntary charges compulsory in 1996. Most visitors to the V&A must now pay £5, which should generate an additional annual income of £2 million. But at the same time as the V&A was introducing charges, the trustees of the British Museum were agreeing to continue to hold out. With the exception of a few months in 1973, admission to the British Museum has always been free. By the year 2000 it is expected to have a deficit of almost £25 million without taking into account money which should be spent on new acquisitions. When the British Library has completed its move to its new site at St Pancras, it will stop paying rent to the British Museum, deepening the hole in its finances because the government will not increase its grants by the full amount lost.

FIG.2/5: FLUCTUATING VISITOR NUMBERS AT THE VICTORIA AND ALBERT MUSEUM

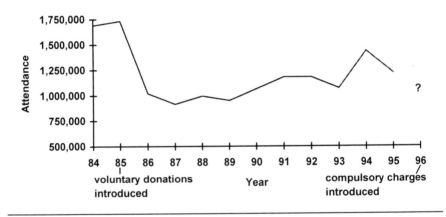

Dr Robert Anderson, director of the museum, fears that attendances would halve if charges were introduced. He also fears they would result in greater pressure to repatriate items like the Elgin Marbles (see Chapter 13). At present he can argue that the museum doesn't make a profit from displaying them. The rug might be pulled from under his feet if this were no longer true. The new government elected in 1997 have stated that in principle it believes in free admission to museums. However, it remains to be seen whether more money can be found to make this possible.

Even when the decision to charge has been made, the level of charge and who should be exempted still has to be agreed. Some museums charge outsiders but admit local people free or at a reduced price. On the continent most museums have entrance fees but also offer free admission on specific days each week. Inevitably the museums are packed on those days, but at least no one is prevented from visiting by the cost. Local residents can also time their visits to take advantage of the free times, whereas tourists with tight schedules will simply pay. Some of the UK museums with charges have a free period in the week; for example there is free admission to the South Kensington museums from 4.30 to 6pm on Mondays to Fridays.

Eight Glasgow museums now close one day a week in an effort to reduce costs without having to bring in charges. This followed a £1.3 million cut in their 1996 grant which threatened 40 jobs. Apart from the practicalities admission charges also present some museums with a moral dilemma. Past donations were sometimes made on the understanding that the gift would be put on show without charge. This was the case with the Wellcome medical collection, now in the Science Museum.

BUSINESS SPONSORSHIP

In the 1990s the government encouraged museums and art galleries to increase their funding through business sponsorship. The appointment of prominent figures from the business community to boards of trustees was intended to help this happen. However, although some museums have found business sponsors it's often easier to interest them in publicity-generating temporary exhibitions or in capital projects like new galleries which could carry their name. The Science Museum has been particularly successful in attracting sponsors, perhaps because its exhibits often relate closely to their work. In 1995 the British steel industry came together to commit £3 million in towards the cost of a new gallery, the largest-ever sponsorship of a British museum The British Museum has fared best with overseas sponsors (particularly from Ireland, the USA and Japan), although it has also received backing from the Wolfson Foundation. As more ventures have been encouraged to seek sponsorship they have come into competition with each other for what is, in any case, a limited pool of resources.

In an extension of the idea of sponsorship, some museums now have businesses as Corporate Partners. The Science Museum's 24 corporate partners, amongst them Eurotunnel, British Airways and John Lewis, have provided £445,000 for educational work over five years. In return they can use museum facilities for corporate entertaining, product launches, etc.

OTHER SOURCES OF FUNDING

Faced with financial problems, some museums have resorted to selling bits of their collections to raise money. In 1985 the Council for the University of Newcastle sold the George Brown Collection of Western Pacific artefacts to the Osaka National Museum of Ethnography for £600,000. However, when Kirklees Metropolitan District Council tried to sell a Francis Bacon painting which had been given to it for permanent display by the Contemporary Arts Society in the 1920s it was prevented from doing so.

In 1995/6 the V&A raised more than £9 million to top up its government grant. V&A Enterprises, which runs its shops, covenanted £520,000 of profits back to the museum. More money came from a commercial picture library, a restaurant, education programmes, admission fees, the V&A Friends and Patrons group, and late opening on Wednesday nights. An additional £1.8 million came from sponsorship; business sponsors include Pierre Cardin, Citibank, Habitat and Frederick Warne & Co.

MUSEUM BUILDINGS: DESIGN, LAYOUT AND FACILITIES

The Buildings

Although some old museums were purpose-built, they were usually designed in the 19th century when people had different expectations. Consequently they often resemble courts, police stations and other institutional power-houses, when nowadays a more homely approach is favoured. The Bowes Museum, the project of 19th-century private collectors John and Josephine Bowes, even manages to look like a French château in the middle of the Durham countryside. However, age can make a building seem more important and, of course, some are architectural masterpieces in their own right. For example, Alfred Waterhouse based his design for the Natural History Museum on Romanesque cathedrals of the Rhine and created a vast edifice of buff and blue terracotta with twin towers and a huge, recessed entrance. Sir Richard Owen, the first Superintendent, added to the extravanganza by having stone animals carved all over the facade.

Museums have been housed in all sorts of buildings, ranging from castles and prisons to boats, barns and old industrial warehouses (Fig.2/6).

FIG.2/6: HOUSING THE MUSEUMS

Name of Museum	Housed in
Colchester and Essex Museum	Colchester Castle
Norwich Castle Museum	Norwich Castle
Colchester Natural History Museum	All Saints Church
National Waterways Museum	Llanthony Warehouse, Gloucester
Robert Opie Packaging Museum	Albert Warehouse, Gloucester
Somerset Museum of Rural Life	Old barn, Glastonbury
Cotswold Countryside Collection	House of Correction (prison), Northleach

When it opened in 1989 the Design Museum showed what could be done when it was possible to start from scratch. The Museum was built at a cost of £7 million over the shell of a 1950s warehouse across the Thames from the Tower of London and with access to it by boat. Its design incorporates a lecture theatre, riverside restaurant, library and galleries for both permanent and temporary exhibitions.

Museums associated with famous historical or literary figures are often housed in buildings where they used to live or work. Many of these are small and cannot easily handle a large number of visitors. Plans to add an extension to the Bronte Parsonage Museum at Haworth have proved extremely controversial, but it's hard to see how many more people can be squeezed into what was once a family home. The Parsonage received 99,412 visitors in 1995.

Inevitably older buildings become expensive liabilities for institutions with tight budgets. As the years pass maintenance costs tend to rise. Nor were old buildings designed with modern expectations in terms of lighting and heating in mind, so bills tend to be higher than they would be in a new building. Most old museums have also had to pay for improvements to their restaurants, shopping areas and lavatories.

Facilities

Nowadays large museums are expected to offer all the following facilities:

Car/coach park
Refreshments: bar/buffet
                    restaurants
                    vending machines
Shops selling: publications
                    postcards
                    souvenirs
                    posters
Seats
Lavatories: disabled facilities
                    mother and baby rooms
Good, clear signs and maps

Some now have classrooms (Wigan Pier Heritage Centre) while others have their own cinema (Bradford Museum of Photography) or theatre (Richmond, Virginia; Figueres, Spain).

There is also increased emphasis on the needs of minority groups, including the disabled. The Museums and Galleries Commission issues Guidelines and employs a Disabilities Adviser to help museums adapt to provide access for disabled guests.

Layout and Design

With an old building designers have to decide how best to utilise space which may not be ideal for their purposes. This may mean building new rooms inside the old ones or creating modern settings within the old building. The Musée d'Orsay in Paris shows what can be achieved; within the constraints of a 19th-century railway station with a high, vaulted glass ceiling, the designers created a series of rooms and galleries of assorted shapes, flexible enough to display items of varying sizes and guaranteed not to bore or intimidate the visitor.

It is easiest to light showcases along the walls. Since such cases also tend to look more permanent than those in the middle of the room, many museums are lined with glass-fronted cabinets. However, too many of these can look dull so most have some central display stands as well. Most exhibits need to be enclosed behind glass, not just for security reasons, but also to keep off dust. However glass panels can cause problems with reflection so designers prefer to avoid them if possible.

Since museum displays may change, designers must build flexibility into their plans. Sometimes this can be achieved by use of moveable wall panelling. However high quality materials must be used to prevent the end result looking shoddy.

The first museum designers favoured quantity over quality and put everything possible on display. The Pitt-Rivers Museum in Oxford continues that tradition, but since the 1920s restraint has been more fashionable. Some designers took advantage of empty museum galleries during the Second World War to experiment with different sorts of display. Others have been influenced by shop-window display techniques and temporary exhibitions like trade fairs. Since the 1960s some museums have even employed specialists in display, many of them trained in the commercial field. However, the fewer items actually on show, the more storage space is needed for reserve collections; drawers and other storage facilities must then be provided near exhibits.

As with other areas of display, museum work has had its fashions. For example, before the advent of open-air museums period rooms were the most popular way of showing all sorts of different items of the same age in a proper context. Many such rooms can still be found in museums. One side is usually roped off and visitors look in across the rope. Occasionally they peep in through a window. But the rooms often seem dead and it isn't always possible to collect all the necessary authentic fixtures and fittings; walls and ceilings may well be reconstructions. They are also space-consuming, a problem resolved in one Chicago museum by creating miniature period rooms.

Modern museums often choose to piece broken items like pottery back together to make them more interesting for visitors. But when this is done care must be taken to ensure that the public can tell which parts are original and which just speculative.

CHOOSING THE EXHIBITS

The task of deciding what to exhibit normally falls to departmental curators who may be torn between their desire to show as much as possible and the display advisor's preference for fewer items more attractively shown. The public too are torn; some prefer to see just a few particularly attractive items, while others feel cheated if they are not shown as much as possible.

What can go on display is also dictated by what the museum actually owns. Many museums keep lists of items they would like to acquire to fill gaps in their collections. However, with prices rising and their budgets static most have to make do with what they already own. What is displayed is also likely to reflect certain limitations. In the first place most curators are specialists in particular fields which may receive preferential treatment. Many museum collections also tend to reflect the tastes and concerns of the aristocracy since the objects they owned are more likely to have survived. Outside influences can also affect what goes on display. In particular there are worries that commercial sponsors might try to influence what is and isn't exhibited.

Curators may also have to decide what is and is not in good taste. The Egyptian mummies have drawn fascinated crowds since they were first displayed in the mid-19th century. However it is possible that they would not be thought appropriate for display if they were rediscovered today. Several groups of people, including Australian Aborgines, have objected to the bones of their ancestors being displayed. Such objections might once have been brushed aside. These days they are more likely to be respected.

Many long-established museums own more items than they can display; the Science Museum alone has two completely separate storage sites, at Wroughton and Hammersmith. Some surplus objects may be of purely academic interest. However, others would be on display if there was more space.

MUSEUMS AND SECURITY

When it comes to security museums have a triple problem; they must ensure that their visitors can enjoy their visit in safety, but must also make it impossible for anyone either to steal or damage anything. As long ago as 1845 William Lloyd shattered the Roman Portland Vase into 200 pieces which had to be painstakingly stuck together again. He was only the first of many people to have attacked exhibits for a variety of reasons. In 1994 an arsonist attacked the William Morris Gallery in Walhamstow and caused extensive damage. In its guidelines for security the Museums and Galleries Commission lists the following essentials:

- reinforced doors and windows to protect the building's shell
- an intruder alarm system which is constantly monitored
- an automatic fire detector system
- security attendants in each room whose sole job is to guard the exhibits
- an internal security system relating to things like key ownership

THE VISITORS

Little detailed research has been carried out to see who uses Britain's museums and why. However, the UK Leisure and Recreation Survey for 1996 suggested that 28.2% of adults had visited a museum in the preceding 12 months.

The General Household Survey and Social Trends Survey also contain limited data on museum visits. In general most visitors seem to be from the higher socio-economic groups. They are also better educated, younger and more mobile than average. As people's incomes and levels of education rise so does their apparent propensity to visit museums. Apart from casual visitors, who seem to prefer general or on-site museums, there are five other categories of museum attenders:

- researchers
- people who want an object identified
- students/teachers
- volunteer workers, either with spare time or planning to join the museum profession
- overseas visitors

The average visit lasts less than 90 minutes, perhaps because the museum experience is tiring, with few seats available and labels that often require a reading age of at least 17 to be understood.

FIG 2/7: ATTENDANCE AT GREAT BRITAIN'S TEN MOST POPULAR MUSEUMS IN 1995

British Museum	5,745,866
Science Museum	1,556,368
Natural History Museum	1,442,591
Glasgow Art Gallery and Museum	992,320
National Museum of Photography, Film and Television, Bradford	620,000
National Maritime Museum	609,008
Birmingham City Museum	519,807
Royal Museum of Scotland, Edinburgh	514,475
Liverpool Museum	508,228
Imperial War Museum	477,784

Not surprisingly five of the most visited museums in 1995 were in London, the UK's tourist capital. Of these only the British Museum - far and away the most popular - was still free. All the other museums were in large cities with big resident markets. The Bradford museum is free and shows films which would be likely to bring it more visitors.

THE EMPLOYEES

The first museum curators were usually trained in specific disciplines and had little understanding of the museum as a whole or of its role in the wider community. Training was usually done via apprenticeships which hardly encouraged new ideas. In 1858 Civil Service pay and conditions were introduced for staff at the British Museum (until then staff stayed in their posts until they died since there were no pensions) and in return an entrance exam was instituted. It wasn't until 1930 that the Museums Association gave its approval to specific training courses, but by the 1990s one of the most popular ways of getting to work in a museum was by taking the Museums Association Diploma. In 1989 the Association helped set up a Museum Training Institute to approve, promote and provide training throughout the museums world. Funding comes from the Department of National Heritage and the Museums and Galleries Commission.

Small local museums often manage with half a dozen members of staff, but the national museums employ large numbers of people, many of them specialists. As many as 40,000 people, including part-time staff, may be employed in British museums.

Museum work can be divided into the following categories:

- Curatorial Staff: The academic staff are responsible for the care of objects held by the museum and for carrying out research to identify them and place them in context.

- Technical Staff: Many museums employ conservators and people to carry out building and restoration work.

- Commercial Staff: There are an increasing number of jobs as accountants, fund-raisers, marketeers, shop managers, display staff, etc.

- Administrators: They see to the smooth running of the museum.

- Educationalists: Some museums employ qualified teachers to work with school groups.

- Other Specialists: Depending on the type of museum there may be other specialist vacancies; for example, as taxidermists in natural history museums.

The professional jobs often involve work in the evenings and holidays, while attendants often work weekends or shifts, conditions which rarely suit women; only 34% of museum staff are women. There are even fewer women at the top of the museum world. Only 26% of museum directors and 15% of technical staff are women.

Like many public institutions museums employ a lot of volunteers, the majority of them female. In addition people hoping to take museum qualifications are required to spend some time working in one voluntarily.

MARKETING AND PUBLICISING THE MUSEUMS

Increasingly museums employ modern marketing methods to attract larger audiences. Despite their relatively small budgets many independent museums have led the way because their dependence on admission fee revenue makes it essential to attract as many visitors as possible.

Some museums work with the tourist boards to take advantage of their advertising budgets. Others have created immediately recognisable logos which can be stamped on merchandise to keep the museum in the public eye. For example, the Victoria and Albert Museum has "V&A" stamped on all its merchandise and publications.

One way to attract media attention is by winning an award. Perhaps the most prestigious is the Museum of the Year Award given by National Heritage, a national organisation set up in 1971 to support, encourage and protect the UK's museums and art galleries (Fig.2/8).

FIG.2/8: WINNERS OF THE NATIONAL HERITAGE MUSEUM OF THE YEAR AWARD

1976   Gladstone Pottery Museum, Stoke-on-Trent
1977   Ironbridge Gorge Museum
1978   Museum of London/Erdrigg Hall, Wrexham
1979   Guernsey Museum and Art Gallery
1980   British Museum (Natural History)
1981   Hunday National Tractor and Farm Museum, Stocksfield
1982   Stoke-on-Trent City Museum and Art Gallery
1983   Ulster Folk and Transport Museum
1984   Quarry Bank Mill, Styal
1985   Burrell Collection, Glasgow
1986   Beamish North of England Open Air Museum
1987   Manchester Museum
1988   Bradford Museum of Photography Film and Television
1989   National Portrait Gallery at Bodelwyddan Castle
1990   Imperial War Museum/Museum of Science and Technology, Manchester
1991   National Railway Museum, York
1992   Manx National Heritage
1993   Jersey Museum
1994   Tower Museum, Derry
1995   Ryedale Folk Museum, Hutton-le-Hole
1996   Buckinghamshire County Museum, Aylesbury/National Trust's Sun Alliance Exhibition at Uppark

DIFFERENT TYPES OF MUSEUM

Museums can be categorised according to their size or position, but particularly according to their contents (Fig.2/9). Museums and Galleries in Great Britain and Ireland, which is published annually by British Leisure Publications, recognises the following categories:

Aerial Photography	Agriculture
Archaeology & Prehistory	Arms & Armour
Ceramics & Glass	Children's Museums & Toys
Cinematography	Clocks & Watches
Coins & Medals	Costume & Accessories
Embroidery & Needlework	Fine Arts
Folk Collections	Furniture & Woodwork
Geology	Historical & Literary Assocs
Jewellery & Metalwork	Leather
Local History	Medical
Military	Music & Musical Instruments
Natural History	Philately
Primitive Art	Science & Industry
Shipping	Sport
Tapestry & Textiles	Transport

Comprehensive Museums

Perhaps the most old-fashioned type, comprehensive museums developed out of 19th-century belief in encyclopaedic knowledge and attempt to show the public something of everything. In the UK the British Museum is the best example of a museum that started out by trying to be comprehensive, showing archaeological and ethnographical objects, paintings, books and natural history exhibits, but which has become gradually more specialised. The Louvre in France and the Rijksmuseum in The Netherlands are of the same genre. The Vatican Museum is also similar although, in general, Italy, like West Germany, has fewer multi-purpose museums. Neither country was unified until the late 19th century, and it is possible that, without unification, there was not the same automatic assumption that the capital's museum should have first pickings.

Nowadays the great national museums rarely try to be comprehensive; their original natural history, ethnography, archaeology and fine art collections are normally housed separately. Comprehensive collections are more likely to be found in local museums which set out to introduce local residents to a little of everything.

Local Museums

Many local museums, particularly in British cities, also had their origins in the 19th century; about 300 such museums were established between 1850 and 1914. Many were set up as symbols of civic pride with the same overtly educational aims as the national collections. Some are housed in impressive purpose-built buildings, while others re-use redundant local properties, including churches, barns and listed houses. In the 1990s those that were run by local authorities were still marginally less likely to charge for admission than independent local museums.

There are two separate types of local museum: small comprehensive collections, and those that concentrate on topics of purely local interest.

- **Comprehensive Local Museums:**

  A local museum that aims to be comprehensive faces several problems. In the first place the choicest items are usually on show in the national collections. Secondly, it's expensive enough for a large museum with a large budget to employ staff with a wide range of expertise, but almost impossible for a smaller one. Nevertheless such collections serve a useful purpose in making it possible for those who can't travel to the national museums to be introduced to a wide range of topics, so most large towns tend to have at least one museum of this kind. Bristol City Museum and Art Gallery is typical of a local comprehensive museum.

- **Specialist Local Museums:**

  Local museums that opt for purely local displays face different problems. Their collections are likely to be most interesting to a limited local market although in popular tourist areas outsiders may also visit, especially in the peak summer months. One solution is to stage a programme of temporary exhibitions, whether locally put together or designed in collaboration with the larger museums. Alternatively such museums may close or curtail their opening hours in winter. Chepstow Museum is a typical specialist local museum, with details of the 19th-century trans-Severn tourist trade.

Whenever something historically important is discovered the difficult decision must be made between showing it locally where it may have a specific context, and displaying it in one of the national collections where more people will have the opportunity to see it and where it may be put into a broader context, allowing comparison with similar items from other areas. The larger museums may also offer better security arrangements and conservation facilities. Consequently finds like the Sutton Hoo and Mildenhall Treasures are displayed in the British Museum rather than local East Anglian museums.

History and Archaeology Museums

Museums are often thought of as synonymous with history, and indeed very few completely lack a historical thread; natural history museums usually cover the concept of evolution, while scientific museums often trace the development of different ideas and processes. However, the following types of museum are more narrowly historical in approach:

- those dealing with past events (e.g. the Imperial War Museum in London),
- those commemorating an individual, frequently in a building associated with their life (e.g. the Bronte Parsonage Museum in Haworth),
- those dealing with a town's past (e.g. the Museum of London),
- antiquities museums (e.g. the Egyptian Museum in Cairo),
- archaeology museums, often on the site of an excavation (e.g. Fishbourne Palace Museum),
- period houses (e.g. No.1 Royal Crescent, Bath),

Obviously historical museums are about the past although what exactly that means can be debatable. Technically, history only covers those periods of the past for which there are written records; archaeology deals with those periods for which physical remains are the only evidence. However, good history is also about interpreting the evidence of the past. The original museums were only really 'historical' in as much as they presented collections of relics of the past, many of them actually archaeological artefacts. However, most good modern historical museums try to interpret the items as well as simply exhibiting them. This can lead to controversy since the evidence may lend itself to more than one interpretation. Historical analysis is also subject to revision, so reassessment may sometimes be required. A good example of this is what has happened at the Imperial War Museum, once criticised for tending to glorify war. Since its refit in 1989 it now features a 'Blitz Experience' which helps visitors imagine the awfulness of being bombed with the aid of voice-overs and dramatic sound effects. In doing this it has shifted decisively towards emphasising the horrors of war.

FIG.2/9: TYPES OF MUSEUM

Type	Examples
Comprehensive	British Museum; Bristol City Museum and Art Gallery
Local History	Sheffield City Museum; Colchester City Museum; Museum of London
Science/Technology	Science Museum, London; Bristol Exploratory
Natural History	Natural History Museum, London; Colchester
Ethnography	Museum of Mankind, London; Pitt-Rivers Museum, Oxford; Horniman Museum, London
Open-Air	Beamish; St. Fagan's; Blist's Hill; Weald & Downland
Film/Photography	Bradford Museum of Photography, Film & Television; Museum of the Moving Image (MOMI), London; Lacock Abbey
Fine Arts	Victoria and Albert Museum, London; Barber Institute, Birmingham
Industrial Heritage	Ironbridge Gorge Museum; Bristol Industrial Museum; Mr Bowler's Business, Bath
Historical/Literary Assocs	Haworth Parsonage; Dove Cottage; Captain Cook's Birthplace Museum
Archaeology	Corinium Museum, Cirencester
Children & Toys	Bethnal Green Museum of Childhood, London; Eureka!, Halifax
Military	Imperial War Museum, London; Yeovilton Fleet Air Arm Museum; Stoke-on-Trent Spitfire Museum
Maritime	National Maritime Museum, London; Portsmouth Maritime Museum; Bristol Maritime Heritage Centre; Merseyside Maritime Museum
Transport	London Transport Museum; National Railway Museum, York; Great Western Railway Museum, Swindon; National Motor Museum, Beaulieu
Specialist	Museum of Advertising and Packaging, Gloucester; Harvey's Wine Museum, Bristol
Private Collections	Wallace Collection, London; Sir John Soane Museum, London

The museums of Eastern Europe have faced great problems since the collapse of Communism. Many of them have had to reconsider their presentation of events since the Second World War as it would be impossible to explain Communism's collapse if everything had really progressed as smoothly as the museums suggested. For a while some completely closed their modern history sections.

The very object-centred nature of museums presents curators with problems. Where no objects have survived museums can, however inadvertently, imply that they never existed. But the survival of objects depends on many factors: those made of better quality, more durable materials are most likely to survive; those owned by the wealthy are likely to have been most valued, increasing their chances of survival; and objects with sentimental, symbolic or ceremonial significance may have been more carefully looked after, ensuring their survival.

Of course the reverse also applies: objects made of poor quality material and those that were not valued by their owners do not usually survive. So some tools used in early food production were probably used until they fell apart, leaving nothing to show in museums. However, unless this fact is made explicit in accompanying texts the visitor may assume such things never existed. The increasing pace of technological change and the accompanying rapid obsolescence of outmoded artefacts may mean items survive for even shorter periods. However, the sheer quantity of them produced and the materials used guarantee that many will survive for future museums. In fact simply because more items do survive as we get nearer to the present day, it is also possible for museums to present an unrealistically foreshortened picture of history.

Curators may wish to help visitors understand how particular events unfolded or ideas developed. However, they may not possess enough objects to illustrate the complete picture in which case they may use graphics, models and photographs to supplement the objects and provide continuity. Indeed, in some developing countries history museums often consist of little more than a photographic record of their independence struggles.

History museums have also been criticised for virtually ignoring whole groups of the population, especially women and immigrants.

If museums in general have suffered from being thought of as stuffy, history museums have suffered most of all. One way round this was to develop a new, zappier name, and as the word 'heritage' grew in popularity, so many ventures that would once have been called museums chose to call themselves heritage centres instead. A consultant's report on the proposed Wigan Pier Heritage Centre stated that "a heritage centre is not a museum. The main point is to present a theme, not to display a collection of objects." The best history museums would say that was what they were already trying to do. And critics have pointed out that the heritage industry, with its emphasis on continuity, is even more inclined to romanticise the past by removing all suggestion of change or conflict than traditional museums with their emphasis on the unchanging solidity of objects.

Science and Technology Museums

Science and technology museums developed almost a century after the comprehensive museums which had interpreted science purely in terms of geology and natural history. In part they evolved out of the need to promote science and technology in a rapidly industrialising world. So the Science Museum in London developed after the 1851 Great Exhibition which had acted as a showcase for all things technological. The Smithsonian Institute in Washington was founded in 1846

as the result of a £1.5 million bequest from James Smithson. The
Museum in Munich opened in 1903.

Although science and technology are sometimes thought of as
museums usually seem more modern than others since their contents are   ....bly
more recent. They have always seen promoting an interest in and understanding of
science as part of their role, and in this they have the advantage that it's easier to
explain science with the 'hands-on' approach which has proved most appealing to
the public - and children in particular - than with objects behind glass. So the
Science Museum could always rely on objects with buttons to press to interest
visitors in a way that the static objects at the Victoria and Albert Museum could not.

One problem for science and technology museums is that they are working in
an area closely linked with each country's trading performance which could
compromise their objectivity. For example, England's Science Museum makes
much of the British-developed Advanced Gas-Cooled Nuclear Reactor, while the
Palais de Decouverte in Paris prefers to emphasise the French Pressurized Water
Reactor. It might be difficult for an English science museum to put on an exhibition
about an area of technology where Japan rather than Britain was leading the field.
Similarly it would be difficult to present an exhibition about watch-making which
would not show the decline of the English industry; this would be intellectually valid
but might not suit a government which was still holding the purse strings.

Displaying machinery also presents difficulties for technology museums.
Many art objects were produced to be looked at as such, so moving them to an art
gallery changes their setting but not their fundamental purpose. However, machines
were always produced to work, so when placed in a museum they lose not just their
setting but also their meaning. The problem can be resolved by putting the machine
to work again within the museum, but often constraints of space and safety make this
impossible. Alternatively visitors can be taken to the original sites of the machinery,
instead of bringing the machinery to them, an approach adopted at the Living Steam
Museum in Kew. Many open-air museums are more successful in bringing the
reality of industrial processes to life again than conventional museums; while the
reproduction coal-face in Wigan Pier Heritage Centre is certainly effective, it can't
have the impact of a visit to the Big Pit Mining Museum in Blaenafon which was
still a working colliery until 1980. Visitors to the Wigan Pier cotton mill will,
however, come away with a more realistic view of the harsh working life of the mill
workers.

Just as curators in history museums and heritage centres must grapple with
the frequently conflicting needs to entertain and to present the past realistically, so
curators in science museums tread a thin line between using exciting, attractive
technology to entertain and using it to educate. The Planetarium in London just
about gets the balance right, with modern technology, including holograms, used to
make a little-known branch of science (astronomy) interesting by projecting the
night sky onto a giant indoor dome. The hands-on 'exploratorium' idea pioneered in
the San Francisco Science Museum and Ontario Science Centre offers another way
of combining education and entertainment to provide 'edutainment'. This was
copied in The Exploratory in Bristol and Techniquest in Cardiff. In these 'discovery

centres' all the exhibits offer 'hands-on' experiences which encourage people to learn through discovery. This is more practical in a science museum where individual exhibits are not as often priceless and irreplaceable as in other type of museums.

Under Neil Cossons' directorship London's Science Museum has become much livelier. Cossons brought with him the more commercial approach to museum presentation of the successful Ironbridge Gorge Museum. In a five-year restructuring plan, he supervised the revamping of all the museum's facilities; lifts and lavatories were modernised, the shop was expanded and made more prominent, the cafeteria was franchised out and wardens were given a more casual uniform and retrained to treat the public as customers. New exhibits enabled children to create their own bridges and generate electricity in ideas borrowed from exploratoria. Actors were also brought in to bring to life figures associated with the history of science and technology. In 1995 the Star Trek exhibition and the relaunch of the interactive gallery moved the Science Museum up the list of most popular charging attractions from eighth to fifth place.

In 1995 the Science Museum received a government grant of £20,175,000 towards its running costs but since 1988 there have also been entrance charges. Other science museums are independently owned and, like the Science Museum, have attracted considerable business sponsorship, much of it from companies associated with science and technology. Such sponsorship inevitably raises the issue of potential interference again. At a time of financial hardship science museums have the advantage that technological artefacts are rarely unique and so tend to cost less to buy than artistic and historic objects.

Natural History Museums

Several of the earliest collectors were especially interested in natural history and 'Tradescant's Ark', the basis for the Ashmolean Museum, included the remains of a dodo, now extinct. Sir Hans Sloane's collection also included many natural history items so that the British Museum immediately had a department of natural curiosities which was very popular with the public. However, it was quickly plain that one building couldn't do justice to the differing needs of history, archaeology, books and natural history. Eventually the natural history collections were moved into Waterhouse's specially designed building which opened as the British Museum (Natural History) in 1881.

Natural history collections used to consist primarily of glasscases filled with stuffed animals and birds. However, they too have had to move with the times and present their collections more imaginatively and within a context. These days the Natural History Museum (NHM) at South Kensington would be unrecognisable to people who had visited in their youth, not least because it has merged with the old Geological Museum to present the world in its entirety in one set of 'Life' and one set of 'Earth' galleries. The glasscases are now relegated to corridors and remote galleries and in their place have come high-profile galleries concentrating on themes like ecology, evolution and human biology. A fine new gallery for mammals highlights the problems facing endangered species; in contrast the glasscases showing stuffed birds are introduced with apologetic labels stating that new displays will materialise soon. The NHM is now even more high-tech in its approach than the Science Museum; the popular dinosaur exhibition has sound effects, and computers and compressed air make the models move, while visitors can experience something of the impact of an earthquake in a mock-up of a shop destroyed by the Kobe earthquake in Japan in 1995.

The cost of modernising the museum has come in large part from private sponsors. BP, for example, contributed £1 million towards the cost of creating the magnificent ecology exhibition which, perhaps inevitably, mentions the threat to the environment from logging but not from oil exploration.

Many natural history collections are still shown in comprehensive local museums alongside historical and archaeological exhibits. However, there are a few other specialist collections, including the one at Colchester which is housed in the redundant All Saints Church.

Ethnography Museums

Ethnography is the study of the races of man and ethnographical museums usually exhibit costumes, artefacts and handicrafts from different cultures. The early collectors were as happy to snap up ethnographical specimens as fossils and medals, and these were increasingly easy to come by as explorers like Captain Cook roamed further afield in the 18th century. Their finds often excited the public; the South Sea Room in the British Museum was a favourite as soon as it opened.

Once again it was soon realised that the ethnographical collections were better taken out of comprehensive museums and shown separately. As early as 1930 a Royal Commission suggested that the UK should have a specialist ethnography museum in London. However, it wasn't until 1970 that a permanent Museum of Mankind was created at Burlington House. This showed artefacts from Africa, Australia and the Pacific Islands, North and South America, parts of Asia and parts of Europe. (The Museum of Mankind is due to move back into the British Museum.) Other important ethnography collections in the UK include the Pitt-Rivers Museum in Oxford, the Museum of Archaeology and Anthropology in Cambridge and the Horniman Museum in London.

Most countries with a history of colonialism have ethnography museums; the Musée d'Homme in Paris and Tropenmuseum in Amsterdam are the equivalents of the Museum of Mankind in London. Unfortunately many of their exhibits were obtained at a time when developing countries were in no position to prevent the removal of their treasures; some items were even stolen. For example, the Ashanti regalia found their way into the British Museum after British troops helped suppress the Ashanti king. The Benin Bronzes were acquired in 1900 after their king was deposed and his chiefs killed. Most ethnography museums no longer accept items whose origins or ownership are in doubt, but they are not as enthusiastic about returning even items which they hold in storage; the Museum of Mankind alone has 2,000 bronzes which can't be displayed. In the 1990s there were not only demands for the return of some such items but also complaints from aboriginal groups about their ancestors' skeletons being put on public display instead of being returned for burial.

Presentation of ethnographical items can also be tricky. For example, simply displaying some of the African objects without proper explanation can serve to reinforce prejudices about 'primitive' ways of life. However, cuts in university research budgets have meant that plenty of high-calibre anthropology graduates are available to create better thought-out displays. Some of the best of these have been temporary exhibits which recreated entire settings like Indian villages.

The same items which are regarded as exotically ethnographic in Western Europe become more mundane when shown in their countries of origin where they are often used to help create a sense of unity and to emphasise common cultural traits. The Khartoum natural history museum is an example of everything that is awful in museums (fading stuffed birds, specimens falling out of pickle jars, an emphasis on grotesque defects like five-legged goats), but the 'ethnography' museum makes use of some of the best western display techniques to provide an informative museum in a very attractive setting.

Open-Air Museums

Folk museums, or museums of the life and cultures of people from a specific community, started in Sweden where Artur Hazelius established the Northern Museum in Stockholm in 1873 to house a collection of folk art. In 1891 the Skansen Museum near Stockholm was the first of a new type of museum, displaying folk collections in an open-air setting. All sorts of buildings, including a log church, a manor house and farm buildings, were brought to Skansen and reassembled. Craftworkers were also encouraged to work at the site, alongside minstrels and guides in period costume. The new museum was so successful that similar ones sprang up all over Scandinavia where it helped that many buildings were wooden and fairly easy to move. The idea was also widely copied in Europe.

In English the word folk' often implies 'peasant' or 'primitive'. However, it can also means 'popular' or 'of the people', and in the United States folk museums of a different sort developed. The best-known example is Colonial Williamsberg, the brainchild of Reverend A. W. Goodwin. European settlers reached Williamsberg in 1633 and from 1699 to 1780 it was the capital of Virginia. After that it fell into decline. When Goodwin visited in 1926, 85% of its 17th-century buildings, including the William and Mary College designed by Sir Christopher Wren, were still standing.

Goodwin decided the site could be used for a total recreation of 17th-century life. He persuaded John D. Rockefeller Junior to put up $68 million to buy 65 of the 88 remaining buildings. Owners who were reluctant to sell were offered life tenancies. A holding company called 'Colonial Williamsberg' was set up to maintain their properties. Existing documentation was used to reconstruct the old Capitol, the Governor's Palace and the Raleigh Tavern which had been demolished. Even 18th century-style plants were reinstated in the gardens.

Colonial Williamsberg is unique. The present site only measures about one mile by a quarter of a mile, but $100 million was spent developing it. Although the original population is unlikely to have topped 2,000, 1,800 people are now employed just to feed, house and generally look after the tourists who flock there. There are 350 professional curators, architects and historians, with a further 400 carpenters, gardeners, etc, and 900 costumed guides. Two hundred and twenty period rooms are open to the public, each of them containing appropriate furnishings and often looked after by a costumed interpreter. During the day no cars are allowed into the historic central area, although life in modern Williamsberg continues on the periphery.

In 1912 the idea of a British Folk Museum at the Crystal Palace was first mooted. However, the UK's first real folk museum was probably Am Fasgadh (The Shelter) which was set up on Iona in 1936 but later moved first to Laggan and then to Kingussie. In 1955 four Scottish universities took over its maintenance with help from the Pilgrim Trust. The Creg Neash Museum on the Isle of Man, established in 1938 and made up of a group of buildings including a farm, a turner's shop and weavers' cottages, was another early example.

However, it wasn't until the Welsh Folk Museum was established at St. Fagan's near Cardiff in 1946 that Britain had anything to compare with the continent. And it wasn't until 1960 when a UK architect finally managed to lift an entire 14th-century house and move it out of the path of a new road that sites like the Weald and Downland Museum at Singleton where old buildings were reconstructed became practical.

Open-air museums can adopt one of two approaches: they can either try and freeze time as at Colonial Williamsberg, or they can mix dates and styles. The latter approach is favoured in the UK, and the Weald and Downland Museum shows buildings from a range of dates and sites. However, this can be deceptive; visitors to Beamish Open-Air Museum (opened in 1970 but still growing in 1995) could easily assume all the buildings originally stood on the site when in fact the Victorian terrace came from Gateshead, the miners' cottages from Hetton-le-Hole, the Co-Op shop from Anfield Plain and the other exhibits from other parts of north-east England. What's more the farm dates from the 18th century, the colliery from the First World War, the cottages from the 1890s to the 1930s, and the station from 1910.

Using open-air museums to educate can be difficult since too much labelling can detract from the site's 'natural' appearance. The problem is partly overcome where people actually work inside the buildings, showing the processes that would have gone on inside them and answering people's questions. However, this approach also has its limitations; cosy coal fires, the smell of freshly-baked bread and pretty costumes can make the past seem less harsh than it would have been in reality.

Open-air museums often depend on the generosity of individuals to donate suitable buildings. Curators also work closely with local authorities, road-builders, foresters, etc. to discover threatened buildings in time to save them. Most of the buildings used in these museums are original. Conceivably replicas would be as effective.

Open-air museums are certainly popular. In 1995 Beamish had 366,000 visitors, St. Fagan's 363,548, Ironbridge 297,359, the Black Country 228,384 and Weald and Downland 151,005. St. Fagan's also organises a programme of special events, particularly over holiday periods, which are guaranteed to draw capacity crowds.

Specialist Museums

In some ways specialist museums are most typical of late 20th-century museum thinking. Most of the world-famous museums started out as polyglot collections, only to become huge and unmanageable as more and more miscellaneous items accrued to them. Consequently they were broken down into smaller, more specialist entities. Now it's recognised that no one museum can be all things to all people and increasingly museums reflect specialist fields of knowledge, some of them very specialist indeed, like the Bagpipe Museum in Morpeth and the House of Hardy fishing tackle museum in Alnwick.

The Robert Opie Collection in Gloucester is typical of many specialist museums in the UK. It is also proof that, even in the late 20th century, private collectors play an important role in the development of museums. The Museum of Advertising and Packaging started life as the collection of Robert Opie. When the Victoria and Albert Museum showed a small part of it as a temporary exhibition called 'The Pack Age.... A Century of Wrapping' in 1976 it was so popular that the permanent museum quickly followed.

The Museum contains all sorts of packaging, advertising and point of sales materials, dating from the late 19th century to the present day. It's housed in the Albert Warehouse which was built in Gloucester Docks in 1851. Once a crumbling ruin, this has been refurbished to provide an excellent setting for a modern museum. A shop sells all sorts of books, posters and souvenirs to do with advertising. The cafe is beside a screen which reruns old TV commercials.

In the USA special children's museums are very popular. The first one was created in 1899 in Brooklyn, but the Boston Museum (1914), a general museum but with everything chosen to stimulate and entertain children and to complement their formal education, has been the trend-setter. In 1985 the Clore Foundation contributed £5 million to the Eureka! project to create England's first children's museum. This was created within the old engine shed of a Halifax station and in a landscaped park and its designers had already worked on the successful Granada Studios attraction. There are two permanent themes: the city and the world of work, with a mock town square, bank, supermarket and factory; and the body, with giant explanatory models. In 1995 the museum attracted 380,000 visitors.

OVERSEAS MUSEUMS

Different countries organise their museums in different ways. Depending on how their role is perceived they may be administered by departments of education, tourism, culture or the environment.

The United States

In the 18th century a few proto-museums opened in the USA. These included a museum of agriculture and herbal medicines established by the Charleston Library Society of Science in 1773, and the Peale Museum in Philadelphia which opened in 1786 and survived into the 19th century. However, 19th-century America was slow to follow the European lead in creating museums and preserving historic sites. This slow response may have been because North America owed its freedom to a dramatic break with the past. Most conservationists were wealthy landowners descended from the original colonists, like the Daughters of the Revolution group.

Nevertheless in the 20th century the USA caught up with Europe and overtook it when it came to new ideas. Now developments in British museums often follow American leads; for example, there are many more planetaria in the States than in the UK. The States also pioneered the 'non-museum', a sort of exhibition/activity centre concerned with public education through the medium of an exhibition but without the traditional dependence on a collection of original materials.

In the USA many museum buildings are owned by the city in which they stand. The city authorities may provide some financial backing but it is usually minimal and the museums are independently run, often by boards of trustees whose members include financial experts, adept at attracting endowments and one-off gifts. Only the Smithsonian Institute in Washington could be regarded as a 'national' museum like those in the UK. US tax law also helped the development of the Getty Museum (which has the world's biggest purchase budget), the Metropolitan in New York, and other private museums. There are also usually large groups of 'friends' who pay substantial subscriptions and take a more active part in the day to day management and funding of American museums than they do in the UK. The American media tends to take more interest in museums than does the UK's; many museums encourage this by producing regular bulletins.

Europe

In Western Europe state involvement in museums is more widespread than in the USA. In France there are many state museums which are administered and funded centrally by a Director of Museums based in the Louvre. However, most German museums are organised on a local basis through a network of 'Stadtmuseums' and 'Landesmuseums'. In Spain 'provincial' museums are frequently the most important even though this title would indicate something less prestigious in Britain. Until 1991 state control was at its most pervasive in the eastern bloc countries, a situation which will probably change as the countries of Eastern Europe develop new ways of running their economies.

TEMPORARY EXHIBITIONS

There have been temporary exhibitions in England since 1851 when the Great Exhibition at Crystal Palace in London was a resounding success, attracting six million visitors to admire more than 100,000 industrial products. This triumph inspired the New York Exhibition in 1853, the Paris Exhibition in 1855, the South Kensington Exhibition in 1862 and the US Centennial Exhibition in 1876. More recent huge exhibitions have included the Festival of Britain in 1951 and the Washington Revival Exhibition in 1976.

Increasingly museums see temporary exhibitions as a way of showing excess collections, focusing on specific topics or themes, and raising extra money from admission fees and sales of associated merchandise. However, they pose specific problems which include:

- the high cost of staging short shows in terms of staff time and effort, employing outside contractors to set them up, preparing catalogues, etc.
- the prohibitive cost of insuring masterpieces on loan. The Museums and Galleries Commission administers a Government Indemnity Scheme to help smaller museums cope with this cost
- the risk of theft
- the reluctance of some museums to loan desirable objects
- the fact that the public can be very disappointed if they've travelled a long way to see something which is on temporary loan elsewhere

Some museums, like the British Museum, now have a gallery which is specifically devoted to temporary exhibitions. Such galleries are designed to be flexible, and other galleries need no longer be disrupted. Outside sponsorship is frequently sought to cover the extra costs. This can come from foreign governments, the Arts Councils or commercial companies who hope to benefit from having their name on publicity materials; for example, the Victoria and Albert's blockbuster William Morris exhibition in 1996 was sponsored by Pearson plc whose name and logo appeared on all promotional materials.

Temporary exhibitions have always spawned posters, postcards and other revenue-generating back-up materials. However, recently some of their catalogues have become much more detailed, more like real books than traditional guidebooks. Inevitably they have also become more expensive. Exhibition catalogues are now expected to contain high-quality reproductions of all the exhibits with written descriptions and detailed contextual essays as well. It is now standard to charge in excess of £10 for these books. Sponsors usually provide a foreword and put their logo on the cover; however, the museum normally retains responsibility for the contents.

Some temporary exhibitions have actually promoted interest in other tourist attractions. For example, the huge exhibition entitled 'Treasure Houses of Britain', held at the Washington National Gallery of Art in 1985-6, contained items from 200 British stately homes and acted as a showcase for the UK stately home industry.

CHAPTER 3 : STATELY HOMES, CASTLES, PALACES AND GARDENS

Until the end of the Second World War Great Britain still had a flourishing aristocracy. Since then, however, although there are still many wealthy, titled families, few of them have been able to keep up the sort of lifestyle their ancestors had enjoyed. For many even maintaining their ancestral homes has proved difficult; an increasing number depend on revenue from visitors to their homes to survive.

THE ROYAL FAMILY

British aristocracy can be seen as a pyramid with the Royal Family at its apex. Royalty holds great appeal for tourists, particularly those from overseas who find their past history and modern lifestyle fascinating. This is so much the case that the part they play in the tourism industry and the revenue thus generated are sometimes given as reasons why tax-payers should continue to support the Royal Family. The figures for visitors to palaces and houses associated with royalty are impressive: in 1995 1,212,305 people visited the State Apartments at Windsor Castle, 594,000 went to Hampton Court Palace, 290,000 to Holyroodhouse in Edinburgh, 175,104 to Osborne House on the Isle of Wight (a favourite with Queen Victoria), 120,255 to Carisbrooke Castle where King Charles I hid during the Civil War and around 90,000 to Balmoral Castle.

FIG.3/1: VISITORS TO THE HISTORIC ROYAL PALACES IN 1995	
Tower of London	2,536,680
Hampton Court Palace	594,000
Buckingham Palace	412,000
Kensington Palace	91,178*
Kew Palace	44,000
Banqueting House	28,000*

(*1994 figures)

Buckingham Palace, the best known of all the royal homes, started opening to the public in 1993 to raise money for repairs to Windsor Castle after the 1992 fire. Despite charging £8.50 per person and opening only from August to October, it was visited by 412,677 people in 1995. In addition 84,616 people visited the Royal Mews where the state carriages, including the Coronation Coach, are displayed.

Royal homes have been at least partly open to the public for many years. Hampton Court, for example, has had visitors almost from the day work began on it in 1514 and quickly established itself on the circuit travelled by 16th-century foreign visitors who were usually shown around by a housekeeper in return for a gratuity. By the 19th century a standard fee of one shilling had been introduced for viewing the State Apartments. However, the number of visitors greatly increased after 1838 when the charge was dropped; by 1842 the Palace was receiving over 122,000 visitors, with the number rising to almost 370,000 in 1862. By the turn of the century organised day trips to the Palace were common.

Since 1989 the Historic Royal Palaces agency has cared for Hampton Court Palace, the Tower of London, Kew Palace, Banqueting House and Kensington Palace. It has also been successful in turning round a 25% decline in visitor numbers during the 1980s, in part by arranging improvements like the new Crown Jewels exhibition in the Tower of London, in part by joint marketing initiatives. In 1995 it received a government grant of £9.1 million.

Like Windsor Castle, Hampton Court now has admission charges again. Guidebooks, postcards and merchandise are also on sale, so a direct profit can be made from the royal heritage. The sale of Buckingham Palace merchandise was so successful a second gift shop had to be opened to cope with the rush.

Royal Pageantry

Special ceremonies associated with the royal family also have considerable touristic pulling power; an estimated 200,000 people a year watch the daily Changing of the Guard and the Trooping of the Colour in June when the Queen herself can be seen. These events are, of course, free. However, local shops and restaurants do better business as a result of them. Despite the high cost of staging such ceremonies it is also probable that fewer people would choose London as a holiday base without them.

Modern Tourist Attractions Associated with Royalty

By their very nature attractions associated with royalty tend to be old and traditional. However, in the 1980s there were several attempts to create new 'royal' tourist attractions to cash in on this popularity. The most long-lived was the 'Royalty and Empire' exhibition which was set up by the Madame Tussaud's group in 1983 in Windsor and Eton Central Station and showed the original Brunel station as it was in 1897 when Queen Victoria celebrated her Diamond Jubilee. 'Royal Britain' was a high-tech look at royalty which opened in the Barbican in 1987. Both these attractions have since closed, proving that a link with royalty is not in itself enough to guarantee success.

It has also been pointed out that the royal family's continued existence limits access to the royal palaces. In 1995 an estimated seven million people visited the palace and/or garden at Versailles, which is 13 miles from the centre of Paris. Arguably, the abolition of the monarchy could actually lead to an increase in visitors to attractions with a royal link.

Royal Parks

Tourists to London in particular also benefit from another royal legacy in the form of the Royal Parks: Hyde Park, Kensington Gardens, St James Park, Green Park, Regent's Park, Richmond Park, Hampton Court Gardens, Primrose Hill, Bushy Park, Greenwich Park and Windsor Great Park. Some of these are relics of the 11th century when one-sixth of England was reserved as royal hunting grounds. Others, like Hyde Park, were developed on ex-monastic land by Henry VIII. Most of the Parks were taken over by Parliament after the execution of Charles I and returned to his son Charles II when the monarchy was restored. As early as 1737 Kensington Gardens was open to suitably dressed members of the public on Sunday afternoons as long as the king wasn't in residence; by the early 19th century visitors were welcome every day and the Round Pond quickly became a popular place for children to bring their toy boats. Charles I had provided six gates and ladder-stiles to allow the public into Richmond Park. However, arguments about their right to access rumbled on until 1904 when Edward VII decreed that as many of the woods as possible should be open to everyone.

With no charges for going into the Parks it's difficult to assess how many people visit them and how many are tourists as opposed to Londoners lunching in attractive surroundings. However, more than 100,000 people may pass through Hyde Park on a summer Sunday.

The Royal Parks have been administered by the State since the reign of George III, and there is a special Royal Parks Department of the Department of the Environment, with a Central Parks sub-division to look after St James Park, Green Park, Hyde Park and Kensington Gardens. A special constabulary looks after all the parks except Hyde Park which has been policed by the Metropolitan Police Force since the Reform League Riots there in 1866, which also led to the creation of Speaker's Corner to provide a legitimate outlet for voicing grievances.

The Royal Parks Department looks after the park infrastructure, providing litter bins, lavatories, chairs and deck-chairs. It also provides the special crown-topped green and white signposts which direct people round the parks and employs the gardeners who care for them. Most of the general maintenance is contracted out to save money.

Since there are no admission charges to the parks, no direct profits can be made from them. Even when special events like concerts take place they are usually free. Nevertheless most of the parks now have cafes or restaurants and some sell guidebooks to recoup part of their running costs. During the summer there are regular performances of Shakespearean plays at the open-air theatre in Regent's Park.

CASTLES AND STATELY HOMES

While castles and stately homes are often thought of together, the word 'castle' actually means a large, fortified building or set of buildings, while 'stately home' means a large, magnificent house. In fact the two types of building belong, with some exceptions, to two different periods of history. Castles belong to the Middle Ages, to a time when life was uncertain and outbreaks of fighting could be expected at any time. Consequently they are found in greatest concentrations in towns which needed defending, along coasts and in areas regarded as potentially rebellious like the Scottish and Welsh borders. In contrast stately homes belong to the more settled, post-medieval world. Those built in the 16th century sometimes look as if their owners weren't quite sure about this, but by the 18th century the descendants of the medieval knights were building what were clearly houses for all their grand scale. What's more they were usually building them well away from towns. In his book on *English Castles* for the ETB Richard Humble identifies a cross-over group of 'fortified stately homes' belonging to the 14th and 15th centuries when life was more settled and owners were thinking primarily of comfort but when the Peasant's Revolt was a potent reminder that they might need to be able to defend themselves as well. The fortified house at Ashby-de-la-Zouch in Leicestershire is typical of this group.

CASTLES

Many British castles are preserved as ancient monuments and some, like Pleshey Castle in Essex, are little more than earthworks. Others, like Corfe Castle in Dorset, are picturesque ruins, sometimes deliberately destroyed by the victorious Parliamentary forces at the end of the Civil War in 1649 because their owners had supported King Charles. A few, like Arundel, Windsor and Warwick Castles, are still very much intact. Sometimes this was the lucky result of historic accident (Warwick), sometimes because they were heavily restored in the 19th century when medieval architecture was once again fashionable (Arundel), and sometimes because they were carefully maintained, even if no longer inhabited (Bodiam Castle in Sussex). Castles which have been continuously occupied up to the present time are obviously more likely to have survived in one piece than those whose owners long ago abandoned them.

Although many British castles date from the Norman conquest and are of mainly medieval or later date, fortifications also survive from the Roman period. Such fortifications include those along Hadrian's Wall and the forts of the Saxon Shore along the south coast, including those at Richborough and Porchester. Such 'castles' are better regarded as archaeological sites since the ruins would mean little without excavation and explanation.

Who Owns the UK's Castles?

Most British castles are now looked after by English Heritage, Historic Scotland and Cadw (for Wales). By far the most visited British castle is the Tower of London which is in the care of the Royal Historic Palaces agency. Its popularity stems in part from its important and colourful history but also from its situation beside the Thames in London, the UK's single biggest tourist destination. Even when English Heritage doesn't actually own a castle it has been able to make grants of up to 50% towards the costs of essential repairs since 1989.

Other castles are cared for by local authorities. Of these, the most visited in 1995 was Norwich Castle which, like Colchester and Newcastle castles, now houses a museum. Durham Castle (a World Heritage Site) is owned by Durham University. The National Trust also looks after some castles; in 1995 the most visited were Bodiam and Corfe Castle, both picturesque ruins.

A few castles are still privately owned. These include Berkeley Castle which has been lived in by the same family since the reign of Henry II, and Alnwick and Bamburgh Castles in Northumberland. In 1995 the most visited privately owned castles were Windsor and Warwick (part of the Tussaud's Group), but Hever (owned by the Broadland property company), Arundel and Dunvegan also attracted more than 100,000 tourists each. Lewes Castle is cared for by Sussex Archaeological Society. Leeds Castle belongs to a charitable trust for medical research.

FIG.2/3: BRITAIN'S MOST VISITED CASTLES IN 1995

Tower of London	2,536,680
Windsor	1,212,305
Edinburgh Castle	1,037,788
Warwick	803,000
Leeds	578,171
Norwich	520,000
Stirling	337,530
Dover	315,273
Hever	250,121
Blair	216,606

Castles probably play a more important role in tourism in Wales than anywhere else; of the 20 most visited historic properties in Wales in 1995, 14 were castles, with Carnarfon topping the list. They are also very important to Scottish tourism where 53 castles attracted 3,301,672 visitors in 1995. Carrickfergus Castle was Northern Ireland's most visited historic property in 1993, 1994 and 1995.

The Appeal of Castles

Some of the most popular castles owe their popularity to aesthetics; Leeds and Bodiam Castles in particular are everybody's idea of fairy-tale moated castles (Leeds is used for international conferences which helps explain its outstanding figures). Caerphilly, Conwy and Caernarfon Castles in Wales are also strikingly beautiful, as are Blair Castle, the third most visited castle in Scotland, and Eilean Donnan. It helps that many castles have remote or dramatic settings, Bamburgh Castle would be striking anywhere; set on the edge of the cliff overlooking the Northumberland Heritage Coast it is stunning. Stirling Castle dominates the Scottish landscape for miles around.

Other castles, like Windsor, Hever (Anne Boleyn's childhood home) and the Tower of London, benefit from royal connections. The castles at Norwich and Lincoln probably gain from being close to particularly popular cathedrals, while Clifford's Tower, not in itself the most impressive castle, has drawn more visitors since it took part in a joint marketing campaign with other York attractions. Like Conisborough in the 18th century, Tintagel owes much of its popularity (176,051 visitors in 1995) to romantic associations, in this case with King Arthur. Apart from its links with Charles I, Carisbrooke on the Isle of Wight probably benefits from being on an island with large numbers of visitors where sightseeing possibilities are relatively limited.

WARWICK CASTLE

In December 1967 Lord Brooke inherited Warwick Castle, a mainly 13th century building with a Norman core to which state apartments had been added in the 17th and 18th centuries. It had been receiving visitors since the 18th century and by the late 1960s up to 200,000 tourists arrived every year.

Lord Brooke employed the firm of Strutt and Parker to manage his estate as a tourist attraction. By 1975 the gatehouse, armoury and dungeon had all been opened to visitors, while from 1977 his private apartments could be viewed whenever he was away, on payment of an extra fee. By the end of 1978 the Castle was attracting more than 500,000 visitors a year. The site was then sold to Pearson plc, owners of the Tussauds Group, who started an expensive restoration programme, paying £50,000 just to repair one stretch of collapsed wall. The work included building a bridge to an island in the River Avon which offers a wonderful view of the Castle, and expanding the parking space to accommodate 350 cars and 25 coaches. A further £350,000 was spent on converting the stables into a reception centre with lavatories and a shop.

Once Lord Brooke moved out of the Castle the State Apartments lost their focus but research into the Castle's history showed that they had been the setting for fashionable weekend house-parties in the late 19th century. When it was revealed that members of the Royal Family had attended these parties, the Apartments' future was guaranteed. Lord Brooke loaned his furniture to the Castle, and the Tussauds' design team created 30 figures, including models of the Prince of Wales and the young Winston Churchill, as centrepieces for an exhibition called 'The Royal Weekend Party, 1898'. By 1984 Warwick was the UK's most visited non-royal stately home.

Work on developing the Castle continued. The mound of the old Norman castle was opened up to reveal a view of the Cotswolds. A Victorian Rose Garden was replanted, and the stable haylofts were converted into a restaurant. The 19th-century boathouse acquired an exhibition of local flora and fauna, and a bureau de change and tourist information centre were installed. In 1994 £4 million went to create the 'Kingmaker...A Preparation for Battle' exhibition which shows the last hours of the medieval baron known as Warwick the Kingmaker.

Warwick Castle is an example of a basically traditional tourist attraction which has widened its appeal by incorporating modern features, especially the Kingmaker exhibition with its animatronic models. By continuing to add new features the Castle hopes to attract vital repeat visits. They also provide a justification for price increases; after the Kingmaker exhibition opened in 1994 the standard admission charge rose by £1. In 1994 the castle was the English Tourist Board's Visitor Attraction of the Year and in 1995 it was visited by 803,000 people, many of them North Americans.

Changing Popularity of Castles

In the Middle Ages castles regularly offered hospitality to travellers. However, travelling was so difficult that no one did it just for enjoyment; there were no tourists, only embryo business travellers. Although some visitors took a passing interest in the architecture of their lodgings, no one seems to have assessed castles purely in terms of their aesthetic appeal.

When foreign tourists first started visiting Britain in the 16th century they tended to visit the Tower of London as well as the newer royal palaces. However, English tourists seem to have preferred the new to the old. It wasn't really until the 18th century and the coming of the Romantic Movement that visitors became more interested in ruined medieval buildings, including the many castles that littered the landscape. Conwy and Berkeley Castles began to receive increasing numbers of visitors. When Sir Walter Scott set scenes from his stories in Kenilworth and Berkeley Castles, they also began to feature on the itineraries of educated travellers. Conisborough Castle became so popular that iron rods had to be set into walls to strengthen them, while railings were put round the well to make the site safe for its many tourists.

Presentation of Castles as Tourist Attractions

The Romantic Movement which first popularised the castles placed great emphasis on 'active visiting'; tourists were encourageed to use their imaginations to supply whatever was missing from the site. In keeping with such ideas most of the castles now in the care of English Heritage are still shown to the public as ruins. However, wooden drawbridges may be reinstated to provide access in its original form, and moats may be cleared of rubbish and refilled, as at Tattershall, Caerphilly, Bodiam and Beaumaris, restorations which may involve installing new sluice-gates, waterproofing and concealed concrete support beams. New roofs may also be added to protect internal structures. Castles were usually built with thicker walls than abbeys and so often survived even deliberate destructive attempts fairly well; few have had to be as extensively excavated as ecclesiatical ruins. However, the ground plans of Bolingbroke and Montgomery Castles have been recovered and marked out by archaeologists. When restoration work has been carried out (as at Alnwick Castle where the decoy defenders on the barbican were repaired in the 18th century) site guidebooks should make this clear; different materials are sometimes used to avoid confusing what is original with replacements. Further alterations may be needed to ensure visitors' safety and to provide access to towers or walls; where possible replacement stairs and hand-rails should be made from wood rather than concrete. Sometimes wooden stairs can be placed over old stone ones to prevent further wear and tear.

The public often need assistance to make the most of their visit. English Heritage/Cadw/Historic Scotland sites usually have a sales booth, selling guidebooks as well as tickets and merchandise. Signs giving information about opening hours and prices are designed to be unobtrusive and are usually secured directly to the walls. There may also be plaques identifying different parts of the castle; boards warning against climbing on the walls, damaging the site or using a metal detector; and maps indicating when different parts of the site were built. Most popular castles also have a car/coach park and public lavatories. Most also sell refreshments.

Increasingly English Heritage/Cadw/Historic Scotland castles also host special events which may include vehicle displays, reconstructed battles and tournaments, concerts of music through the ages, falconry displays, flower festivals, craft fairs, guided tours, re-enactments of historical events, historical entertainments and dramas.

Privately owned castles which are still inhabited are usually shown in the same way as stately homes, with visitors invited to ponder a privileged way of life, now almost vanished. However, a lot can be done to make them more interesting. At Bamburgh in Northumberland there are waxwork prisoners in the 'dungeon', lavatories in the stables and a large restaurant and shop. Hastings Castle now houses The 1066 Story which attracted 84,337 visitors in 1995.

STATELY HOMES

According to the Historic Houses Association about 3,500 British country houses still retained their land and contents in 1990. Of these, perhaps 2,000 were still owned by families with long-standing connections with the house.

Stately homes evolved out of the fortified manor houses of the late Middle Ages which combined as much comfort as possible with the necessities for defending the houses if necesssary. In the 16th century the growing business class of Tudor England was able to buy land which had once belonged to the monasteries for grand new houses. Many were clearly built for display, implying that an audience was expected.

As Adrian Tinniswood has pointed out in his *History of Country House Visiting*, the new owners inherited the medieval tradition of hospitality to travellers just as travel was becoming easier and people began to move around for pleasure. Even in the 16th century John Leland had described visits to Denbigh and Sudeley Castles and Ewelme Manor, while William Camden visited Windsor Castle and Hardwick Hall. But foreign visitors, especially from Central Europe, were also starting to arrive in Britain, and they too toured the houses of the wealthy like Theobalds and Holdenby which were within easy reach of London. They were received as travellers traditionally had been, and were shown around the houses by a servant, usually for a tip.

By the 17th century country house owners were often wealthy enough to travel abroad and bring back souvenirs which formed the basis for private museums or 'cabinets'. Some of these became well known and people visited houses just to view them; diarist John Evelyn recorded visits to both Knole and Wilton House in search of curiosities. By the 18th century it had become more fashionable to collect paintings than objects, and Daniel Defoe writes of visiting Burghley House to see the works of art.

Early country house visitors were rarely drawn by interest in their architectural history. In fact many actively preferred the newer houses to the old; in the late 17th century Celia Fiennes admired Uppark, Chatsworth and Burghley Houses more than the older Haddon Hall, and expressed much greater enthusiasm for the 30-year-old gardens at Bretby than for the house itself.

In the 18th century a house building boom led to a rise in the number of visitors. More people started to tour country houses as the cultural climate changed and it became fashionable to know something about art and architecture. By the end of the 18th century Houghton, Holkham Hall, Blickling Hall, Oxburgh, Raynham, Chatsworth House, Hardwick Hall, Kedleston Hall, Wilton House, Wardour Castle, Longleat House, Stourhead, Mount Edgecumbe House and Saltram were particularly popular with visitors. Wilton House seems to have received 2,324 visitors in 1776, while Strawberry Hill had 300 visitors in the short season between May and September.

As visitor numbers rose, old ideas about hospitality became less appropriate. By 1760 Chatsworth had two regular opening days a week, and by the 1790s Blenheim was only open in the afternoons, while Woburn Abbey received guests only on Mondays. To visit Chiswick House or Strawberry Hill it was necessary to buy a ticket in advance; Strawberry Hill even had rules, including a ban on children. Only the smaller houses could afford to continue with casual admissions.

In the late 18th century visitors' tastes changed. Horace Walpole spoke disparagingly of the Baroque work at Blenheim, while Robert Adam's work at Kedleston Hall became particularly popular. Medieval architecture also increased in popularity as Romantic ideas took root, and erstwhile little-visited houses like Little Moreton Hall, Compton Wynyates and Haddon Hall began to attract attention. Visitors also travelled to houses associated with famous people: Shakespeare at Charlecote, Spenser at Penshurst and Byron at Newstead Abbey.

However, it wasn't until the late 19th century that country house visiting really began to take off. Until then only a small, elite group had had the time and money for such activities but with an increasing emphasis on educating the working classes, letting them into the stately homes with their fantastic art collections was seen as desirable. Queen Victoria led the way by opening Hampton Court Palace to the public free in 1838. The new railways also made it easier for people to reach country houses; by 1849 Chatsworth House was receiving about 80,000 visitors a year, most of them arriving on the Midland Railways train from Derby and then paying omnibus or carriage drivers to run them from the station.

After the First World War the advent of private cars and the popularity of country walking and cycling brought even more people to the country houses. In particular the boom in seaside holidays meant that houses and castles within easy reach of the resorts experienced an upsurge in visitors. Thus Corfe Castle was ideally positioned for people staying in Bournemouth. In general, with most of the population now living in towns, there was increasing nostalgia for the rural life which the country houses were seen as exemplifying.

By 1920 most stately homes charged for admission, and some also charged for parking. It cost 6d to visit Little Moreton Hall, Beaulieu Abbey, Corfe Castle and Brighton Pavilion, 1/- for Penshurst, Studley Royal and the State Apartments at Windsor, and 2/- for Wilton House, Knole, Warwick Castle and Blenheim Palace.

Financial Problems For 20th-Century Stately Home Owners

In 1894 the British government introduced death duties, signalling the start of financial difficulties that have plagued country house owners throughout the 20th century and have resulted in many houses becoming tourist attractions first and foremost. The amount owed by an heir could be enormous even if only paid once in a generation. However, the carnage of two world wars meant that duty sometimes had to be paid more than once in a relatively short period of time. By 1919 the amount owed could amount to 40% of the value of an estate worth £2 million or more. Inevitably the only way to find the money to pay these debts was to sell part of the estate; 8,600 acres of the Longleat estate were sold to raise £350,000. Under such pressure many owners allowed their houses to be demolished; between 1918 and 1945 458 country houses were demolished, amongst them Drayton Manor and Agecroft Hall which was dismantled and shipped to Virginia in 1926. In 1929 the unsold remains of Nuthall Temple were actually burnt to get rid of them.

In the 1920s and '30s the National Trust lobbied Parliament for tax concessions for owners who would allow access to their properties, something some of them were still reluctant to accept. The 1937 National Trust Act eventually permitted the Trust to accept a country house with its contents and enough land to maintain it so that it could be opened to the public while the original owners continued to live in it as tenants. The National Trust Country House Scheme quickly acquired Blickling Hall, Cotehele House, Penrhyn Castle, Melford Hall, Hardwick Hall, Ickworth House, Sissinghurst Castle, Saltram House and Sudbury Hall. By the early 1950s the National Trust was caring for 98 country houses, which attracted 700,000 visitors between them.

It wasn't until 1946 that the 'listing' of historic buildings (see Chapter 5) offered routine protection to the most important stately homes. In the same year the Labour MP Hugh Dalton created the National Land Fund which was intended to buy a wide range of properties for the public as a reminder of those who had died in the two wars. It had a theoretical annual income of £50 million, some of it used by the Treasury to compensate the Inland Revenue for tax revenue lost when houses like Hardwick, Saltram, Shugborough and Sudbury were transferred to the National Trust. In 1948 the government embarked on a survey of the surviving country houses which led to the 1950 report, Houses of Outstanding Historic or Architectural Interest. This in turn resulted in a clause in the 1953 Historic Buildings and Ancient Monuments Act which allowed Historic Buildings Councils to make grants for repairs and maintenance of houses which were open to the public.

The huge cost of maintaining these houses meant that yet another 712 were demolished between 1945 and 1974, 431 of them in England, 175 in Scotland and 23 in Wales. Age was no guarantee of protection; in 1965 16th-century Rawtensall Manor was demolished. Even the work of renowned architects disappeared; in 1964 Hawksmoor's work at Panton Hall was also pulled down. However, the value of land was rising so fast that some house owners who had moved out actually moved back home again. Enterprising owners also started to think up alternative ways of raising money; in 1949 the Marquis of Bath introduced lions to Longleat, in 1952 Lord Montagu opened the National Motor Museum at Beaulieu and in 1955 the Duke of Bedford instituted nudist camps and jazz festivals at Woburn Abbey.

In 1974 the Labour government floated the idea of a wealth tax which would have had serious consequences for stately home owners. At the same time the Victoria and Albert Museum staged the influential Destruction of the Country House (1875-1975) exhibition, which focused on a 'hall of destruction' and a voice slowly reading the names of all the houses which had been demolished 'as if they were names on a war memorial' (Marcus Binney). One million signatures protesting at this new threat to their future were collected at assorted country houses, and the wealth tax idea was dropped. In *The Heritage Industry,* Robert Hewison argues that this episode was crucial in the development of the idea of 'the national heritage'.

In 1975 pressure from the Historic Houses Association helped ensure that death duties were replaced with Capital Transfer Tax, giving tax exemptions to owners who opened their houses to the public for at least 60 days a year. The first charitable trusts were also set up to 'own' houses and their estates. But in 1977 the sale of the Rothschilds' old home at Mentmore highlighted the continuing problems facing those who thought such houses should be acquired for the nation. Lord Rosebery offered the house, its contents and the grounds to the government for £2 million, but although the National Land Fund had a balance of more than £17 million, the government refused to release the necessary funds. The house was sold privately and became a centre for transcendental meditation. The public outcry eventually led to the clause in the 1980 National Heritage Act which replaced the National Land Fund with the National Heritage Memorial Fund (NHMF). Unlike its predecessor, the NHMF could not only buy land, properties and artefacts but could also make endowments which made it easier for the National Trust to take over any houses it saved. Since then the NHMF has been instrumental in saving Belton House, Fyvie, Kedleston Hall, Nostell Priory and Weston Park. (In Northern Ireland the Ulster Land Fund serves a similar function.)

The wealth tax idea was raised again in 1979. Heritage In Danger, a pressure group formed to fight the previous proposals, warned that this could lead to the sale of £200 million of artworks and books to pay the tax and once again the idea was abandoned.

Even so, heirs to country houses continued to have difficulty maintaining them. In 1982 Henry Harpur-Crewe, the heir to Calke Abbey in Derbyshire, was faced with a capital transfer tax bill of £8 million. He offered the Abbey with its contents and enough land to maintain it to the government (who would then give it to the National Trust). However, the Treasury refused to accept the land, and the National Trust wouldn't take the house without it. Calke Abbey was remote and little known. However *Country Life* magazine ran a series of illustrated features highlighting the fact that its contents were virtually intact, and SAVE Britain's Heritage launched a campaign to save it. Finally in the 1984 budget the Chancellor agreed to give the National Heritage Memorial Fund enough money to buy Calke for the National Trust. Altogether £4.5 million (£65,000 of it from the English Tourist Board) was then spent on restoring Calke Abbey, with a car park installed in a paddock and the cattle sheds, stables and barns converted into shops and restaurants.

In the mid-1990s a new source of funding came along with the introduction of the National Lottery. Since 1996 both trusts and private owners of castles and stately homes have been able to apply to the Heritage Lottery Fund for grants to pay for repairs.

The National Trust and Stately Homes

In 1894 when the National Trust was created its remit was to preserve open countryside; it was only in the 1920s and '30s that it became involved with the fate of country houses. In 1923 the Trust asked the Treasury for tax concessions for

---

RESTORING UPPARK

Uppark in West Sussex is a fine 17th-century house with 18th-century interior which came into the care of the National Trust in 1954. The Trust accepted it with an endowment consisting of grants from the Pilgrim and Dulverton Trusts, some timber forests on the estate and an anonymous donation. In accordance with the wishes of previous owners, it was maintained with as few changes as possible beyond routine maintenance and descendants of the original owners continued to live there.

In 1989 a terrible fire swept through the house, bringing down the roof and destroying the first floor and much of the decor. Although some people argued for its demolition, reconstruction or rebuilding in a modern idiom the Trust opted for restoration and spent the next five years, and some £20 million, returning it as far as possible to the state it had been in immediately before the fire. The decision was in part dictated by the fact that the house was insured for the cost of 'reinstatement'. Thanks to the efforts of the fire brigade, volunteers and conservators on the night of the fire, almost 90% of the furnishings were rescued, including an Axminster carpet and curtains in good enough condition to be restored. However, during the course of the work conservators had to sift through 3,806 dustbins filled with debris dug out from the charred interior.

In 1995 Uppark reopened to the public and received 69,459 visitors. The multi-media exhibition on the fire and the ensuing restoration work was joint winner of the National Heritage 1996 Museum of the Year award.

---

country house owners who kept them in good order. This was refused, but the 1931 Finance Act allowed exemption from death duties for properties given to the National Trust; in 1937 this exemption was extended to owners who kept a life interest in their property despite giving it to the Trust to maintain. The 1937 National Trust Act acknowledged the Trust as a suitable protector for buildings of national, architectural, historic or artistic interest and allowed it to keep land and/or investments that came with the houses in order to maintain them. Local authorities were enabled to bequeath land to the National Trust and help with maintenance costs. The Trust could also covenant with owners to protect trees and prevent alterations to buildings in return for reduced death duties. In 1940 the first country house acquired through the new scheme was Blickling Hall in Norfolk, once home of Lord Lothian who, as chair of the Trust, had worked to interest it in old houses. By 1945 the National Trust was caring for over a hundred historic houses and by 1990 it was caring for almost one-third of the historic houses open to the public. However, its bids for houses are not always successful; while it was able to take over Cragside in Northumberland from the government in 1977, it failed to buy either Hever Castle or Shottesham Park.

Not all the houses cared for by the Trust come to it via the government in lieu of tax. Erddig in Wales, Basildon Park in Berkshire and Wimpole Hall in Cambridgeshire were all given to it directly by their owners.

In general the National Trust likes to maintain properties as living entities and encourages owners to continue to live in them even when they are managed by the Trust.

DefrayingThe Costs of Running Stately Homes

Maintaining a country house is tremendously expensive. The buildings themselves may need huge sums spent on repairing the fabric simply because of their age. The fittings usually need similar sums spent on them, and since much of the work required is of a delicate, specialist nature it cannot be done cheaply. Heating large buildings is formidably expensive and, of course, if they are to remain in use, they must be suitably lit and ventilated. Then there are security costs. If the building is open to the public security guards may be needed, together with alarms to protect the fittings. Even if the building is closed some security will be needed to prevent it falling prey to vandals or squatters. Opening to the public brings in money to help defray the costs but initially involves further investment: in printing tickets, guidebooks and other materials, in installing lavatories, litter bins, car parks and other amenities, in salaries for guides and custodians. Capital investment may also be required, for example to convert stables into a shop or restaurant.

Stately home owners have shown considerable ingenuity in dreaming up cash-generating schemes:

- Their biggest asset is often that their houses are the centre of large estates, offering space for other activities; the grounds of Knebworth House are used for large pop concerts and the grounds of Longleat House now contain 13 separate attractions as well as a safari park. Loseley Park, once in a poor state of repair, now has a dairy farm which supplies health food shops and restaurants; the house is also hired out for film-making and is open to the public to qualify for valuable government repairs grants. Others offer grouse or pigeon-shooting in their grounds. Jousting and falconry displays are also popular ways of attracting extra visitors; there are falconry displays at

Sudeley Castle. Most such ventures are blatantly commercial. However even the National Trust uses the grounds of its houses for other activities, with regular Classical music concerts in the grounds of Parham House. Kenwood House (English Heritage) in London is a popular venue for outdoor concerts.

- Medieval banquets are held at Caldicot Castle and Elizabethan ones at Hatfield House. A specialist agency called Heritage Events runs the Stately Homes Musical Fesival. Many historic houses, including Althorp, Hatfield, Hagley, Warwick Castle and Ripley Castle, market themselves as bases for corporate entertainment. Others offer themselves as conference venues.

- Turning stately homes into hotels enables them to keep external and internal features intact. This idea has been particularly successful in Spain and Portugal where the upmarket 'paradores' and 'poussadas' are hotels in reused historic buildings, including castles and country houses. In the UK Thistle Hotels spent £4 million refitting 12th-century New Hall in Warwickshire as a hotel, and another £3.5 million on Cannizaro House on Wimbledon Common. In 1988 Amberley Castle also opened as a luxury hotel and restaurant and the late Bob Paynton turned 18th-century Stapleford Park in Leicestershire into an upmarket country house hotel with 35 individually designed bedrooms. Such houses may not be real visitor attractions but are still accessible to tourists, with much of their appeal (and the justification for their high prices) coming from their architectural beauty and historic interest.

- At Kentwell Hall in Suffolk the public are invited to take part in large-scale recreations of the past each summer.

The grounds of Beaulieu and Woburn Abbeys are showcases for what is possible. The core of the Beaulieu site is a ruined medieval abbey, now overshadowed by Palace House which displays costumed figures in keeping with the Montagu family history. A monorail links various attractions in the grounds. Foremost amongst these is the National Motor Museum with its collection of vintage cars and commercial vehicles. Within it 'Wheels' is a Jorvik-style exhibition with time cars to take visitors past the history of the car. The grounds also contain an audio-visual exhibition called Transporama (see also Chapter 8).

In 1953 when the 13th Duke of Bedford inherited Woburn Abbey he also inherited £5 million of death duties. His response was to start marketing his home as a tourist attraction in a more adventurous way. Although the family actually lived elsewhere he sold the Abbey as a family home and toured the house regularly so guests could see him. When he served in the shop takings soared by between 30 and 50%.

The 11th Duke had brought a few Chinese Père David's deer to Woburn Abbey. On their own they wouldn't have been enough to draw the visitors, so the wildlife stock was greatly expanded. Other parts of the grounds were used for concerts. In the first year of opening Woburn Abbey attracted 181,000 visitors, rising to 234,000 in the second year. By 1995 it was attracting almost a million people a year.

Some properties, like Hopetoun and Chatsworth House, are now operated as charitable trusts. The Duke of Marlborough has hosted 'at home' parties in Blenheim Palace for wealthy Americans prepared to pay between £6,000 and £30,000 for a ticket. All proceeds go to the Blenheim Foundation, a private trust set up to maintain the 18th-century palace.

Presenting and Caring for Stately Homes

When a stately home is to be opened to the public decisions must be made about how it should be displayed. Whereas castles are often presented as ruins, country houses are usually shown as homes with furnishings and artworks intact. There are some exceptions: 19th-century Belsay Hall is one house open to the public bereft of furniture. Sometimes the furnishings will have been donated with the house itself, sometimes they will have been given at a later date or bought separately. Unlike museums, country houses display the fine and decorative arts side by side. Many people find it easier to appreciate art when it has a proper context like this, so some museums reproduce whole rooms in an attempt to emulate stately homes.

Fittings and furniture can need almost as much maintenance as the building itself and the National Trust employs an army of conservators to carry out the work. Furnishings must be protected against pests like silverfish, death-watch beetle, moths and mice which can seriously damage them. Humidity levels in most houses must also be controlled; if it's too dry paint and wood may crack, while if it's too damp mould may grow on books and fabrics. Sudden changes in humidity can also cause paintings to flake. Ideally, a low, steady temperature should be maintained throughout the day or dehumidifiers should be put in every room to remove excess moisture. Fabrics, furnishings and paintings can also be damaged by too much light. At the brightest times of day blinds may need to be pulled down. Using ultra-violet filters on the windows can also help. When the house is closed blackout curtains should be pulled or shutters used to protect the contents. Although flash photography is often forbidden in stately homes it is more because sudden bright light can trigger alarms or spoil other people's view than because the flash will damage the fittings.

To protect furnishings and paintings from the damage caused by constant touching visitors must often follow a roped-off route. Ropes are usually kept low and unobtrusive. Modern carpeting is often laid over antique carpets where the public will walk, and extra carpeting supplied near entrances where mud might be walked in. British visitors can usually walk through rooms in normal footwear; abroad, however, they may have to don cloth overshoes to protect the floors.

In the winter when many houses are closed to the public furniture may be covered with dustsheets to protect it. Items like chandeliers may be taken down for cleaning. All maintenance work is carried out using soft hand brushes and non-abrasive polishes to do the least possible damage. This whole process of 'putting a country house to bed' for the winter has been turned into an event attraction in its own right at several National Trust properties.

In 1995 583 historic properties, amongst them several stately homes, offered guided tours. Others, like neo-Norman Penrhyn Castle in Wales, offered audio tours, enabling visitors to move round at will.

Many stately homes have outhouses - perhaps stables, a barn or lodge cottages - which have great potential for conversion, often allowing blatantly commercial activities to be carried out away from the house itself. Stable blocks frequently become ticket offices, shops, restaurants or lavatory blocks. Sometimes they are let as offices or workshops, as at Sudeley Castle where the Dungeon Tower contains several craft workshops. Occasionally extraneous buildings like gate-houses or follies are also sub-let to bring in extra revenue.

Visitors

Stately homes are probably most popular with the older, wealthier end of the UK market. They are also especially attractive to overseas visitors; in 1995 overseas tourists made up 34% of the visitors to English historic properties, the highest percentage for any type of attraction. Those who visit don't always know a lot about architectural history; often they are more curious about the way of life represented by the stately homes. Castles may appeal to a wider audience, including more children. Obviously adding other attractions to the grounds of a property will influence the audience it attracts.

Opening Hours and Admission Charges

Some stately homes open every day, all year round. Others either close for the winter (usually defined as the end of October through to the end of March) or curtail their opening hours. Since castles are frequently ruinous and less suitable for cold weather visiting they are more likely to close in winter; in Scotland in 1995 84% of visits to castles took place between April and September compared with 73% of visits to historic houses. The average historic property in Britain was open for 206 days in 1995. The English Tourist Board produces a special Open House regional guide to historic properties. In the winter edition it highlights special winter events (fireworks displays, concerts, crafts fairs, antiques shows) and dates when stately home shops will be open for Christmas shopping.

In general, visiting historic houses is more expensive than visiting ruined castles because of the high costs of heating, lighting, conservation, custodianship, etc. Nevertheless the National Trust doubts if high prices are a deterrent to its particular market, partly because they tend to come from higher socio-economic groups, partly because they have often made a special journey to view the property and won't be put off unless the price is out of line with the average.

MARKETING STATELY HOMES AND CASTLES

Since 1987 the Historic Houses Association (which represents the interests of about 1,400 historic houses, parks and gardens in private ownership) has published the Historic Houses Directory which lists opening hours and admission fees for about 150 properties. Houses in the care of the National Trust are listed in the Trust handbook. The annual Historic Houses and Gardens directory published by British Leisure Publications also gives details of most properties.

National Trust signposts with their distinctive 'acorn' logo and English Heritage ones with a red square alert passing motorists to attractions they might not know about. Other properties benefit from brown and white tourist attractions signs (see Chapter 1).

The Treasure Houses of England

There are distinct benefits for properties which agree to work together, especially when it comes to marketing. Consequently ten of England's most popular privately-owned houses - Beaulieu, Blenheim Palace, Castle Howard, Chatsworth, Harewood House, Leeds Castle, Longleat, Warwick Castle, Wilton House and Woburn Abbey - have formed a consortium called the Treasure Houses of England.

FIG.3/3: POSITION OF TREASURE HOUSES OF ENGLAND

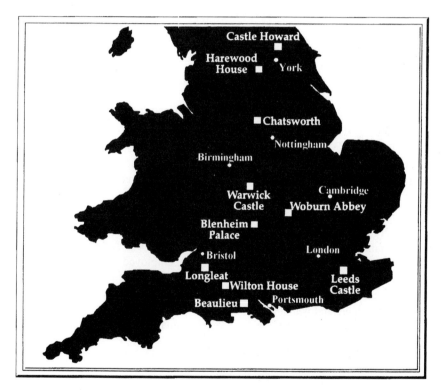

The Treasure Houses concept facilitates cost-effective advertising for its members since they only need one leaflet with details of each property, a picture of its coat of arms and a route map showing its position vis-à-vis the other properties. A visitor to any one house can pick up literature advertising the other nine. The leaflets are produced in several languages including French, Spanish, Italian and Japanese. In addition they contain discount vouchers as an incentive to visit the other properties, in the same way that National Trust or English Heritage members have an incentive to visit several properties to get full benefit from their subscriptions.

FIG.3/4: VISITORS TO THE TREASURE HOUSES OF ENGLAND IN 1995

Property	Visitor Nos.	Area of Group Responsibility
Warwick Castle	803,000	Promotions
Leeds Castle	578,171	Advertising
Blenheim Palace	436,332	Sponsorship
Beaulieu	415,600	Secretariat
Chatsworth	395,302	Travel Trade Liaison
Harewood House	266,446	Workshops & Exhibitions
Castle Howard	200,000*	Print
Longleat House	136,000	Distribution
Wilton House	108,159	Public Relations
Woburn Abbey	200,000*	Finances & Video

(* estimated figure)

Different marketing tasks are also spread around the houses, instead of each having to be undertaken by all of them (see Fig.3/4).

The houses also collaborate with Kodak who sponsor a 'Treasure Houses of England Photography' competition.

Employment in Stately Homes and Castles

While ruined castles often need little more than a ticket-seller and skeleton staff, larger stately homes offer job opportunities as keepers, guides, cleaners, gardeners, shop and maintenance staff. However, some of this work is seasonal. In 1995 the Tower of London, with 2,536,680 visitors a year, employed 115 staff, 40 of them full time and permanent, 75 full time and seasonal. Warwick Castle employed 200 permanent and 100 seasonal staff. National Trust properties also employ volunteer guides, shop helpers and waiters (see Fig.3/5).

The need to employ staff with modern languages is increasingly recognised although many staff remain rigidly monolingual.

GARDENS OPEN TO THE PUBLIC

Until the 16th century most gardens were simply utilitarian vegetable patches. However, in Henry VIII's reign a walled garden was laid out at Hampton Court with features like knot gardens and arbours. Greenhouses used to store plants through the winter gradually evolved into the orangeries of the 17th and 18th centuries; several of these still survive. The first real botanical garden was the Oxford Physic Garden, laid out in 1621. During the Inter-Regnum of the 17th century many people travelled to the continent, returning with ideas for gardens based on what they had seen there, particularly in France where Le Nôtre had developed large formal gardens. Increasingly plants were brought to England from overseas, especially after heated greenhouses were developed to house them. In the 18th century formal gardens became less popular and Capability Brown and Humphrey Repton developed park-like gardens with streams and woods, many of them adorned with mock temples, follies, gazebos, etc. In the 19th century smaller houses also had gardens added to them. By the mid-century William Robinson inspired interest in gardens with beds of flowers alongside expanses of wild rhododendrons and azaleas, etc.

FIG.3/5:HOURS WORKED BY NATIONAL TRUST VOLUNTEERS, 1990-1995

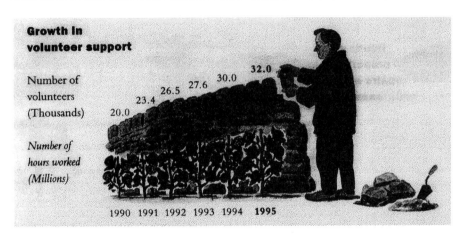

Growth in volunteer support

Number of volunteers (Thousands)

20.0   23.4   26.5   27.6   30.0   32.0

Number of hours worked (Millions)

1990 1991 1992 1993 1994 **1995**

At least 790 historic properties also have gardens and 57 have parks, some of them now popular tourist attractions. At Athelhampton and Hever Castle nearly as many visitors visit the grounds alone as visit the house and grounds combined. Even a non-traditional tourist attraction like Alton Towers has beautiful gardens that add to its appeal by providing a refuge for those who find the rides too alarming.

English Heritage maintains a Register of Parks and Gardens of Special Historic Interest which includes 1,267 entries, 10% of them of Grade 1 standard and 29% of them Grade 2. It is being revised to cover municipal parks too. The National Trust owns 50 historic gardens and the National Trust for Scotland a further 23. In all, in 1995 an estimated 75,526 British gardens were open to the public for at least part of the year.

People have been visiting gardens for almost as long as the houses to which they were attached; in the 17th century Celia Fiennes commented on the gardens at Bretby Park in Derbyshire, and by the 18th century there are records of visitors to Hagley, Stowe and Stourhead. Some gardens already had guidebooks with plans; by the end of the 18th century others had tea rooms as well. Hawkestone even had entertainment in the form of a custodian who dressed as a hermit and jumped out at visitors, waving apparently bloody stumps for arms. By 1760 so many people were visiting Stourhead that the local inn was sometimes full up.

FIG.3/6: BRITAIN'S MOST VISITED GARDENS IN 1995	
Hampton Court Gardens	1,200,000
Kew Gardens	1,060,000
Tropical World, Roundhay Park, Leeds	958,190
Royal Botanic Gardens, Edinburgh	785,732
Wisley Gardens	612,229
Glasgow Botanic Gardens	400,000
Uiversity of Oxford Botanic Gardens	340,000
Wakehurst Place Gardens	258,123
Stourhead	251,081
Ventnor Botanic Gardens	250,000

In 1862 the gardens of Biddulph Grange were open to the public every Monday from May to September. Those who bought tickets in advance could also visit on any Friday except Good Friday. Foreigners were admitted at other times as well, although the Gardens were completely closed on Sundays.

By 1977 the UK Committee of the International Council on Monuments and Sites (ICOMOS) estimated that almost three and a half million people were visiting the gardens in its provisional schedule. By 1995 the number had risen to 16.3 million, with another million visiting gardens open through the National Gardens Scheme. The weather obviously has a disproportionate influence over people's readiness to visit gardens, and the significant rise in the 1995 figures reflected the unusually hot summer. The number of people visiting Sissinghurst Gardens, for example, rose from 163,395 in 1994 to 178,698 in 1995.

The National Gardens Scheme

In 1927 the National Gardens Scheme was set up as a memorial to Queen Alexandra, patron of the Queen's Institute of District Nursing. Garden owners were asked to open to the public on specific days in spring and give the proceeds to a fund to help district nurses. In the first year 600 gardens held open days and the number has grown ever since. In 1995 3,500 gardens in England and Wales collected over £1.3 million from open days, the money going to various different charities.

Gardens that are open regularly also donate their takings from set days to the Scheme. Some National Trust gardens take part, as do the royal gardens at Sandringham and Frogmore.

Scotland has had a similar Gardens Scheme since 1931 and in 1989 almost 280 gardens opened to the public, the proceeds being donated to the Queen's Nursing Institute (for Scotland) and the maintenance of National Trust for Scotland gardens. A similar Ulster Gardens Scheme operates in Northern Ireland.

Who Owns the Gardens?

The Royal Botanic Gardens at Kew are owned by the government. Under the terms of the 1983 National Heritage Act they are funded by a grant from the Ministry of Agriculture, Fisheries and Food (MAFF) and administered by a board of trustees. Until 1988 the buildings were maintained by the Property Services Agency (PSA). However, the trustees now have responsibility for them as well. Other gardens belong to the National Trust along with their houses. Kew's southern offshoot, Wakeham Place, is owned by the National Trust but leased to the Royal Botanic Gardens for research work. Many of the gardens open to the public through the National Gardens Scheme are privately owned. Yet others, including Westonbirt Arboretum, belong to the Forestry Commission. The Gardens of the Rose at St. Albans are owned by the Royal National Rose Society, a registered charity.

Opening Gardens to the Public

While gardens are very popular with the public, most only open during spring, summer and autumn. In 1995 the average English garden opened for only 219 days in the year and 72% of visitors were received between April and September (in Scotland almost 96% of people visit in spring, summer and autumn). Although many gardens are at their best in spring and early summer Kew Gardens publishes a calendar indicating what visitors can expect to see at different times in the year. Because floral displays vary from season to season, gardens have considerable potential for attracting repeat visits. However, they can be badly affected by natural hazards. The worst such disaster in recent years was the hurricane of 1987 which swept southern England, destroying more than 1000 trees at Kew alone. Such catastrophes may lead to temporary closure and a fall in visitor numbers.

Some gardens, like those at Hampton Court, are open free which make it difficult to tell exactly how many visitors they receive. Well-known gardens like those at Stourhead, which came into the care of the National Trust in 1946-7, attract thousands of visitors every year. Elsewhere figures can be boosted by specific, short-term considerations. So the Lost Gardens of Heligan in Cornwall received 150,000 visitors in 1995 as the press focused on the restoration taking place.

While visitors to gardens are usually drawn by a love of flowers and scenery, many such properties offer much more than natural beauty. Some are, for example, the work of distinguished landscape gardeners like Capability Brown at Burton Constable and Humphrey Repton at Sheringham Hall. The grounds of Kew Gardens also contain an imitation Chinese pagoda, a Japanese ceremonial gateway, several museums and a gallery devoted to flower paintings. Other gardens display exotic waterfowl. Many can be visited either with a country house or separately, like Tatton Park in Cheshire where a ticket for the gardens alone costs £2.50, compared with £8 for an all-inclusive ticket.

Gardens can contain general collections and be of many different dates. However, some are more specialist; the Gardens of the Rose obviously concentrate on roses and the Rococo Gardens at Painswick on special winter snowdrop displays.

Physic gardens like the one first planted at Chelsea in 1673 were originally developed to grow a variety of medicinal plants for research.

Inevitably gardens are labour-intensive to maintain, offering plenty of job opportunities for gardeners, may of them full time and year round; in 1995 Scottish gardens employed 144 people, 41% of them in full time permanent jobs. To defray the costs many gardens now boast garden centres selling plants and garden accessories; National Trust properties at Bowood in England and Bodnant in Wales both do this.

Protecting Historic Gardens

Most European countries protect historic sites as well as monuments, so that some gardens are covered. In contrast UK legislation only protects archaeological sites and the surrounds of ancient monuments. The gardens of Biddulph Grange in Staffordshire were laid out in the 19th century and included rockeries, ferneries, a collection of monkey-puzzle trees and various assemblages of roots, stems and tree stumps. Two sections had Egyptian and Chinese themes. Since the 1920s the gardens had been part of the grounds of an orthopaedic hospital and lack of supervision resulted in considerable damage. However, in 1977 Staffordshire County Council succeeded in having them designated a conservation area. In 1986 the Council and the National Trust between them acquired the land, with the Trust taking over responsibility for the gardens in 1988. By then they were in such disrepair that excavation work was required to recover features like the Dahlia Walk. The National Heritage Memorial Fund made a grant of £300,000 towards this work. The Trust has since spent £2 million restoring the gardens. Work finally finished in 1996.

In 1989 the National Trust also took over Stowe Gardens, one of the best 18th-century landscape gardens in Europe and containing 37 Grade I listed buildings. Funding came from an anonymous donor of £2 million, the National Heritage Memorial Fund (£450,000), English Heritage and the Landmark Trust. The National Trust plans to spend £10 million on restoring these gardens which received 59,520 visitors in 1995.

In 1965 a Garden History Society was established to try and protect the interests of important gardens.

KEW GARDENS

The Royal Botanic Gardens at Kew were the UK's most popular gardens in 1995, with 1,060,000 people visiting them. Their popularity springs in part from the fact that they are in London and so offer easy access to overseas visitors as well as Londoners in search of somewhere green to spend their weekends. They are also famous for their botanical research.

Kew Gardens stand on land which was once part of the Sheen (later Richmond Palace) estate but was sold by Parliament during the Cromwellian era. While Charles II regained many of the old royal estates, he didn't bother with this part which was rebought by George II in 1721 and extended by his son in 1730.

Eventually the new estate covered 300 acres which were turned into an 'exotic' garden in the latter part of the 18th century by Queen Augusta and her advisor, Lord Bute. Under Sir Joseph Banks' directorship, collectors were sent round the globe to collect unusual species and lay the foundation for the Royal Botanic Gardens.

When George III died, Kew fell from favour. In 1841 the government took over its administration, under the guidance of Sir William Hooker, the first official director. Since the 1760s most of the gardens had been open to the public on Thursdays. Now only a few buildings remained closed. In 1897 Queen Victoria celebrated her Diamond Jubilee by bequeathing Queen Charlotte's Cottage to the nation, and in 1904 King Edward VII passed Cambridge Cottage, now the Wood Museum, to the State. For many decades the Kew entrance fee was one penny. However, by 1995 it had risen to £4. In 1995/6 the £17.08 million MAFF grant to Kew amounted to roughly 70% of its running costs. The remaining 30% came from admission charges, catering, summer jazz concerts, the sale of books and merchandise, and other commercial activities. Most trading activities are handled by RBG Kew Enterprises which covenanted back profits of £428,000 in 1995/6. Since 1995 Kew Gardens have been licenced as a venue for civil weddings and the hire of function facilities should bring in increasing revenue.

The cost of running Kew is enormous. A 20-year programme to maintain its historic buidings is underway but restoring the old glasshouses can be expensive; just restoring the 19th-century Grade I listed Palm House required £8 million, although it's hoped that regular investments of smaller sums will prevent other buildings deteriorating as badly. Additions to the range of attractions have also swallowed sizeable sums of money. The latest newcomer is the Evolution House which opened in 1995 and features Kew's first example of 'landscape immersion'; visitors travel through 4,000 million years of plant evolution with the help of models of extinct vegetation alongside living examples of ancient plants. Some of the cost was met by Enterprise Oil.

Under Director Professor Prance, who previously worked for the New York Botanic Gardens, Kew has worked hard to attract more visitors. The glasshouses now close an hour later in summer, and a spring Orchid Festival has been introduced to bring in more visitors during a relatively quiet period. Plans exist to turn the old Nash Conservatory into a second visitor centre and to expand the catering facilities in the Orangery. Since 1993 regular surveys have been carried out to assess visitor satisfaction. More use has been made of advertising, and people living near Kew have been encouraged to buy season tickets allowing repeat visits for a fixed fee. The RBG Kew Foundation and Friends have also worked hard to raise funds for specific projects, including the Millennium Seed Bank which will be part-funded by the Millennium Commission.

Some gardens contain features which are attractions in their own right. These include assorted mazes, like the one in the National Trust's Glendurgan garden, and assorted follies, buildings like mock-Gothic ruins with a purely decorative function. A fine example is The Pineapple, an 18th-century summerhouse with a giant pineapple carved on the roof which is owned by the National Trust for Scotland but leased to the Landmark Trust to be rented out as a holiday home.

PARKS

Britain also has many parks, some of them deer parks attached to stately homes, others pleasant leafy oases in the heart of the cities. While such parks may not actually generate touristic visits, their existence certainly adds to the quality of many towns which do receive visitors. Forty per cent of the local population also use the parks, with an estimated 8 million visits a day. The Royal Parks (see above) will certainly be visited by many of London's overseas visitors.

Many of the urban parks were laid out during the 19th century and boasted fine fittings, including hot-houses. However, in the 1990s pressure on local authority finances led to the decline of many of these parks which were left, unsupervised, to the vandals; a Boathouse in Dartmouth Park, West Bromwich had barely been restored at a cost of £70,000 in 1990 than it was burnt down again. In 1996 a National Lottery grant of £50 million over three years was earmarked to help local authorities restore the great urban parks along with town squares, seaside promenades and local cemeteries.

CHAPTER 4 : RELIGIOUS HERITAGE

Britain's cathedrals, churches, chapels and ruined abbeys and priories attract thousands of visitors every year. In 1992 there were an estimated 32.4 million visits to Britain's churches and cathedrals. Some of the world's greatest tourist attractions are also religious buildings.

THE BRITISH CATHEDRALS

Cathedrals are churches which contain the seat or throne of a bishop. The name is derived from the Greek word 'cathedra' meaning seat. A few British cathedrals are also called 'minsters', from the Greek 'monasterion' meaning monastery. Some English cathedrals, like those in Sheffield and Manchester, started life as churches but were extended and promoted to cathedrals as the local population grew. Although Britain also has Roman Catholic and Scottish Episcopal cathedrals, the most architecturally interesting and therefore the most popular with tourists are the Anglican cathedrals which have the longest history. In 1992 they received an estimated 14.6 million visits compared wth 600,000 to the Roman Catholic cathedrals.

FIG.4/1: THE UK'S MOST VISITED CATHEDRALS IN 1995

St. Paul's Cathedral, London	2,220,000
York Minster	2,000,000
Canterbury	1,900,000
Chester	1,000,000
Salisbury	600,000
Norwich	520,000
Durham	431,586
Exeter/Gloucester	400,000
Winchester	360,000

There are 48 Anglican cathedrals in England and Wales alone. Although Truro, Coventry and Liverpool cathedrals were built in the 19th and 20th century, the majority date back at least in part to the Middle Ages.

Scotland also has several ruined or restored cathedrals which are very popular with tourists. These include those at St. Andrew's, Dunkeld, Kirkwall and Elgin.

Since some cathedrals don't charge for admission, approximate visitor figures must be extrapolated from sales of tickets to visit towers and crypts, guidebooks sales, etc.

The popularity of the top three cathedrals is easy to explain; St. Paul's benefits from being in London, the UK's single biggest tourist destination; Canterbury is within day trip reach of London and is famous both for the story of St.

FIG.4/2: POSITION OF BRITAIN'S CATHEDRALS

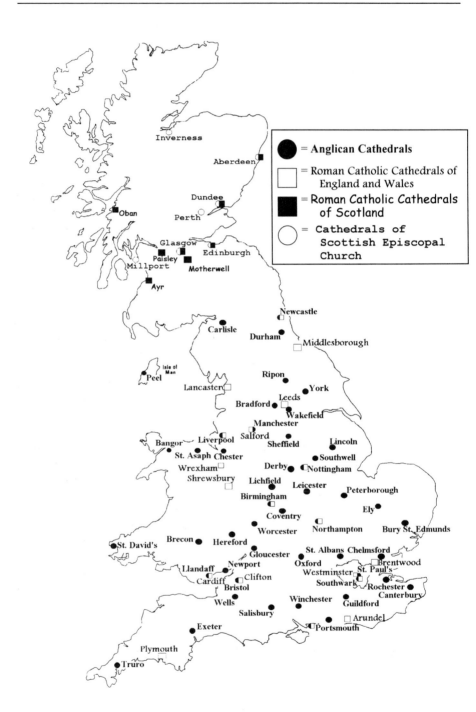

Thomas-à-Becket and as the seat of one of England's two archbishoprics; York is the UK's second biggest tourist centre and seat of the second archbishopric. Both Canterbury and York cathedrals are also magnificent examples of Gothic architecture, while St. Paul's is the work of England's most famous architect, Sir Christopher Wren.

Of the other 'most visited' cathedrals Norwich, Salisbury, Winchester and Durham are particularly beautiful. However, beauty on its own doesn't always guarantee large numbers of visitors; Southwell Cathedral has some of the finest Decorated architecture in England and yet attracted only about 110,000 visitors in 1995, presumably because it's in a small town on the way to nowhere. Chester Cathedral is not as impressive architecturally. However, it's in a 'milk run' town which is very popular with tourists because of its Roman remains and Tudor buildings, and because it's conveniently positioned to act as a stopping place for coach tours heading north or south. Salisbury was the first English cathedral to introduce charges but they haven't deterred tourists who are drawn by memories of Constable's painting of the cathedral and because Salisbury can be combined with Stonehenge for day trips.

Cathedral Visiting

Cathedrals were amongst the first buildings in the world to inspire people to travel away from their homes. In the Middle Ages pilgrims regularly covered great distances to visit cathedrals (and churches) which contained relics of the Holy Family or the saints. The most famous of these cathedrals was at Santiago de Compostela in northern Spain which drew pilgrims from all over Europe to see its relics of St. James. English pilgrims also travelled to Rome and to Jerusalem, while overseas pilgrims came to Canterbury to visit the shrine of St. Thomas-à-Becket. However, these visitors were drawn by religious considerations rather than interest in the buildings' architectural merits.

By the late 17th century people became aware of cathedrals as buildings rather than just as religious centres and Daniel Defoe described Lichfield as one of the most beautiful cathedrals in England. By the 1920s some cathedrals were already asking visitors to pay for admission. Both Wells and Hereford charged 6d, while Gloucester charged 6d for the crypt, cloisters and chapter house, 3d for the triforium and 1/- for the tower. Salisbury and Exeter preferred to request donations.

Today, visiting cathedrals is so popular that roughly half the dioceses have a member of the clergy who acts as a tourism officer, organising guides, promotional events, etc. The better-known cathedrals attract a high proportion of foreign visitors, many of them coach tourists from North America and Northern Europe. Tourists tend to come from the higher socio-economic groups and are thought to spend on average 19% more in local shops during their stay than domestic visitors. Almost half the visitors are over 45 and over half are female. Most travel considerable distances, usually by car, to visit the cathedral. Only around 25% of visitors drop in by chance.

Problems Facing the Cathedrals

By their very nature cathedrals are usually ancient and in constant need of repairs, many of them of a specialist nature and therefore expensive. Apart from the natural effects of wear and tear, some cathedrals like St. Paul's were damaged in the war and needed partial rebuilding. Others stand at the heart of modern cities, exposed to traffic fumes and industrial pollution. Unexpected disasters, like the fire in York Minster in 1984 which destroyed much of the south transept, can also necessitate expensive restoration.

This work is largely funded from donations and there have been many spectacular appeals for funds; Wells Cathedral has raised £1,300,000 to restore its West Front, while Canterbury Cathedral raised £3.5 million, much of it to repair its stained glass. In 1994/5 Salisbury Cathedral needed more than £500,000 for stonework, roof lead and window repairs while Liverpool's Roman Catholic Cathedral needed a similar sum to repair its external cladding. By 1996 it could cost in excess of £1,500 to restore a single buttress, £4,000 to repair an 18th-century monument, £65,000 to restore and overhaul an organ and £70,000 to repair a major stained-glass window.

The most recent research suggests that the average visitor only makes a voluntary donation of 26p. In 1992 all the English cathedrals between them managed to raise £11.2 million from special appeals but by 1995 this had fallen to £4.9 million. Much time and energy has to be spent on fund-raising, some of it controversial. Lincoln Cathedral has never really recovered from a fund-raising scheme which involved taking its copy of the Magna Carta on a tour of Australia but which ended up losing £56,000.

THE MAPPA MUNDI

In 1989 relatively undervisited Hereford cathedral tried to raise £7 million to pay off an overdraft, fund repairs and rehouse its Chained Library by auctioning the priceless 13th-century Mappa Mundi at Sotheby's. Despite a public outcry, the Dean and Chapter refused an offer of £3 million made by John Paul Getty II and the National Heritage Memorial Fund to buy the map. When another attempt to raise money by selling 'shares' in the map also failed, they were forced to renegotiate with the NHMF. In 1996 a new 'high-tech medieval' visitor centre with an admission fee of £4 opened at Hereford Cathedral to display the Mappa Mundi and the Chained Library.

Because of these difficulties a 'National Trust' for cathedrals which would aim to raise £20 million a year from individuals, institutions and even the government has been suggested. Recognition of the cathedrals' difficulties came in May 1990 when the National Heritage Memorial Fund, which doesn't usually fund repairs, gave Ely Cathedral £500,000 to strengthen the 14th-century lantern which had been damaged in storms. Some of the cost was recoverable through insurance, but the Cathedral had only just completed a £4 million restoration and had no money left to pay for more work. A few cathedrals have also managed to obtain financial help from the European Regional Development Fund; Coventry was given money to help strengthen the ruins of the old cathedral, while Lichfield was helped with the cost of restoration. In 1995 Peterborough Cathedral approached the Heritage Lottery Fund for a grant of £1.5 million towards the cost of restoring its vaults.

The cathedrals are still owned by the Church and although all except Blackburn are Grade I listed buildings government repair grants used not to be available to them. Unfortunately the Church of England no longer has adequate funds to maintain the cathedrals, especially following a series of disastrous property investments in the 1980s. Since 1990 English Heritage has been able to help finance essential repairs through the Cathedral Grants Scheme. In 1994-5 £4.2 million was made available to 30 cathedrals, with grants of £500,000 given to Liverpool's Roman Catholic Cathedral and Salisbury, £250,000 to Ely and £246,000 to York Minster. For the first time grants allowed cathedrals to install proper fire detection systems. However, Jocelyn Stephens, the Director of English Heritage, has identified the Church of England's shortage of money to pay for its buildings as one of the 'greatest threats to emerge in the...history of England's heritage.'

The 1991 Cathedrals Measure imposed some external control on what a cathedral's dean and chapter could decide to do. Any extensive reconstruction or the sale of any important object must now be referred to the Cathedral Fabrics Commission which can consult with the relevant national amenity groups before deciding whether to approve it or not. Recent work referred to the Cathedral Fabrics Commission included that on the Lincoln Cathedral rose window and structural changes being made to improve access to Coventry and Worcester cathedrals.

Voluntary help comes from people aged 18 to 30 who pay £40 a week to join 'Cathedral Camps' and work on restoration projects at cathedrals and some of the larger churches. Typical of the work carried out by the volunteers was the scrubbing of the Big Tom bell at Lincoln Cathedral and the clearing of undergrowth from Southwell Cathedral.

CATHEDRALS AS MONEY GENERATORS

Charging for Admission

Many continental cathedrals charge for admittance to all but a small part of the building; for example, in Spain there is normally a charge to visit the central *coro*. In Britain charging for admission to cathedrals is at least as controversial as charging for entry to museums. Those in favour argue that the charges help provide the money to support the buildings and make it less necessary to rely on other commercial activities. They also point out that they make it possible to provide more accurate statistical information on the number of visitors and could offer a way to control the inflow of tourists by means of peak-priced tickets or tickets for specific time periods. Those against argue that there is no place for commerce in a house of God and that charges may deter people from visiting.

There is indeed some evidence to suggest that, like museums, cathedrals see visitor numbers drop after an admission charge is introduced. In any case collecting the fee has to be handled carefully or they can end up losing more money than they make. Most cathedrals still prefer to ask for a set donation. In the early 1990s the Anglican cathedrals between them seem to have raised about £6,400,000 a year from entry fees, donations, catering and other sources. Those with entrance fees fared best; St Paul's Cathedral, for example, took 32% of the net income while receiving only 10% of the visitors because of its admission fee.

Other Sources of Revenue

Even without a fixed entrance fee cathedrals can raise money by charging for visits to towers, crypts, triforia, chapter houses, cloisters and special exhibitions; in 1995 York Minster was charging 70p for admission to the chapter house, £2 for the tower, £1.80 for the foundations and treasury, and 60p for the crypt on top of the suggested donation of £1.50 for coming in. As well as selling guidebooks, postcards and religious books, cathedral shops often sell souvenirs too. Chichester, Coventry, Durham, Ely, Exeter, Gloucester, Guildford, Lichfield, Liverpool, Lincoln, Peterborough, Southwark, Truro, Wells, Winchester and York cathedrals all have full-scale restaurants. Those at York, Gloucester and Southwark are run by the same professional catering firm responsible for the cafe at the Victoria and Albert Museum. Others, like Bristol, have smaller-scale tea shops. Although most catering is provided in the cloisters or chapter houses, some cathedrals, like St Alban's, have purpose-built extensions to house such facilities. In a two-week period in the summer of 1993 Wells Cathedral was found to have raised £17,511 from catering and a further £18,948 from the sale of other goods. In that same period only five cathedrals were found to be taking more in donations than from retailing or catering.

The great musical heritage of the cathedrals also offers scope for making money. Almost all the cathedrals have wonderful acoustics and some also have marvellous organs and/or choirs. Consequently cathedrals (and the larger churches) often host concerts particularly of organ or choral music; Bach's St. Matthew's and St. John's Passions are great favourites. Although some such concerts are free, tickets are sold for others as for any musical events. There are also cathedral music festivals. For example, since the early 1700s the Three Choirs Festival has been held in Gloucester, Hereford or Worcester Cathedral each August. It is the oldest such festival in Europe.

It isn't only the cathedrals that profit from their visitors. The results of a 1975 survey carried out in Canterbury suggested that more than a million tourists, 45% of them foreign, were visiting the city, and 93% of those questioned said that they had visited or would be visiting the cathedral; 77% said they were visiting Canterbury specifically to sightsee, while 58% gave the cathedral as their main reason for visiting. A more recent survey suggested that 71% of visitors to the cathedral spent money locally on snacks, 54% bought gifts, 42% paid for meals and 30% for drinks, and 24% bought guidebooks, 23% clothes and 18% clothes. The shops that do best from tourists are those in the streets nearest to the cathedral (High

St/Parade, Burgate, Longmarket), and more than 25% of the shopping space in that area is devoted to shops selling souvenirs and other items likely to appeal to tourists. A similar trading pattern is obvious in York, with the shops in The Shambles and Stonegate catering almost exclusively for tourists.

A cathedral's presence may also help generate extra visitors for other attractions which, on their own, might not have such pulling power. So some of Canterbury Cathedral's many visitors probably go on to visit St Augustine's Abbey, Westgate Towers and Eastbridge Hospital, while visitors to York Minster may also visit the Castle Museum, Clifford's Tower, the Jorvik Viking Centre and other city centre attractions. What's more because of the number of visitors to popular cathedral towns it can be easier to find new uses for otherwise redundant old buildings. St. Radegund's Hall in Canterbury is now a restaurant, while old half-timbered buildings in York house souvenir shops.

Facilities for Cathedral Visitors

Most cathedrals use volunteers as guides and general assistants. Most also sell guidebooks, ranging from glossy Pitkins to detailed studies of the stained glass, roof bosses, misericords, etc. The age of different parts of the structure is usually shown by shading the ground plan in different colours to indicate different dates, a convention first introduced in the mid-19th century. Often guidebooks are available in French, German, Spanish and Italian. In addition there are usually free leaflets with ground plans, often in several languages.

Some cathedrals provide mirrors on wheels so visitors can study details of the roof vaults without getting a crick in the neck. In the south transept of York Minster these mirrors let visitors examine bosses designed by *Blue Peter* viewers after the 1984 fire.

Many cathedrals now have wooden ramps at their entrances to allow wheelchair access. Such ramps are usually also provided at the entrance to the cloisters when that provides access to the toilets and cafeteria. Durham and Ripon have induction loops to help the hard of hearing. Lichfield and Coventry have also pioneered an approach to cathedral visiting which uses scale models of the building and its plan, together with cassette recordings and large print leaflets, to aid the blind and partially sighted.

Some cathedrals also provide audio-visual presentations of their history for which a charge is made.

The Worshipful Company of Goldsmiths has provided funding or part funding to enable several cathedrals, including St Paul's in London, to display church plate, vestments, and other valuable items in special treasuries. Sometimes a charge is made for visiting.

THE UK CHURCHES

Marcus Binney and Max Hanna have described churches as the 'Cinderellas of tourism' which is particularly ironic given that some of them, like the cathedrals, were drawing visitors from great distances at a time when travel was still difficult.

Nevertheless there is much truth in the observation. In comparison with other historic buildings little has changed in the presentation of British churches to make them appeal to a wider audience, perhaps reflecting the unease some people feel about introducing commercialism into buildings which still have religious significance.

Visiting the Churches

In the Middle Ages a few English churches received visitors because they housed saintly relics. St. Mary's, Warwick claimed to have a piece of St. Stephen's hair, a fragment of the manger and a splinter from the Burning Bush; Wimborne Minster had a piece of the True Cross; and the priory church at Walsingham owned a crystal phial supposedly containing some of Mary's milk. In the early 16th century Erasmus visited Canterbury Cathedral and Walsingham. His written accounts make it clear that some of the trappings of tourism were already well-established at both places: attendants pointing out the relics to guests, boxes conveniently placed for offerings, inns to accommodate guests, street stalls selling food and souvenir badges.

FIG.4/3: ENGLAND'S MOST VISITED CHURCHES IN 1995

St Martin-in-the-Fields	350,000
St Mary the Virgin, Oxford/	
Holy Trinity,Stratford-upon-Avon	300,000
Bath Abbey	285,000
St John the Baptist, Cirencester	275,400
St Mary in the Castle, Dover	244,000
Bolton Abbey	209,790
Tewkesbury Abbey	200,000
St Mary the Virgin, Rye	145,000
Christchurch Priory	142,200
Round Church, Cambridge	140,000
Lancaster Priory	135,000

After Henry VIII's break with the Roman Catholic church in 1534, relics fell from favour and church visiting lost its raison d'être. It was only in the 19th century that church visiting came back into vogue, with archaeological societies organising excursions to look at them. Such visits were usually made on weekdays and mainly appealed to the middle and upper classes. However, the coming of the railways in the 1860s meant a wider range of people gained access to country churches. Part of the popularity of church visiting probably sprang from the fact that it was seen as a respectable activity. Nor did historically-minded people have the wide choice of alternatives now available; few archaeological sites had been excavated, let alone displayed, and many historic houses were still in private hands.

It's difficult to know exactly how many people visit churches since admission is usually free and there are no convenient ticket stubs. Many churches have visitors' books, but surveys suggest that only between one in four (Selborne, Hampshire) and one in fifteen (Bolton Abbey) people actually sign them, making them unreliable sources.

Nevertheless in 1995 there were probably 12 million visits to Anglican churches in the UK, with two-thirds of those visits being to 200 particular churches. In 1995 the English Tourist Board estimated that 67 churches received more than 30,000 visitors, with 45 of them probably receiving more than 50,000 visitors each.

Once again architectural significance alone is not enough to guarantee visitors; Bath Abbey and St. John's, Cirencester are much more impressive architecturally than Holy Trinity, Stratford but are estimated to have received fewer visitors. Dover drew a high proportion of overseas visitors because it's situated in a major Channel port. What's more it stands in the grounds of a dramatic, highly visible and much visited castle (Lancaster Priory is similarly next door to a prominent castle). The Oxford and Cambridge churches undoubtedly benefit from the number of tourists attracted to the towns by the colleges, while Holy Trinity, Stratford owes its popularity to the fact that Shakespeare is buried there. Rye village is renowned for its prettiness, to which the church contributes. Only Bolton and Tewkesbury Abbeys, and Christchurch Priory seem to owe their popularity purely to their intrinsic qualities. Even then Christchurch probably profits from being within easy reach of the seaside resort of Bournemouth, while Bolton Abbey is part of a larger ancient monument in a particularly picturesque setting.

Churches as Tourist Attractions

Churches should have great potential for attracting visitors. They are often the most interesting buildings in a town or village and hold the key to interpreting local history. What's more some contain fittings which are as interesting as the building itself; almost 90% of surving English medieval art may be in Church of England care. However, not all churches can be supervised, partly because they don't receive enough visitors to justify it and partly because the custodians are usually volunteers; in small villages there are unlikely to be enough to organise realistic rotas. The resulting security problems mean that valuable items often have to be removed to safekeeping elsewhere. A casket containing relics of St Petroc was stolen from Bodmin church in Cornwall in 1994, while the church at Walton-on-Thames displays a replica scold's bridle after the original was stolen. The church at Bamburgh now has security cameras screening visitors as they go in, while nearby Alnwick is locked most of the time despite brown and white signs to attract visitors' attention. Insurers believe half Britain's churches now face problems with thieves and vandals.

Many churches which would once have been open round the clock are now locked as a result of theft and vandalism. Although this is mainly a problem in towns, even country churches are increasingly likely to be closed. A key is usually available to those prepared to hunt around, but casual visitors are unlikely to take the trouble, particularly if, as is often the case, it means calling at the vicarage. In Scotland, Wales and Northern Ireland it is usual to find churches locked.

In 1995 the Open Churches Trust was set up to give grants to enable churches to install security devices and open to visitors, with staff to supervise them. The scheme was started by Sir Andrew Lloyd-Webber with a donation of £1 million. So far 39 churches are taking part, amongst them St Anne's, Limehouse, a beautiful Hawksmoor church in London.

Many country churches, including some of the most beautiful like Salle and Walpole St. Peter in Norfolk, are difficult to reach without private transport which immediately limits the likely number of visitors. One helpful initiative is the Country Churches Visitors Handbook which lists the opening times and contact phone numbers for churches in Hereford and Worcester, Shropshire and Warwickshire.

Visitor numbers can be increased by better signposting and publicity (especially on TV), particularly following an appeal for restoration funds. In 1995 Boston church believed lunch-time concerts had drawn more people while St Mary Redcliffe in Bristol had appointed an administrator to publicise the church and so attract more visitors.

Most churches provide only rudimentary visitor facilities. Guidebooks range from simple leaflets to glossy Pitkin booklets. In 1988 75 of the most visited churches reported selling 218,012 copies of their guidebook between them. Thirty-one churches also had free leaflets and distributed 265,238 of these (Holy Trinity, Stratford-on-Avon gave away 165,000 leaflets while Lancaster Priory got through 51,500). In most cases churches rely on visitors' honesty to pay for these guidebooks, with safes often set into the wall near the door or into pillars. In many cases guidebooks are not expected to produce a profit. A few churches provide printed information pasted on to boards which can't be removed.

Some churches also sell postcards while most sell religious publications at the rear of the church. Larger churches like St. John the Baptist, Cirencester may have volunteer stewards to look after the bookstalls and answer queries. Where this is the case small souvenirs, like bookmarks, may also be on sale. There are small restaurants at St. Mary-le-Bow, St. Martin-in-the-Field's and St. James' Piccadilly in London, and at St. Andrew's in Rochester and St. John the Evangelist in Edinburgh. At St. Paul's in Jarrow, which is closely linked to Bede and England's conversion to Christianity, visiting school children can don monastic robes for history lessons aimed at making the church more interesting to them.

To save money churches are usually left unlit. Occasionally coin-in-the-slot time-switches are available so visitors can illuminate particularly interesting features like paintings or roof booses.

Since the 1970s churches with memorial brasses set into the wall or floor have been able to reap an extra income from people wishing to make rubbings as wall hangings. Unfortunately the most popular brasses could be damaged by the number of people wishing to rub them. Churches like Acton in Suffolk get round this problem by providing a facsimile brass which can be rubbed instead. (This facsimile process has spawned 13 purpose-designed Brass Rubbing Centres where visitors can rub copies of brasses from all around the country. Some of these Centres, like the one in St. Nicholas, Bristol, are themselves situated inside redundant churches. In 1995 the London Brass Rubbing Centre attracted 80,000 visitors, while the one in Bristol had 36,622.) Some churches even sell suitable materials for brass rubbing on site.

Some larger churches charge visitors for taking photographs, particularly where a tripod will be used. Like cathedrals, some also charge for climbing their towers, and Holy Trinity, Stratford charges for access to the area containing Shakespeare's memorial. However, the potential for churches to levy extra charges is limited, given that they are small buildings, usually without crypts and private chapels, and that they can't afford custodians to collect entrance fees.

It's hard for church authorities to sanction more forceful courtship of tourists since commercialism sits uneasily in buildings which are still primarily places of prayer, visited by people for religious reasons even when services are not in progress. However, Crewe and Nantwich Borough Council decided to promote the church of St. Mary's by opening a visitors' centre in a room near the porch and providing guides and light refreshments. A Press Officer was appointed and the town's heritage trails were reorganised to start or end at the church. After the possibility of party visits was publicised, Nantwich recorded 35% more people signing its visitors' book. It also managed to sell 1,128 guidebooks and 2,056 leaflets. Northumbria also has a Christian Heritage leaflet, drawing attention to historically significant churches like the tiny Saxon one at Escomb which also has its own brown and white tourist signposts.

Churches don't make much money from tourists. In 1988 75 told the ETB they had made £764,048 from their visitors. Of this 50% was from the sale of guidebooks and souvenirs, 38% from donations and 12% from catering, brass rubbing, charges to visit the tower, etc. Only three churches had an income of more than £70,000, with one raising £60,000 from sales and another £45,000 from donations.

Special Events

Churches can attract more vistors by hosting exhibitions or special events. In 1988 the authorities attributed a rise of 34% in visitors to Lydford church to a successful exhibition on local history. Tetbury church also received more visitors after it staged a production of the musical *Godspell*.

Many country churches organise flower festivals. The church will be decorated with flower arrangements, sometimes with a specific theme, and there may be associated activities, like cake stands, refreshments, a bring-and-buy stall, etc. Since the work is usually carried out by volunteer parishioners, most of the money raised from entrance fees, sales of guidebooks, etc. is profit. In 1995 Beverley Minster church attributed a rise in visitor numbers to a successful flower festival.

Recently some tourist authorities have organised other events to attract more tourists. So in 1990 visitors to Shropshire churches were offered tea in the local vicarage in return for a donation to church funds (see Fig.4/4). The church at Ranworth in the Broads now provides refreshments and acts as an information centre for the surrounding area. English Heritage declared 1997 the year of England's

Christian Heritage and produced a map showing the sites of 200 important churches in an attempt to attract more visitors to them.

FIG.4/4: SOME CHURCHES NOW OFFER TEA AT THE VICARAGE AS A WAY TO ATTRACT MORE VISITORS

(Source: ETB The Clarion, 1989)

Problems Facing Britain's Churches

The biggest single problem facing British
churches is the declining number of churchgoers. Many of the most beautiful, like the 'wool' churches of East Anglia and the Cotswolds, were built by wealthy patrons at a time when there were large congregations to fill them. Over the centuries industry has moved away, leaving them isolated in villages with small churchgoing populations who can't cope with their maintenance costs. The congregation's religious needs can often be met more cheaply and efficiently by moving into smaller, purpose-built accommodation which is cheaper to heat, but that leaves the beautiful medieval building to be maintained without a congregation. Even in towns the falling number of churchgoers has left many Victorian churches without a function.

With more than 8,500 Anglican churches dating back to the Middle Ages, repairs bills are mounting up. Some of the problems are dramatic; the Perpendicular church of Hickleton in South Yorkshire is gradually subsiding because of mining activity. Even some newer buildings have problems; the spire of All Souls, Halifax is already crumbling although it was built in the 1850s.

In 1913 when the Ancient Monuments Act offered financial aid to many historic buildings church buildings were excluded. Although this meant the Church kept absolute control over them, it also deprived them of repair grants from the Historic Buildings Council. In 1977 an influential exhibition, Change and Decay: the Future of Our Churches, was held at the Victoria and Albert Museum. By then 176 churches, 30 of them listed, had already been demolished since 1968. Within a month of the exhibition the government had agreed to provide help with repairing historic churches.

The Quinquennial Inspection Measure requires all churches to undergo a five yearly inspection by an architect who will report on the repairs needed. From 1978 English Heritage and Cadw were able to provide grants to Grade I and II churches. Between 1978 and 1995 English Heritage gave £105 million to restore historic churches. However, it could only contribute to the bill rather than pay it in full and the payment system was slow and bureaucratic. Unlisted and Grade II churches could apply to the National Heritage Memorial Fund for help. In 1996 English Heritage formed a partnership with the Heritage Lottery Fund to double the sum available for repair grants and speed up the process for obtaining them. Christ Church, Spitalfelds, in London was the immediate beneficiary of a grant of £2.8 million. The Historic Churches Preservation Trust (HCPT), set up in 1953, is another potential source of funds. In 1995 it helped with grants or interest-free loans of £1,136,600 to 325 churches, although such grants only averaged £2,300 per church against average bills of £48,000. Further small-scale help was available from County Trusts.

If providing money to maintain church buildings is a problem, finding the cash to restore fixtures and fittings can be even harder. Churches in financial difficulties are often tempted to sell individual items to raise cash, particularly when they are too valuable to be displayed in the church; the Advisory Board for Redundant Churches has found both benches and benefactions boards being sold through the antiques trade. In 1983 it was agreed that the fittings of a redundant church shouldn't be sold before its fate had been decided, a time when they are at greatest risk. The National Heritage Memorial Fund has provided grants to restore important fittings. For example, it gave £29,978 to pay for restoration of the 18th-century ceiling and wall paintings in St. Lawrence, Little Stanmore; £15,000 to restore and display Anglo-Saxon sculptures in St. Paul's, Jarrow; and £72,500 towards restoring the 14th-century stained glass and the monuments in St. Nicholas, Stanford-on-Avon. It also helped Burghfield Church after a six foot medieval effigy was stolen and sold to a Belgian collector. Under Belgian law Burghfield had to buy its own property back which would have been impossible without NHMF aid.

Redundant Churches

The worst dilemmas are presented by churches which have outlived their original purpose, a problem which increased after parishes were reorganised in the 1950s, especially in towns. No Colchester churches had been lost since 1878; however, pastoral reorganisation in 1952 meant that four of its seven Anglican churches were declared redundant. In 1975 St Nicholas, a Sir Gilbert Scott church, was pulled down to make way for a supermarket. All Saints was turned into a natural history museum and Holy Trinity became a rural craft museum. In 1977 St. Mary's was also abandoned, leaving only two churches still in use.

Since 1968, 1,511 Anglican churches or parts of churches have been declared redundant. According to the 1968 Pastoral Measure the Church Commissioners have three possible options in dealing with redundant churches:

- They can be demolished. Between 1968 and December 1995 this was the fate of 316 churches. Amongst those demolished were the mainly Saxon St Peter the Less in Chichester, and the Grade I listed The Saviour at Bolton in Lancashire.

- They can be converted to alternative uses. Although this seems sensible, people sometimes object on the basis that churches are consecrated buildings. Once a church has been sold it is almost impossible to put restrictions on its future use. Reuse of a church can lead to the loss of its fittings and of traces of its archaeological history. Nevertheless between 1968 and 1994 801 churches were found alternative uses, 19 of them as museums, 33 of them as arts, drama or music centres.

- Churches of historic, archaeological or architectural interest can be preserved intact, usually by the Churches Conservation Trust (CCT), but sometimes by other conservation bodies; for example, Rycote Chapel in Oxfordshire is cared for by English Heritage. However, it's not always simple to find them a new owner. Neither the Churches Conservation Trust nor the Department of the Environment wanted to take on All Souls, Haley Hill in Halifax when it was made redundant in 1979. It was only saved when a local group created a Trust to care for it and persuaded the National Heritage Memorial Fund to contribute to the restoration of the tower and spire.

In 1994 the Templeman Commission recommended closing 26 Grade 1 churches in the City of London and converting them into conference or exhibition centres, concert halls or wine bars. The crypt of St Dunstan in Fleet St was earmarked for conversion into a wine bar or museum, while All Hallows, London Wall was suggested as a possible new theatre.

Some forms of reuse still let tourists see the church. This is particularly the case where they become museums, heritage centres, craft centres or brass rubbing centres. But although much imaginative rethinking has gone on in other areas of heritage tourism, little of it has spilled over into the presentation of churches. Marcus Binney's visit to All Souls, Haley Hill, Halifax, set him thinking: 'I began to wonder whether we could not bring parties of visitors and seat them in the pews and tell them something, not about the church but about churchmanship and the style of worship it was built to serve and proclaim. The Church has so much spectacular music and liturgy... A dramatically presented programme with recorded voices and music, principally serious and thought provoking but occasionally light-hearted and witty, might reveal far more about the purpose the church was built to serve than a normal visit to a church ever could.' Sadly, his vision has not been translated into reality.

FIG.4/5: REUSE OF REDUNDANT CHURCHES AND CHAPELS IN ENGLAND	
Church	**Reused as**
Christchurch, Downside, Somerset	Private dwellings
All Saints, Oxford	Lincoln College library
St Mary Castlegate, York	Heritage centre
St. George's, Brandon Hill, Bristol	Concert hall
Holy Trinity, Ship St, Brighton	Local history museum
United Reformed Church, Lightcliffe, Halifax	Crafts emporium
Headingley Hill United Reformed Chapel, Leeds	Open-plan offices
St Saviour, Highbury	Centre for creative art
Idle Old Chapel, Bradford	School of speech, dance & drama
Holy Trinity, Richmond	Regimental museum
Holy Trinity, Wareham	Tourist information centre
St Mark, Byker	Children's activity centre and restaurant
St Peter's, Wickham Bishop	Stained-glass workshop
St Luke's, Chelmsford	Community health, training and recreation centre

Redundant Churches as Tourist Attractions

Most redundant churches which are not sold for reuse are cared for by the Churches Conservation Trust, previously the Redundant Churches Fund, a registered charity funded by the Church Commissioners and the Department of Culture, Media and Sport. Others are cared for by local amenity groups like the Norwich and Ipswich Churches Trusts. Yet another 20 which are, perhaps, less architecturally impressive are cared for by the Friends of Friendless Churches group.

By 1996 the Churches Conservation Trust was caring for 304 churches, fewer than had been expected when it was first set up in 1969. Its original remit was to preserve these churches 'in the interests of the nation and the Church of England' although the 1983 National Heritage Act added the need 'to promote the public's enjoyment of them'. Given the joint State/Church funding this broadening was probably inevitable.

Churches which have lost their primary religious function but which are preserved intact have considerable potential as tourist attractions. It could even be argued that that is the only justification for preserving them. Those in towns sometimes fulfil this potential although there are still problems with access since the small number of expected visitors makes it hard to justify paying a custodian; perhaps half of all the churches belonging to the Churches Conservation Trust are kept locked although they normally display information on the key's whereabouts. However, many are in remote areas, hardly accessible except by private transport: Inglesham church in Wiltshire is tucked away behind a farm and St. Michael's, Upton Cressett is at the end of a long dead-end road. Some are also very small which makes it difficult to add bookshops, refreshments or a visitor centre. They also remain consecrated buildings, open for occasional services or special events. Not all their visitors would want them turned into 'ecclesiastical mini-museums' (Bowles) since some of the unique appeal of churches comes from the fact that they offer oases of peace in an increasingly frenetic world.

In the period from 1984 to 1989 the Churches Conservation Trust had a budget of between £6 and £8 million, with 60% coming from the government and 40% from the Church (some of this was raised through the sale of other redundant churches). In addition the CCT raises about £30,000 a year from donations, fund-raising events, etc. The money is used to make each church wind-, weather- and vandal-proof and to conserve its fittings so that its original significance can be appreciated. It also tries to provide guidebooks for its churches and employs three Field Officers to look after them.

'Listing' of Churches

Until 1970 churches were listed in different categories to other historic buildings (see Chapter 5). Those listed in Category A were of exceptional or pristine character, no matter what their age. Those in Category B were more modest medieval churches and those that were heavily overlaid with later reconstruction, together with later churches of particular importance but which could not be regarded as exceptional. Category C covered minor post-Reformation buildings which were only just of statutory quality. However, once made redundant churches were listed in the same way as other buildings. Since 1970 all churches are graded in line with other historic buildings.

So long as a church continues in ecclesiastical use listed building consent is not needed to alter, extend or partly demolish it. Nor is this needed once it has been declared redundant under the 1968 Pastoral Measure provisions. However, where a church stands in a conservation area consent is needed to alter it even when it is not listed in its own right.

In 1995 there were 16,255 Church of England churches in the UK, 8,500 of them dating from before the Reformation. Including the cathedrals there were 12,970 listed churches, 2,959 of them Grade I. The majority of listed churches were wholly or largely medieval and 49% of them were in remote areas of the East Midlands, East Anglia and the West Country. In addition there were around 450 listed Roman Catholic churches, most of them Victorian. Of the listed churches 645 were redundant. However, between 1968 and 1995 only 79 redundant churches that were actually demolished were listed buildings and they represented 0.61% of all listed Anglican buildings. In a shorter period 0.88% of listed secular buildings disappeared, suggesting that listed churches have a greater chance of survival.

CHAPELS

In addition to the cathedrals and churches Britain has thousands of chapels and meeting houses built by Non-Conformist groups like the Quakers, Methodists, Baptists and Unitarians. Although many chapels are plain and simple, others, like St. Mary's-on-the-Quay, Bristol, the Octagon Chapel, Norwich and the circular chapel at Saltaire in West Yorkshire, can be large and impressive, with interesting architecture. However, of the chapels listed in the 1801 census four-fifths have now disappeared. Since 1945 almost 400 chapels of listable quality have been lost; between 1960 and 1970 the Methodists alone closed a quarter of their chapels. There are still about 1,200 listed Non-Conformist chapels and in 1993 the Historic Chapels Trust was set up to conserve architecturally important non-Anglican places of worship. It receives a grant from the Department of Culture, Media and Sport. When chapels are sold they are even more likely than Anglican churches to wind up as garages and storehouses, their potential as tourist attractions completely lost.

ST. GEORGE'S CHAPEL, WINDSOR

St. George's Chapel is unusual in that it is the private chapel of the Knights of the Order of the Garter. It's also used by the Queen when she is staying at Windsor and is a 'royal peculiar' (i.e. subject to the jurisdiction of the sovereign rather than the bishop of the diocese). It's a magnificent example of fan-vaulted late 15th-century architecture and is particularly interesting because members of the royal family including the saint-king Henry VI and Henry VIII are buried there. It's usually open to the public and there's an admission fee which must be paid at a booth inconspicuously built against an outside wall. In 1995, 1,212,305 people visited Windsor Castle and many of them will have visited the chapel too.

As with churches, age and architectural quality can't guarantee a chapel a future once its congregation has vanished; the 18th-century Unitarian chapel at Crediton has been demolished as have the 19th-century Mint Methodist Church in Exeter and Unitarian Church in Kensington. Some chapels, like the 18th-century Lewins Mead Chapel in Bristol, have been found uses that allow an attractive facade to be maintained, but even then regular public access is not guaranteed.

To add to the problems Non-Conformist chapels are usually locked except during services although many Friends Meeting Houses are open to visitors. Not surprisingly even chapels which have played an important part in Non-Conformist history, like Little Baddow United Reformed Church which was built in 1707, have trouble attracting visitors.

Chapels are popular with foreign tourists who are trying to trace their family trees, including many North Americans whose families left the UK to escape religious intolerance and helped found the North American colonies in the 17th century. So many Friends Meeting Houses in North Lancashire and Cumbria receive a steady trickle of visitors. One of Britain's most visited chapels is Come to Good, near Truro, a particularly pretty building with a thatched roof.

KING'S COLLEGE CHAPEL, CAMBRIDGE

King's College Chapel is an integral part of the college and plays a major part in its calendar, hosting popular events like the candle-lit Nine Lessons and Carols concerts on Christmas Eve and regular performances of the Bach Passions. It, too, is a fine example of 15th-century architecture with magnificent fan vaulting and a superb organ. Since 1962 Rubens' *The Adoration of the Magi* has served as its altarpiece. In 1995 the Chapel received 333,938 visitors; at peak times access had to be restricted to prevent overcrowding.

As with churches, chapels attract more visitors if they are associated with someone well-known. Probably the most famous of all is the Bunyan Meeting in Bedford which was built on the site of a building where John Bunyan, author of Pilgrim's Progress, preached. Despite being tucked away in Bristol's Broadmead shopping centre, the New Room, the first purpose-built Methodist Chapel with links to Wesley, receives around 20,000 visitors a year. Chapels associated with royalty like St. George's Chapel, Windsor, are also popular with visitors, as are those near related attractions, like the college chapels at Oxford, Cambridge and Eton.

CHURCHYARDS AND CEMETERIES

Some people visit churches because they enjoy looking at churchyard monuments. Churchyards may also contain interesting ancient crosses, old biers and ancient yew trees. Inevitably it's the churchyards where someone famous is buried which attract most attention; hundreds of coaches stop in the Oxfordshire village of Bladon so tourists can see Sir Winston Churchill's grave. Nevertheless the tent-shaped tomb of the Victorian explorer, Sir Richard Burton, in Mortlake, Surrey goes virtually unnoticed despite its oriental exoticism. Recently there has been growing recognition that churchyards can act as refuges for wildlife, especially in built-up urban areas. Some churches now provide nature trails for visitors.

As churchyards became too full for more bodies separate cemeteries were created. The monuments in them are usually of later date and not as historically interesting as those in the churchyards. 'Novelty' cemeteries like the one for cats and dogs in Paris appeal to visitors. They will also be drawn to cemeteries which contain the graves of the famous. The Cimitière Père-Lachaise in Paris is popular with those keen to examine the graves of figures as diverse as Molière, Piaf, Colette, Balzac, Proust, Oscar Wilde and Jim Morrison; the custodians supply maps for a small fee.

London's best-known cemetery is in Highgate where Karl Marx is buried. The cemetery, once described as a Victorian Valhalla, boasts many fine monuments apart from his memorial. However, without the lure of the famous father of Communism it's unlikely that it would attract so many visitors. Highgate's

HIGHGATE CEMETERY

In 1836 an Act of Parliament authorised the London Cemetery Company to build cemeteries in Surrey, Kent and Middlesex. The Company paid £3,500 to buy seventeen acres of land and work started on Highgate Cemetery in 1839. From the beginning it was intended to be beautiful and an architect and landscape gardener both worked on it. Although some burial plots were available for as little as £2 10s, space in either the Egyptian Avenue or the Circle of Lebanon cost much more. By the 1860s people were already visiting the cemetery to view the magnificent monuments; in his record of a visit William Justyne commented not just on the tombs but also on the birds and foliage.

In 1854 another nineteen acres of land were purchased to create the Eastern Cemetery where Marx was later buried. The cemetery continued to receive corpses and visitors until 1975 when United Cemeteries Ltd closed it for all but occasional funerals. By then staff and maintenance costs had outstripped what could be made from burials. Graves had also been desecrated and the cemetery used for occult practices.

A registered charity, the Friends of Highgate Cemetery, was formed and volunteers began to clear the undergrowth choking the graves. Funding came from donations, subscriptions and grants from Camden Council. Representatives of the National Trust, the Historic Buildings Council, the Victorian Society and the Highgate Society also formed an advisory group. In 1981 the cemetery was sold for £50 to two of the Friends as a limited company. By 1984 more than 2,000 Friends were working with Manpower Service Commission staff under a full-time Projects Director and with guidance from a landscape gardener. Although trees still keep out views of surrounding houses, others have been cut down and much of the ivy and undergrowth removed to reveal the tombs in all their Victorian splendour.

In 1994 the Cemetery received 60,071 visitors. It's still looked after by the Friends but admission charges now make it possible to cash in on its popularity.

popularity has drawn attention to other interesting cemeteries and a Friends group has been set up to protect Arnos Vale in Bristol which contains the grave of Rammohan Roy, the first Hindu to have visited England. Before visitors can be attracted such groups must often clear decades of undergrowth from neglected graves and then record the headstone inscriptions. Like churchyards, cemeteries are increasingly seen as wildlife havens, and nature trails are often included in plans for clearance.

ABBEYS AND PRIORIES

When Henry VIII broke with the Roman Catholic church and dissolved the abbeys and priories in 1536 he destroyed a lifestyle which had endured for centuries and left its mark on the landscape in the form of innumerable ecclesiastical settlements, often in remote parts of the countryside. Much of the land was sold to private owners and the buildings were left to collapse, their roofs stripped of lead, their bricks removed for use elsewhere.

FIG.4/6: THE UK'S MOST VISITED ABBEY RUINS IN 1995	
Beaulieu Abbey	415,600
Fountains Abbey	311,071
Battle Abbey	157,665
Glastonbury Abbey	134,411
Iona Abbey	120,000
Whitby Abbey	117,972
Tintern Abbey	79,631
Rievaulx Abbey	75,896
Cartmel Priory	75,000
Lindisfarne Priory	68,378

The ruins stood virtually ignored until the 18th century when they were rediscovered by the Romantic Movement. In 1765 William Aislabie bought Fountains Abbey to incorporate in Studley Royal Pleasure Grounds although his attempts to tidy up the site didn't find favour with those who thought the rubble should be left in place as a stimulus to the imagination. By the 1790s boat trips were carrying tourists along the River Wye to visit the ruins of Tintern Abbey.

In the late 19th century visitors became more interested in the architecture of the ruins. However, the remote setting of many abbeys made them virtually inaccessible until the advent of the private motor car. By the 1990s most abbey and priory ruins were in the care of English Heritage or its regional equivalents and some received thousands of visitors every year. A few, like Jervaulx Abbey in Yorkshire, remained in private hands.

Having something 'extra' certainly helps attract more visitors. In the case of Beaulieu the abbey ruins are a very small part of what is on offer; on their own they would probably receive few visitors. Glastonbury has the lure of the legend that it was King Arthur's burial place, while Battle will forever be linked with stories of the Norman Conquest and King Harold's death with an arrow through his eye. Whitby has its wonderful, dominating position on a cliff above the winding shopping streets of a fishing port. But whereas Tintern is a convenient stopping point for anyone travelling along the M4 to South Wales, few people would bother to travel to the remote island of Lindisfarne unless they intended to visit the priory (and castle) ruins.

Protection and Presentation of Abbey Ruins

Some abbeys have few visitors and in his book on the presentation of ruins M.W. Thompson points out that they are particularly difficult for most people to understand because the monastic life is so uncommon now. Once taken into guardianship abbey ruins need to be made safe and intelligible for visitors and simultaneously protected from further decay. Vegetation may have to be removed from the walls which also need resetting and repointing. Steel rods set in concrete may have to be used to secure crumbling masonry; this strengthening work may then need to be disguised, as it has been very effectively at Tintern. Sometimes mouldings have to be reconstructed to prevent them being lost, and millions may have to be reconstructed to make them strong enough for reglazing.

FOUNTAINS ABBEY

Fountains Abbey in North Yorkshire was founded by the Cistercians in 1132. Its ruins were later incorporated into the grounds of the Studley Royal estate where there is a 16th/17th-century house and 18th-century landscaped gardens. A fire destroyed part of the house at Studley Royal in 1946 and in 1966 West Riding County Council bought the site (it was later taken over by North Yorkshire County Council). In 1983 the site was acquired by the National Trust with a grant of £2 million from the National Heritage Memorial Fund, although the Abbey ruins are cared for by English Heritage. In 1987 it was declared a World Heritage Site. With 311,071 visitors in 1995, Fountains is now the most visited National Trust property with an entrance charge.

Since 1983 the National Trust has spent more than £2 million on improving the site, with English Heritage paying even more to restore the Abbey ruins. A new Visitor Centre opened in 1992, and poor car parking arrangements have been greatly improved. Financial help has come from the National Heritage Memorial Fund, the Countryside Commission, the Historic Buildings Council and independent sponsors including Lord Forte and several high street banks.

Fallen rubble is usually cleared away from the lower walls so they can be secured and the ground plan excavated. During this process old tiled floors are sometimes uncovered. Unfortunately tiles (particularly decorative ones) weather badly once exposed to the air and may have to be moved into a museum. Removing rubble can be a major undertaking; at Rievaulx, where clearing was carried out in 1919, a special light railway was built to remove the stones. Later additions to the building may also be removed. However, the 18th-century landscaping at Fountains was left in place because it was regarded as attractive and historical in its own right.

Where the ground plan of previous buildings on the site has been excavated it is often marked out on the ground in brickwork or tile. Provided the markings are set flush with the ground it is easy to cut the grass around them, although it will quickly encroach again in summer. However, if the markings jut up from the ground mowing will be difficult. Where missing pillars are indicated by low concrete shells filled with gravel, these need to be tall enough to prevent the gravel overflowing on to the grass. Ruinous sites can also be made easier to understand if those parts which would once have been indoors have gravel floors, while those which would have been outdoors have grass.

Modern Abbey Buildings

Some abbey churches are still in use, usually because they were taken over as parish churches when the abbey itself was dissolved. Some of these churches are amongst the finest and most visited in the country. Tewkesbury Abbey, for example, received 200,000 visitors in 1995. Westminster Abbey is another example of an abbey church which is still a flourishing concern, receiving something like 2,245,000 visitors a year despite having an entrance fee. Westminster benefits from its impressive history and links with royalty and other famous figures. However, its central situation, across the road from Big Ben and the Houses of Parliament and down the road from Trafalgar Square and Downing Street, also guarantees it a visit from most foreign visitors.

Although the flow of tourists may detract from the pursuit of a contemplative life, several modern abbeys also welcome visitors. Prinknash Abbey in Gloucestershire, where the pottery produces pots with a pewter-effect glaze, attracted about 100,000 people in 1995 and also courts visitors in search of a 'retreat', the sort of holiday that has more to do with spiritual renewal than sightseeing.

RELIGIOUS BUILDINGS OUTSIDE THE UK

Europe

The continental cathedrals are just as popular with tourists as Britain's. In France the cathedrals at Amiens, Chartres, Limoges, Paris (Nôtre Dame), Rheims, Rouen and Tours are particularly important. In Germany Aachen, Cologne, Mainz, Speyer, Trier and Worms are popular, while in Spain tourists flock to Burgos, Cordoba, Granada, Leon, Palma, Salamanca, Santiago, Seville and Toledo. In Italy the

---

FIG.4/7: FAMOUS RELIGIOUS BUILDINGS/SITES WORLDWIDE WHICH ARE POPULAR WITH TOURISTS

Blue Mosque, Istanbul	Wailing Wall, Jerusalem
Holy Sepulchre, Jerusalem	Dome of the Rock, Jerusalem
Church of the Nativity, Bethlehem	Taj Mahal, Agra
Wats Po/Arun, Bangkok	Borobudur, Indonesia
Shwedagon Pagoda, Rangoon	

---

cathedrals at Amalfi, Cefalu, Florence, Milan, Monreale, Pisa, Ravenna, Rome (St. John Lateran and St. Peter's), Siena, Torcello and Venice are very important. St. Basil's in Moscow is also world-famous. Outside Europe it's possible to find very

European-looking cathedrals in ex-colonies like Hong Kong and even New York. These also tend to attract the curious.

The Rest of the World

Some of the greatest tourist attractions outside Europe are, or were originally, religious buildings. Many Christians visit Israel to see the churches in Jerusalem, Bethlehem and Nazareth, while Jewish visitors take in the Wailing Wall, all that remains of Solomon's Temple. Some people visit these sites for religious reasons, but others do so because they enjoy seeing famous historic buildings. Sometimes a mixture of both reasons may be involved. In contrast all the people making the *hajj* (pilgrimage) to Mecca every year will be doing so for religious reasons; non-Muslims are forbidden to enter the city where Mohammed is buried.

The Trouble with Visitors

These different reasons for visiting can cause conflicts, which become even sharper where religious forms are more strictly observed than they are in Northern Europe. Visitors to Southern European churches will be expected to cover their heads, shoulders and legs in accordance with Catholic sensibilities and men in shorts will be frowned upon. Sadly not all tourists readily adjust their behaviour so church porches are often plastered with signs prohibiting the taking of photos, wearing of shorts, eating of ice-creams, etc. inside the church.

The potential for conflict is even greater where tourists are visiting the religious buildings of faiths whose tenets they neither know nor understand. There are few rules for behaviour in Hindu buildings, although visitors to Sikh gurdwaras, like the Golden Temple in Amritsar, are expected to remove their shoes and refrain from smoking. Shorts and short skirts are unacceptable in otherwise relaxed Buddhist temples. In contrast all visitors to mosques must take their shoes off and women must cover their heads and dress with extreme modesty. Sometimes non-Muslims are forbidden to enter mosques; this is the case in Morocco although Egyptian mosques are open to everyone. At its most extreme the conflict between the wishes of tourists and the needs of local worshippers can lead to violence; tourists are said to have been lynched for photographing Mayan Indian religious rites in southern Mexican villages.

Most religious faiths open their buildings free of charge. However, many European cathedrals charge for admission to all but a small part of the building. Foreign tourists are charged for visiting some of Cairo's mosques.

Ruins

Visiting disused or abandoned religious buildings of whatever faith is usually simpler and some of the world's great ruins, like the Indonesian site of Borobudur and the Cambodian site of Angkor Wat, were once religious shrines. However, once the faith that sustained them has gone, many such buildings face a perilous future, especially in developing countries with little money to spare for conservation. The fate of the religious buildings of minority faiths is even more precarious. Cairo is a predominantly Muslim city with a clutch of medieval buildings in its suburbs. Few of these are well-maintained, with even the mosques slowly crumbling. The likelihood of the churches and synagogues surviving without outside funding must be very doubtful.

CHAPTER 5 : OTHER HISTORICAL ATTRACTIONS

While museums, castles, stately homes and religious buildings play an important part in drawing tourists with an interest in history, there are other attractions whose main appeal is also to a love of the past. There are, for example, many archaeological sites and ancient monuments both in Britain and elsewhere which play a crucial role in attracting visitors. There are also an increasing number of heritage centres and heritage trails which focus on the past in a specific locality. In addition many old buildings, while not in themselves important enough to attract tourists, nevertheless help create the sort of environment within which tourism flourishes.

ARCHAEOLOGICAL SITES

The word 'archaeology' means the study of human antiquities, regardless of their age. Until about 1910 it was taken to mean the study of the past based upon its physical remains without any suggestion that these would have had to be excavated from below ground. However, by the 1950s the meaning of the word had narrowed and archaeology began to be thought of in terms of holes in the ground and people with trowels. Since the 1960s there has been more interest in the physical remains of the immediate past and 'archaeology' is once again being interpreted more widely. 'Industrial archaeology' is now a subject in its own right (see Chapter 8).

Britain is rich in relics of the past, ranging from the prehistoric causewayed camp at Windmill Hill in Wiltshire which dates from around 4000 BC to more recent survivals like the 19th-century Sibsey Trader Windmill in Lincolnshire. Most people would certainly regard Windmill Hill as a traditional archaeological site; Sibsey Windmill is an example of an industrial archaeological site.

The term 'rescue archaeology' is used to refer to excavations and surveys undertaken in circumstances where a site is threatened with serious alteration or destruction.

ANCIENT MONUMENTS

That the expressions 'archaeological site' and 'ancient monument' are effectively interchangeable was illustrated by the 1979 Ancient Monuments and Archaeological Areas Act which defined the word 'monument' so that it encompassed most archaeological sites as well. According to the Act a monument is:

- any building, structure or work whether above or below the surface of the land and any cave or excavation:
- any site comprising the remains of any such building, structure or work or any cave or excavation.

The remains of vehicles, vessels and aircraft are also regarded as monuments according to the 1979 Act, as are any machines that could not be detached from the monument without dismantling it.

In 1977 the English Tourist Board surveyed 11,789 'ancient monuments' and divided them into categories which indicate the scope of the term and the clear overlap with archaeology (Fig.5/1).

Ancient monuments can be divided into those that are upstanding, where little or no excavation is needed before they can be shown to the public, and those that are below ground where excavation is essential. Most pre-Saxon remains lie below modern ground levels and need to be excavated. Upstanding monuments are usually of most interest to tourists. However, some below-ground ruins are also of interest because of their great age. For example, the Roman palace at Fishbourne was very much a below-ground site which required extensive excavation to reveal its ground plan and mosaics. Nevertheless it attracted 250,000 visitors within six months of opening to the public in the 1960s. The Jorvik Viking Centre would be no more than a particularly unusual below-ground site were it not for the imaginative presentation that turned it into an award-winning attraction.

Fig. 5/1: CATEGORIES OF ANCIENT MONUMENT

Type of Ancient Monument	% of surviving total number of monuments
Burial mounds and megalithic monuments	29
Camps/settlement sites	15
Linear earthworks	3
Roman remains	6
Crosses/inscribed stones	5
Ecclesiastical ruins	6
Castles/fortifications	10
Deserted villages/moated sites	7
Ancient bridges	4
Industrial monuments	2
Other secular sites/buildings	13

(Source : ETB)

Traces of the pre-industrial world are relatively scarce so that almost any site of any substance is likely to be regarded as an ancient monument, whether protected or not. The more recent the date, the more remains tend to survive and the tougher the decisions over which should be given statutory protection. Industrial archaeologists have fought for recognition of a wider range of monuments. Their success means that old tin and coal mines are now as likely to be protected as ancient monuments even though they're not ancient at all.

In England most monuments are looked after by English Heritage (the Historic Buildings and Monuments Commission for England). In Wales they are cared for by Cadw (the Welsh Historic Monuments Commission), in Scotland by Historic Scotland and in Northern Ireland by the Department of the Environment. A few monuments remain in private hands. Since the 1980s local authorities have been receiving help from English Heritage to compile computerised Sites and Monuments Records for all sites of archaeological interest within their borders.

Archaeology and Tourism

The link between archaeology and tourism is most vividly illustrated by considering some of the most famous attractions abroad. After all, no one would go to Cairo without visiting the Sphinx and Pyramids (both ancient monuments) and the Egyptian Museum where the treasures excavated from the tomb of King Tutankhamun are on display. Every year regardless of the heat and the risk of illness thousands of people also embark on Nile cruises which take them to Luxor to visit the tombs of the Kings, Queens and Nobles. They are then taken to Aswan to marvel at the temples of Philae and Abu Simbel, lifted from below Lake Nasser and moved, with UNESCO help (see Chapter 13), to sites on land above the lake. Egypt also has sun and sand resorts in Sinai and along the Red Sea coast. However, what puts it in a category on its own as a tourist destination are the relics of the Ancient Egyptian civilisation, without which it would have many fewer visitors each year.

The same could be said of Athens where the temples of the Acropolis, and the Parthenon in particular, still draw thousands of sightseers every year despite bad publicity about the city's pollution. In any list of the world's greatest tourist attractions ancient monuments and archaeological sites would feature prominently: Petra in Jordan; Pompeii and Herculaneum in Italy; Knossos in Crete; Piazza Armerina in Sicily; the Mayan ruins of Central America; the Inca ruins of South America; Persepolis in Iran; the Pont du Gard in France; Palmyra in Syria; Jericho and Masada in Israel; Mohenjo-daro in Pakistan; the Great Wall of China... the list is endless.

In Britain, however, with the exception of the Roman Baths, Stonehenge and Housesteads, none of the archaeological sites can attract the crowds like the great cathedrals or castles (see Fig.5/2).

The Growth of Interest in Ancient Monuments and Archaeology

Despite the modern preoccupation with the past, people have not always been so curious about their ancestors. As early as 1162 the Roman Senate decreed that Trajan's Column should be preserved as a reminder of Rome's glorious past, but in general it wasn't until the Renaissance of the 15th and 16th centuries that an interest in the physical remains of the past and their preservation became apparent in Western Europe. In particular the 16th century brought renewed interest in the ancient civilisations of Greece and Italy. Antiquities were collected, monuments recorded and the first tentative excavations took place.

The popularity of the 18th-century 'Grand Tour' brought many wealthy young men into contact with the Classical world, and some brought a curiosity about the past home with them. Others became interested in the past after reading about other cultures in Classical literature.

Napoleon's invasion of Egypt in 1798 brought the treasures of the Pharoahs to the attention of the western world and a team of draughtsmen started to record the monuments systematically. In 1801 the British took Egypt from the French, and the Rosetta Stone which offered the key to deciphering hieroglyphics was removed to the British Museum. In 1837/8 the Great Pyramid of Giza was first explored and by the 1850s most of Egypt's major sites had been mapped. However, it wasn't until 1922 that Howard Carter and Lord Carnarvon discovered Tutankhamun's tomb with its unparalleled treasures.

FIG.5/2: TOP TEN ARCHAEOLOGICAL SITES IN GREAT BRITAIN IN 1995 (excluding castles, ecclesiastical ruins and industrial archaeological sites and those for which there was no admission charge)

Roman Baths, Bath	872,915
Stonehenge	707,796
Housesteads Roman Fort (Hadrian's Wall)	127,389
Old Sarum earthworks	81,446
Fishbourne Roman Palace	77,803
Arbeia Roman Fort, South Shields	74,383
Vindolanda Roman Fort (Hadrian's Wall)	65,595
Chesters Roman Fort (Hadrian's Wall)	68,531
Chedworth Roman Villa	69,141
Skara Brae, nr Stromness	52,518

In Egypt some monuments had to be dug out from under centuries of sand. Elsewhere uncovering them was even more difficult. In the early 19th century archaeologists scoured Middle Eastern mounds for Babylon and Nineveh. In the 1840s Stephens and Catherwood uncovered the Mayan ruins of Mexico and Honduras, many of them surrounded by jungle. Then between 1871 and 1890 one of the most famous archaeologists of all, Heinrich Schliemann, carried out systematic excavations of mounds in Asia Minor (modern Turkey) in search of Troy. Following his successes there he moved to Greece and uncovered the remains of Mycenae and Tiryns in the Peloponnese, now amongst the most visited ruins in Greece. In 1899 Sir Arthur Evans began work at Kephala in Crete (now Knossos), uncovering another site visited by thousands of tourists every year.

The earliest excavations took place within a limited framework of historical understanding. For example, although an exhibition at Copenhagen Museum in 1819 had established the concepts of the Stone, Bronze and Iron Ages as a chronological background for European archaeology, the British Museum didn't adopt it until 1871; without this framework many early excavations made little sense. Men like William Camden and John Leland had been writing about England's prehistoric monuments since the 16th century, and in the 17th century both Inigo Jones and John Aubrey drew and wrote about Stonehenge. In the 18th century William Stukeley's writings refer to a variety of field monuments. Excavations started seriously in the 19th century but often lacked coherence. Then towards the end of the century excavations at Silchester and Cranborne Chase set new standards for British digs. At Cranborne in particular General Pitt-Rivers introduced some of the features of modern archaeology, recording even trivial finds and acknowledging the importance of broken pottery sherds as well as real treasure.

Protection of Monuments in Great Britain

Archaeological sites and ancient monuments, once uncovered, are often fragile and wouldn't survive without protection. Nevertheless until the 1870s little thought was given to safeguarding British monuments; it was only in 1882 that Sir John Lubbock, the MP for Maidstone, persuaded Parliament to pass a law restricting the right of landowners to do what they wanted with monuments on their property. The 1882 Ancient Monuments Act recognised 68 sites, including the Stonehenge and Avebury stone circles, as worthy of government protection, and appointed General Pitt-Rivers (who later founded the Pitt-Rivers Museum in Oxford) as the first Inspector of Ancient Monuments.

Further Ancient Monuments Acts were passed in 1900 and 1910. In 1911 the owners of Tattershall Castle proposed to dismantle it and sell it to the USA. This led to the 1913 Ancient Monuments Consolidation and Amendment Act which set up an Ancient Monuments Board and created Inspectors and Commissioners of Works whose job was to draw up lists of monuments in need of protection. For the first time compulsion was introduced into the law; owners could no longer alter protected monuments without permission. Local authorities were required to set up preservation schemes for monuments and the areas immediately around them (parts of Hadrian's Wall had been threatened by quarrying activities). By 1931 3,000 monuments were under state protection. The 1946 Acquisition of Land (Authorisation Procedures) Act entitled the Secretary of State for the Environment to compulsorily purchase ancient monuments and adjacent land required to manage them and provide access. The 1953 Historic Buildings and Ancient Monuments Act extended protection to industrial remains as well. In 1979 the Ancient Monuments and Archaeological Areas Act consolidated all the existing legislation, and in 1987 protection was extended to cover 12,800 sites in the UK, still only a tiny percentage of approximately 635,000 archaeological sites identified in the country.

In 1989 English Heritage started a Monuments Protection Programme which will survey each county in detail with a view to scheduling a further 45,000 sites. New scheduled sites include deserted medieval villages, a Norman motte and bailey castle and a Roman villa. By 1996 16,023 sites had been scheduled under the programme which is due for completion by 2003.

In 1996 Scotland had 4,700 protected monuments, Wales 2,800 and Northern Ireland 1,100.

Under current legislation ancient monuments can be protected in several ways:

- Those of national importance are taken into *guardianship* by English Heritage or its equivalents. Most such monuments are upstanding remains like Stonehenge, Tintern Abbey and Dover Castle.

- Other monuments thought worthy of protection because of their fine state of preservation or academic significance can be *scheduled*. This prohibits building, farming or forestry work that is likely to damage them without three months' notice being given to the Department of the Environment. However, as long ago as 1968 the Walsh Report pointed out that of 640 monuments scheduled in Wiltshire, 250 had still been destroyed or seriously damaged, while another 150 had suffered minor damage. Often scheduling only covers the outer earthworks of a site, freeing the landowner to do whatever s/he wishes with the area inside. The Walsh Report suggested star grading scheduled sites to indicate their relative importance. The 1972 Field Monuments Act ignored this advice but did offer 'acknowledgement payments' to farmers who actively protected monuments on their land. In deciding which sites to schedule any or all of the following criteria can be taken into account:

  - whether it is characteristic of a specific period
  - its rarity
  - whether surviving documentation adds to the site's importance
  - its value as part of a group of monuments
  - its survival/condition
  - its fragility/vulnerability
  - whether its significance lies in one feature or a group of features
  - its potential

- Finally, monuments that are in imminent danger of destruction can be served with an *interim preservation order* to delay the work being carried out. However, such orders can be challenged in court and are expensive since the Department of Culture, Media and Sport has to compensate anyone prevented from carrying out their work as a result of the order.

In 1973 the Protection of Wrecks Act extended state protection to ruins beneath the sea. Once a wreck has been scheduled no one should visit or interfere with it without the permission of the Secretary of State for Culture, Media and Sport. Without such protection it's unlikely that many more *Mary Roses* would survive to be dredged up from the seabed and turned into tourist attractions.

Ancient Monuments Legislation in the United States

In the USA the 1966 Registered National Historic Landmarks Act provided for the scheduling of monuments in a similar way. The federal government is required to identify and record archaeological sites in each state. These are usually American Revolution, Civil War or Indian battlefield sites, log cabins and river crossings associated with the opening up of the west, and industrial relics like coal mines and steel mills. By the late 1980s there were more than 900 of these sites. In contrast to Western Europe the USA places greater emphasis on the place than the actual monument; for example, the log cabin where Lincoln was born is preserved inside a grand, pedimented modern memorial in Kentucky.

Developers are obliged to produce 'environmental impact statements' before they can start work on any site, and one per cent of their costs must be spent on rescue archaeology where this is deemed necessary. Perhaps because evidence of the past is less common in the States greater emphasis is placed on its preservation than in the UK. The US National Park Service actually looks after more historical sites than country parks (for example, it looks after the Statue of Liberty).

THREATS TO ANCIENT MONUMENTS AND ARCHAEOLOGICAL SITES

Monuments that have already been identified and/or excavated need physical as well as legislative protection to ensure they survive into the future for scholars and tourists alike. Those that have been taken into guardianship are usually well protected. The process of scheduling may also help.

Some of the threats to monuments are new (atmospheric pollution, metal detectors) but others are not. As early as 1721 there were reports that passing carriages had damaged Waltham Cross (one of 12 crosses set up by Edward I as memorials to his dead wife). In 1733 Bristol's High Cross was dismantled to make way for traffic despite protests from those who thought its age should be respected.

Weathering

Once uncovered any monument is exposed to the elements (wind, rain, frost, sun) and can be damaged unless shelter is provided. The degree of danger often depends on the materials used and on the building's position; the harm done by salty wind beating on the ancient stonework of Whitby Abbey on an exposed hilltop is only too sadly plain. In general timber rarely survives except in exceptionally wet conditions (as in the Somerset Levels and Jutland in Denmark) or very dry conditions (as in some of the Egyptian tombs). Purbeck marble and alabaster quickly erode in the open air, and chalk and clunch are not long-lasting. In contrast limstone survives weathering well. The granite stones and crosses on Bodmin Moor also stand up to a great deal more battering than more fragile sandstone elsewhere.

Huge stones like those at Stonehenge are reasonably resistant to weathering (although early drawings show that many of the stones have fallen down). However, the remains of the Roman Painted House in Dover were too delicate to be left uncovered in our damp climate. Roman villas with impressive mosaic floors, as at Lullingstone, Chedworth and Fishbourne, are at least partially covered. In the drier climate of Morocco the Roman mosaics at Volubilis survive uncovered without harm.

Where protection can't be guaranteed in situ the problem can be resolved by moving fragile objects and structures into temperature-controlled museums and replacing them with fibreglass copies. This may not suit the purists but does at least ensure the survival of the originals. Consequently it is the policy pursued at Pompeii. A secondary advantage of moving original structures is that it is usually easier to protect them from thieves and vandals inside a museum.

Pollution

Similarly, once exposed to the open air monuments, particularly in towns, are at risk from atmospheric pollution which eats away at stonework and blackens surfaces. In Athens the situation is so bad that the famous caryatids from the Erechtheum on the Acropolis have been moved into a site museum; copies have taken their place on the temple facade.

Removing industrial pollution is a long, expensive process. Some buildings can be sandblasted quickly and cheaply, but most are too fragile and must be painstakingly washed with sand, water and nailbrushes.

Farming

Sites in rural areas can also be damaged by farming practices. For example, annual ploughing up to the edges of earthworks can erode their outline, while deep ploughing can damage structures beneath the surface of the soil; in 1987 the Marquis of Hertford was convicted of damaging a scheduled Roman settlement by ploughing up two meadows. Mechanical peat-cutting can also be very damaging..

Building Work

Almost all building work, whether for ring roads and motorways, new towns, houses or offices, is potentially damaging to archaeological sites; for example, a new supermarket in Colchester was built on the site of the Temple of Claudius. In Scotland, the 1970s oil boom led to particular threats as new towns sprang up and pipelines were laid. The development of aerial and laser photography has made it easier to identify the position of unexcavated sites. Sadly, few are important enough to halt planned work; the best that can usually be hoped for is a delay while a rescue dig is carried out to record the site and retrieve significant finds. However, £72,000 was raised to preserve the Roman Painted House in Dover which was discovered while a bypass was being built.

The widening of the A66 for six miles from Bowes to the Northumbrian border destroyed a series of unexcavated sites. Parts of the site of the Battle of Naseby (which took place in 1645 during the English Civil War) also disappeared beneath a link road to the A1, although the furore this caused was instrumental in leading to the setting up of a Register of Battlefield Sites (see Appendix I).

Quarrying

Quarrying and gravel digging also present serious threats to the sites of ancient monuments. Once again rescue digs can retrieve a lot of data before a site is destroyed. However, once work has begun, little will be left for tourists to view.

Damage by Visitors

Sadly some monuments are also damaged by the number of people visiting them. This is a particular threat to the earliest archaeological sites, often little more than fragile earthworks and foundation stones. In summer the number of people passing through the Roman Baths in Bath have to be monitored by custodians with walkie-talkies who can spot potential bottlenecks forming. Efforts have been made to divert visitors to Hadrian's Wall from crowded sites like Housesteads, Vindolanda and Chesters to less popular ones like Birdoswald, Carvoran and Corbridge. In 1996 English Heritage published a five-year Management Plan for the Wall which proposes, among many other things, 'monitoring the impact of tourists...and encouraging them away from areas at risk of erosion.'

The most extreme example of a conflict between protecting a site and allowing access to the people who want to visit it is Stonehenge which lies at the heart of an area of prehistoric earthworks. The stone circle itself is under the guardianship of English Heritage while the surrounding farmland and most of the earthworks belong to the National Trust. Since the late 19th century visitors, including modern Druids, have been coming to the site to watch the sunrise at the summer solstice. Although there were already disputes over their right to do this in the 1920s, by the early 1930s 15,000 people were turning up each June. However, in the 1980s English Heritage decided that travellers who arrived each year and held a free festival on the adjacent land threatened to do irreversible damage to Stonehenge and the earthworks. Consequently they barred visitors from holding solstice ceremonies and surrounded the monument with barbed wire. This controversy rumbled on into the 1990s, although it never again quite reached the level of turmoil of 1985 when police forcibly evicted travellers in what became known as the Battle of the Beanfield.

Vandalism

Damage is also done by souvenir-hunters and those determined to leave their mark on everything they visit. Even in the 18th century there were reports of visitors removing chunks of Stonehenge as souvenirs. There are also Roman graffiti on the Pyramid of Cheops and 18th-century signatures on the rock at the top of Mount Sinai.

More serious vandalism is not unknown. In 1996, paint was daubed on the Avebury stones, on the Cherhill White Horse and on the tower on top of Glastonbury tor.

Treasure Hunting

Since the 1970s archaeological sites have been threatened by treasure hunters with metal detectors who can wreak havoc in their efforts to find saleable items. Metal detectors have even been used at well-known sites like Old Sarum and Mildenhall in Suffolk. By removing finds from sites before they have been recorded treasure hunters not only damage the site itself but also destroy the items' value as historical evidence which requires that they can be set into a specific context. According to the law governing treasure trove anything which was probably buried by its owner with the intention of returning for it (coins, gold, silver, etc.) belongs to the Crown, interpreted in practice as the relevant national museum; the gold armlets from

Lockington which are on show at the British Museum were discovered in 1994 and declared treasure trove a year later. To encourage finders to report their discoveries they are usually given the full market value of the items involved. However, objects which were not necessarily buried to be recovered later are not regarded as treasure trove and belong to the owner of the land or to whoever finds them. Scottish treasure trove law is broader and covers copper, bronze, shale, jet and other items.

The 1979 Ancient Monuments and Archaeological Areas Act prohibits use of metal detectors on the sites of scheduled monuments. Those which are in guardianship normally have notices to that effect. However, not all sites are clearly indicated and people have been able to claim they didn't realise what they were doing was illegal. Where there is no site custodian life is obviously much easier for treasure hunters.

Military Manoeuvres

Some ancient monuments, particularly on Salisbury Plain, stand on land used by the army for training. Since defence cutbacks started in the 1990s, such sites have had to be used more intensively, presenting a greater threat to the monuments on them.

Discovering New Archaeological Sites

New monuments still come to light as a result of the work of archaeologists. Although bomb-sites in London were excavated after the Second World War, in the 1960s archaeology was usually associated with greenfield sites where excavations could often take place without rigid time constraints. However, many town sites have been occupied since earliest times. To uncover the story of their past, archaeologists need to work beneath the existing sites. The first urban archaeology unit was set up under Martin Biddle at Winchester in 1961.

Urban archaeology presents serious problems. Some of London's most important sites have come to light when an old building was being demolished to make way for a new one. So the Roman Temple of Mithras was discovered in 1954 during redevelopment of a site in Queen Victoria Street for offices. In 1959 it was lifted to a new position and reconstructed; 30,000 people visited the site while it was being excavated. Any such discovery can lead to costly delay to work on the site, so urban archaeology has often been viewed with suspicion by developers.

Since the early 1970s when important sites like Baynard's Castle and Leadenhall Market were almost redeveloped without any study being made first, rescue archaeologists have usually been allowed time to inspect sites before all traces of earlier buildings are bulldozed. Until the 1970s the pace of change in London was relatively slow. During the boom years of the 1980s, however, it speeded up, putting more potential sites at risk. In the early 1980s the Museum of London's Urban Archaeology Unit was investigating roughly 10 to 14 London sites a year, but the 'Big Bang' in the City brought ever faster development and in 1987 it investigated 54 sites in Central London alone.

What is recorded is often of purely academic interest, and any important finds are removed to the Museum. However, in 1989 there was controversy over the fate of Roman baths discovered in Huggin Hill. An almost complete hypocaust (heating system) had been uncovered which meant the site had obvious potential as a tourist attraction. It was already scheduled as an ancient monument but consent had been given for its redevelopment. If this was revoked English Heritage would have had to pay £70 million in compensation to the site developers, an impossibility given that its total grant from the government in 1988/9 was £66.1 million. By the end of 1990 Huggin Hill was once again covered over.

Even greater controversy greeted the discovery of the site of the Rose Theatre where Shakespeare is believed to have acted. When planning permission was given for work on the site the London Borough of Southwark required the developers to provide a 'reasonable opportunity' for an archaeological survey to take place. The developers agreed to allow two months for evaluation, with further time to be agreed depending on what was discovered. However, they then sold the site to new developers who felt that two months should be long enough for all investigations. By then the archaeologists had uncovered the foundations of the Rose and wanted another 17 weeks to complete their work. The developers would only agree to ten weeks although they provided £150,000 towards the cost of the dig. English Heritage advised the government that the remains should be re-covered at the end of the ten weeks, with the planned office block built on piles to protect them. Had they advised that the monument should be scheduled and development work stopped altogether they might have had to pay out £7 million in compensation. A Rose Theatre Trust was founded to fight for a museum on the site but by 1990 the foundations were once again covered up. Luckily when the Globe Theatre was also discovered in 1989 it received more generous treatment, with the Hanson Trust financing archaeological evaluation of the site before planning proposals were submitted. The site of the Globe is now a scheduled ancient monument, although its future is still uncertain because much of the site lies under nearby housing.

The 1979 Ancient Monuments and Archaeological Areas Act tried to prevent these difficulties by designating 'areas of archaeological importance' where site development could only take place after a six month pause for excavations. The centres of Canterbury, York, Chester, Exeter and Hereford are protected in this way, although local authorities in Gloucester and Lincoln managed to prevent their cities being included in the list. In 1986 a British Archaeologists and Developers' Code of Practice was drawn up and many developers now provide money for digs to take place in advance of building work in return for good publicity and a guaranteed date when the site will be returned to them. In 1994-5 English Heritage made £8.2 million available for rescue digs.

Nevertheless problems still continue. For example, in 1989 York archaeologists uncovered the remains of what could be the palace of the Emperor Septimius Severus in the Micklegate area of the city on the site of a planned car park. The city's MEP called for York to be listed by the United Nations as a 'City of International Importance' (like Bath, Canterbury, Durham and Strasbourg) in the hope that this would offer it greater protection. In the same year, York Minster showed what could be done with a more imaginative approach to preserving sites when it started to charge visitors to view the remains of a Roman fort discovered underneath the cathedral when work to shore it up was being carried out.

Funding for Archaeology

During the 1980s English Heritage was a prime source of funding for English archaeological sites. However, in the 1990s such grants were drastically cut and archaeologists were supposed to draw up excavation contracts for developers to fund digs before work began. An illustration of how draconian the cuts were is that Flag Fen saw its income drop from £121,000 in 1993 to just £7,000 in 1996. In theory local authorities could make good some of the cuts but since most are under pressure this is unlikely to happen. Lottery funding can only help with capital projects and not ongoing maintenance.

Presentation of Ancient Monuments

When the first excavations took place in the UK the sites were usually left much as they had been found, with no attempt made to interest the public in them. Nevertheless in the 1890s people were already curious enough to make day trips by train to see the excavations at Roman Silchester, a journey made practical because of the Great Western Railway link between London and Reading. Sir Mortimer Wheeler played an important part in changing attitudes towards visitors to archaeological sites. In 1930 he excavated Maiden Castle in Dorset. While the dig was taking place he regularly showed people round and gave lectures, as well as giving weekly briefings to local journalists. Interesting features like skeletons in open graves were labelled and students used as guides. Pieces of pottery were sold as souvenirs, and 60,000 postcards and 16,000 site reports were sold. Sites like this can still be found all around the world. But while they are certainly an improvement on what had gone before and archaeology students may find them satisfactory, many other people visit such sites and come away little better informed than when they arrived.

Not surprisingly archaeological sites are often thought of as dull. Television has done much to make the public more interested. In the 1950s and 1960s the archaeologists Sir Mortimer Wheeler and Glyn Daniel appeared in 'Buried Treasure' which featured the West Kennet Long Barrow and the Lascaux Caves in France. Magnus Magnusson continued the work of popularising archaeology with programmes like *The Archaeology of the Bible Lands* and *The Vikings*. Michael Wood took up where he left off with programmes like *In Search of the Trojan Wars*.

Controversy has raged over whether it's appropriate to reconstruct some structures so that they are easier for the public to understand. In 1970 the Vindolanda Trust was set up to rebuild a stretch of the turf wall, rampart walk and timber palisade of Hadrian's Wall, using volunteer labour, much of it from a local school. Images on Trajan's Column, the Rudge Cup and Amiens Skillet were used to decide what the Wall would have looked like, since little more than foundations actually survived. In 1974 the project was extended to include the reconstruction of a stone turret and timber milecastle gate. Opponents of schemes like this claim that

STONEHENGE... TRADITIONAL PRESENTATION OF ARCHAEOLOGY

The stone circle and associated earthworks at Stonehenge in Wiltshire are ancient monuments in the care of English Heritage but standing on National Trust land. Unlike the Jorvik Viking site, Stonehenge is an upstanding monument which has always been visible to passers-by; indeed, it provided the climactic setting for Hardy's 19th-century novel *Tess of the D'Ubervilles*.

The site consists of an earthen ditch and circle enclosing the more famous stone circle of sarsen trilithons. Associated monuments include The Avenue, Vespasian's Camp, Woodhenge and many barrows. In 1995 707,796 people visited Stonehenge.

Stonehenge is not only famous worldwide but also a UNESCO-designated World Heritage Site. In spite of that fact many visitors come away disappointed. At the moment the site is hemmed in between the busy A303 and the A344 and traffic noise detracts from peaceful enjoyment of it. Visitors approach the circle via a grim concrete underpass and, since the solstice clashes of the 1980s, have been prevented from wandering among the stones. So depressing is the situation that the House of Commons Public Accounts Committee described it as 'a national disgrace' in 1992.

English Heritage and the National Trust want to see the A303 enclosed in a tunnel and the A344 rerouted to create a Stonehenge Millennium Park. A new visitor centre would be built up to a mile away, allowing visitors to approach the site more atmospherically but with environmentally-friendly transport available for less able visitors. The car park would be resited away from the stones. They hope to involve the private sector, through the government-backed Private Finance Initiative (PFI), in the design, construction, financing and operation of the new visitor centre. (The Tussaud's Group has won the competition to design this visitor centre.). However, in 1996 the government shelved the project to build a road tunnel as prohibitively expensive.

it is unhistorical since some of the work is based on speculation. Supporters would say it performs a useful educational function and may divert people away from more fragile original structures. Perhaps the crucial factor is that no deception should be involved. At Vindolanda it is perfectly clear which parts of what is on show are reconstructions. Elsewhere different building materials are often used to indicate sections of a monument that have been reconstructed. At Flag Fen near Peterborough, Bronze Age excavations which would normally have held little appeal for the public were turned into a successful attraction by reconstructing some of the

THE JORVIK VIKING CENTRE... BRINGING THE PAST TO LIFE

In the 1970s a team of archaeologists excavated a large area of the Viking settlement beneath the modern centre of York using funds partly contributed by Scandinavian banks. When the work was completed it was exhibited to the public in an entirely new way.

By the time the Jorvik Viking Centre opened in York's Coppergate shopping centre in 1984 a total of £2.7 million had been invested in developing a state-of-the-art tourist attraction, characterised by the use of 'time cars'. These carry visitors around a reconstructed 10th-century Viking village, run them past a reconstruction of the actual excavations and drop them off in a small conventional museum displaying finds from the site. Visitors leave the building via a shop selling a range of 'Viking' merchandise designed to appeal to all ages and socio-economic groups. By 1996 Jorvik had attracted more than 10 million visitors.

Jorvik works by recreating Viking York in every detail. Visitors can hear what sounds like authentic Viking-talk (actually reconstructed from 20th-century Icelandic). They can see life-size fibreglass models going about their daily life, right down to using the toilet. They can watch farmyard animals running around and a ship being unloaded. They can even smell the pungent smell of the medieval world (recreated by a chemist who now exports his expertise in aromas of the past).

The time cars take twelve and a half minutes to take their occupants back in time, a length of time that suits the average concentration span. To make the journey more interesting the cars start by running backwards past ghostly images representing different periods in York's past, before turning round to face forwards when the Viking village is reached.

The Disney Empire pioneered the 'time car' idea in the United States, but Jorvik was its first introduction in Europe. The cars themselves were designed so that people in the rear seats would be able to see as well as those in the front. Speakers in headrests at the back allow the commentary to be given in English, French or German; with separate front and rear amplifiers it's even possible to have commentaries in two different languages running at the same time. Side flaps can be lowered to let wheelchairs into the cars.

The cars run on heavy-duty batteries which are recharged overnight in the service area. They can run for ten hours a day and manage four trips in an hour, covering nine miles a day on a busy day. With 20 cars in all, the circuit can be covered 800 times a day.

This high-tech approach to archaeology has several advantages. It removes the 'boring' image while allowing the proprietors to control how long each visitor spends on the premises. However, it has drawbacks too. Greater care must be taken over safety, with video cameras and television screens monitoring strategic points along the route and engineers on hand to deal with mechanical problems. No more than 400 people can be inside the building at any one time which means that queues build up at peak periods. A daily inspection routine involves cleaning the tape heads and ensuring that the tapes are properly wound, charging the cars' batteries, checking the motors and lubricating all the bearing surfaces. Between seven and ten cars are given a complete service each day. To protect the exhibits from damage everything is just out of reach. However, in themselves none of the exhibits are valuable since they are all models.

Critics also point to the 'prettifying' of history this kind of presentation tends to produce. Jorvik has fine academic credentials, but the reproduction Bayeux Tapestries in the gift shop could lead to confusion in the minds of those for whom the Dark Ages are still pretty dark. And while the Stonehenge approach errs in favour of those with specialist knowledge, the Jorvik approach removes the chance for leisurely study of anything other than the collection of finds at the end.

Jorvik is a commercial success story. Like most modern tourist attractions it charges an entrance fee of £4.95 which is topped up with revenue from the shop. Not surprisingly Jorvik quickly spawned imitations in Oxford, Canterbury, Dover and Nottingham, some of them created by the same design team.

In 1995 York was still one of England's most visited historic cities, although the number of visitors was in decline. Of its attractions only the Minster (with about 2,000,000 visitors) received more tourists than Jorvik, the most visited site with an admission fee in York. Over the last twenty years several other local attractions have opened, including the National Railway Museum, the York Story, Friargate Wax Museum and the York Dungeon. Many of these attractions probably received a boost to their admission figures as a result of the increased number of people coming to the city specifically to visit Jorvik. In addition local shops, hotels and transport operators have seen their takings soar; a survey by Cambridge Economic Consultants suggested that the tourism multiplier figure for York might be as high as 7.14, meaning that for every £2.5 million spent by visitors, £17.5 million was generated for the local economy.

Like many UK attractions Jorvik receives more visitors in the summer than the winter, although the Jorvik Viking Festival every February aims to pull in more people However, by 1995 it looked as if it had passed its prime. In 1995-6 visitor numbers fell by 9% to 604,726, a situation it will be hard to reverse in a small, confined site and which highlights the problem for attractions which can't add new features to pull in repeat visits. But Jorvik is not resting on its laurels; in 1996 11 of the old models were replaced, a coin striker's workshop was installed, a new Education Pack developed and costumed interpreters introduced.

Profits from Jorvik go to fund the work of the York Archaeological Trust. In 1990 the ARC (Archaeological Resource Centre) opened in the redundant St. Saviour's church. It aims to show visitors more about real archaeology than is possible within the constraints of the Jorvik site, using interactive videos and other imaginative methods to make the processes more interesting. In 1995-6 it received 51,664 visitors, 75% of them school children.

houses (Unfortunately visitor numbers fell steeply in the 1990s, and the removal of government grants left Flag Fen facing   closure).

Archaeological reconstructions have also taken place elsewhere. For example, the Stoa in the Ancient Greek market-place in Athens was rebuilt by the American School of Classical Studies and now houses a small archaeological museum. The ruins of Persepolis in Iran have also been completely rebuilt. Even at Knossos some of what visitors see is reconstruction.

Given that many archaeological digs will be filled in again once records have been made, it's important that the public are offered access to the site while work is in progress. If that is done they are more likely to develop an interest in and sympathy for the work involved, making future digs more likely. At some sites, particularly in the countryside, visitors can be allowed to walk around the trenches, perhaps on temporary wooden walkways to protect their feet from the mud. Archaeologists may be prepared to act as guides, perhaps on a rota basis. In cities where access may not be practical viewing platforms can still be provided to let people watch what is going on from a safe distance. It helps to provide maps and diagrams to explain the various structures that are being uncovered, with perhaps an information board to set the site in context. Ideally viewing platforms should be sited against the sun and with shelter from the wind.

The presentation of archaeological sites should aim to safeguard the remains, while also presenting them safely and intelligibly to the public. Sites open to the public usually need to be supplied with ticket offices, visitor centres-cum-shops, toilets, car parks and museums. Even where the site is unsupervised there should still be information boards to help visitors interpret the ruins. Main structures should have discreet labels identifying them and colour-coded plans indicating the dates of different parts of the site. Ideally guidebooks should be sold either at the site or nearby.

The public are admitted to all monuments held in guardianship unless there are problems over safety. However, there is no automatic right of public access to scheduled monuments unless the local authority or Secretary of State for National Heritage has reached agreement with the local landowner.

At sites like Stonehenge there is little to bring the prehistoric past to life; visitors must use their imagination to people the monument and inject life into it. However, at other sites efforts are made to help non-experts interpret what they're seeing. The Jorvik Viking Centre in York led the way in showing what was possible.

LISTED BUILDINGS

While ancient monuments and archaeological sites often become tourist attractions in their own right, many other buildings of historic or architectural interest may contribute to the generally pleasant environment that draws tourists to an area even though they can't be visited. No doubt tourists would still come to Bath to visit the Roman Baths, the Pump Room, the Abbey and the Museum of Costume even if it wasn't such a beautiful town. However, many come specifically for the elegance and ambience created by the many Georgian buildings or stay longer than they would normally do in a town with the same sort of attractions but in a less pleasing setting. Similarly Chester's popularity springs more from its generally pleasant environment than from its specific tourist sites.

However, if it took until 1882 for Parliament to acknowledge the need to protect the major ancient monuments, it took until 1947 for the Town and Country Planning Act to offer mandatory protection to historic buildings which were usually in private hands and couldn't always be made accessible to the public. The 1947 Act made it possible for the Secretary of State for the Environment to 'list' buildings; which could not then be altered or demolished without specific permission. Listing is now the responsibility of the Department of Culture, Media and Sport, although the Department of the Environment handles appeals against listing. In 1995 the then Department of National Heritage brought in new rules to ensure greater consultation with owners and other interested parties before a building is listed.

Listed buildings are divided into three categories:

- Grade I (A) buildings are of national/international importance or are fine, little altered examples of a particular style
- Grade II* (B) buildings are of regional or special local importance or major examples of a particular style which may have been altered
- Grade II (C) buildings are of local historic or architectural interest. This category includes some buildings which are only of value within a group.

Buildings which don't quite justify preservation but which could possibly be upgraded form an unofficial Grade III category. For purposes of listing 'building' is taken to include walls, fountains, sundials, statues, bridges, bandstands and telephone boxes.

Although most buildings are listed because of their external features, some are protected for their interiors or their links with historical events or characters. All buildings dating from before 1700 in anything like their original condition should be listed, as should most of those built between 1700 and 1840. Of buildings erected between 1840 and 1914, only those fitting one of the following categories are likely to be listed:

- planned streets, villages or burghs
- works of well-known architects
- good examples of buildings connected with social and industrial history and the development of communications
- distinctive regional variations in design and use of materials
- good examples within individual building types
- technological innovations

An increasing number of inter-War buildings (including the Hoover Factory in West London and Battersea Power Station) are now listed. In 1988 18 post-War buildings including Coventry Cathedral and the Royal Festival Hall (both Grade I) were listed. Since 1987 any building more than 30 years old has been eligible for listing. In exceptional circumstances buildings that are only ten years old can also be listed; such buildings usually reflect changing building technologies, like the first use of concrete, or are street furnishings like telephone boxes or Nissen huts. Some of the recent listings are extremely controversial. Not everyone feels, for example, that Centre Point in London, Technical Block A at Heathrow or Birmingham's New St signal box should be listed.

In 1995 England had 447,470 listed buildings. Of these 6,090 were Grade I and about 23,000 Grade II. But just as ancient monuments are not always completely protected by scheduling, listed buildings can also be lost or damaged. In 1995-6 listed building consent was given for the demolition of 51 buildings, including two Grade Is. A further 23,000 buildings may be at risk from neglect or decay. Barns, farmhouses, chapels, mills and other industrial buildings seem to be most vulnerable. In 1996 there were 42,000 listed buildings in Scotland and about 18,800 in Wales.

The lists are not final documents. In 1995 2,056 buildings (including 12 new Grade Is) were added to the English lists, while 264 were removed because they had been listed in error, reassessed and found wanting, or had lost the particular features that made them worthy of preservation.

Deciding whether to list a buildings can be contentious, with the quantifiable financial benefits of demolition often having to be weighed against the less easily quantifiable environmental benefits of preservation. Consequently it can be difficult to get even the finest buildings listed; the NatWest Tower in London now stands on the site of Philip Hardwick's elegant 19th-century City Club Building, and Euston Station's great entrance arch was ruthlessly ripped down to make room for more cars in 1962. Nor are unscrupulous developers beyond pre-emptive strikes where they suspect a building may be about to be listed. So the fine Art Deco Firestone Factory was demolished on a Bank Holiday Monday in 1980, presumably to prevent it being 'spot listed' (an emergency procedure rather like interim preservation orders for ancient monuments) the next day. Even when a building has reached the lists the Secretary of State can still be persuaded to grant listed building consent to demolish. Between 1983 and 1994 4,620 listed buildings were demolished, often so local authorities could build new roads. Even in Bath, one of the finest examples of a town where the environment is a pull for tourists, almost 2,000 listed buildings were demolished in the 1960s and 1970s (Bath still has nearly 600 Grade I buildings). In 1987 an auction of the contents of Orchardleigh, a Victorian mansion and listed Grade II building, also highlighted the problem of defining how much of a building is protected by a listing order; it was argued that the wall ornaments and fireplace fittings which were sold were not part of the building's structure and not therefore covered by its listing.

What Listing Means

Once a building has been listed local authorities can make grants to ensure its preservation; English Heritage and its regional equivalents may also be able to help with grants of up to 33% of the cost of making the property structurally sound and weatherproof (often the owner must agree to admit the public for at least 28 days a year in return). If the building is being neglected the local authority can serve a compulsory repairs order on its owner or even compulsorily purchase it. Structural alterations can only be made with permission from the local authority but are then free of VAT.

In 1996 restoration of the fine Grade I crescent in Buxton reached completion, creating a new focus for the town centre.

The Royal Commission for Historic Monuments is responsible for the National Monuments Record (NMR) which keeps details of all listed buildings in England, Scotland and Wales.

CONSERVATION AREAS

In the same way that the scheduling of specific monuments has been broadened to cover entire 'archaeological areas', so the listing of individual buildings has been widened to offer protection to 'conservation areas'. While these may contain or be centred on specific listed buildings, this isn't always the case when it's felt that an area's overall appearance is what needs protecting. Thus although individual buildings in Bath's Royal Crescent are listed in their own right the entire street is also protected as a conservation area, limiting the changes individual owners can make, particularly to the exteriors of their properties.

The Civic Amenities Act introduced the first four conservation areas in 1967 and stated that 'every local planning authority shall from time to time determine which parts of their area... are areas of special architectural or historical interest the character or appearance of which it is desirable to preserve...' The 1974 Town and Country Amenities Act brought buildings in conservation areas under the same controls as individual listed buildings and put the Department of the Environment (now the Department of Culture, Media and Sport) in charge of designating areas. 'Conservation area consent' is required before alterations can be made to buildings in the designated areas. English Heritage and its regional equivalents can provide grants or loans for repairs to the exterior and structural roof work. All trees in the area are also protected and local authorities must be given six weeks' notice of any work which is to be done to them. In 1989 protection was extended to nine London 'views', including those round St. Paul's Cathedral and the Palace of Westminster.

In 1994 English Heritage began forming partnership with local authorities to look after conservation areas. In 1995 it allocated £8.5 million in grants to 127 authorities with Conservation Area Partnership Agreements. One recipient of £300,000 was Grainger Town in Newcastle where sterling efforts are being made to revive the Victorian townscape by converting old buildings into flats for reasonable rents.

By 1995 England had 8,435 conservation areas, 60% of them in rural areas, as well as 248 town centres with special planning controls over them. Forty per cent of all English conservation areas are in ten counties, with 34% of them covering an entire settlement (perhaps a village) and 37% covering most of one. Greater London alone has 814 conservation areas, including the areas around the Royal Hospital in Chelsea, Cheyne Walk, St. James, St. John's Wood and Westminster Cathedral. Sixty-two per cent of all London's conservation areas are in 13 boroughs with which English Heritage has drawn up London Borough Agreements on funding and management (see Fig.5/3). The first of these agreements covered Greenwich, a proposed World Heritage Site but blighted by traffic. English Heritage provided £200,000 to repair old buildings, repave and provide better street furnishing, while the London Borough of Greenwich undertook to remove unsuitable and unauthorised signs and clutter and to improve general street maintenance. However, the relationship has become strained since the Borough suggested demolishing a group of 17 historic buildings so the land could be sold and the profits used to pay for a new Underground station.

FIG.5/3: ENGLISH HERITAGE'S LONDON BOROUGH AGREEMENTS, 1995

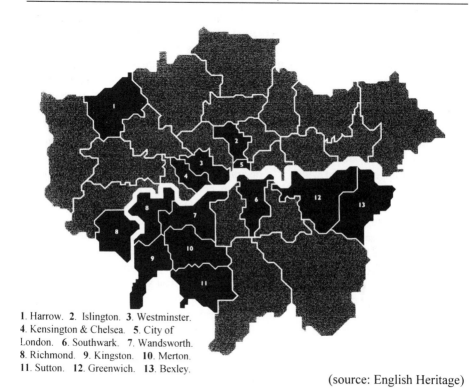

1. Harrow. 2. Islington. 3. Westminster. 4. Kensington & Chelsea. 5. City of London. 6. Southwark. 7. Wandsworth. 8. Richmond. 9. Kingston. 10. Merton. 11. Sutton. 12. Greenwich. 13. Bexley.

(source: English Heritage)

Elsewhere, the majority of conservation areas are in southern counties although North Yorkshire has 294. In 1996 there were 598 conservation areas in Scotland and 470 in Wales.

A particularly interesting conservation area is Portmeirion, near Porthmadog in Wales. Here Sir Clough Williams-Ellis set about proving that you could develop a beauty spot without ruining it by creating an entire Italianate village overlooking a pretty bay. Set in extensive woodlands, Portmeirion has its own hotel, restaurant, shops (including one dedicated to the cult television film 'The Prisoner') and self-catering accommodation. In 1995 it was one of Wales's most popular attractions with 258,605 visitors.

HERITAGE CENTRES

The Civic Trust defines heritage centres as 'permanent exhibitions with the evolution of the whole community as their theme'. An increasing number have opened in the last 15 years. Some concentrate on the architectural history of a particular area, while others focus on a particular date, event or tradition; there is a Shipwreck Heritage Centre in Hastings, and a National Fishing Heritage Centre in Grimsby. Some heritage centres are really museums given a punchier name.

WIGAN PIER HERITAGE CENTRE

In 1973 Wigan was a decaying industrial town with two claims to fame: George Formby had made a joke about it, and George Orwell had featured it in his book, *The Road to Wigan Pier*. The banks of the Leeds and Liverpool Canal passed through the pier area and were lined with crumbling warehouses belonging to the British Waterways Board. In 1982 the Board applied to demolish some of these and redevelop the site. However, by then the main warehouse had been designated a Grade II listed building. The original pier, a metal contraption for tipping coal into waiting barges, had been removed in 1929.

Eventually a decision was taken to redevelop the site as a heritage centre. Work was carried out between 1982 and 1986 with £3.5 million in funding from the following sources:

- European Regional Development Fund
- EC Social Fund
- English Tourist Board
- Greater Manchester Council
- Department of the Environment
- Countryside Commission
- North-West Museums and Galleries Service
- National Coal Board
- British Telecom
- Peter Walker group of companies

Visitors to the site enter between two large restored 18th-century warehouses. One now houses an exhibition called 'The Way We Were' which recreates many aspects of local life in the year 1900. Modern museographical techniques, including models and hands-on machines, are used to make visits as interesting as possible. Nevertheless detractors claim that the past is prettified; while it's possible to walk through a stretch of reconstructed mine-shaft, this is inevitably short and clean and can't possibly reproduce the real heat, dust and claustrophobic conditions below ground. Critics also argue that history is presented in an unquestioning way that belies its real purpose. So the Maypole Pit Disaster of 1908 in which 76 miners were killed is mentioned but without much analysis of its cause. As Robert Hewison says in

The Heritage Industry 'the main purpose of Wigan Pier is to create, not so much an informative as an emotional experience, a symbolic recovery of the way we were.'

The second warehouse now contains the independently managed 'George Orwell' pub and restaurant, and a large shop and Heritage Interpretation Centre used mainly by schools and colleges. Like many modern tourist developments in the UK, Wigan Pier puts great emphasis on education. Not only is there a floating classroom ('the Kittywake'), but actors and actresses of the resident Wigan Pier Theatre Company re-enact scenes from turn of the century life, including a popular school-room scenario.

Visitors with more time can cross the Changeline Bridge and enter the Trenchfield Mill which houses the UK's largest working steam mill, a cotton machinery exhibition (with live demonstrations), the Courtaulds mill and the Mill at the Pier concert hall. The site ends where the Leeds and Liverpool joins the Leigh Branch Canal (Fig.8/3).

Development work is not complete and although the canal banks are part of a conservation area many of the buildings still need repairing. In 1997/8 work is expected to start on a new Museum of Memories.

In 1995 Wigan Pier received about 250,000 visitors. Personal stereos with taped commentaries in French and German were available, and some staff had been taught French and German in anticipation of more visitors from the continent. Because Wigan is close to the M6 connecting north and south England, it makes a convenient stopping point for coach trips.

The success of Wigan Pier is a triumph of marketing over material. Like many modern tourist developments the Pier has a special, easily identifiable logo (Fig.8/3) which appears on all its merchandise, press releases and tickets (these also feature a site map).

The first heritage centre opened in June 1975, European Architectural Heritage Year, and was typical in being housed in St. Michael's, a redundant Chester church. It was funded by Chester City Council and the Department of the Environment and presented the city's history through expensive audio-visuals. In 1975 The York Story in St. Mary's, York became the second heritage centre. In 1995 there were at least 74 heritage centres, the newest being Purfleet Heritage Centre which is housed in the Royal Gunpowder Magazine of 1760.

Considerable capital investment is needed to create a heritage centre from scratch. To be successful it will need a central position which is likely to be expensive. While some of the older heritage centres display conventional museum exhibits, the newer ones tend to be completely artificial, with fibreglass models rather than original artefacts. Some differ little from traditional museums, but others make use of the imaginative techniques pioneered at Jorvik. So visitors to Edinburgh's Whisky Heritage Centre view the industry's history from barrel-shaped electric cars, while visitors to The Tales of Robin Hood in Nottingham travel round in metal cars like those used in an abbatoir. The White Cliffs Experience in Dover, which has 13 exhibitions including a World War II 'blitz experience' set round an archaeological site, had cost £14 million when it opened in 1991.

Heritage centres have been criticised for making the past look more appealing than it really was. While the best go to great lengths to ensure historical accuracy, the Crusades Experience in Winchester at least implied the Crusades had something to do with the city when they didn't. However, such economy with the truth served it badly and it has since closed down.

Wigan Pier Heritage Centre is typical of what can be achieved even in unpromising circumstances.

HERITAGE TRAILS AND GUIDED WALKS

During Architectural Heritage Year in 1975 several towns and villages created 'town trails', linking places of architectural interest or with a particular theme. Visitors follow these self-guided trails using signposts, plaques, guidebooks or tape recordings which give additional information about buildings and monuments along the way. By 1995 613 English towns or suburbs offered town trails. Devon has 66 trails and Hampshire 45. Some towns have several trails; Bristol has a Maritime Heritage Trail to guide visitors round the Historic Harbour, and a main heritage trail linking buildings within easy reach of the town centre. London has 167 different trails. Sometimes local connections lend themselves to trail creation; so Whitby has its 'vampire walk', cashing in on links with Bram Stoker, the creator of Dracula, while Dublin has a rock and roll trail linking sites associated with U2, Sinead O'Connor and other Irish musicians.

Another 137 towns offer guided walks. Some are arranged by local amenity groups and may even be free. Others are organised by Blue Badge Guides who charge for their services. While some guided walks are simply tours of buildings of architectural or historic interest, others are more imaginative and bring together buildings with specific themes. London, Bath, York and Edinburgh all offer 'ghost walks', with the guides bringing to life the gorier episodes of their town's past. London also has Sherlock Holmes Walks, Dickens Walks, even Jack the Ripper Walks round the East End.

In some districts the town trail idea has been taken further and visitors can pick up leaflets guiding them round wider areas. In Scotland a Malt Whisky Trail takes tourists round a series of world-famous distilleries, a Fishing Heritage Trail links the fishing ports between Aberdeen and Hopeman, and a Castle Trail unites more than 70 castles including Balmoral in north-east Scotland. In 1995 the BTA produced a Movie Map of Britain showing sites associated with films and television programmes.

THE HOMES OF THE FAMOUS

Local authorities often attach plaques to the walls of properties once owned or lived in by famous people. London, in particular, has had a system of blue plaques to identify the homes of the famous since 1864. Originally the research was carried out by the Royal Society of Arts and then by the Greater London Council; since 1986 it has been done by English Heritage who have to decide which building of many that may have links with any one individual should bear the plaque. A working party sits twice a year to pick the people to be commemorated. To qualify they must:

- have been dead for more than 20 years
- have been born more than a hundred years ago, or
- be considered eminent by their own profession or have contributed greatly to human welfare or happiness.

In 1996 London had 600 blue plaques commemorating everyone from Keats to Hendrix.

Plaques identifying famous domiciles add to the interest of a stroll round town, but many of the homes of the famous which are actually open to the public are among the most popular tourist attractions of all. One has only to think of Dove Cottage, home to Wordsworth, and Hill Top, home to Beatrix Potter, both of them in the Lake District; the Shakespearian Properties in Stratford; and the Haworth Parsonage, home of the Bronte sisters. Abroad, Graceland, once home to Elvis Presley, is one of North America's most popular attractions.

In London alone tourists can visit houses once lived in by the dictionary-writer Dr Johnson, the historian Thomas Carlyle, the author Charles Dickens, the poet John Keats and the psychiatrist Sigmund Freud. However, in general the most popular houses open to the public are those of great writers. In 1996 work began on repairing Down House in south London, once home to Charles Darwin, the scientist who developed the ideas of evolution and natural selection. Despite the existence of a small Darwin Museum, the house is thoroughly dilapidated and undervisited, something which has been attributed to the British lack of interest in science in general and suspicion of Darwin in particular. Between them the Wellcome Foundation, the Natural History Museum and English Heritage are putting up £2.5 million of the funds required, but much of the remaining £500,000 will probably have to be raised abroad.

HISTORIC PUBLIC BUILDINGS

During the 1990s, cutbacks and changed government policies towards defence and health left many historic buildings redundant in what has been called 'the greatest disposal of public buildings since the dissolution of the monasteries'.

The Ministry of Defence, in particular, planned to sell off many properties. In 1994 it appointed a Historic Buildings Advisory Group, with representatives of English Heritage, to decide the fate of 700-plus listed buildings, some in a poor state because the MOD had Crown exemption from being forced to carry out repairs. A particular cause for concern was the fate of the 17th-century Royal Naval College at Greenwich with work by Vanbrugh, an obvious candidate for opening to the public if money could be found. However, current plans envisage it becoming a campus for cash-strapped Greenwich University. In 1994 Plymouth Urban Development Corporation took over John Rennie's 19th-century Royal William Victualling Yard, a Grade I listed building; English Heritage is advising on its redevelopment. The

Portsmouth Naval Base Property Trust may eventually be able to open the 19th-century Portsmouth Blockmills to the public.

Several historic airfields are also at risk. For example, in 1996 the MOD wanted to sell Britain's oldest airfield at Farnborough which is the site of a biennial air show. The CAA warned that the historic buildings of the Royal Aircraft Establishment would probably have to be demolished before it could be used as a civil airfield. However, the Farnborough Air Services Trust wanted to create an air and space sciences museum to showcase not just the historic structures but also the latest technological developments. The air show organisers also wanted to continue using the site, so sale plans were put on hold.

In 1994 English Heritage also set up a working party with National Health Service Estates to consider the future of around 120 large historic hospitals which face redundancy over the next decade. Some, including Brompton Hospital in Chelsea, have architecturally important chapels which may be lost to redevelopment. The care in the community policy for the mentally ill also means that 98 of 121 English mental hospitals will close by the year 2000.

In 1996 the Phoenix Trust was set up to try and direct money from the Heritage Lottery Fund towards these, and other, threatened buildings. It will also encourage a self-financing method of development whereby parts of a building are converted into housing or offices and sold, the proceeds of the sale then being used to fund the conversion of another section, and so on.

BRITISH BATTLEFIELD SITES

Scattered across Britain are many sites where battles have been fought. The English Heritage Register of Battlefields lists 41 such sites in England alone (see Appendix I). Often there is nothing for the tourist to see at the battlefield itself. However, Visitor Centres have been created at many sites to provide information and make it possible to levy a charge. At Bosworth Field where Henry VII defeated Richard III in 1485 to become the first Tudor king of England the site is marked by a film theatre, exhibitions, models and a battle trail footpath. At Bannockburn in Scotland where Robert the Bruce defeated Edward II in 1314 the National Trust for Scotland operates a heritage centre with an audio-visual exhibition on 'The Kingdom of the Scots'; in 1995 it was visited by 60,700 people. The Visitor Centre at Culloden where Bonny Prince Charlie was defeated in 1746 was visited by 125,128 tourists in 1995. At Battle where the Battle of Hastings was fought in 1066 an Abbey now stands on the site; in 1995 157,665 people visited it.

OTHER MONUMENTS

Some of the world's most famous tourist attractions are actually monuments, although not of the ruinous kind. These include Nelson's Column in Trafalgar Square, the Statue of Eros in Piccadilly and Cleopatra's Needle on the Victoria Embankment. By their nature these are rarely the sort of attractions where visitor numbers can be assessed. However, some monuments do admit visitors and charge

THE ALBERT MEMORIAL

One of London's rising stars in 1995, with over 50,000 visitors, was the new visitor centre adjoining the Albert Memorial in South Kensington. In 1994 English Heritage started work on restoring this Victorian monument which is expected to cost £14 million, £8 million from the Department of Culture, Media and Sport, £2 million from English Heritage and £4 million raised through the Albert Memorial Trust. The visitor centre enables people to see the work in progress while finding out about Prince Albert, husband of Queen Victoria, and the memorial's artistic significance.

them; these include the Statue of Liberty in New York, the Eiffel Tower in Paris and The Monument in London commemorating the spot where the Great Fire started in 1666. The Scott Monument in Edinburgh, which can be climbed, was visited by 77,138 people in 1994.

CHAPTER 6 : THE ARTS

Sir William Rees-Mogg, ex-Chair of the Arts Council, once commented that 'the arts are to British tourism what the sun is to Spain'. Many visitors to the UK are attracted by its great cultural traditions, by the many art galleries, theatres, concert halls and opera houses. Despite government reluctance to subsidise the arts there is growing recognition that they make a valuable contribution to the gross national product, albeit one that is sometimes difficult to quantify. By the early 1990s the arts were estimated to have had an annual turnover of roughly £10 billion, or 2.5% of all spending on goods and services in the UK. The arts were increasingly seen both as a catalyst for urban renewal (as in the case of Bradford's Alhambra Theatre) and as a stimulus to tourism (as with the creation of the Tate of the North in Liverpool's Albert Dock and the Tate St Ives). One hundred thousand visitors to a temporary exhibition at the Royal Academy are estimated to benefit the economy to the tune of £6.3 million. Although the arts are often condemned as elitist the Policy Studies Institute has showed that as many people visited London's theatres in 1993/4 as attended Premier League football matches and twice as many people visited the museums and art galleries as frequented the bingo halls.

WHAT ARE 'THE ARTS'?

In its broadest sense the expression 'the arts' encompasses not only the creative arts, crafts, art galleries and the art trade, but also theatres and concerts, the music industry, publishing, broadcasting and the museums. Museums have already been considered in Chapter 2. The other arts of particular relevance to tourism are the visual arts which include fine arts (painting, sculpture, etc.) and decorative arts (textiles, furnishings, porcelain, etc.), and the performing arts (drama, concerts, etc.).

The Arts and Tourism

Surveys show cultural attractions high up on the list of reasons overseas visitors give for coming to the UK. This is particularly the case with those who come to London, and many arts venues in the capital receive a high percentage of overseas tourists; in 1993 an estimated one in three people in the audiences at West End theatres came from overseas, while perhaps 50% of visitors to the National Portrait Gallery are foreigners. The bias towards London is probably most pronounced because the best known national art collections, theatres, opera houses and concert halls are all in the capital. However, overseas visitors are less likely to attend concerts, ballets and plays while in the UK, perhaps because music sounds the same at home, while plays present an obvious language barrier. Outside London tourists probably make up only 5% to 10% of visitors to arts venues. Places like the Royal Shakespeare Theatre in Stratford and the Aldeburgh Festival with an international reputation are the exception.

Domestic tourists form a high percentage of visitors to art galleries and other arts attractions; an estimated 26% of audiences at West End theatres are from elsewhere in the UK, while 60% of a typical audience at the Royal Shakespeare Theatre has usually travelled more than 50 miles to get there.

Some money is made out of tourists directly as a result of admission charges to art galleries, theatres, concerts, etc. However, even more is made on sales of food and drinks, guidebooks, postcards and other items during the course of their visit. Visitors to concerts and plays tend to spend more at the actual venue, while visitors to museums and galleries spend more in the vicinity of the attraction. In general tourist visitors spend more at cultural attractions than local visitors, contributing as much as two-thirds of what is called the 'customer effect'. Many cultural tourists are from North America or Europe and tend to be older. In general they appear to stay longer and spend more than other tourists to the UK.

FIG.6/1: DOMESTIC ATTENDANCES AT ARTS ACTIVITIES BY SOCIAL CLASS

Visit to:	(% visiting at least once in the year)				
	AB	C1	C2	DE	All
Cinemas	46	39	29	24	33
Historic Buildings	41	29	19	12	23
Theatres	33	24	16	10	19
Museums/galleries	34	23	14	10	19
Exhibitions	24	17	10	8	14
Rock/pop concerts	8	9	8	6	8
Classical concerts/opera	15	9	3	3	7

(Source: Social Trends, 1995)

ART GALLERIES

In Great Britain the fine arts are usually displayed in art galleries, although the decorative arts may be shown in museums. This division is not universal; for example, in the United States paintings are often shown in museums, like the Museum of Modern Art (MOMA) in New York. Even in Britain the divide is not absolute; paintings from non-European traditions also tend to be kept in museums. So the National and Tate Galleries display the best European, British and North American paintings, while the Victoria and Albert Museum shows Moghul Indian paintings alongside other objets d'art, like bronzes, pottery and statues.

Sometimes fine art museums use the expression 'beaux arts' which was first coined in the 18th century to distinguish those arts which brought aesthetic pleasure to their viewer from the more utilitarian 'arts' of agriculture, etc.

Evolution of Art Galleries

Paintings found on the walls of caves at Lascaux and Altamira show that human beings have always been interested in art. In the 5th century BC there was also a 'pinakothekai' on the Acropolis which was like an embryo art gallery. Throughout the Middle Ages churches and monasteries were the main repositories of works of art, which were viewed by the public as part of religious observances rather than as beautiful objects in their own right.

In the late 15th century the Renaissance brought a new interest in art for its own sake; wealthy patrons like the Medici in Florence sponsored the production of works of art and built up their own private collections. Paintings came to be valued purely as works of art, set apart from any other context. Artists also began to be valued for their talents. In temperate climates most paintings had to be kept indoors where they could only be seen by a favoured few. However, as late as the 18th century there were regular outdoor exhibitions in Rome which brought art to a wider audience.

The Grand Tour encouraged both a wider interest in art and a greater number of private collectors. By the 18th century some of them were prepared to show their collections to the public. The first public exhibition of contemporary art in the UK was held in the Strand building of the Society of Arts in 1760. Admission was free in the mornings but there was a 6d charge for catalogues. This early experiment was not quickly repeated; when a second exhibition was held later in the year an admission fee of 1/- was introduced to deter lower class visitors.

Just as many museums started life as private collections, private art collections often formed the basis for later public art galleries. However, their survival was sometimes precarious, particularly on the death of the original collector. In the 18th century Robert Walpole's Houghton Collection was sold to Catherine the Great. Collections at Stowe and Marlborough were also sold abroad. In 1824 the government agreed to buy John Julius Angerstein's collection for £57,000, housing it temporarily in Pall Mall. In 1838 it was moved to Trafalgar Square to form the nucleus of the National Gallery. When Henry Tate gave 60 modern British paintings to the National Gallery in 1890, he prompted the creation of a brand-new gallery for modern art; the Tate Gallery opened in 1897. Private collectors continue to influence the art world today, partly because individuals sometimes build up collections of works that only become fashionable later on. In 1973 Sir Robert and Lady Sainsbury bequeathed their entire collection of modern and non-European art to the University of East Anglia. Their son David also provided a £3 million endowment to build the Sainsbury Centre for the Visual Arts and to provide for future purchases. The Saatchi brothers, who made their name in advertising, are also well-known collectors of modern art who have opened their collection, in a converted London paint factory, to the public.

Like museums, art collections were seen as serving an educational purpose. So when the Victoria and Albert Museum opened in 1852 it aimed to promote good design and improve standards of public taste. An experiment in bringing art to a wider audience took place in 1853 when the Bristol and West of England Society of Arts took an arts and manufacturing display to the Barnstaple Show to be seen by agricultural workers. However, as the concept of 'art criticism' evolved in the 19th century it built a barrier between ordinary people and works of art, elevating art into something remote from everyday experience.

The Arts Review Yearbook lists almost 600 art galleries in England, 100 in Scotland and 40 in Wales (in Northern Ireland most paintings are displayed either in the Ulster Museum or the Belfast Gallery). Some of these galleries, particularly in London, are commercial ventures offering short-term exhibitions alongside their main business which is selling works of art. The BTA lists 232 non-commercial art galleries. About 150 of Britain's stately homes also contain major art collections.

In addition to the full time galleries London in particular has several venues offering regular temporary art exhibitions, particularly the Hayward and Barbican Galleries and the Royal Academy.

FIG.6/2: THE UK'S MOST VISITED ART GALLERIES IN 1995

National Gallery, London	4,469,019
Tate Gallery, London	1,769,662
Victoria and Albert Museum, London	1,224,030
Glasgow Museum and Art Gallery	992,320
Royal Academy, London	881,000
National Portrait Gallery, London	849,223
Birmingham City Museum and Art Gallery	519,807
National Gallery of Scotland, Edinburgh	462,606
Tate Gallery, Albert Dock, Liverpool	454,678
Arnolfini, Bristol	450,000

Although half England's population lives in the North and the Midlands, three quarters of the art galleries are concentrated in East Anglia and Southern England, with 46% of them in London.

Types of Art Gallery

Just as most of the national museums started life as comprehensive collections, so the national art galleries tend to show a wide range of paintings of all dates and by a variety of artists. However, some are more specialised. For example, several galleries, including the Tate and the Modern Art Gallery in Oxford, specialise in modern art, while the Musée d'Orsay concentrates on 19th-century art including Impressionism. Portrait galleries, a relatively late development, concentrate on pictures of famous people. Other galleries focus on individual artists; for example, the Marianne North Gallery at Kew, the Stanley Spencer Gallery in Cookham, the Van Gogh Museum in Amsterdam and the Rodin Gallery in Paris. Photographic galleries can also be seen as a form of specialist art gallery.

Who Owns the Art Galleries?

Several art galleries have 'national' status and are funded directly by the government, through the Department of National Heritage. These are:

- National Gallery
- Tate Gallery
- National Portrait Gallery (branches at Montacute House, Beningborough Hall and Bodelwyddon Castle)
- Wallace Collection
- National Gallery of Scotland

Others are owned by local authorities and may be housed in the same building as the local museum (the Castle Museum and Art Gallery, Nottingham; the City Museum and Art Gallery, Stoke); in 1995 the most popular local authority gallery was Glasgow Museum and Art Gallery which received 992,320 visitors. Some galleries are independently owned, perhaps by a board of trustees like the Stanley Spencer Gallery in Cookham. Others are owned and run by private individuals or companies as purely commercial ventures.

THE VICTORIA AND ALBERT MUSEUM

The Victoria and Albert Museum in South Kensington was set up in 1852. It owns the biggest collection of applied art and design in the world, including Chinese porcelains, Moghul miniatures, fashions, furnishings, pottery, photographs and the national collections of sculpture, silver and glass. The building was purpose-designed by Sir Aston Webb and has 145 galleries. There are several branch museums: Apsley House (the Wellington Museum), the Theatre Museum in Covent Garden and the Bethnal Green Museum of Childhood. The Victoria and Albert is now officially the National Museum of Art and Design, a dual designation which has caused occasional problems; the needs of a museum dealing with primarily modern and ephemeral design artefacts are not necessarily the same as those of a museum required to handle historic and irreplaceable decorative arts collections.

Like all the national collections in the mid-1990s the Victoria and Albert found its grant for running costs outstripped by inflation and its purchase grant frozen. Introducing 'voluntary' admission fees brought a drop in attendances that was not quickly reversed. In 1996 voluntary charges were replaced with a fixed entry fee after the government reduced the grant by 3%. There is also a backlog of expensive repair work to do. Just refurbishing the Raphael Gallery to provide better lighting, install automatic fire curtains and uncover the original Victorian floor had cost £2 million when it reopened in 1996.

In 1996 the Victoria and Albert announced that Daniel Libeskind had won a competition to design a new Boilerhouse Gallery to house an active learning centre and temporary exhibition space. His extraordinary design looks like a series of contorted tile squares, transparent at the top, and is likely to prove as controversial as the Pyramid built to house the Louvre ticket office. The work is expected to take five years and cost £42 million, although an initial application for a grant from the National Lottery has been turned down.

The Visitors

In general art galleries tend to appeal to the higher socio-economic groups. There is some evidence that they are more popular with men than women and that they are attracting an increasing number of under-35s. A survey carried out at the Pompidou Centre in Paris found that 40% of visitors were students and 30% regarded themselves as executives or professionals; only 3% were manual workers. Seventy-five per cent of visitors were under 35 and 40% were from Paris itself, with another 18% coming from the Paris area. However, the Pompidou Centre has such a stridently modern image that it would be unlikely to attract as many older, conservative visitors as the more staid Louvre. Many of those surveyed had come to see one specific exhibit.

Art Galleries and Display

Like museums, many art galleries are housed in old buildings which are not necessarily well adapted to modern presentation techniques and may even make conservation of the collections difficult. When the Victoria and Albert Museum took over the running of its building from the Property Services Agency in 1988 it inherited fire hazard wiring, leaky central heating, inadequate drainage, leaking roofs and a ceramics department which had to be evacuated while fire exits were cut through the wall. The trustees estimated that it would cost £50 million just to put right the problems they inherited and that £125 million would be needed to maintain the building over the next ten years. In 1989 the Museums Association believed the national museums and art galleries needed an additional grant of £200 million just to make good past problems. This was not forthcoming although the arrival of the National Lottery holds out hope that things may gradually improve.

There are a few modern purpose-built galleries including the Pompidou Centre in Paris and the Sainsbury Centre for the Visual Arts in Norwich. The modern Clone Gallery was also built onto the Tate Gallery specifically to house the collection of Turner paintings. The Musée d'Orsay in Paris is a fine example of the adaptation of an old building (the disused Orsay railway station) for a new use. In a similar vein, the Bankside power station, designed by Sir Giles Gilbert Scott and decommissioned in 1986, is scheduled to become a second gallery for the Tate in London with the aid of a £50 million Millennium Commission grant.

Art galleries are completely unnatural. Almost all works of art were designed as individual entities and were meant to be appreciated as such rather than gathered together with other competing works. Many items that now hang in art galleries were not even created as works of art, but as religious objects, perhaps for medieval church altars. Removing such items to an art gallery alters their relationship with the viewer, turning what was once an emotional experience into an intellectual one.

Like museums, art galleries have had to adapt their display techniques to take account of changing tastes. The walls of 19th-century art galleries were literally papered with paintings, a layout which can still be seen in the Marianne North Gallery in Kew Gardens. During the Second World War the National Gallery stayed open showing just one picture at a time thus helping to bring about an enduring change in attitude towards display. Now the preference is for fewer pictures, individually displayed and lit. Since then British curators have been much influenced by the pioneering work done at the New York Museum of Modern Art and the Guggenheim Museum.

Ideally some paintings should be shown alongside decorative art items like furnishings as they would have been in their original homes. So stately homes often make more natural settings for pictures, although they attract less attention because of competition from the building's architecture, fittings and history.

Inevitably the more pictures are spaced out on the walls, the more display room is required. Most of the big national collections own more items than they can

THE SAINSBURY CENTRE FOR THE VISUAL ARTS

In 1973 Sir Norman Foster was commissioned to design a building to house the Sainsbury Collection of Fine Arts alongside the University of East Anglia's School of Fine Arts, its Senior Common Room, the University restaurant and a 40-acre lake. The resulting building, although not very popular with the public (in 1995 only about 29,000 people visited it), is an example of what is possible when a gallery can be built from scratch.

All the different parts of the project are enclosed within one umbrella building, with a linear layout which follows the contours of the valley. The roof and walls are made from well-insulated interchangeable panels and the exterior has been designed to reflect heat and keep the interior cool. Relatively little energy is needed for heating and much use is made of natural top lighting. The building has also been designed to offer views of the lake and woods outside, while the gallery itself acts as a path through to the restaurant and common room.

The interior is divided up by internal screens, mezzanine floors and conservatory courts which provide security and privacy. The gallery is treated as a 'living' environment, with seats, tables and books to encourage people to linger. Plenty of storage space has been built in and the building has been designed for easy servicing; for example, air filters can be changed without exhibits being disrupted.

put on show, but the National Gallery has virtually all its paintings on display. A 1988 government report criticised the Tate Gallery and the Victoria and Albert Museum for not displaying all their possessions (the Tate only shows 24% of its collections at any one time). However, curators argue that many are of mainly academic interest and can be seen by scholars on request. Some of the Tate's reserve collections are now on show at the Tate of the North Gallery in Liverpool. The opening of the Theatre Museum in Covent Garden let the V&A put a specialised collection on show, albeit in a different building.

Traditionally paintings have been displayed according to different 'schools' in accordance with Vasari's *Lives of the Artists*. So Dutch and Italian paintings of the 16th century would appear in different areas of the gallery. However, Neil MacGregor, the Director of the National Gallery, broke with this tradition and rehung its paintings in a continuous time line running from 1260 to 1910. Eventually the Tate and National Galleries intend to swap some of their paintings so that the National will show foreign pictures from before 1900 while the Tate will show those dating from 1900 onwards. In another break with tradition, the Tate's Director Nicholas Serota now rehangs all the gallery's pictures once a year. Although this means people may travel a long way and be disappointed that a picture they expected to see is no longer on display, it does offer an opportunity to show more of the collection than was possible before.

Labels in art galleries only used to give the name of the picture, and the name of the artist and the his/her dates. This is trickier in an age when few people study the Classics from which much of the subject matter of Renaissance paintings came. In a secular society it is unsafe even to assume that all visitors know the Bible stories and recognise the references in medieval pictures of saints; nor will these necessarily mean anything to overseas visitors from different religious traditions. The National and Tate Galleries now provide labels which offer basic information about their subjects as well.

Art Galleries and Security

Like museums, art galleries must be designed and laid out with security in mind. As the price of paintings has risen there have been more thefts, sometimes of well-known paintings and apparently by thieves with a specific hit list. For example, in 1994 Edouard Munch's famous 'Scream' was stolen from an Oslo Museum (it has since been recovered). The risk can be minimised by fitting adequate alarms, stationing custodians in each room and by hanging small pictures away from doors and windows.

Pictures also need to be protected against physical attack. Paintings in the National Gallery and National Portrait Gallery have been slashed, as has the Rubens' altar-piece in King's College Chapel in Cambridge. Guarding against such attacks is particularly difficult and may require the installation of special security devices. In the Rijskmuseum Rembrandt's *Nightwatchman* must be viewed from behind bullet-proof glass following an attack. Picasso's *Guernica* (which was returned to Spain from New York after Franco's death, in accordance with his wishes) used to be displayed in a separate annex to the Prado which could only be entered after submitting to airport-like security checks; its political subject matter made it a likely target for attack.

Paintings also need to be protected against damage from changes in humidity and from the elements. Modern galleries usually have dehumidifiers in all the rooms to ensure there is not too much moisture in the air. Air conditioning may also be installed. Pictures also need to be kept out of direct sunlight as much as possible to prevent the colours from fading. Some paintings are protected by glass, but this can create reflections, making it difficult for visitors to appreciate them.

THE ARTS AND FUNDING

The national art collections, including the V&A, the Tate Gallery, the National Gallery, the National Gallery of Scotland and the National Portrait Gallery, receive grants direct from the Department of Culture, Media and Sport. Traditionally they didn't charge for admission. However, since the 1983 National Heritage Act gave them 'trustee status', the amount of public money given to them each year has been frozen. In 1988 they were also required to take over the running of the buildings from the Property Services Agency. By March 1989 the Victoria and Albert Museum calculated that the real value of its grant had fallen by 90% over the previous five years, at a time when staff salaries were rising at more than the rate of inflation and art prices at auction were soaring.

In 1988 a system of three year rolling funding was introduced. The idea was that the museums and galleries should be given a grant for one year and told what they could expect over the next two, with allowance being made for rising costs. At the end of each year a new third year would be added to make forward financial planning easier. However, the level of inflation was underestimated, leaving little for running costs once this had been taken into account; in 1989 grants rose by 2.9%, even though salaries (linked to Civil Service pay scales and agreed with the Treasury) rose by 10%. With its government grant cut for the second year running, in 1996 the V&A finally introduced compulsory entry fees (see above).

Since the 1948 Local Government Act, local authorities have been entitled to use money from the rates (now the council tax) to support art galleries By 1987/8 they were spending £93 million to support roughly 750 museums and art galleries. In 1881 the government set up a Purchase Grant to help local museums and galleries purchase suitable items. This scheme is now administered by the Victoria and Albert Museum under the financial control of the Museums and Galleries Commission. Wherever possible local galleries are helped with grants of up to 50% of the purchase price. However, there isn't enough money to meet all the requests for assistance and sometimes the value of individual items is so high as to make it impossible to provide 50% of the cost.

The Corporation of the City of London is a generous sponsor of the arts. For example, in 1993/4 it gave £21 million towards the running costs of the Barbican arts complex with another £9.7 million towards its refurbishment.

Other government grants to the arts come from assorted sources like the City Challenge scheme to help the inner cities. For example, in 1993/4 Merseyside received £2.3 million in City Challenge funds, some of which was ploughed into arts projects. Altogether it's estimated that non-cultural government departments spent £168 million on the arts (including museums and the built heritage) in 1993/4.

Not all galleries receive grants and life can be tough for those that don't. The Royal Academy in London is funded through admission charges, sponsorship and membership fees. In 1996 it earned £4.5 million from exhibitions, £2.4 million from suscriptions, £2.27 million from retailing and roughly £1 million from other trading activities, but by 1997 it was believed to be £3 million in debt.

The Arts Councils and Regional Arts Boards

In 1946 the Arts Council of Great Britain was set up as successor to the war-time Council for the Encouragement of Music and Arts (CEMA). In 1967 it was given a royal charter which stated that its aims were:

- to develop and improve knowledge, understanding and practice of the arts,
- to increase public access to the arts, and
- to advise and co-operate with government departments, local authorities and other bodies over arts' issues.

In 1994 the Arts Council of Great Britain was split into the Arts Council of England (ACE), the Scottish Arts Council and the Arts Council of Wales. The Arts Council of England is funded by the Department of Culture, Media and Sport but provides 'arm's length' funding, rather than direct government funding which is what happens with the national galleries. The Arts Councils tend to support the performing arts and avant garde art in particular, and in the 1990s were particularly concerned to ensure that arts venues were providing access for the disabled and to encourage the cultural diversity appropriate to a multicultural society.

In 1995/96 the government grant to the ACE was £191 million, 2.7% more than the previous year but £17 million less in real terms than in 1993/4. Although Lottery funding was available for capital costs, it couldn't make up this shortfall in core funding, leading the ACE's Secretary-General to foresee a dismal future of 'companies...presenting shrunken programmes in lavish Lottery-funded facilities.' However, in 1997 Lottery money enabled the Arts Council to set up a pilot stabilisation project which gave one-off grants to 15 arts organisations to settle their debts. Beneficiaries included the English National Opera, Yorkshire Playhouse, the London Symphony Orchestra and Birmingham Repertory Company.

Many local galleries receive support from the Arts Councils. In the mid-1980s *The Glory of the Garden* report set out a strategy for subsidising local arts ventures. It concluded that funding was disproportionately slanted towards London and proposed a changed emphasis to get more money to the regions. In 1993/4 the Arts Council gave £99 million to the performing arts and of this one-third went to the London-based English National Opera, Royal National Theatre, Royal Opera and Royal Ballet. The London Arts Board also accounted for 25% of all expenditure by the Regional Arts Boards (see below). Figures for 1995/6 show that London still receives a per capita grant of £4.01 compared with one of £1.31 to the South East and £1.41 to the Eastern region. However, since many of the best-known national companies are London-based this imbalance is hardly surprising.

Many local art galleries in England and Wales receive money from ten Regional Arts Boards (RABs) which are, in turn, funded by the Arts Councils, local authorities, the Crafts Council, the British Film Institute and the Welsh Office. Even large-scale ventures like the Halle Orchestra, the London Symphony Orchestra, the Aldeburgh Festival and Bristol Old Vic are funded by the RABs. In 1995/6 the Arts Council for England gave £59.6 million to the RABs.

The Arts Councils adminster National Lottery funds for the arts. By April 1996 the ACE had dispensed 533 grants amounting to £340 million. The single largest grant of £55 million went to the Royal Opera House, and overall London won 70% of available funding compared with the North which got only 1.5%. The one-third of projects chosen which will probably benefit tourists will have absorbed 80% of the grants. Typical of such a project is the reconstructed Globe Theatre in London which won a grant of £12.4 million.

NEW LIFE FOR THE GLOBE THEATRE

Many of Shakespeare's plays were first performed at the Globe Theatre in Southwark which was built in 1599. In 1613 the original Globe - described by Shakespeare as a 'wooden O' - burnt to the ground. Disappointed not to find a Globe Theatre on Bankside when he visited London in 1949, film director Sam Wanamaker set up the Globe Playhouse Trust in 1970 to ensure a new Globe would one day stand there. Work began on the site in 1987 and is expected to end in 1999. The Globe Theatre now forms part of an International Shakespeare Globe Centre where an exhibition explains how archaeologists worked out what the original Globe looked like and how a team of craftsmen meticulously recreated it. The theatre itself offers the chance to see Shakespeare performed as it would have been in the 17th century with half the audience standing in the pit of the theatre, as the 'groundlings' would have done in Shakespeare's day. In 1996 the Globe won the European Tourism Initiative Golden Star Award as the best new tourist attraction in Europe. By then the exhibition centre had already been visited by more than 300,000 people. When work on creating the centre finally finishes it is expected to have cost £30 million, of which £12.4 million will have come from the National Lottery and most of the remainder from individual or corporate donors.

Sponsors and Benefactors

Arts Council figures show that art galleries, like museums, are having to raise more of their income from sources other than public subsidy. In 1988 28% of the income of visual arts associations could be attributed to box office receipts or other earned income; by 1995/6 this proportion had risen to around 30%. But charging for admission to art galleries is controversial. When the Victoria and Albert Museum introduced 'voluntary' charges for visitors, attendances plummeted by about 700,000 (see Chapter 2). Charging for temporary exhibitions is less controversial; the Royal Academy routinely does this, as does the Tate Gallery even though admission to the main collection remains free. Some local art galleries, particularly the privately owned ones, also charge for admission. (Fig.6/3 shows the comparative sums different arts organisations were getting from box office receipts, subsidy and other sources in 1995/6.)

FIG.6/3: SUMMARISED INCOME OF ARTS ORGANISATIONS FUNDED BY ARTS COUNCIL OF ENGLAND AND RABs, 1995/6

	Visual Arts & Photography £000s	Drama £000s	Dance £000s	Music £000s
Earned income	8,125	71,565	19,908	63,479
ACE/RAB subsidy	10,542	44,429	24,616	45,567
LA/other subsidy	3,326	18,693	2,343	6,384
Contributed income	1,949	5,956	4,703	13,554
TOTAL SUBSIDY/INCOME	24,143	140,643	51,570	128,984

(Source: Arts Council of England)

In 1976 the Association for Business Sponsorship of the Arts (ABSA) was established. This now administers the National Heritage Arts Sponsorship Scheme: the Pairing Scheme for the Arts (previously the Business Sponsorship Incentive Scheme), with the Department of Culture, Media and Sport matching money given by new sponsors on a pound for pound basis, and by old sponsors on a one pound to three pounds basis. A similar scheme operates in Northern Ireland. In 1993/4 business sponsors provided £70 million of funding for the arts, 70% of it in cash, the remainder in corporate membership and donations, and assistance in kind. Roughly half this sponsorship went to the performing arts and 40% of it went to London.

FIG.6/4: BUSINESS SPONSORSHIP OF THE ARTS, 1993/4

	Living Arts £000s	Visual Arts/Collections/National Libraries £000s
Cash	36.7	8.3
In kind	4.1	1.6
Corporate membership	6.3	1.1
Corporate donations	3.8	1.3
TOTAL	51.0	12.2

(Source: ABSA)

It's easier to attract sponsorship for specific, high profile exhibitions or capital projects than it is to get companies or individuals to underwrite annual running costs. So the Gallery of Japanese Art and Design at the V&A was sponsored by Toshiba International but no one has come forward to make up the shortfall in its wages bill. Nor do corporate sponsors usually act out of kindness or from a pure love of art; instead they see sponsorship as providing relatively cheap and cost-effective advertising. Consequently their decision on what to sponsor is likely to be conservative and London-centred. Typically Pearson plc sponsored the V&A's popular William Morris exhibition of 1996. It's much harder to get sponsorship for modern, innovative work or for exhibitions in the provinces. For example, no major sponsors could be found for the Royal Academy's exhibition of

FIG.6/5: FUNDING FOR THE ARTS, 1993/4 (£million)

	Umbrella funding bodies (ACE, etc)	Living arts (performing, combined, arts festivals)	Visual arts, collections (includes national libraries)	Built heritage
European funding		27.9	12.7	37.0
Central government: Department of National Heritage*	230.3	1.3	334.1	139.3
Scottish Office		1.0	46.1	5.8
Welsh Office			24.3	13.4
Northern Ireland Office	7.5	3.8	14.5	3.5
Other government depts.		34.8	45.7	12.1
Tax relief				125.0
Local authorities	3.1	219.0	150.1	33.0
Charities		12.7	18.7	5.6
Business sponsorship		51.0	12.1	1.0
Volunteers' contribution		19.0	3.6	4.4
TOTALS:	**240.9**	**370.5**	**661.9**	**380.2**

*Now the Department of Culture, Media and Sport

(Source: Policy Studies Institute)

the work of Egon Schiele, seen as controversial because of his sexually explicit pictures. Business sponsors can also have too much say over the content of an exhibition. Thus when Coca Cola sponsored the 'Designing a Megabrand' exhibition at the V&A critics argued that it became little more than a showcase for the company. During a recession sponsorship is also likely to dry up as companies struggle to make painless economies.

In the United States the National Endowment for the Arts calculates that individuals give more than companies to the arts, probably because the tax system encourages private giving. In the UK there have been some particularly generous one-off gifts; for example, Paul Getty gave £50 million to the National Gallery for new purchases, Gerald Godfrey provided backing for the V&A's new Chinese Export gallery, the Sainsburys funded the new wing of the National Gallery and Walter Annenberg, a former American ambassador, gave the National Gallery £5 million to restore its Impressionist and post-Impressionist collections. However, in general sponsorship has tended to come from companies rather than individuals.

Attracting business sponsorship is also costly. The Royal National Theatre employs five people and the Royal Shakespeare Company two, to work full time on finding and keeping sponsors. It has been estimated that as much as 45% of a sponsorship's value can be lost in servicing the account, providing corporate hospitality, etc. This is obviously a problem for smaller arts bodies, so consortia like South West Arts receive and distribute sponsorship funds on their behalf.

The most recent figures published by the Policy Studies Institute suggested that public subsidy to the arts in the UK was much lower than in other European countries. In the UK the subsidy worked out at £9.80 a head, compared with £17.50 in Sweden, £20.50 in the Netherlands, £21.40 in France and £24.00 in Germany.

European Union Funding for the Arts

In 1993/4 the European Regional Development Fund gave £53 million for infrastructural projects with a cultural component, like restoring theatres, museums and inner city heritage sites. Manchester Art Gallery was one recipient of an ERDF grant.

PURCHASING PROBLEMS

Since 1985 the national art collections have seen their purchase grants (the annual sums available to buy new items) frozen. Although some already own more items than they can display, there are always gaps in their collections which need filling. The purchase of contemporary art also needs to be an ongoing process, and major art works in private collections occasionally come on the market, clamouring to be bought for the public collections.

Originally a work of art's value was assessed according to the materials used to make it. Then the cost of the workmanship involved was added to the value. Until recently art objects were valued more highly than paintings, with tapestries fetching more than Old Masters; the largest amount ever paid for an art work until the 1880s was the £32,000 paid for a mid-16th-century parcel-gilt and enamel cup. From the 1950s onwards the value of art also began to reflect the artist's reputation. The first collectors were private individuals who bought pictures for aesthetic reasons or as status symbols. However, even in the 1920s some collectors saw art purchases as potential investments. By the 1970s the place of private and public collectors in the art market had largely been taken by speculators, some of them, like

British Rail, buying on behalf of pension funds. Large companies also started to invest in art to improve their working environments; so the Chase Manhattan Bank spent £500,000 on 100 paintings and sculptures in the 1950s. The combined effect of these trends was to force prices up.

Between 1830 and 1880 only one sale per decade at Christie's raised more than £50,000. Between 1880 and 1914, 50 sales raised more than £50,000. Since then prices, particularly for 19th- and early 20th-century paintings and Old Masters, have soared; in 1952 Cezanne's *Pommes et Biscuits* sold for $94,280, in 1958 his *Garcon au Gilet Rouge* sold for £220,000 and in 1961 Rembrandt's *Aristotle* sold for more than £1 million. Then in 1987/8 64 works of art were sold for more than £1 million, including *Yo Picasso* which was sold in New York for £28,825,301 and Van Gogh's *Irises* which was sold for $53 million (about £31 million) at Sotheby's. Such high prices provided incentives for sales which might not otherwise have taken place.

The combination of static purchase grants and soaring art prices meant that the public collections were effectively frozen out of the market. However, with the recession of the 1990s, prices began to fall again and some collectors were unable to recover the high prices they had paid just years earlier. By the mid-1990s the market appeared to be recovering and prices were picking up again.

The Taxation System

Since the mid-20th century capital transfer tax has not been payable on works of art bequeathed to the next generation, thus removing some of the incentive to sell. If the heirs decide to sell the Treasury can levy tax at the rate that was effective when the previous owner died which could mean paying up to 80% tax, the top rate in force in the late 1970s.

Less tax is payable when private owners sell to the national collections. The purchase price will be calculated as the agreed value of the work minus the assumed tax liability. Twenty-five per cent of the tax due is then added back to the purchase price as an incentive to sell this way. So a painting valued at £100,000 might incur a tax liability of up to £80,000. Sold on the open market it would only make its owner £20,000. However, through a private treaty sale 25% of the tax liability would vanish, raising the profit to £40,000. In 1993/4 the National Heritage Memorial Fund assisted purchases through the private treaty sales scheme to the value of £1.7 million. Frequently items sold in this way stay in situ provided public access is agreed.

An Acceptance-in-Lieu Scheme also allows private owners to bequeath works of art to the nation in lieu of inheritance tax or capital gains tax. The Museums and Galleries Commission advises the government on whether something should be accepted through this scheme and then decides where the item should be displayed. Sometimes it concludes that it is best preserved in its historic setting but where this happens the owner has to agree arrangements for public access. In 1993/4 works of art worth £3 million were accepted through this scheme.

Export Licences

Pictures sold on the open market often end up overseas. To prevent important works being lost abroad export licences for art and antiques were introduced in 1952. Works of art worth more than £39,600 and photographs worth more than £6,000 manufactured or produced more than 50 years before the intended date of export may need licences. Items which have been imported to the UK within the last 50 years can usually be exported again without difficulty. Since 1992 the EU has also had a licensing system to regulate the flow of works of art outside the EU. This applies to many works of art worth more than £11,900.

Experts from the national collections can object to a licence if they think it meets one of the Waverley Criteria, namely:

- that the item is so closely linked to the UK's historical or national life that its loss would be a misfortune
- that it's of outstanding aesthetic importance
- that it's of outstanding significance for the study of art or history

The Reviewing Committee on the Export of Works of Art then decides whether the item does fit into one of these categories. If they agree that it does, granting of a licence can be deferred to allow the public collections to try and raise the purchase price. The would-be exporter can still refuse to accept their offer in which case an indefinite stop procedure can prevent a licence being granted for ten years.

SAVING CANOVA'S *THREE GRACES* FOR THE NATION

When a sculpture of the *Three Graces* originally designed for Woburn Abbey by the Neoclassical sculptor Canova came on the market in 1990, the Victoria and Albert Museum had insufficient funds to buy it but organised an appeal for public donations to prevent it being exported. The appeal having failed, the sculpture was sold at auction for £7.6 million. However, the Export Reviewing Committee refused it an export licence and in 1994 it was finally purchased for the V&A and the National Gallery of Scotland by means of grants from the National Heritage Memorial Fund and the National Art Collections Fund, and donations from philanthropist John Paul Getty and private collector Baron Thyssen.

Even when an export licence has been delayed, there's no guarantee that a national collection will be able to match the auction price; the combined price of Van Gogh's *Sunflowers* and Manet's *La Rue Mosnier aux Paveurs* exceeded the entire purchase grants of all the UK national museums for the previous two years. In 1990 the purchase grant of all the national museums and art galleries put together was only £9 million. Nicholas Serota would have liked to buy *Ghost*, a work by the then unknown but now prize-winning artist Rachel Whiteread, for the Tate Gallery but had to watch it go to the private Saatchi Collection instead. In 1996 the Tate's purchase grant was only £1.9 million, worth, in real terms, only a tenth of its value in 1986.

In 1991 a group of Old Master drawings from Holkham Hall in Norfolk were sent to auction despite the protests of a group of museums who wanted to buy them and keep them together. At auction the drawings fetched more than the estimated price but the museums appealed against the sale. Although the Export Reviewing Committee then blocked export of some of the sheets the museums were faced with finding the higher auction price. By 1992 15 of the drawings had been bought for British museums or galleries but seven had been exported.

FIG.6/6: HELP TOWARDS PURCHASING FOR MUSEUMS AND GALLERIES, 1993/4

National/non-national museums' allocations for purchase from grant-in-aid:		£million
Department of National Heritage*		8.9
Scottish Office		3.2
Welsh Office		1.5
Northern Ireland Office		0.5
	Total:	14.1
National libraries spend, including grant-in-aid:		**15.1**
Other grants:		
MGC/V&A Purchase Grants + grants for Preservation of Industrial and Scientific Material		1.7
National Heritage Memorial Fund (NHMF)		4.4
	Total:	6.1
Tax concessions:		
Acceptance-in-lieu (AIL)		3.0
Private treaty sales		1.7
	Total:	4.7
Private sector support:		
National Art Collections Fund (NACF)		2.5
	TOTAL:	**42.5**

*Now Department of Culture, Media and Sport

(Source: Museums and Galleries Commission, 1994)

In 1993/4 the Department of National Heritage, the Scottish Office, the Welsh Office and the Department of Education in Northern Ireland between them provided £40 million for purchases including museum purchases. Increasingly the National Heritage Memorial Fund (NHMF) and the National Art Collections Fund (NACF) have been bridging the gap. The National Heritage Memorial Fund exists to help secure anything regarded as important to the national heritage, including works of art. The size of its grants varies enormously: it contributed £4,000 to the £16,000 needed to buy Stanley Spencer's *Chestnuts* for the Wolverhampton Art Gallery and Museum; £103,350 towards the costs of Millais's *Spring: Apple Blossoms for the Lady* Lever Art Gallery; and £900,000 towards the cost of Picasso's *Weeping Woman* for the Tate Gallery. The National Art Collections Fund, set up in 1903 to give purchase grants to museums and art galleries, has helped with the purchase of several of the National Gallery's most famous paintings including the *Wilton Diptych*, the *Rokeby Venus* and Leonardo da Vinci's *Virgin and Child* cartoon. In 1995 it awarded grants to the value of £2.5 million. The National Heritage Memorial Fund and the National Arts Collection Fund also make occasional joint purchases; for example, El Greco's *Allegory* was bought for the National Gallery of Scotland with the help of the NHMF and the NACF

In 1995 the Lottery Heritage Fund gave £26 million to buy works of art. However, when Abbot Hall Art Gallery and Museum in Kendal applied for funds to buy a painting by Lucien Freud it was turned down on the grounds that it was too new; to be eligible for a purchase grant a work of art has to be at least 20 years old.

The only other alternative is for curators to persuade private collectors to loan items to the national collections in their lifetime and bequeath them on their death as Sir Denis Mahon has done with his Italian Baroque paintings (see Chapter 1).

TEMPORARY EXHIBITIONS

Temporary exhibitions are particularly important in the visual arts field and attract the sort of publicity which makes them appeal to business sponsors. Several of London's national art collections hold regular exhibitions which are a useful source of funding, particularly because they generate spin-off sales of catalogues, postcards and other merchandise. The Tate Gallery usually has three big temporary exhibitions every year and these can be very well-attended; for example, in 1996 an estimated 400,000 people paid to see the Cézanne exhibition.

Other galleries like the Hayward and the Royal Academy are primarily temporary exhibition halls. The Royal Academy of Arts was established in 1768 as the UK's first fine arts society and has been based at Burlington House in the Strand since 1868. Every year it plays host to major exhibitions which attract queues and many overseas visitors. Amongst the most popular were the Genius of Venice exhibition which attracted 4,000 people a day in 1983, the Marc Chagall exhibition which attracted 3,536 people a day in 1985 and the Age of Chivalry exhibition which attracted 2,915 people a day in 1987. In addition the Royal Academy hosts the annual Summer Exhibition of work by contemporary artists which has drawn more than 100,000 visitors a year since 1983 and produces sales valued at over £1 million a year. In 1995 the RA raised £4.5 million from its exhibitions. The Hayward Gallery opened in 1968 and was, until 1987, administered directly by the Arts Council. It is now run by the South Bank Board and regularly hosts popular temporary exhibitions.

A particular problem for organisers of temporary exhibitions is the cost of insuring borrowed items. However, the Museums and Galleries Commission runs a government idemnity scheme for non-national galleries to save them the prohibitive cost of commercial insurance.

WORKS OF ART IN SITU

Not all paintings are on show in art galleries. For example, one of Michelangelo's masterpieces is the ceiling of the Sistine Chapel in Rome which has been extensively (and controversially) restored. *The Last Supper*, one of Leonardo da Vinci's few surviving works and a World Heritage Site, is on the wall of a church, Sta. Maria delle Grazie in Milan, where it's proving difficult to stop it flaking because of the experimental fresco technique the artist used. In England Stanley Spencer's masterly anti-war paintings decorate the walls of the Sandham Memorial Chapel at Burghclere in Berkshire, now in the care of the National Trust.

In Europe most paintings which are not in galleries are in churches or stately homes. However, in Mexico the revolutionary frescoes of Rivera, Orozco and Siquieros decorate the walls of schools, law courts and administrative buildings, mostly open to the public free of charge.

Works of sculpture often stand outdoors where they can be seen by anyone free of charge. Many are in public parks and gardens. Occasionally sculptors even carry out their work in public so people can see the processes involved.

THE CRAFTS

Crafts can be defined as occupations or trades like embroidery, pottery and basket-making that require special skills, particularly manual dexterity. Nowadays an increasing number of tourist attractions have craft centres in their grounds or sell craft goods in their shops, and to that extent tourism can be seen as having played a part in the crafts revival of the 1990s. In 1995 the BTA listed 70 craft centres among the UK's tourist attractions.

In addition the Crafts Council estimates that there were some 3,000 commercial crafts fairs in 1993/4. However, many of these would have been purely local affairs.

In 1993/4 the Crafts Council have grants of £4.6 million to develop crafts activities. Some of this was distributed via the Scottish and Welsh Arts Councils or via the Regional Arts Boards. In Northern Ireland the Local Enterprise Development Unit provides grants for crafts activities.

THEATRES

The word 'theatre' can be used to describe either a type of performance (drama, opera, 'theatre of the absurd') or the place where it takes place (theatre, opera house, street theatre, theatre in the round). It's also used in such descriptive phrases as 'mainstream theatre', 'alternative/fringe theatre', 'commercial theatre' and 'subsidised theatre'.

Some theatre buildings, like the Royal Shakespeare Company at the Barbican Theatre, have regular companies attached to them. In Eastern Europe and Scandinavia such buildings-based companies are common, while in Germany every town with a population of about 100,00 has a civic theatre with a company attached.

Some theatre companies don't have permanent bases and tour a lot using theatres all round the country. Finally there are theatres which don't have companies based in them but which are available for use either by touring companies or by casts brought together for specific open-ended runs of commercial plays.

Evolution of the Theatre

Theatres have existed since Classical times when the Greeks staged plays in semi-circular outdoor arenas. However, it wasn't until 1576 that London got its first real playhouse, an unroofed, circular building called simply 'The Theatre'. In 1597 this was pulled down and some of its timbers reused to build the Globe Theatre in Southwark where Shakespeare later performed. During the Commonwealth period theatres were closed down as frivolous, only to open again in 1660 with the monarchy's restoration. It wasn't until the 18th century that most theatres took on the horseshoe shape with tiered balconies which is now standard. One such 18th-century theatre survives in Richmond, Yorkshire, and is a tourist attraction in its own right, as well as staging plays for audiences of up to 280 people.

In the 18th century theatres became very grand inside, a trend which continued in the 19th century when civic pride dictated that they should be built with impressive exteriors, complete with porticoes and colonnades. Inside plush velvet and gilt fittings became de rigueur. Sometimes the decoration even got in the way of the purpose, with pillars obscuring the stage view from some seats (as at the Aldwych). Despite the grand decor theatres could still be uncomfortable; for the first ten years after it opened in 1874 air had to be pumped down to audiences at the underground Criterion until proper ventilation was finally installed.

In Britain many local theatres started life in the late 19th/early 20th centuries as part of a policy to lure tourists to seaside resort. Some have since been taken over by local authorities as commercial backers vanished.

In the 1920s and '30s there was a move towards simpler theatre design although buildings like the Adelphi still made use of popular Art Deco motifs. This trend continued after the Second World War when theatre architecture also became more adventurous. Some theatres like the Roundhouse (now closed) staged plays in the round with minimal scenery, while others did away with the proscenium arch that traditionally framed the stage in favour of wider, more open platforms. New theatres were designed without the sort of balconies and vertigo-inducing upper circles that often offered only partial stage views; when the Barbican Theatre opened in 1982 its three circles only had two rows each and these jutted towards the stage for easy viewing, rather than sloping backwards as in traditional theatres. Both the Lyttleton Theatre (at the Royal National) and the Barbican were designed without permanent space in front of the stage for an orchestra but with adaptable stall seating which could be removed to provide a pit when necessary. The Barbican even has doors which are controlled by electromagnets and can be opened and closed simultaneously and in time with the lighting.

In the mid-20th century when film was at the height of its popularity theatres like the Carlton were turned into cinemas. However, in 1981 the New Victoria (purpose-built as a cinema in 1930) was converted into the Apollo Victoria Theatre where Sir Andrew Lloyd-Webber's *Starlight Express* went on to have a very successful run.

In 1993 the UK had about 300 theatres, seating between 200 and 2,300 people. Most were owned by local authorities and were non-profit making. Just over 30 had resident companies. There were also around 200 art centres, concert halls, open-air theatres and pubs where plays are sometimes performed. In 1993 there were 11,503,358 paid attendances at 15,922 performances in 41 London theatres. These produced a gross box office revenue of £215,619,208, a 10% increase on 1992. The average seat cost £20.08, a 5% increase on 1992 prices even though the retail price index had risen by only 1.4%.

Theatres and Tourism

London theatres in particular attract a large number of overseas visitors with an interest in drama. However, theatres also serve as tourist attractions in other ways:

- The ruins of ancient theatres like the Greek ones at Epidaurus and Segesta attract thousands of history-loving tourists every year. Some are even used to stage modern music and drama festivals, especially during the summer.
- Active modern theatres like the Royal National Theatre in London and the Theatre Royal in Bristol offer guided tours for theatre-lovers.
- Particularly famous historical theatres may even be rebuilt. The Globe Theatre has been reconstructed in Southwark and is proving very popular with tourists (see above).

London Theatres

London's theatres in particular are major tourist attractions. In the West End (an area bordered by Oxford Street to the north, Strand to the south, Kingsway to the east and Regent Street to the west with Shaftesbury Avenue cutting through the middle of it) there are more than 40 theatres (Fig.6/7). In 1993 the Society Of London Theatres (SOLT) estimated that one in three of their audiences came from overseas, while a further 26% came from outside London, making it unlikely that so many could be supported without the tourists. Many theatres had a particularly difficult year in 1991 when fears of retaliation after the Gulf War caused many Americans to stay at home. The majority of overseas visitors come from the United States (16%), followed by Canada and Sweden.

There is some evidence to suggest that theatre audiences come primarily from the ABC1 socio-economic groups. While 34% of theatre goers are aged 45 to 54, the average age of visitors fell during the 1980s and there were a growing number of first-time theatre-goers as well. Surveys suggest that theatre-goers are more likely to

Fig. 32: LONDON'S WEST END THEATRES

164

read the 'quality' newspapers and listen to Radio 4 than average. Theatre appears to be marginally more popular with women than men.

Theatres outside the West End attract fewer tourists because they're not so immediately accessible and don't profit from passing trade. Some, like the Almeida and Riverside Studios, are fringe theatres, showing 'alternative' productions. Others, like the Lyric in Hampstead, are straightforward commercial theatres showing a wide range of productions.

London theatre prices have been rising much faster than inflation; in 1983 the average ticket cost £7.50 but this had risen to £20.08 by 1993. That audience numbers haven't been falling suggests there is a core theatre audience which is relatively uninfluenced by price. There is some evidence that theatre audiences are becoming more sensitive to offputting factors like bomb incidents, strikes and international crises. However, the impact of these events seems to be relatively shortlived; after a two-week drop-off in attendances, figures are usually back to normal again.

The Provincial Theatres

Outside London theatres generally rely on a local clientele. The Royal Shakespeare Theatre in Stratford-upon-Avon is exceptional in being as dependent on tourists as the West End theatres. Nevertheless a successful provincial theatre can play an important part in helping to create a climate in which cultural tourism will flourish. Thus the rehabilitation of the Alhambra Theatre in Bradford played a big part in the city's strategy to attract tourists. The Citizen's Theatre in Glasgow is also thought to have played a part in the general revival of the city's fortunes.

Provincial theatres differ from those in London in that they show a wide variety of performance types in the one venue over the year. Children's shows and modern drama make up almost half of all performances while musicals account for only 10% of performances compared with 59% in London.

Some theatres are run as charitable trusts, with unpaid directors and representatives of those providing the funding on their boards. Trust theatres are usually established as limited companies by guarantee and the trustees have only limited liability. They are normally eligible for a range of tax benefits.

Many provincial theatres are funded and administered by local authorities. They can be more expensive to run than trust theatres because local authority pay scales tend to be higher. By 1990 many of these theatres were struggling as they were expected to generate more money from box office receipts and sponsorship as subsidies were frozen or reduced. Many local authorities were being forced to economise and arts budgets were particularly vulnerable to cuts.

The European Regional Development Fund can provide grants to help local authorities develop deprived areas, but leisure and recreation projects can only be assisted where they will help attract tourism. It was on those grounds that £195,000 was given to the Plymouth Theatre Royal in 1979, £2,125,000 to the Bradford Alhambra in 1984 and £3,422,000 to the Theatre Royal in Newcastle in 1986.

Other important provincial theatres include the Crucible in Sheffield, the Royal Exchange in Manchester (badly damaged by an IRA bomb in 1996), the Playhouse in Nottingham, the Theatre Royal in Bristol and the New Victoria Theatre in Newcastle-under-Lyme (a modern purpose-built theatre in the round).

Since 1991, 200 of the provincial theatres have been represented by the Theatrical Management Assocation (TMA). They estimate that in 1993 there were 27,029 performances in their theatres which raised £113 million, with an average ticket price of £10.05.

The Plays

On any one night in London a wide range of theatrical entertainments will be on offer. These will range from Shakespeare and serious drama at the Barbican and Royal National theatres, to long-running farces, thrillers like *The Mousetrap*, and musicals like *Les Misèrables* and *Cats*. The cost of staging serious plays, particularly with large casts, means that few commercial theatres can afford to risk them. Consequently most of the innovative and experimental plays are at the subsidised theatres; the Royal National, Barbican and Royal Court. After a successful run some plays transfer to West End theatres, as when the Royal Shakespeare Company's production of *Les Misèrables* transferred to the Palace Theatre in 1985. This has led Sir Cameron Mackintosh, the successful producer of *Cats* and *Miss Saigon* as well, to emphasise the interdependency of the subsidised and commercial theatres. At the same time, under pressure to become self-supporting, the subsidised theatres are staging more commercial plays including musicals. If plays are taken to include modern dramas, thrillers and comedies as well as classical plays, then they account for 35% of attendances at West End theatres.

Musicals are particularly important to the West End. They were given a new lease of life in 1972 when Tim Rice and the then Andrew Lloyd Webber staged *Jesus Christ Superstar* at the Palace, introducing a new, younger audience to the medium. Modern musicals now make up roughly 30% of all performances in London auditoria and attract 53% of attendances. They have been showing non-stop at the Palace Theatre (owned by Lloyd-Webber's Really Useful Company) since 1958. Drury Lane Theatre also specialises in musicals, many of them American; it can be cheaper for New York visitors to see productions here than on Broadway. Although musicals are the most popular box office events and did well even in 1991 when other theatres struggled with reduced audiences, 1993 saw audience figures fall slightly for the first time. In the 1980s the staging of musicals became more spectacular, requiring ever more imaginative use of buildings; before *Starlight Express* could be staged at the Apollo Victoria 1000 seats had to be removed to accommodate roller-skating ramps, which meant that the average ticket price had to be higher for it to make a profit. Musicals are inevitably expensive to stage anyway because an orchestra must be paid as well as the actors and actresses.

Plays run for very different lengths of time. The shortest run ever was in 1930 when an audience walked out of the Duchess before the play reached the end of its first night. In contrast *The Mousetrap*, adapted from Agatha Christie's *Three Blind*

Mice, has been running since 1952. Clearly the longer a play runs the more likely it is that much of its audience will be non-Londoners. *The Mousetrap* is now a big tourist attraction as much because of its fame as the world's longest running play as because of its intrinsic dramatic merit.

FIG.6/8 ATTENDANCES AT TYPES OF PERFORMANCES, 1992/3

	% of performances		% of attendances		% of revenue	
	1992	1993	1992	1993	1992	1993
Modern drama	16	16	10	8	7	6
Comedy	14	15	7	6	5	4
Modern musicals	37	30	51	48	52	50
Traditional musicals	8	9	8	11	9	13
Revue/variety	3	2	2	1	2	1
Opera/etta	3	3	6	6	12	10
Ballet/dance	2	2	4	4	4	5
Classical play	10	16	8	12	6	9
Children's show/ panto	1	1	1	1	1	1
Thriller/other	6	6	3	2	2	2

(Source: SOLT Box Office Data, 1993/4)

Until the 1968 Theatres Act producers were restricted in what they could show on stage by the 1737 Licensing Act which allowed the Lord Chamberlain to veto plays regarded as 'obscene'. Nowadays, however, it would be necessary to prosecute a play under the Obscenity Act and prove that it 'tended to deprave or corrupt', something notoriously hard to do.

FUNDING THE THEATRES

Theatres are expensive to run. Although wages are relatively low, theatres are labour-intensive, with not just the actors, actresses and producers but all the stage designers, make-up artists, costume-makers, musicians and stagehands to pay. Rehearsal time must also be financed. Buildings, particularly older ones, may be expensive to maintain and heat. Theatres that depend on tourists will still have to bear the fixed costs of maintenance during winter despite smaller audiences.

Costs can be divided into:

• Overheads...rent, utilities, administration, costs related to the public, general stage costs not tied to a specific production, contingencies

- Production costs...scenery, fees, advertising and publicity, rehearsal expenses, scripts, other miscellaneous costs
- Running costs...fees to stars, authors, designers, the Performing Rights Society, etc.

The Subsidised Theatre

England's main subsidised theatres are those used by the Royal Shakespeare Company (the Royal Shakespeare, Other Place, Warehouse and Swan Theatres in Stratford; the Barbican, Pit and Mermaid theatres in London; and the Theatre Royal, Gulbenkian Studio and People's Theatre in Newcastle), the Royal National Theatre (Olivier, Lyttelton and Cottesloe Theatres) and the Royal Court. However, in reality few theatres can be run on totally commercial lines; most local theatres receive grants from their local authority or Regional Arts Board.

On top of box office revenues and money made from ancillary sales, the subsidised theatres also receive funding from the government. In 1993-4 the Royal Shakespeare Company received £8.47 million from the Arts Council, while the Royal National Theatre received £11.17 million.

FIG.6/9: SOURCES OF RSC FUNDING IN 1993/4

	£million
Box office	14.13
Other trading	1.99
Arts Council grant	8.47
Corporation of London grants	1.45
Sponsorship/donations	1.05
Other	0.94
Total:	28.04

(Source : Policy Studies Institute)

In 1990/1 financial problems forced the RSC to close the Barbican for the winter. Since then it has clawed its way back into surplus, partly helped by royalties from *Les Misèrables* which transferred to the West End in 1985 and has been playing ever since. In 1993/4 6.1% of RSC income came from sponsorship, in particular from Allied-Domecq which had pledged £3 million for the three years to 1997.

Commercial Theatres

The SOLT theatres are the closest to purely commercial theatres in the UK. However, the land they stand on would probably be worth more to developers than the profit from staging plays. They stay open mainly because planning restrictions make it difficult to demolish theatres and because of philanthropic leaseholders.

Plays at commercial theatres are usually financed as individual entities. A producing management assembles a cast and finds investors to put up the production costs for the first few weeks. The producer is paid a weekly fee but won't make real money until the production costs have been covered. Profits are returned to the investors until the break-even point is reached; then they are split, with 40% going to the producers and 60% to the investors. Although a successful run can be very profitable, in general new plays are high risk investments.

When a play is toured, individual theatres are usually expected to put up a guarantee of the weekly running costs and a percentage of the production costs so that investors won't be needed. The amount they put up is usually subsidised, perhaps by a local authority, so it's debatable whether this is really 'commercial' theatre at all.

Commercial theatres make most of their money from box office takings and ancillary sales. In 1993 the average West End theatre ticket cost £18.74, 19% more than in 1990. Ticket prices have been rising faster than the retail price index as theatres moved away from dependence on grants to greater self-sufficiency. Bath Theatre Royal attracts sponsorship for 50% of its shows, but still gets most of its money from the box office, the bars and restaurants, and takings at the adjacent Garrick's Head pub.

Constant inflation-busting price rises are potentially problematic. Although there's some evidence that the average age of audiences is falling, particularly because of the many overseas visitors under the age of 45, there's a danger that younger people won't be able to afford tickets and won't, therefore, develop the theatre-going habit. Theatres try to get round this problem by offering a range of tickets to suit most pockets. Thus those in the stalls indirectly subsidise those in the 'gods' (the upper circle). The subsidised theatres also offer stand-by student concessions, while other theatres sell 'view-impeded' or 'standing' seats at cheaper prices. The Society of London Theatres also offers half-price same-day tickets from a booth in Leicester Square; theatres would prefer to sell unfilled seats at the last minute for half the price rather than lose 100% of their value if the curtain rises with the seat still empty. (New York has a similar scheme to sell Broadway tickets.) Unfortunately many overseas tourists buy tickets from agencies which charge hefty commissions or from touts on the spot who charge exorbitant sums for 'sold-out' favourites like *Cats*.

When capital needs to be invested, a theatre may be able to get help from a local authority or the Arts Council. They may also be able to run up a temporary deficit on the strength of the assumed savings that will result from the investment. The National Lottery now provides the best hope for theatres in need of refurbishment although grants can only be given for capital costs and not losses incurred while the theatre is closed for renovation or for day to day running costs. In 1996 the Oxford Playhouse reopened after a £4 million refit, £2.5 million of which had come from the Lottery. The Cambridge Arts Theatre also reopened after a £8.5 million refit, £5.7 million of it financed by the Lottery. Historic theatres may also be eligible for grants from conservation bodies like English Heritage.

Theatres can also hope for money from sponsorship, although this is usually fairly small scale. In general sponsors prefer to back individual productions rather than the theatre itself. Money can also be raised by selling television and production rights to successful plays. This is an increasingly important source of revenue for the bigger theatres. When a play transfers from the subsidised to the commercial theatre transfer rights must also be paid.

However, despite these varied sources of income many theatres were struggling by the mid-1990s. Musicals are particularly expensive because of the extravagant sets and the need to pay for an orchestra as well as a cast. At the same time the value of grants from the Arts Councils and Regional Arts Boards fell. In 1995, the Salisbury Playhouse, Cheltenham Everyman and Farnham Redgrave were all forced to 'go dark' for periods because of financial problems.

Faced with such difficulty in making ends meet theatre managers have several options:

- They can raise ticket prices (although if they lose some of the audience the revenue increase may not be as great as they hope).
- They can increase the number of performances staged.
- They can market productions more effectively.
- They can pick tried and tested plays.
- They can choose plays with smaller casts.
- They can extend popular pantomime seasons.

However, such decisions strike at artistic credibility and are likely to be unpopular with directors. Price rises that reduce audiences inevitably also result in a diminished income from ancillary sales of programmes and drinks.

Theatre Catering

In the past theatres only came to life just before the afternoon (matinee) or evening performance. During the interval a bar would be open, and chocolate would be on sale. A few theatres also served pre-booked 'matinee teas' which were passed along the rows on trays. Because theatres didn't open outside performances they weren't designed with space to allow for other activities. Those wanting to make more money out of catering may need to extend the building (as at the Nottingham Royal), buy up an adjacent site (as at Bristol Theatre Royal) or reorganise the existing space (as at Norwich Royal). A few, like the Royal National, have enough space to stay open all day. These days catering can be very profitable even though, as all-day cafes, theatres face stiff competition from other venues.

Theatre licences require usher/ettes for safety reasons, so they have traditionally doubled as sales-staff in the intervals. Bar sales are tricky because intervals are so short that there's barely time to serve everyone before the curtain rises again. Most theatres now take drinks orders before the play starts so they can be prepared in advance.

Theatre Box Offices

In most theatres the box office is a glassed-in booth in the foyer which acts as the point of sale for tickets. People can either drop into the theatre to book or phone up and use their credit card.

A few theatres still operate manual booking procedures. A plan in the box office shows the position of each seat. Once one has been sold it's crossed off on a master plan, with different colours indicating sales made by phone, credit card, etc. Seats which have been reserved by phone but not paid for are pencilled on to the plan and inked in when payment is received; they must usually be collected by a specific time before the performance starts. The ticket itself often comes in three parts; one is kept by the box office, one by the customer and the third is given up to the usher/ette. Each one gives the number of the seat and its row (usually indicated by a letter).

Most theatres now have computerised box offices with several telephonists having access to the same master plan. Printers can be attached to the computers to print not only the tickets, but accounts and statistics as well. Some companies have remote selling points for their computers and access to other systems as well.

FIG.6/10: AVERAGE SEAT PRICES FOR LONDON ARTS PERFORMANCES IN 1992 AND 1993

	1992	1993
	£	£
Modern drama	14.77	15.15
Comedy	14.72	16.03
Modern musicals	19.23	20.87
Traditional musicals	21.51	22.63
Revue/variety	17.34	13.58
Opera/operetta	37.83	37.20
Ballet/dance	22.54	24.92
Classical plays	15.92	16.22
Children's shows/pantos	12.92	13.29
Thrillers/others	14.66	15.43

(Source: SOLT Box Office Data, 1992/3)

Some box offices have 24-hour answerphones for enquiries. Discounts will be offered to school groups, pensioners, playgoers' societies, etc. Occasionally free tickets are distributed, perhaps to nurses, to help 'fill' what might otherwise look like an empty theatre. For the same reason ticket sales may be scattered around the building rather than grouped together.

Space for selling tickets in theatre foyers is often limited. The growth of the mega-musicals put particular pressure on them and in the 1990s most theatres also sell seats through agencies. The oldest agency is Keith Prowse, a British company with branches in New York, Amsterdam and Paris. First Call and Ticketmaster are actually American companies but operate in the UK as well. Producers may offer agents 'inside commissions' so they can sell tickets at their face price. However, in many cases the client is charged a booking fee or commission; the mark-up can even be as high as 25%. Even the half-price booth in Leicester Square charges a booking fee.

Theatre Administration

Theatre administration divides into two separate areas: backstage and front of house. Small theatres will usually employ the following front of house staff: an administrator, a house manager, a secretary, a box office manager, an assistant box office manager and several part time usher/ettes and bar staff. They may also employ a public relations executive to handle advertising. Backstage they will usually employ a stage manager and electricians as well as the cast of the show.

In accordance with the 1968 Theatres Act, all premises which stage plays for the public need local authority licences which are renewed once a year (premises for music, singing or dancing must be licenced by local magistrates). In granting the licence the local authority must ensure that the theatre meets its safety standards. Although standards are not set nationally most theatres will observe the same general principles, namely that:

- The building should be structurally safe.
- It should be built from fire retardant materials. Local fire chiefs will usually be expected to check new scenery for safety.
- There should be more than one clearly marked, obstruction-free exit. This can be difficult for very small theatres; Richmond's Georgian Theatre would have been unable to reopen for performances had it not been able to buy an adjacent building for emergency exits, etc.
- Seats must be secured to the floors and should be far enough apart to let people get out quickly.
- Fire-extinguishers must be available and staff trained to use them.
- All wiring must be checked for safety.
- Edges of steps should be lined with paint so they stand out even in smoke.
- Usher/ettes, aged more than 16 and wearing clearly identifiable uniforms, should be on hand to help with emergency evacuations.

Licenced theatres are permitted to serve alcohol during normal licensing hours. The 1972 Sunday Theatres Act permitted theatres to open on Sundays.

MUSICAL ENTERTAINMENT

Once again it's mainly London's Classical music venues and London-based companies that are patronised by tourists. However, even in London audiences are mostly local; figures from the South Bank concert halls suggest that only 7% of their audiences is from overseas and 20% from outside London. Nevertheless the fact that audiences shrank in 1991 when American visitors stayed away implies that tourism plays an important role, especially since few concert venues ever play to capacity audiences.

The most popular Classical music venues are the South Bank concert halls (the Royal Festival Hall, Queen Elizabeth Hall and Purcell Room), the Barbican Centre and the Royal Albert Hall where the Henry Wood Promenade Concerts (the "Proms") are particular favourites; in 1995 roughly 240,000 visitors attended 72 promenade concerts (precise figures cannot be ascertained because many people buy season tickets). Opera at the Royal Opera House in Covent Garden and at the Colisseum, where performances are always in English, is also increasingly popular.

THE FUTURE FOR THE SOUTH BANK

In 1996 plans for a £140 million overhaul of the entire South Bank arts complex were announced. The Royal Festival Hall was built in 1951 and the Royal National Theatre in 1976. The entire complex may generate more than £6 million a year but is often regarded as a user-unfriendly, concrete eyesore. The new proposals envisage placing a transparent roof over the Hayward Gallery, Queen Elizabeth Hall and a refurbished Purcell Room. Associated retail development will include shops, restaurants, cafes, a supermarket and a post office. Provided an application to the Lottery for £113 million is successful, work should start in 1997 and take four years.

All London's big Classical music venues are subsidised by the government via the Arts Council. However, like theatres they are under pressure to become more self-supporting and prices for tickets have risen much faster than the rate of inflation; in 1993 the average opera ticket cost £37.20, £12.28 more than dance, the second most highly-priced arts activity. Perhaps surprisingly there is evidence that audiences have been growing, possibly because of more effective publicity. Opera companies have been particularly tightly squeezed since *The Glory of the Garden* report (1984) suggested that they received disproportionately large subsidies. However, although they have increased their revenues from sponsorship this still brings in only a small proportion of their income. The symphony orchestras have also courted sponsorship fairly successfully, although the majority of their funding actually comes from recording rights and sales of recorded music.

The South Bank Board was set up in 1987 to take charge of the three South Bank concert halls and the Hayward Gallery. Although it's funded directly by the Arts Council of England, efforts have been made to increase the average audience size; the Royal Festival Hall now has an 'open foyer' policy like the Royal National Theatre to attract passers-by into the building (even if they don't stay for concerts they may spend money on food, drink and other merchandise). Themes have sometimes been used to link up activities at all the South Bank venues which has benefits for marketing but can come a cropper if the theme, like the Schoenberg season, proves unpopular.

The Schoenberg experience suggests that, like theatres, music venues can increase their takings by picking tried and tested favourites and avoiding experimentation. However, in the long-term this is likely to lead to stagnation. There's also some evidence that different types of music attract audiences of different ages; thus audiences at performances of Smetana's *Bartered Bride* tend to be over 45, whereas audiences at performances of trendier *Akhnaten* tend to be younger.

EXPANDING THE ROYAL OPERA HOUSE

When the Royal Opera House opened to the public in 1858 it was a state-of-the-art building. However, by the 1990s it was showing signs of its age, with poor heating and ventilation, crowded backstage facilities and limited access for disabled visitors. A major redevelopment plan will see all these problems rectified as well as adding a Studio Theatre as a permanent home for the Royal Ballet. The Victorian Floral Hall, which was badly damaged by a fire in the 1950s, will be restored to provide an impressive foyer.

In 1995 the ROH won a £55 million National Lottery grant, which will be topped up with a further £23.5 million provided certain conditions are met. However, the entire redevelopment is expected to cost £214 million. The extra money will be raised through a public appeal and through shops created within the new complex.

In general, concert audiences are older and from higher socio-economic groups. Up to 59% may also be regular visitors, a figure more typical of leisure facilities in general than of other tourist attractions. Audiences for popular music concerts obviously tend to be younger. Concerts at Wembley Stadium may attract non-Londoners and a few overseas visitors but pop concerts are usually primarily local affairs, with the exception of blockbuster events like the 1996 Oasis concert at Loch Lomond.

Musical Entertainment outside London

Several major orchestras are based outside London. These include the Bournemouth Symphony Orchestra and Sinfonietta, the City of Birmingham Symphony Orchestra, the Halle Orchestra (Manchester), the Northern Sinfonia, the Royal Liverpool Philharmonic, the Scottish National Orchestra and the Ulster Orchestra, as well as the Scottish National Opera, Welsh National Opera, Opera North (Leeds) and Glyndebourne Festival Opera (in Sussex).

Like provincial theatres, local orchestras and opera houses tend to attract mainly local audiences. However, also like the theatres, they play a part in creating a general climate within which city-based cultural tourism can flourish.

Unfortunately, like the London-based companies, many local companies were in financial difficulties by the mid-1990s.

The Aldeburgh Festival's reputation ensures that it attracts overseas tourists as well as visitors from all over the UK. It probably helps that it's within easy reach of London.

DANCE COMPANIES

Britain has an estimated 200 professional dance companies. The best known are the Royal Ballet, the Sadlers Wells Royal Ballet (Birmingham), the Ballet Rambert, the English National Ballet, the London Contemporary Theatre, the Scottish Ballet (Glasgow) and the Northern Ballet Theatre (Manchester). No ballet companies are based in Wales or Northern Ireland.

The ballet companies are dependent on subsidies, from local authorities, the Arts Councils and Regional Arts Boards (which tend to fund mainly ethnic and local dance events). Once again the dance companies are trying to become more self-sufficient, with those in London, like the English National Ballet, having most success at increasing box office takings; the Scottish Ballet remains heavily dependent on the Scottish Arts Council for funding. In 1993 an average dance ticket cost £24.52, a 230% increase on the 1987 price. However, audiences for ballet performances rose by roughly 30% between 1986/7 and 1994/5.

Dance companies attract predominantly female audiences, with 'modern' dance drawing younger people than classical ballet. Audiences also tend to come from higher socio-economic groups. However, tourists make up only a small part of audiences, even in London. Outside London dance companies are just one of the many features that help to make a town attractive to cultural tourists.

CINEMAS

Most cinemas attract a mainly local audience and should be seen as part of the leisure rather than the tourism industry. However, the British Film Institute's flagship cinema, the National Film Theatre on the South Bank, attracts non-London audiences as well partly because of its central position. Visitors to big towns may also choose to visit the cinemas in the evenings; this is particularly the case in London where a wide range of films, many of them new releases and some in languages other than English, will be showing.

The great age of the cinema was the 1930s when going to see a film was a big event, comparable to going to the theatre today. A Wurlitzer organ with flashing lights would rise up from the orchestra pit to announce the start of the show and there would be two films as well as trailers and a news bulletin. Cinemas were built to resemble theatres, with stalls, circles and a stage, and their decor could be almost as elaborate; the New Victoria Cinema cost £250,000 to build, was shaped like an ocean liner with porthole windows to the doors and could seat 2,500 people at a time. Weekend audiences were usually large enough to cover the costs of smaller mid-week audiences. Even in 1950 there were 1,396 million cinema visits, eleven times as many as in 1994. In 1972 the Sunday Cinemas Act permitted cinemas to show films on Sundays.

According to the 1985 Cinemas Act, local authorities must licence all premises which are going to show films. They can set conditions and must impose suitable restrictions for under-16 year olds. All films for public exhibition are also submitted to the British Board of Film Censors to be given a certificate indicating the audiences for which they are suitable. Some cinemas operate as private clubs with a fee for joining on top of the ticket price. This gives them more control over what they can show.

In the 1990s the development of American-style and American-owned 'multiplex' cinemas showing as many as ten different films on the one site, often on the outskirts of town, increased the likelihood that UK residents would make a longer journey to visit a cinema. The first multiplex opened in Milton Keynes in 1984.

Until 1985 the Department of Trade and Industry carried out regular surveys of cinema attendances. Data now comes in the form of estimates from the Cinema Advertising Association based on information supplied by the major distributors and a sample of individual cinemas. However, after the falling sales of the 1950s, cinema audiences started to pick up in 1985/6. After a period of steady growth during the 1980s and early '90s, sales levelled out in the mid-1990s. By 1994 as many as 124 million tickets were being sold each year but this represented an increase of only 10% on the 1993 figure. However, a Target Group Index survey in 1993 suggested that 45% of the population go to the cinema at least once a year compared with 35% who go to the theatre.

In 1994 the UK had 1,919 cinema screens, 60% more than in 1987. Most are controlled by the American companies MGM, Odeon, UCI and Warner Brothers, and by the British Showcase company. But even in 1994 46% of all cinemas still had just one screen, and 15% just two.

THE BRITISH FILM INSTITUTE

The British Film Institute (BFI) was set up in 1933 'to encourage the development of the art of film, to promote its use as a record of contemporary life and manners, and to foster public appreciation.' At first it was funded by a levy on Sunday takings from all English and Welsh cinemas, but by 1995 55.3% of its funding was coming from the Department of National Heritage, and 44.7% from subscriptions, ticket and other sales, donations and sponsorship. In 1995 its grant was increased from £14.97 million to £15.02 million. The BFI offers financial support to 20 Regional Film Theatres (including the National Film Theatre and Bristol's Watershed) and advice to a further 15. It also runs the National Film Archive and provides grants for specific films through its Production Board. It also administers the Museum of the Moving Image (MOMI) on the South Bank, which was largely paid for by John Paul Getty Junior through the British American Arts Association. Both the NFT and MOMI are attracting bigger crowds after a lull in the early 1990s.

The National Film Theatre in turn funds the London Film Festival which attracted record audiences of 88,000 in 1995, a 23.4% increase on the 1993 figure.

The Regional Film Theatres

Regional Film Theatres (RFTs) play a similar role to the National Film Theatre in screening the less commercial films in the provinces. In addition to support from the BFI they receive funding from local authorities, private sponsorship, the Regional Arts Boards and ticket sales. The Scottish Film Council supports six Scottish RFTs, while the Welsh Arts Council supports the Welsh RFTs and the Arts Council of Northern Ireland the Queens Film Theatre in Belfast.

ARTS FESTIVALS

Every year an estimated 500 arts festivals take place in the UK, most of them in the summer. The best known is the Edinburgh Festival which takes place every August, but Glasgow now has its Mayfest as well. The Bath Festival in June is also very popular. Arts festivals usually showcase arts as diverse as street theatre, music and

---

FIG.6/11: SOME MAJOR ARTS FESTIVALS IN THE UK, 1995

May	Brighton Festival
	Covent Garden Festival
	Bournemouth International Festival
	Hay-on-Wye Festival of Literature
June	Greenwich Festival
	Aldeburgh
	Bradford Festival
	City of London Festival
July	Cheltenham Festival
	Llangollen Festival
	Henley-on-Thames Festival of Music and Arts
	The 'Proms'
	Harrogate International Festival
August	Edinburgh Festival
	Three Choirs Festival
September	Cardiff Summer Music Festival
	Manchester Festival
October	Liverpool Visionfest
	Cheltenham Festival of Literature
	Canterbury Festival
	Dance Umbrella (London)
	Belfast Festival at Queens University

(Source: New Leisure Markets)

---

community art, although more than 50 are devoted to literature. Altogether they're estimated to generate around £40.6 million, although the average festival only rakes in around £80,000. Of this total, 58% is estimated to come from box office receipts and retailing, with 25% coming from public funding and the remaining 17% from business sponsorship.

The 1995 Overseas Visitor Survey showed that 21% of visitors regarded arts festivals as very or quite important although only 11% of them actually attended the festivals once here.

CHAPTER 7 : INDUSTRIAL HERITAGE

In the late 18th century Britain was the first country to experience what is now called the Industrial Revolution. Consequently although heavy industry now pays a diminished role in the UK economy, the country is littered with reminders of the industrial past in the form of redundant buildings and obsolete machinery.

There has always been some interest in industrial artefacts for their own sake and some early travellers referred with admiration to industrial landscapes; as early as 1894 visitors to Bangor were diverting to see the quarry at nearby Penrhyn. Ever since the Great Exhibition in 1851 there has also been an awareness that the best industrial artefacts deserve preservation, a belief that originally led to the creation of the Science Museum in South Kensington in 1899. In 1928 the London North-East Railway Company opened the first railway museum in York, and there was already a museum of science and engineering in Newcastle in 1934. However, in general people were slow to appreciate the many surviving mills, mines and factory buildings.

The expression 'industrial archaeology' was probably first used to refer to the physical remains of the industrial boom in the early 1950s even though the sites differed from most conventional archaeological sites in that they rarely needed any excavation; it was popularised by an article in *Amateur Historian* in 1955. The growth of interest in the 1960s may have been inspired by emotional reaction to highly publicised demolitions like that of Euston Arch and the London Coal Exchange at Billingsgate in 1962 which drew attention to the lack of protection afforded such buildings. The first book on industrial archaeology appeared in 1963, the same year that the then Ministry of Public Buildings and Works began a national survey of industrial monuments aimed at deciding which needed to be protected; this task was taken over by the Council for British Archaeology in 1966. In 1964 a *Journal of Industrial Archaeology* was established and in 1974 the Association for Industrial Archaeology was founded to co-ordinate the work that was being carried out in this field. Unlike other amenity groups like the Georgian Group and Victorian Society, the Association for Industrial Archaeology is not statutorily consulted by government when the fate of a building is in question.

Just as the Industrial Revolution itself quickly spread to the continent from Great Britain, so interest in its relics also spread quickly. In 1978 an International Committee for the Conservation of the Industrial Heritage was established, with representatives and correspondents in Argentina, Australia, Austria, Belgium, Canada, China, Czechoslovakia, Denmark, Egypt, Finland, France, Germany, Greece, Guyana, Hungary, India, Italy, Japan, Kenya, the Netherlands, New Zealand, Norway, Poland, Portugal, Spain, Sweden, Switzerland and the USA. By 1978 the US Congress had voted $40 million to create a National Industrial Park at Lowell in Massachusetts where seven mills and a canal had survived the collapse of the textile industry in the 1920s; the mills were converted into flats, shops, offices and exhibition space.

The expressions 'industrial archaeology' and 'industrial heritage' are usually taken to refer to the physical remains of the following:

- power sources...wind and watermills, steam engines, nuclear power stations
- extractive industries...quarries, mines and associated buildings
- manufacturing industries...agricultural produce, clothing, chemicals, potteries
- public services...gas, electricity, water, drainage, sewerage, post, tele-communications
- commercial buildings...shops, corn exchanges
- associated buildings and model towns...workers' houses, factory owners' mansions, docks

In addition the relics of the transport infrastructure, including the preserved railways and canals, are usually regarded as part of the industrial heritage. However, because their remains are so extensive and because they have distinctive new leisure uses these are examined separately in Chapter 8. There are also many museums specialising in particular aspects of the industrial heritage, some but not all of them housed in old industrial buildings (see Fig.7/1).

FIG.7/1: A WAREHOUSE REUSED TO HOUSE A MUSEUM... THE NATIONAL WATERWAYS MUSEUM IN THE LLANTHONY WAREHOUSE, GLOUCESTER

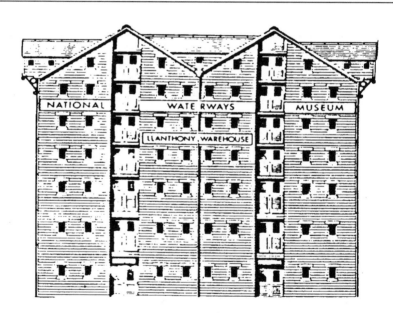

(Source: National Waterways Museum)

In 1995 the BTA estimated that there were about 1,000 industrial heritage sites. Their profile was considerably raised by the 1993 Industrial Heritage Year when 250 attractions banded together to market themselves under the banner

'Experience the Making of Britain.' This campaign is believed to have raised visitor numbers at participating attractions by about 18%.

Location of Industrial Heritage Sites

Some industrial heritage sites cannot, by their nature, be evenly distributed around the country. For example, old tin and copper mines are mainly restricted to the Land's End and Camborne areas of Cornwall, while lead mines are concentrated in Derbyshire, Yorkshire, Northumberland, Somerset, Scotland and Wales. Coal mines used to be widely distributed around the country except in South and South West England and in East Anglia. However, during the 1980s many of them closed down and even in the once-flourishing South Wales coalfields 'heritage tourism' now offers more hope for future income than mining itself.

Potteries tended to develop around good sources of suitable clay as in the Staffordshire region, while cloth mills grew up in sheep-rearing areas like Yorkshire and South Lancashire with plenty of water for industrial processes and transportation. The original canals were built to transport materials from the new industrial sites, but once they were in place new factories were likely to open all along their banks to make use of the improved transportation.

Some power sources were only available in restricted areas of the country. So there are many more redundant windmills in the flat, open countryside of East Anglia than in hillier parts of the UK. Watermills too are only found by fast-flowing rivers and steams, although Britain is well supplied with these. The development of electricity removed the crucial link between industry and localised power supplies, and 20th-century factories are distributed far more evenly around the country, often in towns with ready labour supplies. Relics of the public utilities also litter the towns.

TYPES OF INDUSTRIAL HERITAGE ATTRACTION

Mines and Quarries

Mining was one of the earliest true industrial activities. Some surviving mines predate the Industrial Revolution by centuries. They are not all coal mines. For example, amongst the most impressive surviving remains are the neolithic Grime's Graves, near Thetford in Norfolk where flint was mined in about 400 shallow mines about 30 to 40 feet deep. These are now in the care of English Heritage.

Some mines can be visited in their original situations. Others, like the one at Beamish Open-Air Museum, have been moved and reconstructed. One of the most impressive coal-mines open to visitors in situ is Big Pit at Blaenafon in Gwent. When the mine was closed in 1980 the miners bought it for £1 each and turned it into a museum with the help of £30,000 from the National Heritage Memorial Fund; they now conduct guided tours round the coal faces, haulage engines, workshops and underground stables. The Rhondda Heritage Park was created round the former Lewis Merthyr and Ty-Mawr collieries in South Wales with the help of grants from the Welsh Development Agency, the Wales Tourist Board, the European Regional Development Fund, the Countryside Commission, the Forestry Commission and local councils. The Chatterley Whitfield Colliery in Tunstall was also opened to the public after the mine itself closed. However, in 1986 flooding and a build-up of methane gas meant the original Winstanley Shaft was no longer safe for visitors. Instead a new shaft was built and others were plugged and adapted to let visitors ride in a miner's cage and watch coal winding.

The National Trust owns a Roman gold mine at Dolaucothi in Dyfed. The lead mine at Killhope in Weardale was also opened to the public with the help of money from the European Regional Development Fund and the local authorities. An imaginative 'adopt a rivet' scheme helped pay for the renovation of some of the machinery.

Quarries of particular interest to tourists include the Dinorwic workshops near Llanberis which now form the Welsh Slate Museum. To add to their natural appeal a narrow-gauge railway runs along the foot of the cliff to carry visitors around the site. The Delabole Quarry in Cornwall has the honour of being the largest man-made hole in the UK and is still in use.

The Mills

Most of the disused mill buildings concentrated in the Midlands are reminders of the once booming woollen textile industry. However, Scotland and Ireland boast old flax mills, while the Derby Industrial Museum is housed in a redundant silk mill. The ETB also provided £20,000 towards the start-up costs of the Macclesfield Silk Museum and Heritage Centre, housed in an old Sunday School building.

Some textile mills, like those at Helmshore in Lancashire, have been preserved as reminders of the textile industry itself while others have become industrial museums. In 1995 English Heritage gave grants to House Mill at Newham in London which is to become a Museum of Social History, and to Queen Street Mill in Burnley which is now a Museum of the Lancashire Textile Industry.

More imaginative new uses have sometimes been suggested for disused mills. Bradford has made particularly good use of its old mills. Salt's Mill at Saltaire has been converted into an 1853 Gallery with a collection of small retail and industrial units alongside the paintings of local artist, David Hockney. Shearbridge Mill has been turned into PLS Hotel, complete with covered parking space, while many other mills now house mill shops. Manningham (Lister's) Mill, opened in 1873, has been suggested as a possible future home for some of the Victoria and Albert Museum's South Asian collections, particularly appropriate given Bradford's large Asian population. Rowntree's opened a museum of the chocolate industry in Leetham Mill in York. Arlington Mill at Bibury in the Cotswolds houses an interestingly mixed collection of exhibits, including Arts and Crafts Movement furniture. A large woollen mill at Stroud was restored to provide council offices; clearly it isn't a tourist attraction, although its preservation helps create the sort of attractive environment in which tourism flourishes.

QUARRY BANK MILL

Quarry Bank Mill at Styal in Cheshire was built by Samuel Greg in 1784 in an area south of Manchester where few other mills were established. In 1939 the National Trust bought it as a fine example of an industrial complex complete with textile mill, workers' houses with gardens, Greg's own grand home and a large red-brick building which was home to 100 apprentices. The Mill appealed to the Trust because its site, in the Bollin Valley, was particularly pretty. However, surviving records suggest that while the workers' houses may now look attractive their 19th-century occupants would have found them crowded and uncomfortable.

Normally the National Trust only takes on historic buildings that have funds for their maintenance, but few industrial sites come with such endowments and Quarry Bank was accepted without supporting funds. What's more in the 1950s, before industrial archaeology got into its stride, the mill looms were actually destroyed with the help of government grants to dispose of redundant industrial machinery. Since 1959 the National Trust has spent £300,000 on repairs to the site, setting up the Quarry Bank Mill Development Trust to handle the work. The National Heritage Memorial Fund helped with a grant to reinstate one of the country's largest iron waterwheels on the site. In 1984 Quarry Bank Mill won the Museum of the Year Award and by 1995 it was receiving 192,717 visitors a year. The last part of the site to be opened to the public was the apprentices' house where costumed interpreters now explain 19th-century life to visitors. By taking on a building so unlike those traditionally associated with it the National Trust may even have attracted a new clientele that would not normally have been interested in its work.

Wind and Watermills

Some relics of industrial processes are more interesting than intrinsically beautiful, but wind and watermills are often attractive to look at as well. It's therefore not surprising that many of them have been taken into the care of the National Trust which owns and manages a 15th-century water-powered grain mill at Nether Alderley in Cheshire and a medieval overshot water mill at Cotehele in Cornwall.

Watermills are found wherever there is fast-flowing water. Some are stationary, but others are still in operation as at Redditch. A few are attached to buildings which have been given new purposes. Many have become restaurants or pubs because their situations are so attractive. A few, like Rossett Mill in Clywd, have become private houses. There are still traces of about 20,000 watermills in Britain.

Of perhaps 10,000 windmills once in existence in the UK, there are traces of only about 5,000 now. Most of those in the Somerset Levels and the Wirral Peninsula have vanished and in Anglesey only a few derelict towers still stand.

Those that do survive are mainly in Essex, Kent, Norfolk, Suffolk and Lincolnshire. Some windmills are still in operation and admit visitors to watch the flour-making process, making money out of admission fees and produce sales. Others have had their sails removed and stand as curious relics in the countryside or have been converted into private houses. The Berney Arms Windmill near Reedham in Norfolk is a fine example of a working windmill now in the care of English Heritage. However, the finest working windmills are not in England at all, but in the Netherlands where 14 stand in a dramatic line at Kinderdijk.

During the 1990s new look windmills began to appear in exposed parts of the country. Although their thin white sails are not universally popular, they are certainly eyecatching and some of the new wind farms are already admitting visitors; in 1995 30,000 people visited the wind farm at Delabole in Cornwall.

The Public Utilities

Some of the newest and least aesthetically pleasing industrial archaeology sites are the relics of the water, electricity, gas and waste disposal industries.

Water: Amongst the most striking relics of the history of the water industry are the steam pumps used to raise water from wells or to pump it to storage reservoirs. The water pumping station at Marshall Place, Perth, has been converted into a tourist information centre, while a private preservation trust has turned the Ryhope Pumping Station in Sunderland into a museum of water supply equipment.

    In London the Kew Bridge Engines Trust displays four Cornish pump engines last used in 1944 in the Kew Bridge waterworks.

    Outside the UK old water supply paraphernalia has also been preserved. In Istanbul several underground cisterns are open to the public. Concerts are even performed on an elevated stage in one of them.

Gas: A few old gasworks have been preserved as tourist attractions. Fakenham Gasworks is now an ancient monument while Biggar Gasworks in Lancashire has been turned into an outpost of the Royal Museum of Scotland. The Manchester Museum of Science and Technology also contains a gas industry gallery.

Electricity: The electricity supply industry has its own galleries in the Manchester Museum of Science and Technology, and there's a large display on electricity in the London Science Museum. Visitors to Cragside in Northumbria can also follow a 'power circuit' linking the Armstrong Energy Centre and the original buildings which housed Lord Armstrong's hydraulic and hydro-electric equipment. The decommissioned Bankside power station is due to become a branch of the Tate Gallery by the year 2000.

BATTERSEA POWER STATION

One of the most striking reminders of past electricity generation is Battersea Power Station on the banks of the River Thames. This building (which has been described as looking like an upturned table) was designed by Sir Giles Gilbert Scott and generated electricity for London from 1933 to 1983. In 1980 the power station, with its fine Art Deco interior, was designated a Grade II listed building, so when it was decommissioned in 1983 it couldn't simply be demolished. Instead there was a competition to come up with new ideas for its use. John Broome, then owner of Alton Towers, proposed to turn the 31-acre site into 'The Battersea', a vast seven-storey leisure complex. Unfortunately, expected conversion costs rose rapidly and work stopped when funds dried up. Broome then sold Alton Towers to Pearson plc who persuaded Wandsworth Council to agree to adding two hotels, shops, office and conference space to the original scheme. That project also collapsed and the power station is now owned by Parkview International who propose to turn it into a £700 million leisure and entertainment complex, incorporating a 32-screen 'Power Plex' cinema capable of seating 8,000 people. The main snag seems to be access to the site. Parkview is negotiating with Railtrack for a new station or dedicated rail link from Victoria.

Waste Disposal: A few pumping stations used for waste disposal like the one at Eastney in Portsmouth have been preserved, but one of the most interesting reminders of this side of public provision can be found once again in the award-winning Manchester Museum of Science and Technology which has a whole underground section devoted to the history of the sewerage industry, complete with a length of pipe from an 1830s sewer to walk through.

The Paris sewers are regularly open for walking tours.

Other Industrial Remains

In the last ten years most large towns have opened industrial museums, sometimes in disused warehouses or mills. These often focus on locally important industries. Thus Bristol's Industrial Museum, in a warehouse overlooking the Historic Harbour, has a large section devoted to aircraft engines because of its historic links with British Aerospace. Smaller specialist museums may also concentrate on a local industry. Bristol is also home to a Wine Museum because Harvey's is a local company. In Bath a Victorian brass foundry is now an industrial museum called Mr Bowler's Business, while Abbeydale Industrial Hamlet in Sheffield is housed within an 18th-century scythe-making works, a relic of the local steel industry.

Smaller towns and villages may also have specialist museums devoted to local industries. Northampton has long been a centre for shoe-making and the City

Museum has a large collection of shoes. Hereford has a Cider Museum inside an old cider works. The pretty hamlet of Bucklers Hard in Hampshire is like a natural open-air museum to the ship-building business which flourished there until the 19th century. The Chalk Pits Museum, in a limeworks and quarry near Amberley in West Sussex, is also devoted to an industry specific to the area.

Model Towns

There are also several model towns which were associated with industrial development but which are now particularly pleasant conservation areas:

- Saltaire (see Chapter 11)

- Port Sunlight was founded by William Hesketh Lever in 1888 and housed workers at his soap-making factory in the Wirral. Tudor-style half-timbered houses were clustered around greens and open spaces, with no more than eight houses to an acre, an arrangement which was never financially viable. The village is now home to the Lady Lever Art Gallery which has a fine collection of Pre-Raphaelite paintings and received 51,789 visitors in 1995.

- The 19th-century workers' village at Bournville, Birmingham, was the product of George and Richard Cadbury, who built 8,000 houses with gardens for their factory workers, half-timbered shops, a park and a village green. Cadbury World is a particularly popular reason to visit the village.

- The industrial village of New Lanark in Scotland was created by the factory reformer, Robert Owen, in the early 19th century; at its heart was the Institute for Formation of Character which has been restored with a grant from the National Heritage Memorial Fund.

DOCKLAND REVIVAL SCHEMES

In the 1960s and '70s several North American cities were faced with the same sort of urban decay as towns like Liverpool and Wigan. In 1977 the US government passed the Housing and Community Development Act which allowed for the public and private funding of projects designed to revive these areas. One of the success stories was Baltimore's Inner Harbour area. The Greater Baltimore Committee helped redevelop 33 acres of run-down inner city to create the Charles Centre for offices and businesses. The success of this project inspired the restoration of the Inner Harbour (which had been abandoned in the 1950s) primarily for tourism. A promenade was laid alongside the harbour and attractions, restaurants and amenities interspersed with green spaces were built. Festivals were also created to attract publicity. The 230-acre site now includes a World Trade Centre, the Maryland Science Centre, an aquarium (which attracts 600,000 visitors a year) and Harborplace, a huge development of specialist shops, restaurants, etc. Thirteen thousand new jobs were created and 20 million people a year now visit the Inner Harbour. Similar developments quickly followed in New York, Boston and (further north in Canada) in Toronto.

Like many good ideas this one was copied in the UK and the restoration of decaying British docks has been one of the most striking examples of heritage tourism's capacity to help revive the cities.

Bristol Docks

In 1971 Bristol City Council considered filling in the old 'floating harbour' in the city centre which no longer met the needs of commercial shipping. Fortunately the rising cost of the engineering work involved put paid to that plan. Instead the Council launched a City Docks Local Plan which envisaged improving the area's appearance to encourage re-use and investment. The Plan proposed:

- demolishng or repairing derelict buildings and carrying out environmental improvements
- improving public access to the harbour
- creating event attractions to draw people to the area
- the Council carrying out pump-priming schemes like developing an Industrial Museum in the harbour area
- finding new uses for old buildings like the transit sheds

Little public money went into redeveloping the docks, although the city received an Urban Aid Grant to help rebuild the Albion Dockyard, and the Historic Buildings and Monuments Commission offered some assistance. The Bristol Marketing Board then approached the English Tourist Board for advice on how to attract more visitors to the city. The 'Historic Harbour' became a pilot project for urban tourism within the first Tourism Development Action Programme (see Chapter 1). The ETB provided £1 million in grants over a five-year period to supplement development funds raised elsewhere. By 1987 almost half the usable land in the docks area had been redeveloped, mainly for housing, shops, hotels and tourist facilities. The Historic Harbour is now the tourist heart of Bristol with a youth hostel in one of the old warehouses along the quayside. By 1996 only the polluted Canons Marsh site, partly owned by British Gas and Railtrack, still lay derelict. Lloyds Bank had been allowed to build a head office on part of the site in return for environmental improvements, including the creation of an amphitheatre for outdoors concerts. The rest of the site is expected to be redeveloped courtesy of a £41 million grant from the Millennium Commission.

Other British cities quickly followed Bristol's lead. In the 1980s they were helped by government policies for inner-city regeneration. Increasingly tourism was seen as a way both to improve inner-city environments and provide new jobs. Decaying dock areas, often surrounded by empty warehouses, became prime targets for redevelopment, sometimes through the creation of special government-funded Development Corporations, as in both London and Liverpool.

London Docks

The work of the London Docklands Development Corporation (LDDC) in the run-down docks of East London was a high-profile endeavour costing millions of pounds. However, in touristic terms London has less to show for the money spent than Bristol or Liverpool. The redevelopment of East London was interpreted largely in terms of offices and housing. Because of its position in the booming south-east it was assumed, until the property slump of 1989, that this redevelopment would pay its way as an extension of the City. However, the building of a new light railway as far as Greenwich did make the National Maritime Museum more readily accessible.

St. Katherine's Dock, which is close to the Tower of London and Tower Bridge, was the one area to be redeveloped with tourism in mind and this work was carried out before the advent of the LDDC. The Dock was designed by Thomas Telford and Philip Hardwick in the early 19th century. By the 1960s it was losing money and was eventually closed down. Although it has now been redeveloped for shops, offices, luxury housing, restaurants and pubs around a collection of historic ships on loan from the National Maritime Museum, one of the warehouses had already burnt down, another was demolished and a third was cannibalised to provide a framework for the 'Dickens' pub before restoration work was completed.

The London Docklands Visitor Centre, telling the story behind the dockland redevelopment, was visited by 190,220 people in 1995.

Liverpool Docks

The situation in Liverpool is very different. The docks there had actually overtaken Bristol's in importance by the 19th century. However, by the 1960s they too were no longer financially viable and there were plans to replace them with offices. When this scheme fell through the Mersey Docks and Harbour Company virtually abandoned the docks.

The 1981 Toxteth Riots highlighted Liverpool's economic collapse and the problems of unemployment. In 1982 the Merseyside Development Corporation was set up and gave £2.25 million to turn one of the warehouses in the Albert Dock into a maritime museum; this was later awarded national status, making it eligible for further government grants. A further £2 million was provided to develop the Tate Gallery of the North, £9.25 million for landscaping and engineering work and £16 million for shops, restaurants, offices, etc. An Urban Aid Grant of £1.4 million aided the restoration of the Adelphi Hotel, and private sector funding and a £60,000 ETB development grant helped with the creation of the Beatle City attraction in the Britannia Vaults of a Victorian warehouse. All this enterprise paid handsome dividends. In 1985 a study of the economic impact of tourist and associated arts developments in Merseyside discovered that 26% of leisure visitors to the city thought it a rough, violent and depressing place before their visit, while only 2% felt that way after it. By 1989 it was estimated that the average visitor was injecting £7.70 into the local economy.

In 1995 the new HM Customs and Excise National Museum, Anything to Declare? received 165,361 visitors. Overall, 5,770,000 people visited the Albert Dock, making it the UK's second most popular free attraction.

The Rest of the Country

The success of these schemes led to imitations all over the UK. By 1990 almost every town with docks or canal/riverside warehouses was striving to convert them into shops, offices, houses, tourist attractions, marinas, etc. In Exeter 19th-century warehouses were turned into a Maritime Museum. In Gloucester the Albert Warehouse became home to the Robert Opie Museum of Advertising and Packaging, and the Llanthony Warehouse to the National Waterways Museum. Hull created a regatta and maritime heritage trail for its docks. A Tourism Development Action Programme in Portsmouth helped reinforce the Portsmouth Naval Heritage Project centred on the docks. At Southampton an Ocean Village was developed, in Newcastle the quayside area was redeveloped, and in Barrow-in-Furness a 19th-century ship-repairing dock was restored with the help of the largest single Section 4 grant ever made to north-west England (£294,000). Large-scale dock development activity also took place in Cardiff, Swansea, Edinburgh, Manchester, Lancaster and many other English towns.

PRESENTING INDUSTRIAL HERITAGE ATTRACTIONS

There are some specific difficulties in presenting industrial heritage attractions. In the first place many of the artefacts are too large to be moved to conventional museums, a problem usually solved by creating museums around them instead. So the Leicester Museum of Technology was created around the Abbey Pumping Station, an old sewage works.

Industrial processes were also dynamic and a machine that may be fascinating in use can seem dull when stationary, a problem often resolved by putting it to use again particularly when it's on display in its original setting. This has the added advantage that the machine's produce can sometimes be sold to visitors to raise extra revenue. People can also learn more about the technological processes involved. However, moving industrial machinery can be dangerous so extra precautions must be taken to safeguard the public. This also applies when people are taken into old mine shafts and quarries.

Many industrial artefacts are on display in science and technology museums which are seeking sponsorship. Big companies may be more enthusiastic about sponsoring an exhibition which relates to their own business. However, this raises the possibility of interference and loss of objectivity. Nationalistic considerations may also come into play. Reminders of the early, perhaps less successful, phases of industrial processes may also not survive. Without careful explanation industrial museums may therefore suggest that particular processes came into being already fully-formed.

IRONBRIDGE GORGE MUSEUM... BRITAIN'S FIRST INDUSTRIAL WORLD HERITAGE SITE

In The National Trust Guide to *Our Industrial Past* Anthony Burton compares Ironbridge Gorge in importance to the Pyramids or the Parthenon, pointing out that it was probably more significant in Britain's history than better-known sites like Hadrian's Wall and Buckingham Palace; after all if Britain led the way with the Industrial Revolution, Ironbridge could be seen as the seat of that revolution, the place where Abraham Darby I first managed to produce cheap iron in 1709. The Iron Bridge itself, the world's first metal bridge, constructed in 1779, exemplified what was possible once iron became cheap and easy to manufacture.

The bridge is now the heart of a vast industrial heritage centre which achieved World Heritage Site status in 1986. Work began on the site in 1959, the 250th anniversary of the first successful coke-smelting of iron, when the first Coalbrookdale Museum was opened and the original Darby furnace excavated. In 1967 a working party on industrial archaeology suggested making Coalbrookdale into a living museum and creating a public park at Blists Hill. The Telford Development Corporation had been set up to create a New Town and trustees of the new Ironbridge Gorge Museum believed their ideas could give it a sense of identity and a past to be proud of. The Development Corporation duly leased land to the Trust and provided it with funding, along with the Department of the Environment and local urban councils. The National Heritage Memorial Fund added another £285,000 and a group of 'Friends of Ironbridge Gorge Museum' was set up. Not only did their subscriptions help finance work but many friends provided voluntary labour on the site; to this day some still work as voluntary 'interpretive guides'. Other help was provided by army and prison labour. In 1991 Telford Development Corporation was wound up and the government provided the Museum with a £2 million capital endowment to continue its work.

Today the Ironbridge Gorge Museum is a vast complex covering 9½ square kilometres. Visitors buy tickets designed to look like British passports which give admission to each attraction on the site once at any time. These include:

- the Museum of the River and Visitor Centre housed in the 19th-century Severn warehouse

- the Museum of Iron, Darby's Furnace and the Elton Collection of paintings, engravings and film related to industrialisation collected by the late Sir Arthur Elton

- Blist's Hill Open-Air Museum, a 50-acre reconstructed late Victorian settlement where visitors can change their money into Victorian currency and use it to buy pies and beer in the shops

- Coalport China Museum

- Jackfield Tile Museum in the 19th century Craven Dunnill decorative tile works

- Rosehill House where Abraham Darby I's son lived in the early 19th century

- the Clay Tobacco Pipe Museum at Broseley

To visit all the attractions could take two days because they are so spread out. Blist's Hill is far and away the most popular individual attraction, attracting 227,190 visitors in 1995 compared to 107,579 at the Museum of the River.

In 1978 the Ironbridge Gorge Trading Company was set up to run shops in the Coalbrookdale Museum, the Coalport China Museum and Blists Hill. Annual profits are transferred back to the Museum Trust. In 1988 404,000 visitors paid £1 million in admission fees, 80% of the site's annual running costs. By 1983 the museum's publications list already featured 150 items which were also generating funds.

Ironbridge Gorge attracted considerable free publicity in the past, partly because of the awards it won: 1973 BTA 'Come to Britain' trophy, 1977 National Heritage Museum of the Year, 1978 European Museum of the Year and the 1989 Times/Shell Museum of the Year. After the Museum appeared on the BBC's 'Holiday' programme, visitor numbers soared from an expected 7,000 people to 35,000 over one weekend. However, it has a fairly small publicity budget: just £100,000 in 1996. Much of this goes into joint advertising with Wrekin District Council and local hoteliers, although there have been occasional publicity-seeking events like 'Duck Races' on the river. In 1995 visitor numbers rose by just under 5% after several years of decline during the recession.

Visitor surveys consistently suggest that Ironbridge Gorge attracts most its visitors from the ABC1 socio-economic groups (67% in 1989), and that only 5% of its visitors come from overseas. Forty per cent of visitors come from London and the South-East.

Increasingly industrial heritage sites are 'living museums' which attempt to show how people lived and worked alongside the artefacts. Costumed attendants are on hand to explain what visitors are seeing, as at Quarry Bank Mill and Ironbridge Gorge.

Curators putting together an industrial exhibition have one considerable advantage in that few technological objects are unique or priced for their intrinsic beauty. Consequently they rarely fetch high prices at auction. This also means that exhibits can often be treated more roughly; at the Killhope Lead Mining Centre children are encouraged to play with equipment once used to sift lead from the river. Some run-down industrial sites are also sold for very reasonable prices, so that it can be relatively cheap to set up a new industrial museum.

INDUSTRIAL TOURISM

The success of industrial heritage sites in interesting people in technological processes has led an increasing number of companies to consider industrial tourism as an additional money-spinner. While industrial heritage tourism is concerned with presenting redundant machinery, processes, buildings and ways of life, industrial tourism is about contemporary manufacturing processes. Sometimes the two may even overlap; a modern factory may decide to open a museum on the industry's history while inviting visitors to tour the existing factory as well.

By 1988 the BTA estimated that there were about 5 million visits to industrial tourism attractions in the UK, and that the market was likely to grow rapidly to between 8 and 9 million visits. As early as 1964 69 British companies had some sort of museum on their premises. However, these were rarely actively promoted and development of industrial tourism was generally demand- rather than product-led. In 1988 the ETB and CBI organised a national conference on industrial tourism with a view to promoting it more actively.

The industrial tourism product has several possible components:

* a factory tour,
* a purpose-built visitor centre,
* catering facilities,
* shops selling the company's produce.

It can cost anything from £15,000 to £1 million to provide facilities for visitors but this outlay has been estimated to create a turnover of anything from £20,000 to £1.5 million of which up to 75% can come from shop sales. Most visitors to industrial tourist sites are likely to be British and many of them will be senior citizens or school parties.

Companies become involved in industrial tourism for a variety of reasons. In the case of some products there has always been great interest. At one stage there was, for example, a two year waiting list for coach tours of the Wedgwood china factory. As a result the new Visitor Reception Centre was designed as a central feature of the Barlaston site even though there would have been more space for parking on a peripheral site. It was also designed on one level to suit the needs of disabled visitors and mothers with pushchairs. Sixty staff are employed specifically to deal with tourists, although those working in the craft demonstration hall are ordinary factory workers whose piecework rates have been adjusted to allow time to talk to visitors.

Cadbury World at Bournville, in the Birmingham suburbs, is attached to the famous chocolate factory and cashes in on people's enthusiasm for the product, offering organised tours and the chance to inspect exhibits on the history of the industry and its advertising. Visitors can buy cut-price samples before they leave, as they can at Harvey's Wine Museum in Bristol. In 1995 515,955 people visited Cadbury World.

Not surprisingly the high-profile Body Shop provides tours to enable visitors to watch its products being manufactured. The Visitor Centre at Littlehampton received 103,138 visitors in 1995.

Breweries, too, have always drawn curious visitors. Since 1974 the Carlsberg plant in Northampton has been open to visitors who are provided with free refreshments during their visit. Very little advertising is done except to coach tour operators and yet there were 14,400 visitors in 1994, mainly drawn by word of mouth recommendation. The Guinness Brewery in Dublin has long been another favourite with tourists. The Scottish whisky distilleries have been particularly successful at marketing themselves as tourist attractions, often by linking up to offer 'whisky heritage trails'. One of the most popular is the Glenfiddich Distillery at Dufftown which attracted 116,740 visitors in 1995, 59% of them from overseas. In Northern Ireland the Bushmills Distillery attracted 101,938 visitors in 1995.

Ford Motors at Dagenham has also opened its factory to visitors. Cars are obviously interesting to lots of people and it's not surprising that Germany's most popular industrial tourism attraction is the BMW plant in Munich which receives about 300,000 visitors a year. However, the less glamorous Dagenham plant received only 21,450 visitors in 1995.

In contrast, some industrial tourism has developed partly as a public relations exercise. For example, in 1980 a visitor centre was opened at the Sellafield nuclear fuel plant with the aim of reassuring the public and improving the industry's image. Soon so many tourists were visiting that £5.4 million was invested in a new reception centre. In 1995 107,582 people visited Sellafield Visitor Centre, one of UK tourism's more surprising success stories.

Finally, some companies open their doors to tourists as an alternative to closing them altogether. For example, by 1978 the Walkley Clog Factory at Hebden Bridge (which dates from 1870) faced closure because the market for its products had virtually vanished. Instead it started admitting visitors to watch the clog-making process. After an organised publicity drive helped by the Yorkshire and Humberside Tourist Board and the local council, visitor numbers rose steadily. Craft workshops, a pine showroom, a puppet theatre and bee museum were then added to guarantee its future as an attraction.

Some industrial tourism attractions open to the public free of charge and rely on sales of merchandise to make a profit; the Carlsberg Brewery reckons to sell several hundred pounds worth of goods to coach groups although it then donates the money to industry-linked charities. It's also assumed that people impressed by what they see on their visit may become future customers, so that an indirect profit may be generated. However, the Wilton Royal factory which could hardly expect to sell many carpets to passing visitors charges £3.50 for a tour.

Industrial tourism also plays a role in generating potential visitors for other local attractions, hotels and restaurants. So the success of Sellafield is credited with having drawn more visitors to the Ravensglass and Eskdale Railway and Muncaster Castle. Many potential industrial tourism centres are in towns which didn't traditionally attract many visitors. They also have the advantage that they can be marketed as year-round, all-weather attractions. What's more when company profits are squeezed, they offer a way to boost revenue at relatively small cost, although a reception centre becomes essential once visitor numbers start to rise. Additional staff may also be needed to act as guides/interpreters, and extra safety precautions must be taken to protect visitors from dangerous machinery.

Even in developing countries industrial tourism can be very important. So in Havana, Cuba, the tobacco factories are open to visitors who want to watch cigars being made.

THE POTTERIES

While most mines and mills become attractions when their working life is over, potteries are often places where industrial heritage tourism meets present-day industrial tourism. Pottery manufacture is still very much a flourishing industry and kilns can be found all over the country. However, many of the most interesting sites can be found in the Staffordshire region traditionally known as the Potteries.

Josiah Wedgwood was largely responsible for turning Stoke-on-Trent into the centre of the pottery industry in the 18th century. Not only did he build his Etruria factory there, but he also promoted the development of the Trent and Mersey Canal to get his pots to market and to fetch raw materials from further afield. Sadly the factory was demolished in the 1960s (the Stoke-on-Trent Garden Festival took place on its site) and production of Wedgwood pottery moved to Barlaston. Tourists follow a self-guided route round the museum and art gallery and can watch the famous pots being created in a craft demonstration hall. Inevitably the tour terminates in a shop where pottery is on sale. In 1995 about 200,000 people visited the museum and visitor centre.

For a better idea what the district might have looked like in the 19th century visitors can go to the Gladstone Working Pottery Museum in Longston, Staffs., a group of four typical 'bottle kilns' saved by the Staffordshire Pottery Industrial Preservation Trust and turned into an industrial heritage-cum-industrial tourism centre (see Fig.7/2). In 1990 Stoke-on-Trent City Council bought it from the Trust, since when visitor numbers have been steadily improving; in 1994 it received 29,012 visitors.

Stoke-on-Trent has several other museums associated with the pottery industry including the Minton Museum, the Sir Henry Doulton Gallery, the Heron Cross Pottery and the Spode Museum. Visits can also be arranged to the Minton, Royal Doulton, Crown Windsor and Spode factories. In fact the potteries are so important to local tourism that the city is promoted under the straplines 'Firing the Imagination' and 'Stoke-on-Trent - A China Experience'. Its main target market consists of older 'empty-nesters' with the surplus income to buy the pottery, although Stoke also receives a lot of young professional families with children, visiting as an add-on to a trip to Alton Towers. Seventeen per cent of visitors are thought to be from overseas. Of those, around 44% are from the USA.

FIG.7/2: BOTTLE KILNS REVIVED TO HOUSE A MUSEUM IN THE POTTERIES...GLADSTONE WORKING POTTERY MUSEUM

ENGINEERING PROJECTS AND TOURISM

In the same way that workplaces which originally had nothing to do with tourism have nevertheless become attractions, so several major engineering works also draw large numbers of visitors every year. Fine examples in Africa include both the

Aswan Dam in Egypt and the Kariba Dam in Zimbabwe. In England the Thames Barrier, built to improve London's flood defences, has a Visitor's Centre which attracted 78,707 tourists in 1995. The Eurotunnel Exhibition Centre in Folkestone drew 145,650 people in 1995, even after the Tunnel itself had opened. Perhaps more surprisingly the Docklands Light Railway also appears to be attracting tourists. During the summer it carries an average extra 5,000 people every day, suggesting that it is not just being used to get tourists to Greenwich but also as an attraction in its own right.

The history of transport has been one of constant change, usually in response to new technology. During the Industrial Revolution of the late 18th century a network of canals was built to facilitate the movement of goods being manufactured in the new factories at a time when journeys by road could still be long and uncomfortable. Then as the 19th century progressed the canals fell into neglect as railways tracks were laid, providing even quicker and easier transportation. In the 20th century it was the turn of the railways to feel the pinch as people acquired their own cars and the growth of a motorway network meant that many goods could be transported more quickly and efficiently by road.

However, in the late 20th century tourism has given a new lease of life to some transport systems that might otherwise have outlived their usefulness.

THE RAILWAYS

Most railway tracks in the UK were laid in three bursts of 'railway mania', in the 1830s, 1840s and 1850s. The first railways were distinguished by complex tunnels and earthworks to deal with differing gradients, and by grandiose station buildings, typified by the mid-Victorian Gothic fantasy of St. Pancras, the Elizabethan Revival-style of Brunel's Old Station in Bristol and the Classical style of Huddersfield Station. As the century progressed, however, more powerful steam locomotives could handle steeper gradients, so the routes became simpler. Financial constraints also led to more modest station designs.

By 1870 the majority of the rail network had been laid and Britain had more than 17,600 kilometres of track. A few branch lines continued to be built and when the railways were nationalised in 1948 there were 31,160 kilometres of track together with 8,294 stations. Since then many lines have been axed, particularly as a result of the Beeching Report in 1963, so that today only about 16,452 kilometres remain, together with 2,506 stations. Railways that had served old quarries and other industrial sites were particularly likely to be closed as uneconomic. British Rail inherited more than 20,000 steam engines from the private railway companies in 1948, but by 1968 had taken them all out of service.

Fortunately train enthusiasts were quick to spot the touristic potential of railways that British Rail decided to abandon, particularly when they ran through beautiful countryside. So in 1951 the Talyllyn Railway Preservation Society was created to save a narrow-gauge slate quarry railway running through spectacular scenery in West Wales. This was the world's first successful railway preservation society and was quickly followed by others, some of them, like the Bluebell Railway Preservation Society in East Sussex, run as commercial operations. Preserved railways are particularly important to Welsh tourism (see Fig.8/1).

The railway preservation societies usually had two aims: to restore old steam locomotives and operate them again, and to revitalise old tracks in attractive countryside for the benefit of railway buffs and tourists. This was expensive work since they had to buy both the land and the tracks from British Rail and then restore not only the engines and rolling stock but also the stations, signals, workshops, etc. Before they could carry passengers they also needed a Ministry of Transport licence which would only be granted if they could prove the railway would be run safely and efficiently. The Fairbourne to Barmouth Railway in Gwynedd which carries 50,000 people a year cost almost £1 million to restore, has won a Prince of Wales award for its station architecture and has been voted Railway World's 'best railway in Wales'. When the Bure Valley Railway in the Norfolk Broads reopened in 1990 it had cost £2.5 million to develop and had been helped with an ETB Section 4 grant.

FIG.8/1: THE PRESERVED RAILWAYS OF WALES

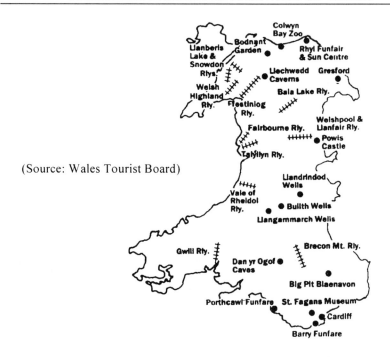

(Source: Wales Tourist Board)

Most of England's railway preservation societies (see Appendix II) now operate as registered charities, ploughing all their takings back into the railway. Many are run entirely by volunteers or by a skeleton staff. Occasionally outside help has been available. Peterborough Development Corporation helped restore the Nene Valley Railway as part of its plan to create a recreation park for an expanding new town in the area. Bury City council collaborated with the East Lancashire Railway Preservation Society to reopen a railway line through the Irwell Valley. In contrast to lines like the North Yorkshire Moors Railway this didn't run through beautiful countryside. In fact the Irwell Valley had become very polluted and the Council saw the railway's redevelopment as a way of regenerating it and attracting tourists to an abandoned area. While the railway enthusiasts reconstructed the stations from a mishmash of items owned by British Rail or private individuals, the

Council created picnic areas and parks along the way. Now local shops are booming, new restaurants have opened and as many as 1,000 people may show up at Ramsbottom Station on an average Sunday.

The Association of Railway Preservation Societies offers technical, legal and administrative advice and liaises with the British Tourist Authority, Railtrack and other interested bodies for publicity purposes.

FIG.8/2: TOP TEN STEAM RAILWAYS IN 1995	
North Yorkshire Moors Railway	267,000
Ffestiniog Railway, Porthmadog	188,262
Bluebell Railway, Sussex	171,000
Severn Valley Railway, Shropshire	167,000
Keighley and Worth Railway/Swanage Railway	150,000
Lakeside and Haverthwaite Railway	145,000
Paignton and Dartmouth Railway	144,180
Snowdon Mountain Railway	141,790
Romney, Hythe and Dymchurch Railway	140,000

Some of the railways that have been restored used to be part of the passenger network, while others served industrial outlets. In some cases new track has been laid to carry restored steam trains, as in the grounds of Bicton House and Bressingham Hall. Stations have sometimes been restored in situ. Elsewhere fittings have been salvaged from other stations and reused. The Midland Railway Trust even moved Whitwell Station in its entirety to Butterley.

Some of the restored locomotives were acquired with the tracks from British Rail, some were brought from industrial concerns like the National Coal Board, and others were brought back from overseas. Many came from Woodham's Scrapyard in Barry which became a graveyard for old engines in the 1960s. In the 1970s a few reproductions of famous locomotives were also built: a copy of *Locomotion Number One* was made for the 150th anniversary of the Stockton-Darlington Railway in 1975, and reproductions of the trains used in the Rainhill Trails were built for the Liverpool-Manchester Railway anniversary celebrations in 1980.

A few preserved railways like the Bluebell operate all year round. Elsewhere winter services may be restricted, as with the Romney, Hythe and Dymchurch Railway. A few, like the Watercress Line which has a connecting station at Alton, link into the national rail network which makes commercial passenger operation more feasible. Others operate special services like 'Santa Specials' (Nene Valley Railway) and Enthusiasts' Days when train buffs will flock from around the country. The Romney, Hythe and Dymchurch Railway, 'the world's smallest public railway', operates open-top carriages in summer, while the Kent and East Sussex Railway offers passengers Pullman luxury and four-course Sunday dinners. The Rail Preservation Society of Ireland also runs 160-mile railtours of Northern Ireland in summer. The smallest railways may only operate on summer weekends and bank holidays.

The Main Rail Network and Tourism

British Rail was slow to appreciate the touristic potential of some of its routes. For example, it was narrowly prevented from closing the Settle to Carlisle line across Yorkshire which was expensive to operate because of the cost of maintaining the viaducts, etc. A Settle to Carlisle Railway Trust was set up to help restore the most important structures and provide interpretation for tourists. British Rail, the tourist boards and local authorities then collaborated to publicise the line, and by 1989 it was carrying more than 500,000 people a year.

Some of the new rail companies now work with the British Tourist Authority to publicise rail routes through exceptionally beautiful countryside like the Inverness to Kyle of Lochalsh and Shrewsbury to Aberystwyth runs.

In the 1990s reopening railways was seen as a possible way of dealing with the congestion at popular tourist destinations. So the Peak Railway Society was hoping to reopen a stretch of railway which ran through beautiful Monsal Head until 1968. With the Peak District sinking beneath the weight of an annual 22 million visitors, a new railway is seen as one way to alleviate traffic pressure on Bakewell in particular. But with the cost of just one bridge over the existing A6 likely to cost £500,000 there's no certainty over the outcome of its plans.

The Ffestiniog Railway Society has also been given a £6 million grant from the Millennium Commission to restore the railway line from Caernarfon to Mount Snowdon by the year 2000. Caernarfon has been without a station for 30 years and its visitor numbers have been falling. A new line might help reverse the decline.

Ironically the success of the restored railways caused British Rail to reconsider using steam trains. Steam services were reintroduced on the York-Leeds-Harrogate, and Carnforth-Sellafield routes in 1978. Occasional steam trains also operate on the Mallaig line in Scotland and on the York to Scarborough route.

In 1995 the Railway Heritage Trust estimated that Britain had 1,383 listed railway structures, 59 scheduled railway monuments and 1,147 railway buildings in conservation areas. In 1994-5 Railtrack and British Rail gave the Trust £1.8 million to carry out restoration work on some of these monuments, including Bristol Temple Meads Station, the Ribblehead Viaduct, the Midland Grand Hotel, St Pancras Station and the roof of Paddington Station.

The Preserved Railways and Tourism

Many of the preserved railways are mainly local tourist attractions and carry relatively few people. Others attract visitors from further afield and carry increasing numbers of people each year. The North Yorkshire Moors Railway, running through a bleak area of National Park, managed to draw about 262,000 passengers in 1995, while the Bluebell Railway and Romney, Hythe and Dymchurch Railways, both in the easily accessible south-east area of England, drew 171,000 and 140,000 passengers respectively. The West Somerset Railway, operating out of the holiday town of Minehead, also attracted 128,378 passengers, while the North Norfolk Railway, operating out of the holiday town of Sheringham, drew 125,000.

Joint publicity ventures have given a higher profile to some of the preserved railways which offer 'scenic rail journeys' and made it easier for them to get their publicity to its potential audience. Publicity can do a great deal to boost passenger numbers. For example, the number of people travelling on the Keighley and Worth Railway, which passes through Haworth (a popular destination because of the Parsonage Museum associated with the Bronte sisters) tends to rise whenever the film *The Railway Children*, in which it appeared, is shown on television.

A list of the UK's preserved railways appears in Appendix II.

OTHER RAILWAY ATTRACTIONS

Museums

The UK also has several railway museums, including the National Railway Museum (a branch of the Science Museum) in York, the Great Western Museum in Swindon, the Didcot Railway Centre, the Midland Railway Centre at Butterley and the Steamport Museum in Southport. Many railway preservation societies also run small museums alongside the tracks, as at the Lytham Motive Power Museum and Lytham Creek Railway. A problem for railway museums is that the movement which is essential to what they are showing is rarely possible. The National Railway Museum therefore makes use of videos, films and working exhibits to try and bring the museum to life. Visitors can board some of the trains or look through the windows at wax replica passengers, again to try and make the experience more real. Occasionally some of the trains actually run on Railtrack lines, although this can't be done often because the museum's main priority is to preserve the trains undamaged.

Stations

The Manchester Museum of Science and Technology (joint winner of the 1990 National Heritage Museum of the Year award) was created in and around the old buildings of Manchester's Liverpool Road Station, while the royal waiting room at Wolferton Station near Sandringham has been restored to its 1868 appearance and opened to visitors. The newest restored station is Hulme End, a rural station on the Leek and Manifold Light Railway in the Peak District, which now houses a visitor centre.

Other Buildings

Railtrack is responsible for about 400 buildings of architectural or historic importance, including the Midland Grand Hotel at St. Pancras and Kings Cross Station which are Grade I listed buildings. In the past British Rail's record on caring for old buildings was not good; the Victorian Society was set up largely in reaction to the demolition of the huge arch outside Euston Station in 1962, and in 1984 the beautiful station at Derby was ruthlessly pulled down, despite being in a designated 'railway conservation area'. Fortunately by the 1990s the political climate had become more favourable to restoration and some listed buildings, including Liverpool Street Station, were restored to their former grandeur after years of neglect. Others like Bath's Green Park Station, a listed Grade II building and now a Sainsbury's supermarket, have been sold to private owners for redevelopment.

Other Leisure Possibilities

Sometimes the loss of a railway has produced other leisure opportunities. So the High Peak Trail for walkers, cyclists and pony trekkers was laid out along the route of the old Cromford and High Peak Railway track once train services stopped.

The marketing of Stockton-on-Tees centres on its importance as 'the birthplace of railways'. A Rail Heritage trail runs from the town hall, where the idea of the railway was first mooted, to the first ticket office. A Railway Heritage Centre has also been added to Preston Park Museum.

THE CANALS

Although locks were being added to English rivers to make navigation easier as early as the 16th century, it wasn't until the mid-18th century that true canals started to be built, usually to link up rivers or to connect a town to the sea. When the Duke of Bridgewater built a canal complete with aqueduct to carry coal from the mines at Worsley to Manchester he sparked off the first burst of canal fever. This was followed in the 1790s by true 'canal mania', characterised by great feats of engineering like the building of the Ellesmere Canal from Nantwich to Llangollen, and the Manchester Ship Canal joining Manchester to the sea. This canal, one of the last to be built, was completed in 1894.

The canals' popularity was shortlived since it was soon obvious that the new railways offered an even better way of moving industrial products around. Work only began on the Kennet and Avon Canal, linking the two rivers, in 1810, but already by 1841 the creation of the Great Western Railway threatened its profitability. Like most of the canals it was in complete decay by 1948 when about half the canals were nationalised and taken into the care of the British Transport Commission (BTC).

Fortunately canal enthusiasts, like railway lovers, could see a life beyond heavy goods transportation for the waterways. Many canals run through areas of unspoilt countryside, are lined with industrial monuments and are home to mammals and birds. Even in the 19th century some individuals were holidaying on the waterways at home and abroad and some of the Canal Acts specifically allowed for recreational use of the canals provided the locks weren't involved. Many of the canals were also designated 'water highways' which meant they couldn't be closed unless no one had used them for three years.

In 1946 the Inland Waterways Association (IWA) was founded to restored some of the canals. By 1949 the Lower Avon Navigation Trust had been set up to oversee the rebuilding of crumbling locks and the dredging of navigable channels. In 1961 the National Trust took over the South Stratford Canal from the British Transport Commission. Then in 1962 the British Waterways Board (BWB, now British Waterways) replaced the BTC. Its remit was to develop amenity and recreational use of the inland waterways. Almost half Britain's rivers and canals were taken into its care and a Waterways Recovery Group was set up to run volunteer restoration programmes. The 1986 Transport Act set up an Inland Waterways Amenity Advisory Council to suggest new ways of running the canals which were categorised into those with cruising, commercial or 'other' potential.

But just as restoring the railways was extremely expensive, so was restoring the canals. Many had been left to rot and were not only full of rubbish and choked with weeds and silt but also crumbling as well. In 1960 the National Trust agreed to invest £53,000 in restoring the Stratford-upon-Avon Canal. Between 1965 and 1981 the Kennet and Avon Canal Trust raised almost £750,000 to restore 43 locks, re-line parts of the canal and restore the Claverton and Crofton pumping stations. By 1973 £190,000 had been spent on restoring the Upper Avon Navigation from Evesham to Stratford, and it was the same all over the country.

THE KENNET AND AVON CANAL

The Kennet and Avon Canal, stretching 87 miles from Bristol to Reading, was the work of John Rennie who also designed the Dundas and Avoncliff aqueducts. As well as wildlife habitats, the canal boasts 161 buildings and structures of historic or arcitectural importance. The single most striking feature is the Caen Hill flight of 19 locks.

In 1996 the Heritage Lottery Fund awarded the canal a grant of £25 million towards a £29 million programme of heritage and environmental conservation and visitor improvement works. New access points with ramps and better parking facilities are to be provided and there will be a new marina and waterside restaurants. Once these are completed it's hoped that an extra £28 million a year will be injected into the local economy and that jobs for 2,600 people will have been created. The £4 million of matching funds will come from the Kennet & Avon Canal Trust, British Waterways, private sector businesses near the canal and an assortment of local authorities.

Like the railway preservation societies, the canal preservation trusts relied heavily on volunteer labour. They also received considerable help from various government job creation schemes in the 1970s and 1980s. The Kennet and Avon Canal Trust even used labour from Winson Green Prison.

Funding also came from a variety of sources. The preservation trusts have been very active as fund-raisers, but money has also come from local authorities, British Waterways, the Department of the Environment, the Countryside Commission, the National Parks Authority (Brecon and Abergavenny Canal), the Tourist Boards, the Sports Council (Upper Avon Navigation), the Science Museum (Coalport Canal) and private individuals. In addition government funding has sometimes been available through Land Drainage Grants and Derelict Land Restoration Grants, or through the Single Regeneration Budget or City Challenge Scheme. By 1979 perhaps £55 million had been spent on restoring and improving canals and rivers in the care of British Waterways. The result was the creation of almost 14,000 jobs, many of them in rural areas with few other openings. In 1993 the first National Waterway Walk was opened to follow the Grand Union Canal towpath for 145 miles from London to Birmingham.

In 1996 British Waterways was managing around 3,200 kilometres of canals in England, Scotland and Wales.

Canals and Tourism

Restored canals offer opportunities for barge and canoeing holidays. The towpaths are also ideal for walkers and cyclists. Horses are not allowed on some towpaths but in other areas like Calderdale horse-drawn canal trips are available. Anglers and birdwatchers may also enjoy canal holidays. In some areas like Little Venice in London and Farmer's Bridge in Birmingham towpaths and buildings have been designated conservation areas. Some canals like the Grand Western in Devon, are now linear country parks, and some local authorities have created picnic areas beside them. Attractive pubs with outdoor eating areas often stand beside the canals, especially near the locks. British Waterways must maintain designated 'cruising' canals so they can be used by powered boats, although by-laws usually limit their speed.

Many canals, particularly those that pass through towns, are lined with industrial monuments which can be promoted as tourist attractions in their own right; a good example is the Wigan Pier Heritage Centre which was created out of decaying warehouses on the banks of the Leeds-Liverpool Canal (Fig.8/3). The National Tourist Boards of England, Scotland and Wales and the British Marine Industries Federation have also promoted the following 'Seven Wonders of the Waterways':

- Anderton Vertical Lift in Cheshire
- Pontcysyllte Aqueduct on the Llangollen Canal
- Standedge Tunnel on Huddersfield Narrow Canal
- Barton Swing Aqueduct which carries the Bridgewater Canal over the Manchester Ship Canal
- Bingley Five Rise Locks in Yorkshire
- Burnley Embankment on the Leeds-Liverpool Canal
- Caen Hill flight of locks on the Kennet and Avon Canal

Publicity is very important, and some canal trusts have Interpretation Officers to make the most of the opportunities. The Kennet and Avon Canal Trust has an information centre at Devizes and also produces a guide/map to what to see along the canal.

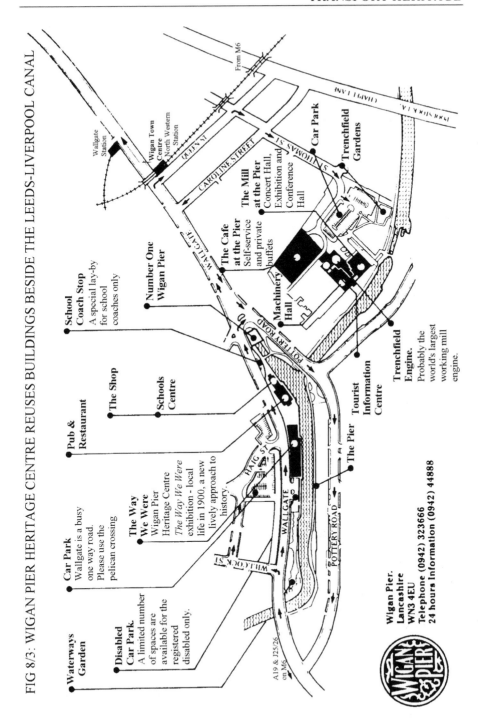

FIG 8/3: WIGAN PIER HERITAGE CENTRE REUSES BUILDINGS BESIDE THE LEEDS-LIVERPOOL CANAL

Waterways Garden

Car Park
Wallgate is a busy one way road. Please use the pelican crossing

Disabled Car Park.
A limited number of spaces are available for the registered disabled only.

School Coach Stop
A special lay-by for school coaches only

The Way We Were
Wigan Pier Heritage Centre *The Way We Were* exhibition - local life in 1900, a new lively approach to history.

Number One Wigan Pier

Pub & Restaurant

The Shop

Schools Centre

The Cafe at the Pier
Self-service and private buffets

The Mill at the Pier
Concert Hall, Exhibition and Conference Hall

Car Park

Trenchfield Gardens

Machinery Hall

The Pier

Tourist Information Centre

Trenchfield Engine.
Probably the world's largest working mill engine.

**Wigan Pier.
Lancashire
WN3 4EU
Telephone (0942) 323666
24 hours Information (0942) 44888**

Wallgate Station

Wigan Town Centre North Western Station

From M6

CAROLINE STREET

ST THOMAS ST

CHAPEL LANE

WALLGATE

POTTERY ROAD

HAIG ST

WALLGATE

WHELOCK ST

A19 & J25/26 on M6

Because of the many leisure activities possible on the canals it is difficult to give precise figures for the numbers of people making use of them. However, British Waterways estimates that 12 million people use its canals every year.

Figures for how many people are visiting buildings associated with the canals are more exact. There are, for example, several major waterways museums. In 1995 the Canal Museum at Stoke Bruerne on the Grand Union Canal received 38,663 visitors; the Boat Museum at Ellesmere Port, where the Shropshire Union joins the Manchester Ship Canal, 57,094; and the National Waterways Museum in Gloucester, in the old Llanthony Warehouse on the banks of the Gloucester-Sharpness Canal, 72,000.

SHIPS

As an island Great Britain has always been particularly dependent on its navy and shipping companies. Not surprisingly several of its major tourist attractions are ships.

London

Once a great port, London is home to several popular ships. The HMS *Belfast*, a Second World War Cruiser now owned by the Imperial War Museum, is moored near Tower Bridge and received 232,821 visitors in 1995. Nearby in the restored St. Katherine's Dock several old boats, including the *Challenge* and the *Nore*, are permanently moored although visitors can't board them. Ferries also carry tourists along the Thames to Greenwich, home of the National Maritime Museum, where the *Cutty Sark* (a 19th-century tea clipper) and *Gypsy Moth IV* (in which Sir Francis Chichester sailed round the world) can be visited. In 1995 the Museum received 609,008 visitors and the *Cutty Sark* 233,502.

Portsmouth

Portsmouth is also home to several famous ships, including the *Mary Rose* and Nelson's flagship the HMS *Victory*, which are moored together in an area developed as a 'naval heritage project' by the city's Tourist Development Action Programme. Also displayed here is the 19th-century iron-hulled HMS *Warrior*. In 1995 the Portsmouth Historic Ships attraction drew 544,032 visitors. What's more other local attractions which might otherwise have drawn only small number of visitors also benefited from Portsmouth's overall appeal to visitors; thus the Royal Naval Museum attracted 244,122 people in 1995. Portsmouth is due to receive £40 million from the Millennium Commission as a grant towards the £86 million cost of the Renaissance of Portsmouth Harbour Millennium Project.

Bristol

One of Bristol's most popular tourist attractions is Brunel's SS *Great Britain*, the first iron ship ever built which was abandoned in the Falklands in 1886 but later towed back to the dry dock where it was originally built for restoration. This work was funded by donations and ticket receipts, although the National Heritage Memorial Fund also assisted with grants totalling £50,000. It's now moored outside the Maritime Heritage Centre and attracted 91,735 visitors in 1995.

Dundee

The research ship the *Discovery* was originally built in Dundee in 1901 and, after many years of being moored on the Thames near Cleopatra's Needle, has now returned there. In 1995 105,677 people visited it.

Unfortunately most historic ships, and particularly the well-known ones, are no longer seaworthy or are too precious to risk putting to sea. Visitors therefore look at them in unnatural circumstances. Attempts are made to reveal what life would have been like on board ship: there are guides to take people round the *Victory*, while visitors to the SS *Great Britain* can watch a video about the ship before going on-board.

However, a few British steam boats still carry passengers. For example, the National Trust has restored an 1859 steam yacht to carry people across Lake Coniston. A steamer called the *Sir Walter Scott* has also operated on Loch Katrine since 1899. The UK's last sea-going paddle-steamer, the *Waverley*, has also been preserved by the Paddle Steamer Preservation Society and offers Bristol tourists the opportunity to travel along the Severn Estuary to Lundy Island in old-fashioned style.

ROADS AND ROAD TRANSPORT

Carriages

Many museums preserve old carriages from pre-motoring days. Maidstone has a particularly good collection, as does the Yorkshire Museum of Carriages and Horse-drawn Vehicles in Aysgarth. Sometimes carriages are an additional attraction in stately homes; a few are preserved in the stableyard at Donnington House. Others have been returned to service to carry tourists short distances, as at the National Waterways Museum in Gloucester.

Veteran and Vintage Cars

Just as old boats and trains hold great appeal for certain sectors of the tourist market, so there are many enthusiasts for *veteran* cars (those built before 1916) and *vintage* cars (those built between 1917 and 1930). Britain's best-known collection of motor vehicles, the National Motor Museum at Beaulieu, is also one of the most popular attractions in the whole country, receiving 415,600 visitors in 1995. However, there are smaller collections of old vehicles in most transport and many industrial museums. Some stately homes also keep collections of cars to broaden their appeal to visitors.

Beaulieu was the brainchild of Lord Montagu who inherited the Abbey in 1951. In 1952 he established the Montagu Motor Museum in the grounds. By 1962 there were more than 100 vehicles and in 1968 he decided to create a charitable trust to continue the work. In 1970 the National Motor Museum Trust was set up, opening to the public in 1972. It now has more than 200 exhibits, including four cars that have broken world land-speed records and some interesting old commercial vehicles. Recognising that it isn't always easy for visitors to stand in front of old cars and imagine what it would have been like to drive them, he introduced 'Wheels', an exhibition which takes people back through the social history of motoring from the comfort of time cars with synchronised commentaries. The commercial vehicles are shown in a recreated 1930s setting, complete with recorded sounds of street life. The prize exhibits are shown in a 'Hall of Fame'; normally a 1909 Rolls-Royce Silver Cloud is the centrepiece. Visitors can even look down on the restoration area where work is constantly going on to keep the cars in roadworthy condition.

While the basis for the museum was Lord Montagu's own collection which he made available to the Trust in 1970, cars are still bought, borrowed or occasionally donated to the Museum. Funding has been provided by the Area Museums Service for South Eastern England, the ETB and the Science Museum's Fund for the Preservation of Technological and Scientific Materials. The National Heritage Memorial Fund also gave £63,750 of the £85,000 needed to buy the *Bluebird* in which Donald Campbell set a new land speed record in 1964. Individual motor companies have also sponsored the Museum: for example, the 'Wheels' exhibition is sponsored by the Kenning Motor Group and the 'Hall of Fame' by *Motor* magazine. Like many charitable trusts the Museum also has a group of 'Friends' who receive free admission in return for their subscriptions.

The museum at Brooklands, near Weybridge, stands on the site of what was, in 1907, the first purpose-built racing circuit in the world. Visitors can visit the test-circuit hill with its steep gradients, the original clubhouse and the 'Fastest on Earth' exhibition.

Public Transport

Northern Ireland's most popular museum in 1995 (and 1983's Museum of the Year) was the Ulster Folk and Transport Museum in Belfast which was visited by 192,984 people. Almost as popular is the London Transport Museum in Covent Garden which attracted 182,000 visitors in 1995, probably because of its excellent position at the corner of a busy shopping centre. Both show a variety of different types of public transport vehicles including trams and buses. The London Transport Museum also shows a range of underground train compartments (London's underground system may be an amenity rather than an attraction, but some underground stations, particularly in Moscow, have become attractions in their own right). The Museum of British Road Transport in Coventry was visited by 63,473 people in 1995.

A few trams still trundle along the seafront in British holiday towns and on the promenade outside Derby Castle, but the only horse-drawn tram still in passenger service is at Douglas on the Isle of Man. Elsewhere trams are restricted to museums; Hull Transport and Archaeology Museum displays a horse-drawn tram from about 1867, while at Crich in Derbyshire a Tramway Museum shows the sort of electric trams that could eventually return to some city streets.

Road Structures

As yet there are no road preservation societies because roads are rarely closed, merely rebuilt. Nor are there many traces of older roads which are interesting enough to become tourist attractions. Part of a Roman road can be seen at Wade's Causeway on the North Yorkshire Moors and the Chalk Pits Museum at Amberley has reconstructions of different road surfaces. Otherwise the only touristic potential currently offered by the roads lies in the bridges and buildings associated with them. For example, a stretch of road designed by Thomas Telford has been reconstructed at Blists Hill complete with the 18th-century toll-gate that went alongside it.

Several bridges are tourist attractions in their own right, because of their age, because they are aesthetically pleasing or because they are associated with a famous engineer. The pretty bridges are usually the older ones, like the medieval clapper bridges of Dartmoor and the 14th-century three-sided Trinity Bridge at Crowland. Clifton Suspension Bridge in Bristol is the best example of a bridge associated with a particular engineer. Designed by Brunel (who was also responsible for the Royal Albert Bridge over the Tamar at Saltash) and finished in 1864, it still carries cars, charging a toll for the journey over the picturesque Avon Gorge.

Suspension bridges are always impressive. Britain's oldest is the Union Chain Bridge at Berwick which was constructed in 1820. The Forth Road Bridge was completed in 1890. More recent but just as impressive are the Severn and Humber Bridges which charge tolls. Sydney Harbour Bridge and the Golden Gate Bridge in San Francisco are examples of bridges overseas which are very popular with tourists.

Tower Bridge in London, with its familiar profile, was first opened in 1894. Until recently visitors could only admire it from afar, but it's now open as a real attraction offering fine views of the Thames and exhibits on its history. In 1995 404,130 people visited it.

The case of London Bridge, a very ordinary Thames bridge designed by John Rennie in 1831, shows how important a part a bridge can play in tourism. By the 1960s London Bridge was sinking into the clay of the Thames riverbed and the City of London Corporation decided to sell it. There were 500 requests for further information and 50 firm offers, from New Zealand, Canada, Korea, France and Japan. McCulloch Properties, part of an American oil company, finally paid £1,025,000 for it. The bridge was dismantled and each stone numbered. Then it was shipped from Surrey Commercial Docks through the Panama Canal, up to Long Beach California and across the desert to Arizona to be reconstructed on dry land on the shores of Lake Havusu. The surrounding area was then flooded and the bridge became the centrepiece of a new attraction which was soon drawing 2 million visitors a year, becoming the second most popular site in Arizona after the Grand Canyon.

AIR

Most planes that are preserved as attractions for the public are in military museums, including the Royal Air Force and Battle of Britain Museums in London. However, both Edinburgh and North Berwick have Museums of Flight. There is also an Aerospace Museum in Wolverhampton and an Air World at Caernarfon. Visitors can also see inside a reconstructed section of Concorde in Bristol's Industrial Museum.

The main problem with museums of flight is that they give no idea of the excitement of flying. However, there was a division of the Vickers aircraft company at Brooklands near Weybridge and the new museum there will include flight simulators in an attempt to overcome this difficulty.

CHAPTER 9 : COUNTRYSIDE ATTRACTIONS

If historic buildings are the mainstay of the UK tourist attractions industry, the countryside is also vitally important despite the fact that the British climate makes much of it inaccessible for much of the year. Countryside attractions are particularly important to the Highlands and Islands area of Scotland, parts of Wales and the Lake District.

A DEVELOPING APPRECIATION OF THE COUNTRYSIDE

Although the appeal of the countryside seems obvious in the 1990s, this has not always been the case. In fact it wasn't until the Romantic Movement of the late 18th century that people started to look on the countryside as intrinsically interesting. For example, Celia Fiennes' account of her travels in the north of England in 1698 makes only fleeting reference to the Lake District.

Nevertheless as early as 1639 an English climber had journeyed to Mount Snowdon, becoming its first recorded tourist. The poet Thomas Gray who visited the Lake District in 1769 is generally thought of as its first tourist, but as roads improved, making the countryside more accessible, others quickly followed in his footsteps. This trend was probably reinforced by political unrest in late 18th-century Europe which made the popular Grand Tour too dangerous; touring Britain was seen as a good alternative. By the end of the 18th century Gainsborough, Turner and Constable had all visited the Lake District and appreciated its beauty. It was William Wordsworth who gave it the final stamp of approval when, in his *Guide to the Lakes* written in 1810, he commented that 'persons of pure taste deem the district a sort of national property in which every man has a right and interest who has an eye to perceive and a heart to enjoy'.

The first visitors to the Welsh mountains and the Lake District tended to be most impressed by their 'horrible grandeur' and wildness. In his *Picturesque Tours* written in 1782 William Gilpin commented on the rugged beauty of the Lake District and suggested that visitors should use their imaginations to people and flower it. However, many tourists found the countryside alarming and carried Claude eyeglasses which let them view it neatly framed and tinted to whatever colour suited their tastes.

Appreciation of the countryside increased as the railways brought it within reach of more people. In 1843/4 just 12,000 passenger vehicles passed the turnpike on the Kendal to Windermere road. Then in 1846 trains started to operate between London and Carlisle, with a branch line running to Windermere. Links to Coniston, Keswick and Cockermouth quickly followed. By 1847/8 the new railways were bringing 120,000 people a year to the Lakes, with two-thirds of them arriving between May and October. Naturally hotels were built and boats provided to enable them to explore. On Whit Monday in 1883 10,000 day trippers went to Bowness, 8,000 of them arriving on the Kendal line and 2,000 on the Furness one.

FIG.9/1: PROTECTED AREAS AND NATIONAL COUNTRYSIDE INITIATIVES IN ENGLAND

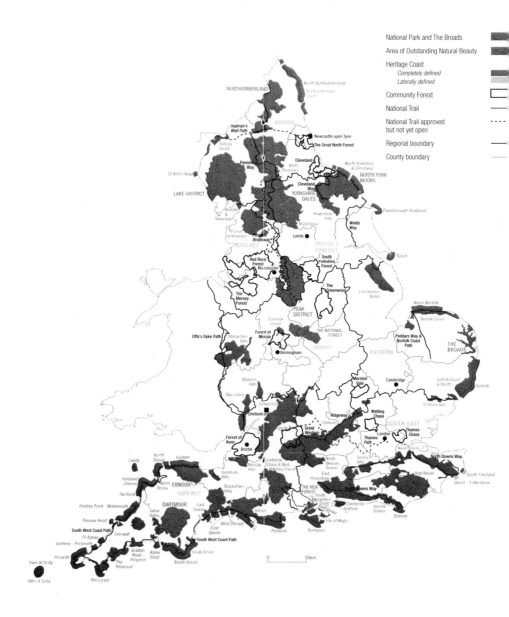

National Park and The Broads

Area of Outstanding Natural Beauty

Heritage Coast
  Completely defined
  Laterally defined

Community Forest

National Trail

National Trail approved
but not yet open

Regional boundary

County boundary

From the start some people feared that the countryside would be destroyed by the volume of visitors. In 1844 Wordsworth was already complaining about the impact of the Kendal to Windermere railway, and by 1883 a Lake District Defence Society had been set up to guard against intrusions on the scenery including touristic development. A century later the problem was even more pressing as private cars gave everyone who wanted it access to as much of the countryside as they liked.

COUNTRYSIDE CONSERVATION

If people are to be able to enjoy the countryside it must be protected against the constant threat of redevelopment, destructive farming practices and so on. In the USA this was acknowledged as long ago as 1864 when President Lincoln signed an Act of Congress giving Yosemite Valley and Mariposa Grove to the State of California as a public park, to be 'inalienable for all time'. In doing so he created the world's first national park in all but name. Then in 1872 Yellowstone, home of the 'Old Faithful' geyser, became the first official national park in the USA. By the 1990s two million people a year were streaming through Yellowstone, the vast majority of them during the summer months. The US national parks have been owned and administered by the federal government since the 1916 National Park Service Act.

In the UK most land, even in the remotest areas, is privately owned. Its preservation depends on control of development and incentives to encourage beneficial use of it. The basis for protection of the most scenically beautiful areas of England and Wales is the 1949 National Parks and Access to the Countryside Act which authorised the creation of ten National Parks, mostly in upland areas (see Fig.9/2). It also established National Park Direction Areas in Scotland, where specific planning rules would apply. In addition the act designated Areas of Outstanding National Beauty (AONBs), National Nature Reserves (NNRs), Local Nature Reserves (LNRs) and Sites of Special Scientific Interest (SSSIs). All these were to be subject to special protective measures to conserve them. The National Parks Commission was set up to advise on running the new parks. In 1968 the NPC became the Countryside Commission, with extended responsibilities for the countryside as a whole. Since 1991 the Countryside Commission and the Countryside Council for Wales have shared responsibility for the national parks.

The National Parks

The International Union for the Conservation of Nature and Natural Resources (IUCN) promotes the creation of protected landscapes to 'maintain nationally significant natural landscapes which are characteristic of the harmonious interaction of man and land, while providing opportunities for public enjoyment through recreation and tourism within the normal lifestyle and economic activity of these areas.' According to the IUCN the expression 'national park' should be applied to wilderness areas not materially altered by human exploitation or occupation. They should also be owned or managed by the government.

COUNTRYSIDE ATTRACTIONS

The first ten national parks of England and Wales were designated by the National Parks Commission under the authority of the 1949 National Parks and Access to the Countryside Act. They are extensive areas of relatively wild country where the landscape's characteristic beauty is strictly protected and the wildlife and historic buildings are conserved. Nevertheless existing farming continues and facilities for public access and enjoyment are provided so they are not strictly wildernesses in line with the IUCN definition.

FIG.9/2: THE NATIONAL PARKS, THE BROADS AND THE NEW FOREST

(Source : Countryside Commission)

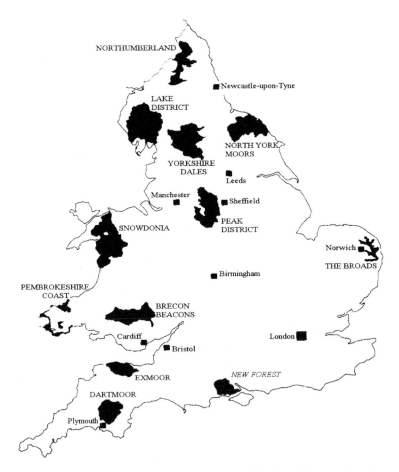

In 1989 the Broads Authority was established, making the Broads a national park in all but name. By 1996 the 11 parks covered 14,011 square kilometres between them (see Fig.9/3).

214

In 1973 an application to designate the Cambrian Mountains was rejected. However, the New Forest in Hampshire is administered by the Forestry Commission under a mandate from the Ministry of Agriculture. It, too, is a national park in all but name. Neither Scotland nor Northern Ireland has any national parks. However, the Countryside Commission for Scotland is pressing for the Cairngorms, the Ben Nevis-Glencoe area, Wester Ross and the Loch Lomond-Trossachs area to be designated either national parks or Scottish Wilderness/ National Heritage Areas.

FIG.9/3: THE NATIONAL PARKS OF ENGLAND AND WALES

Name	Established	Area (sq.kms)	Visitor Days (estimated, 1994)
Dartmoor	1951	954	3,825,000
Lake District	1951	2292	13,925,000
Peak District	1951	1438	12,400,000
Snowdonia	1951	2142	6,568,000
North York Moors	1952	1436	7,790,000
Pembrokeshire Coast	1952	584	4,662,000
Exmoor	1954	693	1,397,000
Yorkshire Dales	1954	1769	8,303,000
Northumberland	1956	1049	1,408,000
Brecon Beacons	1957	1351	3,622,000
The Broads	1989	303	5,361,000

(**Note**: Visitor figures for The Broads and the Pembrokeshire Coast are thought to be overestimated and those for the Lake District, Peak District and Snowdonia underestimated)

(Source: Countryside Commission)

Since 1974 each park has been administered by a National Park Authority (NPA). However, only the Lake District and Peak District authorities are in sole control; the other park authorities work with local councils. Since the 1995 Environment Act the Environment Secretary has been able to appoint half the members of the NPAs minus one. All the NPAs are overseen by the Countryside Commission and 75% of their running costs come from central government.

The National Park Authorities make planning decisions and offer help, grants and advice on land management, public access, etc. to landowners within the parks. Their statutory duties are:

- to protect and enhance the character of the landscape
- to enable the public to enjoy the parks as recreation areas, and
- to protect the social and economic well-being of the local communities

COUNTRYSIDE ATTRACTIONS

The National Park Authorities have the power to purchase land compulsorily, to restrict development and to issue tree preservation orders.

Despite their legal protection, the national parks still face threats, particularly from the changing nature of agriculture. Other threats include:

- military use which makes public access virtually impossible in parts of Dartmoor
- quarrying (a particular threat in the Peak District)
- housing and office developments
- increased afforestation with non-indigeneous species of tree
- new roads.

In 1972 permission was granted for the A66 which runs through the Lake District National Park from Penrith to Workington to be widened to provide better access to the park. As a result the *Sandford Report* ruled that where the preservation

---

FIG.9/4: ASPECTS OF THE NATIONAL PARKS, THE BROADS AND THE NEW FOREST MOST ENJOYED IN 1994 (% OF RESPONDENTS)

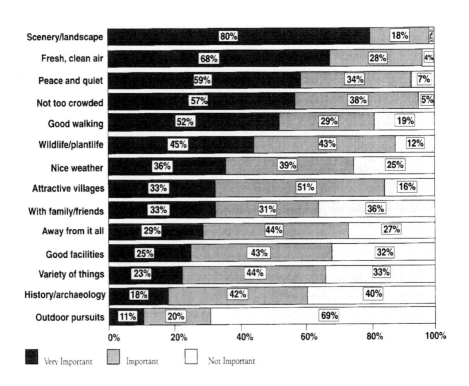

(Source: Countryside Commission)

216

of natural beauty and public enjoyment of the park came into conflict, priority should be given to conserving the park's natural beauty. The Report's recommendations were accepted in 1976 and plans to route the Manchester to Sheffield motorway through the Peak District National Park were dropped. However, since then the Okehampton bypass has been built on Dartmoor, proving that the threat is still alive.

Tourism also presents a threat to the parks, especially to specific over-popular parts of the Lake District and Peak District parks. This is a problem the British parks share with their European counterparts. In *Loving Them to Death?,* the Europarc Federation, representing around 200 protected areas in 29 countries, highlighted the need to develop strategies to protect these fragile areas from their visitors.

Visitors to the National Parks

The 1994 National Parks Visitor Survey suggested that six out of ten visitor days spent in the National Parks are by holidaymakers. Only the Brecon Beacons and the Peak District received more day trippers than holidaymakers. Many visitors were returners already familiar with the park, and 91% arrived by private car. Most came

FIG.9/5: TYPE OF VISITOR TO THE NATIONAL PARKS, THE BROADS AND THE NEW FOREST, 1994

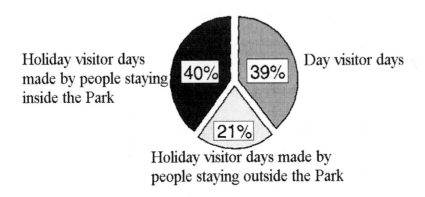

Holiday visitor days made by people staying inside the Park — 40%

Day visitor days — 39%

Holiday visitor days made by people staying outside the Park — 21%

to walk and gave the reason for their visit as 'the scenery and landscape' (58%) or 'the peace and quiet' (29%). On average day trippers spent £6.90 in or around the park, while holidaymakers spent between £8.80 and £13.50 depending on whether they were staying in the park or elsewhere. The average visitor spent £3.22 on food and drink and a further £3.24 on shopping in the area.

FIG.9/6: GROUP STRUCTURE OF VISITORS TO THE NATIONAL PARKS, THE BROADS AND THE NEW FOREST, 1994

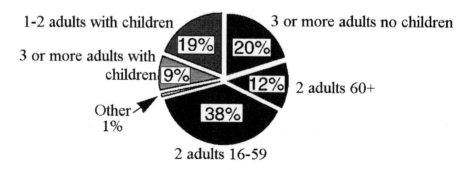

1-2 adults with children

3 or more adults no children

3 or more adults with children 9%

19% 20%

12% 2 adults 60+

Other 1%

38%

2 adults 16-59

THE BROADS

Now Britain's finest remaining wetland, the Norfolk and Suffolk Broads, 200 kilometres of navigable river and 40 lakes, originated as an area of flooded medieval peat workings. In the 1880s the Victorians discovered the Broads using Wroxham Station as their base. Yachting became popular, and by the 1920s the first motorboats appeared on the Broads. By 1986 boating holidays were generating 1400 local jobs and attracting £14 million into the local economy. By 1995 there were 10,640 private boats in the area and another 2,445 for hire, many of them through Blakes and Hoseasons.

The Broads Authority has the task of managing the area in the interests of conservation, public enjoyment and navigation. Two thirds of its £3,124,000 annual funding comes from the Department of the Environment and eight local authorities, the remaining third from tolls levied on boats.

However, the Broads environment is very fragile. By the mid-1980s the wash from the boats was eroding the river banks, plants were disappearing and algae was thriving in the increasingly polluted water. European grants for cereal crops also encouraged farmers to fill in dykes, drain off water with electric pumps and switch from traditional cattle and sheep grazing to growing wheat.

In 1993 the Broads Authority report *No Easy Answers* set out its strategy for sustainable management of the area. From 1993 to 1996 it worked with the EU on a LIFE-funded Restoration of the Norfolk Broads project aimed at ridding the Broads of algae and generally reviving them. The Norfolk Windmills Trust is trying to raise funds to preserve the surviving windmills while Halvergate Marshes, with its historic waterways and 29 drainage mills, is now a conservation area, unusually since most conservation areas are in towns. The Ministry of Agriculture now provides payments to farmers who continue to graze cattle.

FIG.9/7: MAIN PURPOSE OF DAY TRIPS TO THE NATIONAL PARKS, THE BROADS AND THE NEW FOREST, 1994

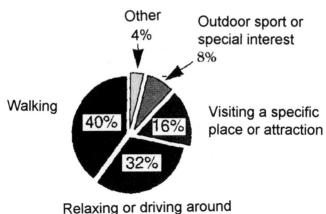

Other 4%

Outdoor sport or special interest 8%

Walking 40%

16% Visiting a specific place or attraction

32%

Relaxing or driving around

THE LAKE DISTRICT NATIONAL PARK

The Lake District is the largest national park and its wonderful lake and mountain scenery has been popular with visitors for two centuries. Roughly 40,000 people live within the park boundaries but they are hugely outnumbered by the 12 million tourists who visit each year. Just over 41% of land within the park is owned by the state, 24% by the National Trust and 21% by private individuals. The rest is owned by the National Park Authority, the Forestry Commission and North West Water. There are 4 national nature reserves, 13 other nature reserves, 16 conservation areas, 79 Sites of Special Scientific Interest, 150 scheduled ancient monuments and 1179 listed buildings inside the park boundaries. The Lake District has also been proposed (although not yet accepted) as a World Heritage Site.

The National Park Authority, or Lake District Special Planning Board, is charged with carrying out the aims of the 1949 National Parks and Access to the Countryside Act. In the course of a year it may deal with up to 1200 applications to build within the park, most of them for housing. It also looks after conservation; town and county planning procedures; providing interpretation, information and recreational facilities for visitors; offering support and advice to the local communities; and on management and administration.

The NPA Visitor Services Department is based at Brockhole where a National Park Visitor Centre is open to the public from March to November each year. In 1995 it was visited by 155,000 people. This department also looks after the visitor centres at Bowness, Coniston, Gosforth, Grasmere, Hawkshead, Keswick, Pooley Bridge, Seatoller, Ullswater and Waterhead which, between them, receive about 700,000 visitors a year. It also provides a weather service to advise fell walkers, looks after the car parks, prepares the park's leaflets, videos and publicity materials, administers a boating centre and caravan/camp site, and provides accommodation in the Blencathra Centre. Administration and planning applications are handled from Kendal, while the park management which is responsible for maintaining footpaths, running the ranger service, providing signposts and negotiating land use agreements with local landowners is based at Brockhole. Altogether the Lake District National Park provides around 100 permanent jobs, although it also makes use of volunteers, particularly as wardens.

Roughly 88% of visitors to the Lake District are on holiday. Only 7% of visitors come from overseas, with more than a third of these coming from North America. Of domestic visitors 31% come from the north west, 20% from London and the South East, and 15% from the north of England. Over a third of visitors arrive during July and August although an increasing number of people visit in the off-peak period.

The most popular specific attractions within the park are the Brockhole and Whinlatter Visitor Centres, the Lakeside to Haverthwaite and Ravenglass to Eskdale Railways, Lowther Park, Dove Cottage and the Wordsworth Museum in Grasmere, Beatrix Potter's house at Hill Top, near Sawrey, the Windermere Steamboat Museum, Rydal Mount and the Cumberland Pencil Museum.

An estimated 15% of Cumbrians work in tourism so the Lake District is hugely important to the local economy. However, it has to be carefully managed if it's not to be destroyed by its own overwhelming popularity. The Regional Tourism Strategy for Cumbria emphasises the need to preserve the quieter parts of the park (the west and east dales, and the northern fringes). It also states that there should be a presumption against granting permission for further major accommodation developments or for new attractions that are not in keeping with the stated aims of the park, i.e. to protect and enhance the natural beauty of the scenery.

Areas of Outstanding Natural Beauty

The 1949 National Parks and Access to the Countryside Act also authorised the designation of Areas of Outstanding Natural Beauty in places of particularly fine landscape quality. There are 40 AONBs covering nearly 14% of England and Wales (see Fig.9/8). It is hoped that the Tamar and Tavy valleys, and the Berwyn Mountains will also be designated in the future.

Once an Area of Outstanding Natural Beauty has been designated, it's easier for planning authorities to justify turning down unsuitable large-scale developments like new roads and reservoirs. Sometimes extra money for conservation also becomes available. Local authorities are not obliged to set up special administrative procedures for AONBs but are encouraged to appoint an officer to co-ordinate procedures and draw up a management plan. They are also encouraged to produce a Statement of Intent and plans to resolve local disputes over land usage.

In Northern Ireland the 1965 Amenity Lands Act authorised the Department of the Environment to designate Areas of Outstanding Natural Beauty, the region's only category of wholly protected landscape. In doing so it was advised by the Ulster Countryside Committee and the Committee for Nature Conservation. As a result of the Nature Conservation and Amenity Lands Order (NI) of 1985, Mourne, the Antrim Coast and Glens, the Causeway Coast and the Ring of Gullion were designated. There are also plans to designate Erne Lakeland and Fermanagh Caveland in the future.

FIG.9/8: AREAS OF OUTSTANDING NATURAL BEAUTY IN ENGLAND AND WALES

1956	Gower Peninsula	1967	Anglesey
1957	Quantock Hills	1967	South Hampshire Coast
1957	Lleyn Peninsula	1968	Norfolk Coast
1958	Northumberland Coast	1968	Kent Downs
1958	Surrey Hills	1970	Suffolk Coast and Heaths
1958	Cannock Chase	1970	Dedham Vale
1959	Shropshire Hills	1971	Wye Valley
1959	Dorset	1972	North Wessex Downs
1959	Malvern Hills	1972	Mendip Hills
1959	Cornwall	1972	Arnside and Silverdale
1960	North Devon	1973	Lincolnshire Wolds
1960	South Devon	1976	Isles of Scilly
1962	East Hampshire	1983	High Weald
1963	East Devon	1983	Cranborne Chase/West
1963	Isle of Wight		Wiltshire Downs
1964	Chichester Harbour	1985	Clwydian Range
1964	Forest of Bowland	1990	North Pennines
1964	Solway Coast	1990	Blackdown Hill
1965	Chilterns	1990	Howardian Hills
1966	Sussex Downs	1994	Nidderdale
1966	Cotswolds		

(Source: Countryside Commission)

In Scotland the Town and Country Planning (Scotland) Act of 1978 authorised the Secretary of State for Scotland, advised by the Countryside Commission for Scotland, to designate 40 National Scenic Areas (Fig.9/9). Most of these NSAs are in north and west Scotland and the islands; altogether they cover 12.9% of the land and inland waters of Scotland.

Once an NSA has been designated special planning procedures apply whenever five or more houses, flats, chalets or caravans or a non-residential development covering more than half a hectare are planned. Roadworks costing more than £100,000, vehicle tracks and buildings which would be more than 12 metres high are also subject to restrictions. All such proposals must be vetted by the Countryside Commission for Scotland. Where there is disagreement the Secretary of State for Scotland may be asked to arbitrate.

FIG.9/9: NATIONAL SCENIC AREAS IN SCOTLAND

(Source: Scottish Natural Heritage)

Sites of Special Scientific Interest

As a result of the 1949 National Parks and Access to the Countryside Act the Nature Conservancy Council (NCC, now English Nature) could also designate areas of land which were of special interest because of their flora, fauna, geological or physiographical features. The owners were then required to give the NCC at least three months notice of changes which were likely to damage the sites.

FIG.9/10: THE WEB OF ENVIRONMENTAL INITIALS

Area of Outstanding Natural Beauty	AONB
Area of Special Scientific Interest	ASSI
Environmentally Sensitive Area	ESA
Local Nature Reserve	LNR
Marine Nature Reserve	MNR
National Nature Reserve	NNR
National Park	NP
National Park Authority	NPA
National Scenic Area	NSA
Site of Special Scientific Interest	SSSI
Special Protection Area	SPA

The 1981 Wildlife and Countryside Act required the NCC to redesignate all the 4000 SSSIs and then contact their 30,000 owners to tell them what activities would be likely to damage the site. The ensuing delay provided an opening for unscrupulous landowners to take preemptive action to prevent their land being designated; between March 1983 and March 1984 156 SSSIs, or 3.7% of the total, were damaged, mainly by ploughing, drainage schemes, reseeding or the use of fertilisers and sprays.

The 1985 Wildlife and Countryside Amendment Act extended the period of notice farmers were required to give before carrying out work on an SSSI to four months. However, the legislation is not always as effective as it should be. Even though Rainham Marshes in Essex is an SSSI, MCA International won the consent of Havering District Council to develop a Universal City theme park on it. Fortunately this plan didn't come to fruition.

There are currently 3,874 SSSIs, covering more than 900,00 hectares and in the care of 23,000 owners. The best are also designated National Nature Reserves (NNRs, see below). Some, which are important bird habitats, are also designated Special Protection Area (SPAs). Other wetland sites are also designated Ramsar Sites or 'wetlands of international importance' requiring special safeguards. English Nature is in overall charge of supervising the SSSIs and NNRs and advises the government on which should be designated sites of European importance.

In Northern Ireland Areas of Special Scientific Interest (ASSIs) are the equivalent of SSSIs.

COUNTRYSIDE ATTRACTIONS

Environmentally Sensitive Areas

By the mid-1970s it was clear that intensive farming methods were destroying traditional landscapes to produce surplus food stocks. For example, between 1946 and 1975 it was estimated that 25% of English and Welsh hedgerows had been dug up to make fields more manageable. As part of a rethink of British agricultural policies, the 1986 Agriculture Act empowered the Minister of Agriculture (advised by the Countryside Commission, Nature Conservancy Council, English Heritage and Cadw) to designate Environmentally Sensitive Areas where farmers would be encouraged to farm in ways that would conserve the wildlife and archaeological features of their land. By 1997, there were 43 ESAs in the UK, including 22 in England.

FIG.9/11: ENVIRONMENTALLY SENSITIVE AREAS OF THE UK

ENGLAND

Lake District	Pennine Dales	North Kent Marshes
North Peak	South West Peak	Shropshire Hills
Clun (Shropshire border)	Radnor	Cotswold Hills
Upper Thames Tributaries	Brecklands	Broads
Suffolk River Valleys	Essex Coast	South Downs
Test Valley	Avon Valley	South Wessex Downs
Somerset Levels and Moors	Exmoor	Blackdown Hills
Dartmoor	West Penwith	

SCOTLAND

Machair of the Uists and Benbecula, Barra and Vatersay	Breadalbane	Argyll Islands
	Loch Lomond	Stewarty
Cairngorms Straths	Central Southern Uplands	Central Borders
Western Southern Uplands	Shetland Isles	

NORTHERN IRELAND

Antrim Coast, Glens and Rathlin	Croob	Sperrins
Mourne Mountains and Slieve	West Fermanagh and Erne Lakeland	Slieve Gullion

WALES

Ynys Mon	Lleyn Peninsula	Clwydian Range
Cambrian Mountains	Preseli	

(Source: MAFF)

ESAs are administered by the Ministry for Agriculture, Farming and Fisheries (MAFF) via the Farm and Rural Conservation Agency, and farmers are given incentives to restrict use of herbicides and pesticides, to preserve hedges, ditches and barns, and to protect historical features of the landscape. In 1997, more than 8,000 farmers were involved in the scheme.

National Nature Reserves

The 1949 Act also created National Nature Reserves (NNRs) on some of the UK's finest wildlife sites. By 1995 there were 164 NNRs covering 0.5% of England with at least one in most counties. English Nature owns 46 NNRs and parts of 30 others but most are either leased from the Crown, privately owned but managed by English Nature, or owned and run by approved bodies like the National Trust. The largest NNR in Britain, The Cairngorms, covers 25,949 hectares while the largest in England, The Wash, covers 9,899 hectares. Others cover only a couple of hectares. Most NNRs offer at least limited access to the public.

The National Trust and the Countryside

In 1907 the National Trust was incorporated by Act of Parliament. Amongst its stated aims were 'the permanent preservation for the benefit of the nation of lands... of beauty or historic interest and as regards lands for the preservation... of their natural aspect features and animal and plant life'. By 1996 it owned over 240,000 hectares of land in England, Wales and Northern Ireland, including 18% of the coastline and 10% of the SSSIs. Some of this land is attached to historic houses, but much of it has been acquired purely for its landscape value. After the Forestry Commission and the Ministry of Defence the National Trust is the UK's single biggest landowner. The National Trust for Scotland was set up in 1931 and owns 100,000 acres of Scottish land, including important battlefield sites like Culloden and Bannockburn.

In the Lake District alone the National Trust owns 140,000 acres of land, including 85 farms and 7,300 acres of woodland. It has a policy of planting about 50,000 trees a year, half of them broadleaves. It also repairs and maintains mountain paths, restores properties with local building materials and provides screened campsites and car parks. The National Trust Act of 1971 permitted it to pass by-laws to protect its properties. At many sites fires may not be lit or flowers picked. The Trust can also exclude people from its sites, and levy 'reasonable charges' for admission.

Typical of National Trust countryside properties are Lydford Gorge in Devon which attracted 75,858 visitors in 1995, the 4000-acre Malham Tarn estate in Yorkshire and the mountain peaks in Snowdonia, ten of them owned by the Trust. One problem for the Trust is that many of its countryside properties are unenclosed and cannot therefore be maintained out of admission charges, although optimistic donations boxes can often be seen. Despite this, the land often requires expensive maintenance. In 1995 the Trust received a grant of £217,000 from the Lottery Sports Fund towards the cost of resurfacing eroded parks in the Peak District.

RURAL TOURISM

Just as turning derelict inner city areas into tourist attractions was seen as one way out of the problems of urban decline in the early 1980s, so turning farms into tourist attractions began to be seen as a way out of the increasing problems facing British farmers by the end of the 1980s. Nor was this a trend restricted to Britain. All over Western Europe increasing interest in health and green issues made the countryside seem even more appealing. Concern over the adverse impact of tourism in well-established destinations also encouraged planners to look for new areas to develop; once again the countryside seemed to fit the bill. The English Tourist Board produced its *Visitors in the Countryside: Rural Tourism... A Development Strategy* and the Countryside Commission its *Principles for Tourism in the Countryside*. The Rural Development Commission also appointed a full time national Rural Tourism

Development Officer. Some district councils in rural areas also appointed tourism officers. Many farms have always offered bed and breakfast or camping and caravan sites. Many now have small craft centres or sports facilities and offer farm open days, farm trails and demonstrations of farming techniques.

Surveys suggest that of British tourist nights spent away from home 21% are passed in the country, with 20% of all visits taking place in the West Country. Fifty-two million nights are spent away on holidays of three days or more, while 12 million are spent on short breaks, an expanding market. Seventy-seven percent of rural tourists reach their destinations by car and 24% will have travelled more than thirty miles from their home. Rural tourism may be worth about £3 billion a year to the British economy. However, the countryside seems to have most appeal for the ABC1 socio-economic groups and better educated segments of the market, suggesting a limit to the potential development that can take place.

Tourist development in the countryside presents serious problems. Not all small communities can absorb increasing numbers of tourists without irreparable damage being done to the fabric of the community. In particularly popular areas tourists can do enormous damage to what they have come to see. In the Lake District footpaths and lake edges have been worn away and litter is carelessly dropped all over the place. During August Bank Holidays long traffic jams can build up between Kendal and Ambleside, and ugly yellow no-parking lines now mar the appearance of Glenridding. The Friends of the Lake District have suggested levying a bed tax on visitors to pay for repairs, a scheme which has not so far been adopted.

In 1990 the English Tourist Board and the Countryside Commission agreed a six point plan for future development to prevent further damage taking place. It said that:

- the promotion of tourism should emphasise those activities in keeping with the country's character, history, culture, etc.
- tourism development should aim to assist in conservation, for example, by providing new uses for historic buildings.
- the design, siting and management of new developments should be in keeping with/enhance the existing landscape. So the Countryside Commission opposed Pearson plans to replace Woburn Safari Park with a theme park.
- tourism investment should support the local economy, but encourage a wider geographical and seasonal spread of visitors.
- those who profit from rural tourism should play a full part in its conservation, etc.
- the tourism industry should try to widen the public's understanding of countryside issues through its marketing, etc.

However, the last government had gradually removed some of the restrictions on the development of equestrian centres, camping and caravan sites, forestry, and theme and amusement parks in the countryside.

COUNTRY PARKS

The 1968 Countryside Act authorised the creation of recreational country parks on the outskirts of large conurbations. Many country parks have since been established, especially in the north of England and the Midlands; Center Parcs in Sherwood Forest is technically a country park on old Ministry of Defence land. Many of the parks have been established on abandoned industrial land or in old quarries and reservoirs which have been equipped with picnic facilities, nature trails, etc. Although a few are privately owned, most belong to the local authorities. Ranger services may be supplied by the Countryside Commission. The number of people visiting country parks in 1995 rose by an average 7%, probably reflecting the excellent weather. In 1995 762,521 people visited Rother Valley Country Park near Sheffield, up from 633,392 in 1994.

FIG.9/12: TOP TEN COUNTRY PARKS IN 1995

Strathclyde Country Park, Motherwell	4,150,000
Dunstable Downs Country Park, Bedford	1,500,000
Sandwell Valley Country Park, West Bromwich	1,500,000
Bradgate Park, Leicestershire	1,300,000
Clumber Park, Worksop	1,000,000
Thetford Forest Park, Norfolk	1,000,000
Temple Newsam Country Park, Leeds	831,855
Sherwood Forest Country Park, Nottinghamshire	800,000
Rother Valley Country Park, Sheffield	762,521
River Lee Country Park, Waltham Abbey	750,588

(Source: BTA)

Country parks are especially popular in Northern Ireland where 41% of all visits to tourist attractions in 1995 were to country and forest parks (there are admission charges at most of the forest parks but not at the country parks). Almost all Northern Ireland's country and forest parks are owned by the government or local authorities. Between them they provide 11% of all local employment in tourist attractions. In 1995 the most popular were Cavehill, Peatlands, Carnfunnock, Scrabo, Roe Valley and Castle Archdale Country Parks, and Tollymore and Castlewellan Forest Parks.

COASTAL SCENERY

Heritage Coasts

Some of Britain's most beautiful countryside is to be found along its undeveloped coastlines. However, this scenery is threatened by:

- industrial development
- the creation of marinas
- intensive farming
- housing schemes
- caravan parks
- land reclamation schemes

In 1966 a National Parks Commission study of coastal development resulted in two reports, *The Coastal Heritage* and *The Planning of the Coastline* (1970), which suggested the designation of 'heritage coasts'. In 1972 the government

FIG.9/13: THE HERITAGE COASTS OF ENGLAND AND WALES

1973	Aberffraw Bay	**1979**	Flamborough Head
	North Anglesey		Suffolk
	Holyhead Mountain		
	Gower Peninsula	**1981**	North Yorkshire and Cleveland
	Glamorgan		Purbeck, East
	Sussex		Purbeck, West
	North Northumberland		
		1982	Ceredigion Coast
1974	Hamstead		
	Marloes and Dale	**1984**	West Devon
	South Pembrokeshire		East Devon
	St. David's Peninsula		
	Dinas Head	**1986**	South Devon
	Isles of Scilly		Hartland (Cornwall)
	Tennyson		
	Great Orme	**1988**	Spurn Head
	St. Dogmaels and Moylgrove		
	Lleyn Peninsula	**1989**	St. Bees Head
	St. Bride's Bay		
		1990	Lundy
1975	South Foreland		Hartland (Devon)
	Dover to Folkestone		
	North Norfolk	**1991**	Exmoor
1976	Penwith	**1992**	North Devon
	Godrevy to Portreath		
	St. Agnes		
	Pentire Point to Widemouth		
	Gribbin Head to Polperro		
	The Lizard		
	Roseland		
	Trevose Head		
	Hartland		
	Rame Head		

(Source: Countryside Commission)

authorised local authorities to produce management plans for the stretches of coast suggested by the Commission. To date 45 'heritage coasts', mostly within national parks, AONBs or SSSIs, have been designated (see Fig.9/13). The protected areas cover 1,525 kilometres or 35% of the coast of England and Wales and usually extend to a depth of two or three kilometres from the seafront.

Once a heritage coast has been designated special planning procedures apply and extra management funds may be made available. Three-quarters of heritage coasts now have their own staff, including rangers, and a Heritage Coast Management Plan.

Like SSSIs, 'heritage coasts' have proved vulnerable to developers. In 1989 it was agreed that the new A20 should be routed along the top of the White Cliffs of Dover, regardless of their supposed protection.

LAND'S END

In 1987 Land's End was simply a stretch of rocky coastline popular with cormorants. The hotel on the promontory had closed in 1979. The National Trust hoped to buy the site, demolish the hotel, build a lookout and provide screened car parking in a sunken arena. However, businessman Peter de Savary eventually paid £7 million for it and then invested another £5 million in creating a theme park which attracted 600,000 people in its first year in business. The hotel has been restored, and a 'multi-sensory experience', the *Last Labyrinth*, created. The site also includes a small farm, miniature models of Cornwall's landmarks, a glassblower's studio and a 'Spirit of Cornwall' exhibition. Statistics show that visitors used to spend an average 12½ minutes at Land's End; this has risen to four or five hours as a result of the theme park. Of 5,000 people questioned in 1989 98% thought their visit good value for money. In 1995 521,000 people visited Land's End.

Some individual coastal features are enormously popular tourist attractions. In Northern Ireland the single most visited tourist attraction (apart from the Belfast Botanic Garden) is the Giant's Causeway which received 408,790 visitors in 1995. St. Michael's Mount in Cornwall was visited by 200,790 people in 1995.

The National Trust and Enterprise Neptune

Although the National Trust is often thought of in connection with stately homes, it also plays an important role in looking after Britain's remaining unspoilt coastlines. In fact its first acquisition was Dinas Oleu, four and a half acres of headland above Barmouth in Wales. In 1965 it launched Enterprise Neptune which aimed to acquire 1,400 kilometres of coast. Its first purchase was Whitford Burrows in Glamorgan which was threatened by the industrial development of Llanelli. In 1969 it bought Lundy island, now managed by the Landmark Trust. Other coastal properties acquired through Enterprise Neptune include the Needles on the Isle of Wight, the Farne Islands, Lindisfarne, the Giant's Causeway, Strangford Lough, Murlough Nature Reserve and Golden Cap in Dorset.

By 1993 Enterprise Neptune had acquired almost 900 kilometres of coastland, or one in every five kilometres of coast. One of the most impressive recent purchases was Orford Ness in Suffolk, an important port of call for migratory birds. All this land belongs to the National Trust inalienably; it cannot be sold, mortgaged or compulsorily purchased without Parliament's permission.

Marine Nature Reserves

The 1981 Wildlife and Countryside Act authorised the creation of marine nature reserves. Although only Lundy and Skomer had been designated by 1996, further reserves are planned for the Menai Straits in Wales and Tayvaillich on Loch Sween. There are also eight Voluntary Marine Conservation Areas, including those at Helford River and Roseland in Cornwall, Wemsbury in Devon, St. Abbs in Scotland and Strangford Lough in Northern Ireland.

FORESTS AND WOODLANDS

Around 3000 BC most of Britain was probably heavily wooded; areas like the Midlands may have been entirely covered in trees. However, during the Roman occupation large areas of trees were cleared for agriculture and simple industry. Some areas were naturally refforested during the Dark Ages, only to be cleared

---

THE NEW FOREST

The New Forest in Hampshire was originally created as a royal hunting preserve by William the Conqueror in 1079. It's now administered by the Forestry Commission under a mandate from the Minister of Agriculture and is a national park in all but name. New Forest District Council has designated a New Forest Heritage Area and it's also a Site of Special Scientific Interest. Forty-nine per cent of the land is open forest belonging to the Crown and administered by the Forestry Commission, while 23% is enclosed and 28% used for agriculture, housing and commonland. There are 13 conservation areas, 800 listed buildings and 96 archaeological sites within the Forest boundaries. The 3,000 New Forest ponies are also very popular with visitors. Attractions inside the Forest include the National Motor Museum at Beaulieu and Paultons Park.

Proposed legislation would see the New Forest designated an Area of National Significance with the same status as a National Park but with special administrative arrangements to suit its specific needs.

---

again in the Anglo-Saxon period. Although the word 'forest' is often thought of as synonymous with woodland, in the Middle Ages it referred specifically to land which belonged to the king and was controlled by the 'forest law', which prohibited the killing of game. Forests were certainly wooded, but were not necessarily covered in trees; the New Forest, for example, was probably never entirely wooded. A 'chase' was a noble's hunting ground.

As the population grew the forests came under pressure from the land-hungry. At the same time kings made less use of them for hunting and more for cutting timber for shipbuilding. As early as the 17th century John Evelyn was mourning the speed with which the woodlands were vanishing. Eventually in 1810 the royal forests were taken over by a Commission for Forests. By the start of the 20th century only 5% of the UK was still covered by trees. In 1919 the Forestry Commission was set up to plant 1,770,000 acres of new woods by 1999 by establishing state plantations, providing advice and tree planting grants, and encouraging private landowners to plant more trees. In 1923 the Forestry Commission took over the care and control of the old royal forests.

FIG.9/14: ENGLAND'S HISTORIC FORESTS

Forest of Dartmoor	Forest of Clarendon	Forest of Dean
Duffield Frith	Forest of Exmoor	Savernake Forest
Tintern	Forest of the Peak	North Petherton
Melksham and Pewsham	Forests of Herefords.	Forests of Yorks.
Neroche Forest	Forest of Braden	Forests of Worcs.
Pickering Forest	Forest of Mendip	Forest of Chute
Forests of Warks.	Forests of Shrops.	Powerstock
New Forest	Cannock Chase	Marce or Delamere
Forest of Gillingham	Bere	Forests of Northants.
Forest of Wirral	Forest of Blackmore	Windsor Forest
Huntingdon Forest	Forest of Macclesfield	Forest of Selwood
Forest of Alice Holt & Woolmer	Thetford Forest	Forests of Lancashire
Kingswood	Forest of the Weald	Forest of Rutland
Forests of Cumbria	Cranborne Chase	Forests of Essex
Charnwood Forest	Forests of Durham	Forest of Melchet
Forests of Bucks.	Needwood	Northumberland Forest
Groveley	Forests of Oxon.	Sherwood Forest

By 1939 only 300,000 hectares of new woodland had been planted, and in 1943 a White Paper demanded another two million hectares by 1983. By 1945 the Commission was planting 24,000 hectares of new woodlands each year.

However, between 1947 and 1980 half the trees which had survived from the 16th century were felled. In the 1970s Dutch Elm disease killed a further 11 million trees, while farmers continued to uproot trees that got in the way of intensive farming practices. By 1979 the Nature Conservancy Council was warning that all the remaining broadleaved woods could soon be lost.

Various tax and grant schemes to encourage tree planting have been tried. In 1947 the Forestry Commission's Dedication Scheme allowed landowners to dedicate their land specifically to tree planting in return for grants. This was replaced in 1981 by the Forestry Grant Scheme which offered higher grants for planting native deciduous trees. Those in receipt of grants were encouraged to provide public access to their lands, but this was not compulsory. They were paid 80% of their grant at the time of planting and the remaining 20% after five years. In 1985 the Broadleaved Woodland Grant Scheme offered even better grants, paid in three instalments, to those planting deciduous tree. In 1988 a Farm Woodland Scheme offered farmers grants to switch from food production to tree planting. The tax concessions granted for tree planting have been criticised for encouraging foresters to plant quick-growing conifers even in environmentally fragile areas like the Flow Country of Scotland.

Since the 1971 Town and Country Planning Act local authorities have been able to put temporary tree preservation orders on trees threatened with destruction. In 1972 the Woodland Trust was created to safeguard trees and look after forests that might otherwise be destroyed; it now owns over 800 woods and offers unrestricted public access wherever possible. In its 1987 report *Forestry in the Countryside* the Countryside Commission said tree-planting policies should aim to create attractive sites and enhance the beauty of the land as well as to provide new wildlife habitats and offer an alternative source of rural employment. By 1991 10% of the UK was once again covered in trees, two-thirds of them conifers.

The National Lottery is providing some funds for reafforestation; for example, in 1997 it gave the Woodland Trust £1.4 million to buy a large part of the Glen Finglass estate in the Trossachs and will provide a further £1.3 million to kickstart a 40-year project to restore the deciduous forest that grew here before the Clearances. As a result, an estimated 20,000 more people are expected to walk the drovers' road on the estate each year. The Millennium Commission is also providing the Woodland Trust with £6.5 million to create 200 new woods by the year 2000.

Forest Parks

Since 1935 the Forestry Commission has created 14 forest parks. The first was at Argylls in Scotland and there are others in Snowdonia and the Wye Valley. The New Forest is also a forest park. The Forestry Act of 1967 specifically laid down that the Forestry Commission should provide recreational facilities on its land and protect and enhance the environment. Within the parks Forest Enterprise, a branch of the Forestry Commission, provides picnic areas, camp sites, forest and nature trails, museums and information centres, and forest drives. One of the most popular single attractions administered by Forest Enterprise is Westonbirt Arboretum in Gloucestershire, visited by 248,587 people in 1995. Forest Enterprise also manages several SSSIs and Forest Nature Reserves.

Facilities provided in Forest Enterprise forests include:

- Forest walks/nature trails
- Picnic sites
- Forest cabins/holiday homes

- Youth camps
- Camping/caravan sites
- Arboreta or tree gardens
- Visitor centres and shops
- Forest drives
- Cycle and horse trails
- Facilities for fishing, shooting, sailing, orienteering, etc.
- Deer safaris

The RAC is also allowed to organise car and motorbike rallies on Forestry Commission land; for example, the RAC Lombard Rally is held in Grizedale Forest in the Lake District every November.

Community Forests

Research on the continent suggests that the countryside's popularity with holidaymakers springs as much from desire to escape the cities as from real love of the rustic. Given the pressures that rural tourism can cause, one solution is to bring the countryside closer to the towns, as country parks and city farms already attempt to do. The Countryside and Forestry Commissions plan that by the year 2000 12 major town and cities will have community forests on their doorstep.

FIG.9/15: PLANNED COMMUNITY FORESTS

Cleveland Community Forest
Great North Forest, in the north-east
Great Western Community Forest, around Swindon
Greenwood, in Nottinghamshire
Forest of Avon, around Bristol
Forest of Mercia, in south Staffordshire
Marston Vale, south of Bedford
Mersey Forest
Red Rose Forest, in the north-west
South Yorkshire Forest, around Sheffield
Thames Chase, edge of London
Watling Chase, edge of London

Germany has had urban forests (*stadtwalder*) close to its cities since the 18th century; for example, Bremen Stadtwald starts only five kilometres from the city centre and has a boating and windsurfing lake, cyclepaths, bridleways, adventure playgrounds, a jazz cafe, bandstands and a small zoo. Bos Park on the outskirts of Amsterdam was planted in the 1950s. It covers 2,200 acres and encompasses several canals and lakes, a large artificial hill with a restaurant on its summit and ski slopes.

The forest also has swimming pools, cyclepaths, bridleways, nature trails and an open-air theatre.

The Community Forests planned for the UK will contain both deciduous and coniferous trees. Often they will be planted on areas of derelict wasteland. Funding will come from a variety of sources, including European Union grants for the largest projects.

In 1990 the Countryside Commission produced proposals to create a 502-square-kilometre National Forest to link Needward Forest (near Uttoxeter) with Charnwood Forest (near Leicester) at an estimated cost of £90 million. Funding would come from government and private sources and the forest would aim to encourage economic development of the area, enable farmers to diversify, provide a source of timber and encourage recreation and tourism.

ACCESS TO THE COUNTRYSIDE

Public Rights of Way

The majority of land in the UK is in private hands, with no assumption in favour of public access. In fact at the start of the 20th century very little land could be walked on, even in areas which are now national parks. In the 1930s there was public pressure to change this situation and in 1932 a group of ramblers wound up in jail after a 'mass trespass' on Kinder Scout in the Peak District to assert the public's right to access. Even now the public only has absolute right of access even in the national parks on public footpaths and bridleways and some stretches of common land. There is *de facto* right of access to areas like the Lake District fells and mountains simply because no one is likely to be around to complain. Elsewhere access depends on agreement with farmers, some of them more obliging than others who regularly plough up public paths. Where access is granted the National Park Authorities have the right to enact by-laws to control public behaviour which can be enforced by rangers. The situation is not helped by the fact that the Ministry of Defence owns 850,000 acres of land, including some in Dartmoor, the North York Moors, the Dorset Coast and Salisbury Plain, where access is often restricted for safety reasons.

The situation in England and Wales contrasts with that in Scotland where there is no law of trespass for those passing through. In Sweden people are entitled to walk wherever they want in wild countryside.

When landowners are given forestry grants and tax concessions, efforts are usually made to persuade them to admit the public, but this has never been a prerequisite.

England has 192,000 kilometres of rights of way. According to the 1980 Highways Act these must be maintained in the same way as bridges and road surfaces. Ideally they should be signposted and kept clear of undergrowth; the Health and Safety at Work Act also means that dangerous animals shouldn't be kept in fields containing public rights of way. Farmers sometimes prefer to put stiles which people can't forget to close along footpaths; however, these are hard for the elderly and disabled to cope with. The Countryside Commission is working with local authorities and parish councils to ensure that all the rights of way are actually accessible to the public by the year 2000.

Permitted Rights of Way

In addition to public rights of way there are also permitted rights of way where access has been negotiated with landowners. Charges can be made for access to these routes although they are often low and don't seem to deter visitors. The Duke of Devonshire typically charges for access to the private nature trail along the Wharfe river on the Chatsworth estate.

National Trails

The Countryside Commission has negotiated free access along ten long-distance footpaths or national trails. Hadrian's Wall and the Pennine Bridleway have been approved and will become national trails in due course (see Fig.9/16.). The Cotswold Way may also be upgraded in the next few years. The Countryside Commission funds the maintenance and signposting of these paths. The first such long-distance path was the Pennine Way which was designated in 1965 and extends for 402 kilometres. The existing national trails are:

- The Pennine Way
- The Cleveland Way
- The Wolds Way
- Offa's Dyke Path
- Peddars Way and Norfolk Coast Path
- The Ridgeway
- The South West Coast Path
- The North Downs Way
- The South Downs Way
- The Thames Path

Some of these trails are astonishingly popular; an estimated one million people walked part of the South West Coast Path in 1995, 93% of them attracted by the gorgeous coastal scenery.

The Pembrokeshire Coast Path in Wales is also a designated National Trail. Scotland also has several long-distance footpaths: the Millennium Way, the West Highland Way and the Speyside Way. In Northern Ireland the Ulster Way sweeps round the coast for 800 kilometres.

Recreation Paths

These paths have usually been negotiated by local authorities, voluntary groups or individuals and offer relatively short circular walks. An example would be the informal Apple Blossom Trail in Armagh, Northern Ireland.

FIG.9/16: EXISTING AND PLANNED NATIONAL TRAILS

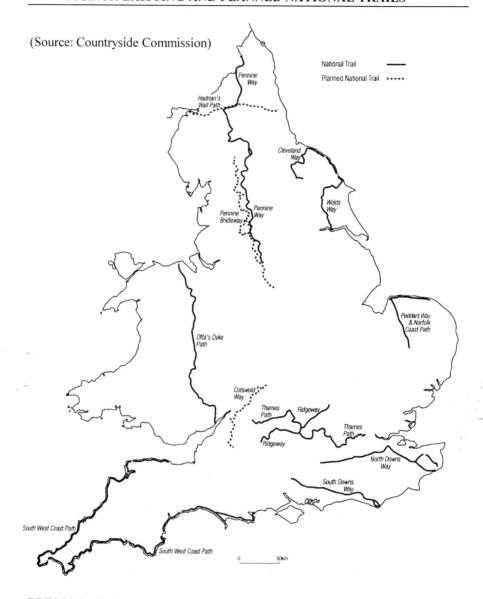

(Source: Countryside Commission)

PRESENTATION OF COUNTRYSIDE ATTRACTIONS

Presentation of the countryside is a particularly sensitive subject. Providing certain basic facilities (lavatories, car parks and rubbish bins) is essential to the good management of any area which will receive visitors. Where more visitors are expected fences, seating, picnic sites and information boards may also be needed. In some places visitor centres and trails of various kinds may also be appropriate. However, where it is the unspoilt nature of the countryside itself which is the attraction care must be taken that none of these facilities detracts from what people have come to see. The more people are expected, the more likely it is that there will be problems.

Wherever possible things like seats, picnic tables, fences and rubbish bins should be made from natural materials which will not stand out. In some cases treated logs may provide adequate seating. The positioning of fences needs careful thought. Clearly it's essential where there's a danger that people might fall; for example, along some cliff-tops. However, sometimes the presence of a fence would ruin the view people have come to see. A compromise may be to fence the stretch of cliff within ten minutes' walk of the car park which is as far as most people will walk. Luckily some evidence suggests that the most apparently dangerous spots (for example, the rim of the Grand Canyon) may actually be safest since people anticipate danger and behave accordingly. Where people must walk across wet or uneven ground, including sand dunes, wooden boardwalks can be laid; these blend in with the scenery and protect fragile plants but make walking easier.

The positioning of litter bins and picnic tables should be carefully considered. Ideally they should be placed round the edge of fields rather than in the centre where they will mar the view. Fortunately research suggests that most people tend to hug the edges of open spaces anyway. The ideal picnic sites are on light, well-drained soil; sites near water are particularly popular. In the UK only benches and tables are routinely provided; in the States and Australia there are usually bases for barbecues too. Lavatories and litter bins should always be provided within easy reach of picnic sites.

Sites without visitor centres still need information boards which state who owns the land, the times and dates when it is open and any relevant by-laws. Ideally these should have a site map showing points of interest. Again, they should be as unobtrusive as possible, and preferably attached to pre-existing buildings. Alternatively they should be secured to posts reaching as much as a metre into the ground to resist wind and vandals. The ground immediately surrounding the post should be covered with compacted gravel or slope downwards to prevent water collecting around the base. Ideally signs should be legible from a metre away.

The best nature trails are no longer than two kilometres, and laid out in a figure of eight shape with spurs to allow people to turn back early if they want to. Perhaps 30 items should be highlighted. Paths should be wide enough for two people to walk side by side; winding paths also mean that it will not be necessary to see people ahead all the time. Where the trail leads to viewpoints a firmly secured telescope can be supplied.

SPECIFIC TYPES OF SCENIC ATTRACTION

Mountains

All around the world mountains act as important foci for tourism. Obviously not all of them can be climbed other than by experienced mountaineers. However, a surprising number are accessible to the reasonably fit. For example, both Mount Kenya and Mount Kilimanjaro (Africa's highest mountain) can be climbed by non-mountaineers. So can Mount Kinabalu in Sabah, the highest mountain in south-east Asia. Even where a mountain cannot be casually climbed it's sometimes possible to trek in its foothills; so many people now visit the Mount Everest Base camp in the Himalayas that special 'clear-up Everest' groups have had to be organised to remove the abandoned litter.

As attractions, mountains offer the chance to experience wonderful views and scenery. Often they also have interesting flora and fauna which can be examined on the way: for example, walkers on Mount Kinabalu have the chance to see unusual and exotic carnivorous pitcher plants.

Mountains are also the focus for winter sports activities, although it's the snow that falls on them, and the angle at which it does so, rather than the intrinsic beauty of the mountain that is the draw.

Where mountains are accessible to visitors they must be supplied with places where people can rest as they climb. The highest mountains will also need accommodation, however simple, on the way up. Ideally there should also be places for climbers to fill up with clean water and buy simple meals. Usually guides and porters will be needed to limit the likelihood of accidents.

Mount Snowdon is the highest mountain in Wales. Almost 300,000 people visit it each year, as many as 142,000 of them taking the easy way up by mountain railway rather than walking. Nevertheless the six paths to the summit are all showing signs of wear and tear. The Snowdonia National Park employs 12 staff and three wardens specifically to look after the visitors. Scafell Pike in the Lake District is England's highest mountain, while Ben Nevis is the highest both in Scotland and in the UK as a whole.

Caves

Like mountains, not all caves are accessible to casual visitors. Nor have all of them always be known; the 30-mile Mammoth Cave complex in Kentucky was only discovered by a hunter in 1799, while the Lascaux Caves in France, with their fantastic prehistoric paintings, were only discovered by teenagers in 1940.

As attractions, caves are frequently beautiful in their own right, with dramatic stalactites and stalagmites, as at Cheddar and the Caves of Drach in Majorca. Some, like Wookey Hole in Somerset, also contain underground lakes. However, caves are naturally dark so for visitors to appreciate these features lighting has to be installed. The ground may also be wet and slippery so a concrete floor may have to be installed; in 1995 266,000 people visited the Cheddar Showcaves which inevitably have to have artificial flooring. The floor is also likely to be uneven so that hand or rope rails may also be needed. The largest cave in Britain, big enough to accommodate York Minster inside it, is Gaping Gill at Ingleborough. Marble Arch Caves in Northern Ireland were the province's eighth most popular miscellaneous attraction in 1995, with 60,228 visitors. Other popular caves open to the public are in the Peak District where the Speedwell Cavern attracted 46,500 visitors and the Treak Cliff Cavern 70,000 in 1995.

Other caves are more interesting for their evidence of a prehistoric lifestyle. Like the Lascaux Caves, the Altamira Caves in northern Spain have bison and other animals painted on their walls. Further afield in Sarawak tiny figures are also painted on the walls of the cave at Niah. Unfortunately such paintings are fragile; in 1963 the Lascaux Cave was closed while temperature and humidity controls were installed to prevent damage being caused by people's breath. Both Lascaux and Altamira are now closed to all but speleologists. Visitors to Lascaux can see a precise copy; there are also many other painted caves in the area.

Finally, a few caves are more interesting for their wildlife. The Niah cave in Sarawak, for example, is filled with millions of bats by day and millions of swiftlets by night. Visitors trek to the cave at dawn and dusk to witness the astonishing moving clouds as bats and birds change places.

A variety of imaginative devices have been used to make caves more appealing to a wider audience. Wookey Hole has long been promoted for its witch, while some of the Cheddar caves now contain holograms and exhibits more usually seen in hands-on science exhibitions. Perhaps most startling of all are the Caves of Drach, the most popular tourist attraction on Majorca, where visitors regularly struggle past the incredible scenery in queues. Eventually they arrive in an underground theatre where banks of seats look down on a lake. The lighting is dimmed and Classical music, particularly Chopin, is played while boats float back and forth on the lake. Finally guests climb into the boats themselves to be rowed to the exit.

Water Attractions

The Lake District's popularity stems from its combination of lakes and mountains. The same applies to many areas of Scotland, where the lochs coexist with spectacular mountain scenery; Loch Lomond and Loch Ness are two of the most popular lochs with visitors. In fact the combination of lakes and mountains is so popular that there is a whole 'lakes and mountains' sub-section of the holiday industry devoted to taking people to the Italian, Swiss and Slovenian lakes and mountains. The Plitvice Lakes in Croatia, where 14 lakes are linked by waterfalls, have been a national park since 1949 and are now a World Heritage Site. In Northern Ireland the lakes, or 'loughs', are also very important to tourism. Lough Neagh is the UK's biggest lake and measures 28 by 18 kilometres. The Upper and Lower Lough Ernes are also very popular with the boating fraternity.

While sites like Plitvice are preserved for people to appreciate their unspoilt natural beauty, other lakes are a focus for water sports, including water skiing and power-boat racing. The same is true of reservoirs which are often used for a variety of watersports. Picnic areas are usually provided on the shores of lakes and reservoirs. However, in the Lake District siting car parks so that they don't intrude on the views or damage the surrounding grass verges sometimes proves difficult.

Where many people walk along a lake shore it will quickly erode and become messy unless edged with disguised sand or gravel.

Waterfalls also make enormously popular tourist attractions. Probably the most famous falls are Niagara Falls, on the US/Canadian border, and Victoria Falls on the Zambia/Zimbabwe border, the latter so dramatic that the spray can be seen from 40 kilometres away in the wet season. The world's tallest waterfall, Angel Falls, receives relatively few visitors because it's in a remote area of Venezuela. The dramatic Iguazu Falls on the Brazil/Paraguay/Argentina border also receive relatively few visitors because they are difficult to get to.

The UK's smaller waterfalls can still be very beautiful. In 1995 181,434 people visited the Swallow Falls at Betws-y-Coed in North Wales. Another popular and dramatic waterfall is High Force in Teesdale where there's a charge to walk along the river to the falls. British waterfalls are usually kept as natural as possible. However, safety precautions must be taken and lifebelts are usually prominently positioned nearby.

Wildlife attractions range from the great game parks of Africa to the many specialist zoos scattered around the world. Within the UK they are becoming less popular, probably as a result of increasing unease about keeping animals in captivity. Since 1991 six British zoos have closed and in 1995 this was the group of attractions showing the steepest fall in visitor numbers.

THE AFRICAN GAME PARKS

Most British wildlife is small and difficult to observe. Consequently national parks in Britain are places where people go primarily to appreciate the countryside. In Africa, in contrast, much of the wildlife is large and easy to observe, so visitors to the national parks are usually more interested in seeing the animals and birds than the scenery.

FIG.10/1: SOME OF AFRICA'S BIG GAME PARKS

KENYA	TANZANIA	UGANDA
Amboseli	Lake Manyara	Kabalega
Marsabit	Gombe Reserve	Ruwenzori
Meru	Ngorongoro Crater	
Masai Mara	Ruaha	**ZIMBABWE**
Nairobi	Rungwa	Hwange
Samburu	Selous	Matapos
Tsavo	Serengeti	Victoria Falls
	Tarangire	
SOUTH AFRICA		**NAMIBIA**
Kruger	**ZAMBIA**	Etosha
Hluhluwe-Umfolozi	Luangwa Valley	
Drakensberg		**CAMEROON**
Bontebok	**BOTSWANA**	Waza
West Coast	Chobe	
Kalahari-Gemsbok	Moremi	**MALAWI**
Addo Elephant Park	Tuli	Nyika Plateau
Karoo		

In the 19th century big game could still be seen in huge herds in many parts of Africa. However, hunters quickly decimated the animals and as early as 1858 a law was passed in the Transvaal (South Africa) to prevent the indiscriminate slaughter of elephants in particular. In 1898 President Kruger declared much of northern Transvaal a game reserve (now the Kruger National Park), offering protection to its wildlife. The first officially designated African national park was Virunga in Zaire which was created in 1925. There are now many parks in Kenya,

Uganda, Tanzania, Malawi, Zambia, Zimbabwe, Namibia, Botswana and South Africa (see Fig.10/1) where tourists can go on safari, taking pictures of animals which might once have been shot. In some parks restricted hunting is still permitted.

The game parks are usually thought of as natural attractions despite the fact that they are carefully managed to ensure that the animals are protected and visitors see what they have come to see. Some of the parks are enormous (the Masai Mara/Serengeti Park straddling the Kenya/Tanzania border covers 10,138 square kilometres). They are nevertheless enclosed with electric fences and deep ditches to keep the game in and keep out domestic animals, which would compete with them for food and help spread diseases like rinderpest. Nairobi National Park, just outside the Kenyan capital, is one of the smallest parks but is still so large that visitors don't see the fences and think what they are seeing is 'natural'. However, most of the animals have been trucked into the park because it's too close to a big city for animals to choose to live there.

Clearly the hotels, huts, tented camps and restaurants provided inside the parks are not 'natural'. Nor is the underwater viewing tank provided to allow visitors to watch hippopotami swimming at Mzima Springs in Tsavo. But there is much more to the management of the game parks as tourist attractions than this. Animals tend to gather round crucial resources, particularly waterholes and salt-licks, so accommodation for tourists is often built within sight of such things. Treetops Hotel in the Aberdare National Park is built right beside a waterhole which is constantly topped up to ensure the animals keep coming. Two buckets of salt a week are also tipped on to the ground, again to guarantee visitors see the animals.

The game parks are an example of tourism as a mixed blessing. On the one hand it's unlikely that poorer African countries could justify devoting so many precious resources to wildlife conservation were it not for the potential return in terms of income from tourism. Thus tourism can be seen as preserving the animals and landscapes. It's then tempting for managers to try and attract as many visitors as possible. However, the parks are ecologically fragile and too many tourists can damage them. In Amboseli the sheer number of visitors and their vehicles started to wreck the grasslands. Consequently they were restricted to specific tracks and routes which made the park seem less 'natural'. Nor do people much enjoy sharing their view of a lion's kill with hundreds of other striped safari vehicles full of sightseers.

Other problems have arisen when the needs of tourists and animals have come into conflict. For example, the best times to see game are at dawn and dusk. However, cheetahs need space for their long runs and suffer from vehicles crowding round them. This may cause them to hunt later in the day when higher temperatures make it harder work. There can also be conflicts with local people. The Masai, for example, traditionally herd cattle, but these are now excluded from the parks. As a result, many of the Masai now live in terrible poverty on the fringes of their ancestral lands.

Other countries also have national parks whose chief attraction is their wildlife. For example the Royal Chitwan National Park in Nepal offers tourists the opportunity to tiger-spot from the back of an elephant.

ZOOS

The word 'zoo' as an abbreviation for 'zoological gardens' was first used to refer to Clifton Zoo in Bristol in 1847. It was then popularised by a music-hall song and replaced the word 'menagerie' which had previously been used to refer to collections of animals in captivity. According to the 1981 Zoo Licensing Act zoos are 'establishments where wild animals are kept for exhibition to the public' but the *Good Zoo Guide* differentiates between Type A zoos which have large animal collections often shown in fairly small enclosures (London, Bristol, Chester, Dudley) and Type B zoos which favour fewer animals but in larger enclosures (Howletts, Port Lympne and most safari parks).

By 1992 Britain had 80 establishments displaying mammals which could be called 'zoos'. Between them they received 14 million visits. In total they held about 50,000 captive animals, about one-fifth of the world total of zoo animals.

The Development of Zoos

People have been collecting animals for almost as long as records exist. The Ancient Egyptians kept lions, baboons and ibises, and Alexander the Great is known to have owned parrots. Ptolemy II may also have had a zoo in Alexandria in 300 BC. Most of the Greek city-states seem to have had animal collections by the 4th century BC, while there were menageries in Rome to keep the animals required for gladiatorial combat. Early menageries also existed in Mesopotamia, and in the 12th century BC the Chinese Emperor Wen-Wang had a 600-hectare 'garden of intelligence' full of animals.

Menageries existed throughout the Middle Ages. In the early 12th century Henry I kept animals, many of them gifts from other rulers, at Woodstock. Henry III moved this collection, which included a polar bear, to the Tower of London where it stayed until 1828. England's first elephant arrived in London in 1254 as a gift from Louis IX to Henry III. In the 13th century Frederick II of Sicily and Jerusalem had a travelling menagerie which he took with him to Worms in 1235 for his marriage to King John's daughter, Isabella. In the 14th century Phillip VI kept lions and leopards in a building called the 'Hotel des Lions du Roi' in the Louvre. In the 15th century Montezuma also seems to have had a menagerie requiring 300 keepers to look after it at Tenochtitlan (Mexico).

However, the first modern zoo is usually regarded as the one Franz Stephen, husband of Empress Maria Theresa, founded in the grounds of Schonbrunn Palace in Vienna in 1752. This was a private collection of the least dangerous animals which could be studied from a viewing pavilion on the site of an old deer park. In 1781 Josef II set up a Society for the Acquisition of Animals and began actively collecting even the most dangerous animals. The public were regularly admitted to the zoo. The first giraffe was displayed there in 1828 and the first elephant bred in Europe was born there in 1906. The zoo still exists although the viewing pavilion is now a cafeteria.

In 1826 there were only three real zoos in England. One was at Chiswick House, another was in the Exeter Exchange in the Strand while the third was the old royal menagerie where the public was already being admitted in the 18th century in return for payment of 1½/d. They could also buy cats and dogs to feed to the lions! There were also several travelling zoos including George Wombwell's which had started life with just two boa constrictors.

In 1826 Sir Stamford Raffles founded the Zoological Society of London, based on an animal collection he had brought back from Malaya. The Society was like a private club for scientists and aristocrats with an interest in animals. Women were not admitted as members of the Society until 1827. From 1828 onwards Society members could bring visitors to the zoo for 1/- each. Sundays were reserved for members.

London Zoo started off with a griffon vulture, a white-headed eagle, some deer and a few monkeys. In 1831 it acquired a quagga (now extinct), while in 1834 it bought an Indian rhino for 1000 guineas. In 1835 the zoo got its first chimpanzee which only survived for six months. By 1839 it also had some gibbons. However, in 1836 Charles Darwin felt that it was in too poor a condition to be allowed to take over the specimens he brought back from his voyages. In 1850 the first hippopotamus was acquired, and in 1887 the first male gorilla arrived. Some animals were bought, while others were given by members of the royal family after visits overseas.

In 1849 the old carnivores' house at London Zoo was converted into the world's first reptile house containing 21 species. This house remained in use until 1883 when a new one was built with the proceeds of selling an elephant to Barnum's circus. In 1853 the Zoo also opened a 'Marine and Fish Water Vivarium', the world's first public aquarium. This was closed down in the 1870s and other zoos didn't copy the idea until the 1920s when aquaria appeared in Brighton, Hamburg and Naples.

Other European zoos were also set up in the 19th century. These included Amsterdam (1837), Antwerp (1843), West Berlin (1844), East Berlin (1854), Rotterdam (1855), Frankfurt (1858), Hamburg (1860), Budapest (1865) and Basle (1873). The first zoos in the United States opened in Philadephia in 1874 and New York in 1899. Zoos opened in Melbourne in 1857, Adelaide in 1878 and Sydney in 1881. Tokyo got a zoo in 1882 and Beijing in 1906. Most of these zoos were started by wealthy animal collectors or circus owners, although some were opened by amateurs.

The war years were especially bad for the zoos. Animals were sometimes killed by falling bombs; of 3,600 animals in West Berlin only about 90 survived the bombs and post-war looting, while five African elephants were killed by a bomb in Munich. Other animals were killed because there wasn't enough food to feed them. Some were even killed to feed humans because of the shortages.

Nevertheless by 1982 the *International Zoo Yearbook* listed 757 zoos worldwide, more than 40 of them over a hundred years old. Of these, 290 were in Europe, 117 in the Far East and 181 in North America. Between them the zoos held 162,874 mammals and 256,413 birds in captivity and were visited by an estimated 357 million people. By 1988 the number of zoos and aquaria listed as being open to the public had grown to 899. There were increasing calls for their closure from those who regard keeping animals in captivity as cruel.

The Zoological Society of London now runs two zoos; the old London Zoo in Regent's Park, and Whipsnade Wild Animal Park which opened in 1931 on 500 acres of farm and downland suitable for paddocks. London Zoo now displays over 8,000 animals. In 1995 it was by far the most popular wildlife attraction in the UK with 1,042,701 visitors, a small drop from 1,046,888 in 1994. It probably owes much of it popularity to its convenient central position, although Windsor Safari Park was also conveniently positioned and yet has closed.

In the late 20th century zoos are threatened by the huge cost of maintaining them, by an ageing population when zoos remain most popular with families with children and by television which can show animals in their natural environments and in a detail zoos can never manage. In 1999 Bristol is due to open the UK's first techno-zoo where people will be able to call up images of animals in their natural environments at the touch of a button.

The Purpose of Zoos

Until the 17th century only the Chinese zoos were run as scientific establishments. Most were seen simply as objects of curiosity and as places for wealthy men to advertise their own importance. Research students tended to use common animals for their studies; even when something more exotic was called for it was not usually obtained from a zoo.

However, in the 18th century a more scientific approach was taken to the study of animals, particularly after Linnaeus produced his classification of plants and animals in 1735. This new approach was reflected within the zoos so that the charter for the Zoological Society of London, granted in 1829, gave the purpose of the Regent's Park Zoological Gardens as 'the advancement of zoology and animal physiology and the introduction of new and curious subjects of the animal kingdom.' When the zoos in Philadephia and Antwerp opened their stated aims were scientific. The Paris and London zoos were particularly successful in establishing themselves as scientific institutions, no doubt helped by their proximity to other academic establishments. Other zoos, including the American National Zoo in Washington, nevertheless continued to operate without even a vet on the premises.

Once zoos were seen as scientific establishments the way was also clear for them to be regarded as serving an educational function. Most modern zoos now put labels on the cages giving details of where the animal comes from, what it eats, etc. and also provide teaching materials for schools. Some also have 'talking labels' allowing people to listen to a commentary through head-sets. Others have 'Meet the Keeper' sessions when the public can ask the experts questions. However, these are expensive in staffing terms and volunteers are often used instead.

In the latter part of the 20th century most good zoos see their primary function as conservation, particularly of endangered species. During the 1980s it was estimated that an animal species was being lost every hour; even previously common animals like the African elephant were threatened. In such circumstances zoos clearly have a role as places where endangered species can be protected. However, it is not enough simply to keep individual specimens in zoos. There are several instances of species which finally became extinct inside zoos: the quagga died out in 1883 in Amsterdam Zoo and the passenger pigeon died out in Cincinnati Zoo in 1914. To safeguard a species an organised breeding programme is required and recognition of this fact has radically altered some zoos. Traditionally they were places where a wide variety of species were on display. Now many good zoos prefer to keep a larger number of animals from a smaller range of species which can be reared in breeding colonies. By 1992 London Zoo kept only 142 species of mammal in captivity. Nowadays it's also accepted that some species of animal cannot be habituated to zoo life. In 1988 British zoos held 18 polar bears but by 1992 just 10 remained; after efforts to help them adapt to captivity failed, Bristol Zoo eventually had its two polar bears put down.

JERSEY ZOO

Jersey Zoo prefers to call itself a 'wildlife preservation trust'. It was originally set up in 1959 by Gerald Durrell who had been a keeper at Whipsnade Zoo. In 1963 it became a charity, holding only endangered species within its grounds. Its stated goals are to identify species in danger of extinction; to preserve endangered wildlife through a carefully controlled breeding programme; to promote fieldwork and research into a species' requirements in the wild; to negotiate with governments for the protection of species; and to communicate the nature of this work to the public and zoo professionals through an education programme. When deciding what animals to show the Trust gives priority to those that might otherwise disappear entirely because of the loss of their habitat, and to the zoo's ability to manage them properly. Currently two-thirds of the animals on show in Jersey have been bred within the Trust's grounds. There have been considerable successes. For example 14 pink pigeons loaned to the Trust were returned to Pamplemousses Botanical Gardens on Mauritius after 12 years' work. Later, 11 more were reintroduced to the native forests with radio transmitters attached so their movements could be charted.

Zoos' captive breeding programmes have successfully saved Père David's deer, Przewalski's horse and the Arabian oryx from almost certain extinction.

However, zoos continue to have a dual function as places of entertainment. This is least evident at somewhere like Howletts where visitors may never see the nocturnal clouded leopard because zookeeper John Aspinall refuses to compromise animal welfare for the convenience of the public, and most evident at somewhere like Chessington World of Adventures where the animals are almost incidental to the theme park.

Where the Animals Come From

Historically many zoos evolved out of collections made by wealthy men. All the animals had come straight from the wild and frequently their capture had involved the killing of other animals. Some died in transit and early zoo histories are full of stories of animals that lived for very brief periods after arrival in their new homes. Animals were also popular gifts in diplomatic exchanges between members of royal families and often ended up in zoos which usually accepted all gifts whether or not suitable accommodation or potential mates were available.

Increasingly zoo professionals think it better to rear breeding colonies and swap animals born in captivity between zoos rather than take more out of the wild. Their ability to do this is helped by computer systems like ISIS (International Species Inventory System) based in Minnesota, and ARKS (Animal Record Keeping System) based in Jersey which enable interested zoos to find partners for their animals elsewhere. By 1977 67% of the animals in London Zoo and 85% of those at Whipsnade had been born in the UK. Doha Zoo was entirely stocked with animals bred in Whipsnade Zoo. Sadly a trade in rare wild animals still continues in some parts of the world.

Countries like Australia now have laws that make it difficult to import any more animals from outside the country; when a pair of koalas went on display at London Zoo they had come from San Diego Zoo. One solution is for zoos to concentrate on local species. As early as 1874 Basle Zoo concentrated on showing Alpine and European species. However, Alpine animals are hard to keep in captivity and the public usually prefer to see elephants and other large animals. Now that so many people live in cities and are as unfamiliar with their own wildlife as anyone else's this solution may become more acceptable.

Presentation within Zoos

Those in charge of designing zoos are faced with a fundamental conflict between what is good for the animals and what is good for the public. Ideally animals require large enclosures with secluded areas offering them privacy. In contrast the public want smaller enclosures which make easy viewing possible, together with restaurants, shops and entertainments.

The original zoos were designed with very little thought for the needs of their animal occupants. Thus London Zoo's original Lion House, designed in 1876, gave the big cats no privacy at all. Many of them were also very bleak environments and it soon became obvious that if zoos were to be attractive places for people to visit they must be designed with that end in mind. (Sadly many zoos in developing countries are just as grim as the first menageries, and the death rate amongst their occupants can be very high.)

In 1907 Carl Hagenbeck opened Stellingen Animal Park, a private zoo near Hamburg. In it for the first time he used moats to create enclosures without bars, making them more attractive by building up artificial hills, etc. Paths and fences were used to keep predators away from their prey in such a way that the public saw only unbroken panoramas. Some of his ideas were picked up by London Zoo in 1913 when the Mappin Terraces were built. Now it is commonplace for zoos to use concrete, epoxy resin and other artificial materials to create natural-looking environments which are more appealing to visitors. Armoured glass, which protects the public from the animals, keeps the animals warm and creates an illusion of openness, was first used in place of indoor bars in the 19th century. However, Frankfurt was the first zoo to use it outdoors when it was put into the new Gorilla House in 1970.

Originally zoos were laid out taxonomically i.e. with the animals grouped according to their biological classification into families. Then in 1974 Metro Toronto Zoo broke new ground by displaying its animals zoogeographically, i.e. according to their place of origin, a scheme now followed by many other zoos. This has the advantage that it enables visitors to see how different animals co-exist within the same environment. However, it can create problems for specialist keepers who may find the animals in their care spread out all over the zoo. To make it easy for the public to see the animals exhibitions can be designed to be long and shallow as in the Africa Plains Exhibition in Philadelphia. This zoo also has a monorail so people can view animals from above.

New zoos have an advantage when it comes to creating attractive settings since they don't have to start by removing the old-fashioned cages (some of the buildings, like London Zoo's 19th-century Camel House, are listed buildings which can't simply be demolished). They are therefore well-placed to take advantage of everything that high-tech makes possible. For example, the Penguin Encounter exhibit at Sea World, San Diego (far more a zoo than a leisure park) exists in an artificially created climate of a constant 2.2° Celsius despite the sun outside. The enclosure covers 465 square metres and every day 500 kilos of crushed ice are blown in to create an Antarctic floor. The pool itself is 30 metres long and extends below an ice shelf so the penguins can swim naturally. The 560,240 litres of water are filtered every 39 minutes to keep them clean and the light is carefully adjusted to mimic the Antarctic. A moving pavement carries visitors past the penguins and into a darkened viewing area where television screens show six-minute features about their lives. In Seattle, Point Defiance Zoo even plays tapes of Arctic winds near the polar bears, while in Chicago's Tropical World tape-recorded thunder precedes artificial rainstorms.

Human visitors are often distressed by the repetitive behaviour of bored animals and several zoos have tried to overcome that problem by providing distractions for the animals that will also entertain onlookers. Usually such distractions are related to feeding. Zurich Zoo, for example, created an artificial termite's nest and filled it with food which chimpanzees could fish out with rods. Copenhagen Zoo pumps honey into a tree to encourage bears to climb up and scrape it out. Seattle Aquarium provides its otters with clams which need to be broken open. However, while the public will happily watch animals catching and eating fish and insects they don't want to watch carnivores hunting for their food which restricts what can be done for them. Some zoos also put animals on display according to a rota which allows them privacy to sleep if they want for most of the time but also allows the public to see animal activity. At Minnesota and Chicago Zoos they even blast cold air into the cage so that the animal which is rotaed to be on display will keep moving around. Other zoos have simply made the decision to stop displaying the larger mammals.

Since the 1960s many aviaries have been designed to allow birds to fly freely. Two of the earliest examples of such aviaries were the Bird House in Frankfurt which opened in 1961 and the Snowdon Aviary in London Zoo which opened in 1965. The largest walk-through aviary in the world is at Singapore's Jurong Bird Park. In 1970 Philadelphia was the first zoo to open a walk-through hummingbird exhibition. These, too, are now commonplace, with double entrance and exit doors to make sure birds can't escape into the cold outside. Finding new ways to display birds of prey has taken longer but London Zoo's African Aviary uses 'invisible' wire made of special stainless steel seven times stronger than usual to create an illusion of open air while still confining the birds safely; 'African' landscapes have been created by the makers of the sets for the Indiana Jones and Tarzan films. The idea of 'walk-through' exhibitions was also picked up in Japan where Tokyo's Tama Park Zoo opened a walk-through 'Insectarium', allowing visitors to mingle with butterflies and dragonflies, in 1969.

One particular presentational problem has been that many animals are nocturnal so that under normal conditions day-time visitors would either not see them at all or see them sleeping. Many zoos have got round this problem by building special houses in which day is turned into night. Often they are underground and always the lighting is very dim. The result is that people get to see animals that are otherwise almost unknown going about their normal lives. The Charles Clore Pavilion for Small Mammals at London Zoo was designed with just such a 'Moonlight World'. In Singapore the Jurong Bird Park even has a nocturnal walk-through aviary.

Some animals are much more naturally popular with visitors than others and less needs to be done to make the public interested in them. However, researchers in Dallas Zoo discovered that visitors to the reptiles and amphibians spent only seconds in front of each display. To get round this problem they removed some of the traditional cases and replaced them with windows which allowed people to watch the keepers handling snakes, etc. They also installed a public address system so keepers could explain what they were doing, provided 'safe handling' displays and installed videos about reptiles with the result that people started to linger and ask questions. In Lousiana the Audoban Zoo made the 'Reptile Experience' more attractive by providing exhibitions along only one side of the corridor to cut down reflection from the glass, by putting in carpets and climate control, and by cutting wording on labels to a minimum to encourage reading.

In *Zoo 2000* Jeremy Cherfas points out that the way animals are presented in zoos can affect people's perceptions of them. Thus crocodiles are seen very differently when presented behind metal bars and notices warning the public that they are dangerous from when they are surrounded by lush vegetation, wooden bridges and fish as in Emmen Zoo in the Netherlands. However, neither presentation tells the whole truth (crocodiles are often from arid areas of the world), so careful labelling is also needed.

In zoos where entertainment is seen as important animal shows will still take place. However, London Zoo long ago stopped the popular chimps' tea parties. In order to take part in them chimps needed to be hand-reared. Unfortunately at puberty they became too unruly to continue play-acting but it was difficult to return them to the captive troupe because they were unused to living with it. However, at the successful and popular Sea World in San Diego there are regular killer whale, seal and dolphin shows. Those sitting in the front six-row 'splash zone' are routinely soaked by the activities but there are always takers for the seats. Some argue that these displays don't degrade animals since they are not taught to do anything that is not part of their natural behaviour.

Zoo Security

Where dangerous animals are being shown to the public there can be a conflict between the desire to show them as attractively as possible and the need to guarantee that no harm will come to the visitors. In 1976 the Dangerous Wild Animals Act was passed to bring private zoos, where some of the worst accidents have taken place, under local authority control. The 1981 Zoo Licensing Act also provided for local authorities to licence zoos for four years at a time and to impose whatever rules they wanted to prevent escapes, record births and deaths, provide adequate insurance, etc.

Fortunately vinyl laminated safety glass is now strong enough to enable people to come close to the most poisonous snakes and sharp-toothed sharks with no ill effects. Nevertheless good zoos have vehicles available to rush visitors to hospital if necessary and a well-practised emergency system. Reptile houses should also have venomous bite alarm systems in place and several locked doors between the snakes and the public. Modern zoos increasingly use deep, wide moats to keep dangerous mammals away from the public while also enabling them to view them as naturally as possible.

For the sake of animals which require specific climate conditions the best zoos have back-up generators to use if the mains electricity supply should fail.

Funding the Zoos

Many zoos around the world have their capital costs paid either by central or local government. However, running costs must often be met from entrance fees and these can be very high. For example, London and Whipsnade Zoos employ about 500 staff, half looking after the animals and half dealing with the public. They also run a library, two research laboratories, a hospital, a pathology department, a quarantine station and an education centre. The cost of keeping different animals varies, with carnivores costing the most in food bills and gorillas the most in medical fees. Since most zoos are outdoor attractions they are unlikely to be financially viable for much of the year. Even in the United States none of the 110 zoos is able to make a profit any more.

Where a zoo depends on admission fees for its income this can influence the animals it chooses to keep. For example, Twycross Zoo which started as a private collection was quickly forced to introduce exotic animals to attract more visitors when it went public. The financial problems of Whipsnade Zoo meant that a commercial partner was sought. However, it was eventually agreed that the changes that would be necessary to produce an adequate return on the capital invested would not be in keeping with the Zoological Society's overall aims in which conservation and education feature prominently.

PROBLEMS AT LONDON ZOO

With around 12,000 animals to feed and care for and a backlog of old buildings, some of them listed, in need of updating, London Zoo is constantly struggling for money. In the past it was heavily dependent on sponsorship and wealthy benefactors for new developments; for example Jack Cotton, Sir Michael Sobell and Sir Charles Clore provided funding for the houses which now bear their names. How fast costs are rising is indicated by the fact that whereas the original Clore Pavilion cost £200,000 in 1965, the trustees of the Clore Foundation provided £1 million for its renovation in 1990.

Initially the government didn't give the Zoo any financial help, but after it was recognised as a 'national institution... a major London amenity, and also an important tourist attraction' in 1970 it acquired a small annual grant. The government then baled it out with a one-off £10 million grant in 1988, but by 1990 the Zoo was £1.8 million in the red. Amid rumours that it might be forced to close, a high-profile 'Save our Zoo' campaign brought in £350,000 of donations in just two months. But visitor numbers remained unchanged and the government came under pressure to do more from zookeepers worldwide.

In 1992 the Emir of Kuwait gave the Zoo £1 million as a thank you for the efforts of British troops during the Gulf War. Since then its future has looked more secure. It's now in the middle of a ten-year, £21 million Forward Strategy project devised by animal conservationists and business experts which will result in major changes to many of the old buildings. The Millennium Commission will also be giving money towards the cost of a £4.4 million project which will focus on showing how animals fit into their particular biological niches. In 1996 the Zoo reported its first ever profit of £1 million.

The continuing importance of sponsorship and donations is indicated by the fact that Esso UK has donated more than £220,00 towards the breeding programme to conserve the Siberian tiger, while Lord Paul of Caparo gave £1 million to build the Ambika Paul Children's Zoo which opened in 1994.

Zoos' dual roles as places of entertainment and education cause certain problems. According to the law, natural history museums, with their stuffed animals, are educational and so not subject to VAT. However, zoos are still treated as places of entertainment and must therefore pay VAT, pushing up their costs.

Taking a serious approach to conservation exacerbates the situation. Keeping a large enough herd of animals to run a successful breeding programme is much more expensive than keeping one or two animals of each species. The rarer an animal is, the more it tends to cost to obtain in the first place, giving the zoos that concentrate on the 'entertainment' favourites (lions, giraffes, zebras) an advantage.

Like most tourist attractions zoos try to make as much money as possible from ancillary sales of food, drink, souvenirs and guidebooks. There is nothing new about this; as early as 1827 when a giraffe was given to the Jardin des Plantes in Paris it led to a glut of giraffe-decorated souvenir plates, paperweights, wall-paper, brooches, etc. The same thing happened in 1850 when London Zoo received its first hippopotamus. One innovative idea in retailing has been the hiring out of video cameras, sometimes helped by sponsorship from Kodak.

London Zoo also raises money through a popular animal 'adoption' scheme. The cost of feeding each animal for a year has been calculated and adopters buy units to help towards the cost of feeding their chosen animal. For £20 they can adopt a gerbil or rabbit; for £6,000 they get an Asian elephant.

London Zoo also runs a Lifewatch membership scheme and offers 'close-up' visits when the zoo opens in the evenings and the public can take a closer look behind the scenes for an extra fee.

Attendances at Zoos

When it was first set up London Zoo was popular and fashionable. In 1831 there were 250,000 visitors, and until 1836 never fewer than 210,000 a year. After that the numbers of visitors declined and by 1843 there were less than 100,000 a year. However, the arrival of a new animal could double numbers, as happened in 1850 when the first hippopotamus was bought from Egypt for £350. The birth of a particularly appealing baby animal could have the same effect; when the polar bear, Brumas, was born in 1950 it pushed London Zoo's visitor numbers back up to 3 million. In general in the late 20th century conventional zoos have had difficulty attracting visitors, partly because of competition from safari parks and partly because of changing attitudes towards keeping animals in captivity.

FIG.10/2: THE UK'S MOST POPULAR ZOOS IN 1995

London Zoo	1,042,701
Chester Zoo	760,580
Edinburgh Zoo	527,655
Twycross Zoo, Atherstone	412,671
Bristol Zoo	326,997
Colchester Zoo	319,093
Drusilla's Zoo Park, Alfriston	300,000
Blackpool Zoo	299,584
Paignton Zoo	279,151
Dudley Zoo	262,206

This is not the case universally. In fact it is estimated that almost two-thirds of Japan's 100 million population visit a zoo or aquarium each year. This is almost twice the ratio of visitors to zoos and aquaria in the UK, even when overseas tourists are included. Tokyo City Zoo can receive as many as 100,000 visitors a day.

Specialisation

New zoos often specialise in particular species or even in animals from a particular area. The Arizona-Sonora Desert Museum zoo at Tucson, Arizona is typical. Set up in 1962, it shows about 200 species which are native to the Arizona and Sonora deserts of the United States and Mexico in simulated natural environments. Visitors can go underwater to watch beavers in action and underground to see skunks and badgers.

AQUARIA

Aquaria are another form of specialised zoo and can be found either within larger zoos or on their own. Fish are both easy to display and easy to maintain provided they are supplied with an adequate quantity of clean water at the right temperature and with the right chemical composition. Filters can be used to remove suspended particles and biological treatment beds to remove waste so that viewers get a clear view. Tanks can be made out of fibreglass or resin and water-weeds usually grow easily. Attention to detail isn't as important in aquaria as in conventional zoo displays, partly because the water masks imperfections and because most people have little idea what the world looks like underwater.

Nevertheless in the late 20th century aquaria, too, have improved in terms of presentation. Tanks in Baltimore and Hong Kong's Ocean Park are huge to imitate the vastness of the sea, and at Seattle visitors actually stand inside a tank let into the sea and look out on it rather than the other way round. There are also underwater aquaria which permit non-scuba divers to examine the wildlife of coral reefs, as at Eilat in Israel. The Shark Encounter at Sea World in San Diego also has a moving pavement which carries visitors through an acrylic tube round which sharks are swimming.

One of the UK's biggest tourism success stories of the 1990s was the chain of Sea Life Centres developed in the main seaside resorts. The most popular, in Blackpool, attracted 497,000 visitors in 1995, but by 1996 there were also Sea Life Centres in Barcaldine, Brighton, Hastings, Newquay, Plymouth, Rhyl, St Andrews, Scarborough, Southend, Tynemouth and Weston-super-Mare. Their owners, Vardon, had also bought out competing attractions like the Kingdoms of the Sea centres in Great Yarmouth and Hunstanton.

A brand-new, three-level London Aquarium costing £25 million opened in County Hall, close to Westminster Bridge, in 1997. It features twin tanks focusing on the fish and marine life of the Atlantic and Pacific oceans, and gives the opportunity to touch stingrays. London Zoo has also approached the Millenium Commission for help towards building a £100 million National Aquarium in London's Docklands.

SAFARI PARKS

Some people have always objected to caged animals. For example, during the French Revolution the crowds demanded the release of the animals in the Versailles Menagerie; the least dangerous were freed, the most dangerous eaten! However, it wasn't until the 1960s that these demands really began to bear fruit. Conventional zoos began to experiment with more imaginative ways to keep animals while other people turned their minds to alternatives. Safari parks built both on the popularity of real safaris and on the success of the African game parks in conserving surplus quantities of giraffes, zebras, lions and antelopes which could be shipped to England for show in more 'natural' surroundings than a zoo.

England's first safari park was set up in the grounds of Longleat House in 1966 when Lord Bath collaborated with Jimmy Chipperfield (of Chipperfield's Circus) to bring lions from various different zoological collections to the grounds of his stately home, then receiving an average 135,000 people a year. The original 'Lions of Longleat' were quickly joined by giraffes, zebras, camels, elephants, baboons, rhinoceroses and other wild animals. Visitor numbers soared to an average 500,000 a year.

FIG.10/3: THE UK'S MOST VISITED SAFARI PARKS IN 1995

Whipsnade Wild Animal Park	415,000
Longleat Safari Park	390,000
Knowsley Safari Park, Prescot	380,000
Woburn Safari Park	230,000*
Blair Drummond Safari Park	180,448
Causeway Safari Park	58,378

(*1994 figure)

Safari parks generally allow visitors to drive through countryside and view the animals from their cars. Safety precautions are meticulous, with notices reminding people to stay in their car and sound the horn if they are in trouble. So far the parks have an admirable safety record despite the horrors forecast by newspapers when the idea was first mooted. Although several elephants were imported from Zimbabwe to Longleat in 1989 before the CITES regulations prohibited further exports from Africa, most of the animals are captive-bred rather than imported from the wild. In fact Longleat has been able to export animals to the ex-USSR, ex-Czechoslovakia, France, Germany, Italy, Nigeria, Mexico, Spain and Australia.

The boundary between a safari park and a leisure park is often blurred, and visitors to Longleat can also explore a maze, visit a Dr. Who exhibition, shop in a garden centre and souvenir shop, while away a few hours in an amusement arcade, and tour Longleat House and its gardens. As with most theme parks many safari parks offer all inclusive tickets; visitors to Longleat can also buy a separate ticket for the house and gardens only.

In addition to the safari parks which offer the opportunity to drive past big game and dangerous animals, Britain also has zoo parks and wildlife parks which exhibit animals in traditional zoo fashion but in more attractively rural surroundings. Zoo parks include Howlett's and Drusilla's, and the zoo at Port Lympne. There are wildlife parks at Cricket St. Thomas and Burford (Cotswold Wildlife Park).

ANIMAL ENCOUNTERS

Occasionally attempts are made to bring the public into even closer contact with wildlife. For example, on Phillip Island in Australia the 'Penguin Parade' has been developed at a site where fairy penguins regularly come ashore. A grandstand with floodlights has been built, and from it 200,000 people a year watch the birds who seem oblivious to their presence.

At Mon Repos in Australia people can also go on to the beach in guided groups to watch giant turtles laying their eggs in the sand, a slow, laborious process during which, once again, the turtles seem oblivious of their audience, only metres away from them.

In *Zoo 2000* Jeremy Cherfas argues that encounters like this succeed in being educational and entertaining at the same time, and that they also serve a conservation role because the animals will be protected by the cold dictates of the tourist dollar. However, even if this is the case in countries like Australia where they take place under strict controls, it's not necessarily the case in poorer countries where the need to make as much money as possible may take precedence over the need to safeguard the animals for the future. So on the east coast of Malaysia, at Rantau Abang, the uncontrolled development of 'turtle-watching' as a tourist attraction threatens to drive away its very raison d'être as people crowd round the turtles, shining torches in their eyes and otherwise disturbing their reproductive processes.

OTHER WILDLIFE ATTRACTIONS

Wildfowl and Wetlands Trust Reserves

In 1946 Sir Peter Scott established the Wildfowl Trust at Slimbridge in Gloucestershire to maintain and breed wildfowl (ducks, geese, swans and waders), especially endangered species, and to educate the public about them. The original reserve was set up on wetlands where geese already wintered. Slimbridge now has about 3,000 birds from roughly 200 different species and sub-species on display to the public in geographically organised settings. Wild birds still visit the reserve, so tourists can be introduced to 'real' birdwatching as a natural extension to their visit.

FIG.10/4: ADMISSIONS TO THE WILDFOWL AND WETLANDS TRUST RESERVES IN 1995

Slimbridge, Glos.	192,812
Martin Mere, Lancs.	180,000
Arundel, Sussex	93,557
Washington, Tyne and Wear	74,670
Peakirk, Cambs.	46,000
Castle Espie Wildfowl Centre, Comber	40,001
Welney, Cambs.	32,000
Caerlaverock, Dumfries	10,000

WILDLIFE ATTRACTIONS

Slimbridge's biggest success story has been the recovery of the Hawaiian goose or ne-ne. In 1952 there were only 52 of these birds left in the world. Now so many have been reared that some have been returned to the wild.

The success of Slimbridge spawned other reserves (see Fig.10/5). There are also two 'refuges' at Welney in Cambridgeshire and Caerlaverock in Dumfriesshire where visitors can watch wild birds, including geese and swans.

FIG.10/5: SITES OF
WILDFOWL & WETLANDS TRUST RESERVES IN THE UK

(Source: Wildfowl & Wetlands Trust, Slimbridge)

The Wildfowl and Wetlands Trust is non-profit-making and raises most of its running costs from admission fees. However, it also runs a membership scheme which had 65,000 subscribing members in 1996. There are souvenir shops at all the sites, and children can make brass-rubbings of birds at Martin Mere. The Wildfowl and Wetlands Trust also runs schemes to allow the public to 'adopt a duck', 'guard a goose', 'nurture a ne-ne', 'foster a flamingo' or 'sponsor a swan' for sums ranging from £8 to £20 a year.

Education plays an important role at all the reserves and there are nature trails and teaching materials available, as well as braille trails with cassettes and guide-dogs for the blind. Talks, tactile exhibits and guided tours can also be arranged. To make life easier for birdwatchers the reserves also have 'hides' from which visitors can observe birds without being seen themselves; binoculars can also be hired. The Slimbridge hides are large enough to allow wheelchair access and have seats. There are also elbow rests and foot rails below the windows for easier viewing. The hides are camouflaged and sited so the sun will be behind them during peak birdwatching hours, and are wind and rain-proof, with floors firm enough to prevent muddy puddles forming. Wallcharts and free-standing charts display pictures to help visitors identify what they see.

The Royal Society for the Protection of Birds Reserves

The Royal Society for the Protection of Birds (RSPB) was set up in 1889 and also operates a network of 98 bird sanctuaries around the country (see Fig.10/6). These are mainly aimed at serious birdwatchers rather than tourists with a general interest. They are usually open all year round from nine o'clock in the morning until nine o'clock in the evening. Dogs are not admitted to the sites and RSPB members and members of the Young Ornithologists Club (YOC) are admitted free.

Binoculars can be hired at Minsmere, Leighton Moss, Bempton, Radipole, Ouse Washes, Blacktoft Sands, Vane Farm, Irish Marshes and Titchwell Marsh.

Falconry Centres

Birds of prey are rarely well-displayed in zoos where they are unable to fly freely. Falconry Centres allow visitors to see these birds flying and are therefore more satisfying. Displays of falconry can sometimes be seen in the grounds of stately homes, especially during the summer, and at the National Birds of Prey Centre in Newent which drew 40,361 visitors in 1995.

Other Bird Attractions

Other attractions like Birdland at Bourton-on-the-Water in the Cotswolds are more like specialist zoos. Some concentrate exclusively on particular species; the Swannery at Abbotsbury in Dorset drew around 100,000 visitors in 1995.

Rare Breeds Farms

Between 1900 and 1973 20 breeds of British farm livestock became extinct. Recognising the problem, the Cotswold Farm Park at Guiting Power in Gloucestershire was set up in 1970 to display rare breeds of British livestock, including St. Kilda sheep, Gloucester Old Spot pigs and West Highland cattle. In 1973 the Rare Breeds Survival Trust was also set up and since then no further breeds have been lost. The Trust now deals with 40 different breeds; some have recovered to the point where they are no longer endangered.

Rare Breeds Survival Trust 'approved' farms are centres 'involved in the

FIG.10/6: RESERVES OF THE RSPB THROUGHOUT THE UK

THE ROYAL SOCIETY FOR THE
PROTECTION OF BIRDS

preservation, breeding and promotion of living breeds of endangered farm animals which are open to the public'. In 1996 the approved farms were:

Oban Rare Breeds Farm Park	Newham Grange Leisure Farm
Cruckley Animal Farm	Farm World, Oadby
Home Farm, Temple Newsam, Leeds	Croxteth Home Farm
Wimpole Home Farm	Cotswold Farm Park
Tilgate Park Nature Centre	Sherwood Forest Farm Park
Shugborough Park Farm	Sandwell Park Farm
Hatton Country World	Wye Valley Farm Park
Dedham Rare Breeds Centre	Aldenham Country Park
Odds Farm Park, High Wycombe	Hounslow Urban Farm
South of England Rare Breeds Centre	Norwood Farm
Cholderton Rare Breeds Farm Park	Isle of Wight Rare Breeds and Waterfowl Park

In 1995 about 70,000 people visited the Cotswold Farm Park.

City Farms

The first city farms were developed in the Netherlands in the 1960s to help put town dwellers back in contact with the countryside. In 1972 a city farm was created on the site of a disused timberyard in Kentish Town, London. Since then another 62 such ventures have been set up throughout the UK, most of them on local authority land. They are funded by local authorities, charitable trusts, local companies, donations and sales of farm produce. Their activities are co-ordinated and publicised by the National Federation of City Farms which was set up in 1980. Most employ only two or three full time workers but have made use of government training schemes. In 1990 roughly 1.3 million people visited the city farms, with about 2,800 schools organising trips. However, the farms remain mainly local attractions.

Heavy Horse Attractions

Amongst the most popular domestic animals are the large farm horses, including shires and percherons. However, their numbers have been drastically reduced during the century; in 1900 there were about 700,000 heavy horses in the UK, but in 1980 there were only 7,000 left. In the late 1980s there was a revival of interest and numbers recovered slightly; several breweries still keep horses to pull their drays while some farmers have reintroduced heavy horses. Several attractions focused on these horses have also opened, including the Horse at Work exhibition in Halifax, the Norfolk Shire Horse Centre at West Runton and the Courage Shire Horse Centre. A few heavy horses are also kept in the grounds of open-air museums like Beamish as an added attraction. At the National Waterways Museum in Gloucester a heavy horse is also used to take visitors for a carriage ride around the site.

Trout Farms

While fish farms are set up as commercial rather than tourist enterprises, some also admit visitors, particularly to feed the fish. The trout farm at Bibury in Gloucestershire, conveniently situated on the curve of a busy road through the Cotswolds, drew 40,885 visitors in 1994.

Butterfly Farms

Of all the millions of insects butterflies are the most immediately attractive and least alarming, so it's not surprising that there are now several attractions focusing on butterflies. These include the Tropical Butterfly Garden at Great Ellingham, Norfolk, the Butterfly Centre in Eastbourne, the Great Yarmouth Seafront Butterfly Farm, the Seaforde Tropical Butterfly House in Northern Ireland and the Butterfly Worlds at Bolton and Stockton-on-Tees.

Local Wildlife Trusts

The UK has 48 local wildlife trusts which, between them, own 1,814 nature reserves. Although they receive some financial assistance from English Nature, each Trust owns and runs its own reserves and is responsible for its own fund-raising. However, their work is co-ordinated by the Royal Society for Nature Conservation.

Other Specialist Wildlife Attractions

People with an interest in specific types of animal sometimes establish trusts or sanctuaries for them. These can be very expensive to run and one way to subsidise them is to admit the public, as happens at the Earsham Otter Trust in Norfolk (visited by 46,844 people in 1994) and the Cornish Seal Sanctuary at Gweek (visited by 190,033 people in 1995). A woolly monkey sanctuary was set up at Looe in Cornwall in 1964; its 20 inhabitants live in extensive enclosures, and the breeding programme has been so successful that it has helped with the reintroduction of monkeys to the wild in Brazil.

Howlett's Zoo Park in Kent specialises in breeding gorillas; in 1996 it boasted the world's largest colony and was visited by around 200,000 people.

CHAPTER 11 : MISCELLANEOUS TOURIST ATTRACTIONS

Some of the UK's tourist attractions don't fit easily into any of the categories so far examined. These include attractions as diverse and popular as Madame Tussaud's Waxworks and Alton Towers theme park.

WAXWORKS

Early History of Waxworks

There were displays of wax figures in London as early as the mid-17th century when a broadsheet of 1647 records 'wonders made of wax' at St. Bartholomew's Fair. In 1685 the Lord Mayor of London gave Jacob Schalek permission to show waxworks in the City, in 1691 a Mrs Mills was showing life-sized wax effigies of Cromwell, Charles II and William and Mary in the Strand, in 1701 Samuel Fry took a series of waxworks to the Angel Inn in Norwich, and in 1703 a Mrs Goldsmith showed an effigy of the Duchess of Richmond at Westminster Abbey. But the best known and most successful of the early workers in wax was Mrs Salmon who exhibited 140 waxworks, some with clockwork mechanisms, at the Golden Salmon near St. Martin-le-Grand and later at a house in Fleet Street. Mrs Salmon's services as a waxworker were in great demand, and amongst her commissions were the figures made to go in Merlin's Cave at Kew Gardens for Queen Caroline, wife of George III. After her death in 1760 the exhibition continued under her name until 1794 when a banking firm bought it and moved the figures into Prince Henry's Room in the Strand.

Evolution of Madame Tussaud's Waxworks

While Madame Tussaud's is by no means the only waxworks exhibition either in the UK or in Europe (there are other displays in York, Blackpool, Edinburgh, Rouen, etc.), it is by far the most famous.

Madame Tussaud herself was Swiss but spent much of her youth in Paris where she was taught to make wax models by Curtius who owned the Salon de Ciré in the grounds of the Palais Royal and another waxworks in the city's theatre district. In her teens Madame Tussaud modelled a head of Rousseau and a likeness of Voltaire from life. For some years she was art tutor to Princess Elizabeth in Versailles Palace which gave her the opportunity to make models of the entire French royal family.

When the French Revolution broke out in 1789 Curtius turned his hand to making models of dead revolutionaries. Madame Tussaud did the same and her wax effigies included Louis XVI, Marie Antoinette and Marat. In 1794 Curtius died and left his collection to his apprentice.

Madame Tussaud created new models for the exhibition, including likenesses of Napoleon, the Empress Josephine and Talleyrand. However, Parisian interest in waxworks eventually flagged and some of the models were sent to London where

"Curtius' Grand Cabinet of Curiosities" was shown in Bond Street and then toured the UK. In 1802 Madame Tussaud herself took 30 wax models to London where they were shown at the Lyceum Theatre alongside Philipstal's new 'Phantasmagoria', the forerunner of modern films. While in London she modelled several English figures, including the Duchess of York and the MP, Sir Francis Burdett.

In 1803 Madame Tussaud took her waxworks to Edinburgh where their novelty value meant she could make £13 a day by charging people 2/- per visit. Philipstal's Phantasmagoria was much less popular. In the next 26 years she took her show to 75 British towns, sometimes showing the historical figures and the revolutionary death-masks in separate galleries. In 1808 a Bristol news-sheet first records the models being shown under her name rather than Curtius' and being called 'waxworks'. An 1819 catalogue for the Cambridge exhibition reveals that the models were seen as having both an educational and an entertainment value. Sometimes they were shown at a reduced rate in the evenings to allow poorer people to see them.

In 1834 a temporary London home was found for the exhibits at the Old London Bazaar in Gray's Inn Road. Next they were moved to the Strand to be shown in an arcade alongside other entertainments and shops. After that they were taken to Camberwell and Hackney before returning to the Old London Bazaar. Finally in March 1835 they moved to The Bazaar in Baker Street. There Madame Tussaud gradually built up the collection of English figures in the exhibition, modelling Princess Victoria from life but using photographs of people like Lord Melbourne. She also began to buy items that could be used to create tableau settings, including King George IV's coronation robes and Napoleon's carriage. In 1837 the waxworks was one of the earliest public exhibitions to make use of gas lighting in a tableau of Queen Victoria's coronation.

In 1850 Madame Tussaud died, leaving the waxworks to her sons Joseph and Francis. They quickly added a Hall of Kings, recouping the huge cost of the work in just one year. In 1882 work began on a purpose-designed building in Marylebone Road which opened to the public in 1884. This building set new standards for fire safety, with ten fire hydrants and two full-time firemen in attendance. By 1888 400,000 people a year were visiting the waxworks and the Tussaud brothers turned them into a limited company while still keeping artistic control. New models continued to be added and drew big crowds; when the murderess Mrs Pearce was added to the Chamber of Horrors in 1891 31,000 people came to see the model on Boxing Day alone.

Improvements to visitor facilities also continued to be made; in 1890 electric lighting was installed, while in 1899 a restaurant replaced the old refreshment room. In 1908 an 'auxetophone' was installed to play the voices of opera singers like Melba and Caruso. In 1909 a 300-seater theatre was installed to show animated pictures related to the exhibition.

Sadly the fire precautions proved inadequate and in 1925 a fire destroyed all but 171 of the 467 figures on display. A new building opened in 1928 and received 8,000 visitors on its first day. Then in 1940 a bomb hit the waxworks, destroying the cinema, the restaurant and the few moulds which hadn't been removed for safety. Although the exhibition reopened at the end of the year it was difficult to replace the damaged models: clothing rations were inadequate to replace the costumes, and there were shortages of suitable soap to wash the wax faces, of hair which had traditionally been imported from the Balkans, and of the blue/grey glass eyes which had been imported from Germany and Czechoslovakia. Constant evacuations and air raid warnings also caused visitor numbers to fall, threatening the viability of staying open. Even after the war there were problems: the plaster needed to make moulds was in short supply and restricted to medical use, while paper rationing prevented catalogues being published until 1949.

Madame Tussaud's and the Pearson Group

Since the war the Madame Tussaud business has expanded. In 1958 the Planetarium was built on the empty site left by the bomb. In 1970 a branch of the waxworks opened in Amsterdam and in 1973 the company bought Wookey Hole caves to use as a store for its moulds. In 1977 the number of visitors at all these sites exceeded 2.5 million for the first time and in 1978 Pearson, a publishing, banking and leisure group, bought the company. In 1989 Pearson decided that Wookey Hole was too small to fit the Tussaud's Group portfolio. It was sold to a management-led group for over £2 million.

In 1996 the Madame Tussaud's Group was the largest private company involved in heritage tourism and consisted of:

- Madame Tussaud's itself, visited by 2,703,283 people in 1995.

- Alton Towers, visited by 2,707,000 people in 1995.

- The Chessington World of Adventures, originally a zoo but now a theme park with a 'World of the Fifth Dimension', 'Circus World', 'Safari Skyway' and other attractions. It was visited by 1,770,000 people in 1995.

- Warwick Castle (see Chapter Three), visited by 803,000 people in 1995.

- The Planetarium in Baker Street, London. In 1996 it reopened after a £4.5 million refit.

- Madame Tussaud's Scenerama, Amsterdam, visited by 572,000 people in 1995.

- The Port Aventura theme park near Barcelona in which Madame Tussaud's has a 40% stake (see below).

- Rock Circus in the London Pavilion at Piccadilly which was visited by 709,000 people in 1995 despite a steep admission fee. Its popularity is no doubt partly due to its excellent position in the heart of tourist London and partly to its subject matter. Rock Circus is devoted to the history of pop music and uses hi-tech robotics to produce waxworks that move. Visitors listen to a commentary through infra-red headphones and end their tour in a theatre with three stages and the world's first revolving auditorium.

Improvements continue at the original Madame Tussaud's with £21 million being invested in the five years up to 1997. Innovations include a new 'Spirit of London' time-taxi-ride through the events of the last 400 years which has replaced the old fixed tableaux.

The Chamber of Horrors and its Successors

The Chamber of Horrors evolved out of the 'Caverne des Grands Voleurs' in Curtius' original exhibition where models of criminals, often made after their execution, were displayed under blue lights. Later the exhibition included images of those killed by the guillotine, modelled directly from their heads. When she came to England Madame Tussaud brought some of the criminal heads with her, showing them in a separate room when she toured Scotland and Ireland. The first English addition to the collection was an effigy of Colonel Despard who had tried to overthrow King George III. Some models, like that of Thistlewood, the Cato Street conspirator, were made while they were still alive, but others, like that of William Corder, the murderer of Maria Marten, were created from surgeon's death masks. Burke and Hare were modelled from courtroom sketches. Individuals were only shown as long as their notoriety lasted; then they were discarded in favour of new villains.

In 1843 a catalogue for the two new Napoleon rooms suggested renaming the 'Separate Room', the Chamber of Horrors. In 1846 in an article critical of the exhibition's emphasis on lavish costumes and grandeur at a time of economic depression, *Punch* picked up the phrase and used it to refer to tableaux showing Irish peasants and handloom workers in rags. The name stuck but was used to refer to the horrors of the guillotine death-heads and models of criminals instead.

Just as the main exhibition displayed historic artefacts alongside the wax figures, so objects were purchased to go in the Chamber of Horrors. For example, in 1878 the Hertford Gaol gallows went on show. In 1891 for the first time the Chamber included a tableau called 'The Story of a Crime' which depicted a hypothetical murder rather than a real scenario. This was later followed with tableaux of an opium den and of forgers at work.

The basement Chamber of Horrors survived the 1925 fire better than the rooms upstairs, but when it reopened eerie lighting and mechanical spiders had been added to make it more spooky. In the first week of reopening 43,225 of the 71,327 visitors to Madame Tussaud's took in the Chamber of Horrors as well. In 1929 exhibits showing torture and brutal punishments were also added.

The ending of the death penalty in 1965 presented problems by depriving the Chamber of its main source of new material. Instead the murderers were regrouped according to the type of crime they had committed and some were redisplayed in upright coffins.

Many people found the Chamber of Horrors distasteful rather than frightening, but others thought it tame stuff. After a mother's children failed to be frightened by the Chamber she went home and developed the idea for the London Dungeon, a gory display of medieval torture and death in a dark dungeon-like setting under the railway arches of London Bridge. In 1995 610,000 people visited the London Dungeon and 135,000 its York equivalent.

The popularity of this type of exhibition has led to its being imitated on a small scale elsewhere; the dungeons of Bamburgh Castle now display waxwork effigies of people undergoing torture. Nor is this fascination with the morbid side of life unique to the UK; in Mexico City visitors to the waxworks can see an Aztec priest ripping the heart out of a sacrificial victim.

Bowing to the inevitable, the Madame Tussaud's Chamber of Horrors is now much more like the London Dungeon with some truly revolting exhibitions, for example, of the mutilated body of one of Jack the Ripper's victims. These sit rather uneasily alongside static exhibits of contemporary prisoners like Denis Nilsen. That this is uncomfortable territory is tacitly acknowledged by the fact that there are no models of the Moors Murderers, perhaps the most famous and reviled of British prisoners.

Problems with Waxwork Exhibitions

The biggest problem with exhibiting waxworks of famous people is deciding who to include and for how long. Most of the displays at Madame Tussaud's consist of single and grouped figures of politicians, show business celebrities, sports heroes, etc. Although it would be inconceivable not to include a tableau of the British Royal Family, deciding which scions to leave out must pose some dilemmas. Sarah Ferguson was removed from the family group as soon as her divorce from the Duke of York became absolute, but Princess Diana remains in place, partly because she is the mother to an heir to the throne and partly because of her great popularity with the public. However, since her divorce her model has been moved further apart from that of Prince Charles. If adding and subtracting figures as marriages, births and deaths take place is relatively easy, it's trickier deciding when an individual has aged so much that their effigy must also be aged to remain recognisable.

It's also relatively easy to decide which politicians are best known and to replace them as elections and depositions take place. However, some politicians stay in power for decades and once again the figures may need updating. It's harder to decide which celebrities to include since fame can be fickle. The expense and time involved in creating new models make it impossible to include each year's new fad in the exhibition. Until the Rock Circus opened this had led to a situation in which the world of pop music was represented only by models of the Beatles, Boy George, Michael Jackson and Dolly Parton.

A survey carried out within the exhibition revealed that people reacted most strongly to figures that meant something to them personally. As a result the rules forbidding people to touch exhibits were scrapped and instead they were encouraged to bring cameras with them. Cameras can now be hired as well.

Letting people touch the exhibits entails greater risk to them, and Madame Tussaud's recent history has included instances of visitors damaging exhibits. During the First World War a model of the Kaiser was regularly defaced. In 1933 the effigy of Hitler was smeared with paint and in 1954 Churchill and three other politicians were attacked by a draughtsman with a hammer who was angered by government education policy. Fortunately the sheer number of visitors and the security arrangements make such attacks rare.

Making the Waxworks

When Madame Tussaud herself was at work waxworks were created by pouring plaster of Paris over a face to make a mask. Living sitters had to have quills or straws pushed up their nostrils to enable them to breathe during this process. A clay mould was then made from the plaster of Paris and wax was poured into it. Finally features were sculpted into the wax and coloured, and the eyes and hair were inserted.

Nowadays a metal frame is used to support a clay mould which is created either from a live sitting or from a bust or photographs. A plaster mould in as many as 12 separate pieces is made from the clay head. The parts are then reassembled, molten wax is poured inside and left to cool and harden, and the mould is removed. Glass eyes are fitted and real hair inserted into the warm scalp. It is then washed, cut and styled. Water colours are used to bring life to the features. It can take three months to complete a model from the first sitting. Sometimes the waxwork is unsuccessful; the York Waxworks uses cast-off models of the famous to create more workaday images.

The Madame Tussaud's studio employs researchers, designers, sculptors, moulders, hair inserters, wigmakers, make-up artists, a wardrobe mistress, carpenters, painters, and lighting and audio specialists.

The 200 Years exhibition at Madame Tussaud's contrasts how the original models were created with a video showing how a cast of model Jerry Hall would be made today.

Funding Madame Tussaud's

The huge number of visitors ensures that Madame Tussaud's is profitable. Nevertheless a pricing policy has been developed to reflect the needs of different visitors and the fact that although a visit may seem cheap to overseas tourists it can seem expensive to local people. There are discounts for groups, students, families and senior citizens, and Madame Tussaud's sometimes joins other London attractions in offering discount vouchers to tourists.

More money is also raised from shops and catering outlets, the aim being to add 20% to what has been raised from the ticket through retail sales. In 1989 the average visitor spent 50p on top of the cost of their ticket; the target was to raise this figure to £1.75 per head. Throughout the Group merchandising themes have been identified. At Chessington all five different 'worlds' have their own shops, while the Emporium near the exit sells everything that was on sale in the individual shops to give people a second chance to buy.

LEISURE AND THEME PARKS

Leisure parks are primarily outdoor entertainment attractions which offer a variety of different activities, including white-knuckle rides, safari parks, animal shows, children's play areas, boats, replica buildings, shops, restaurants and live entertainments. They are usually clearly enclosed and owned by one company rather than a group of concessionaries. There will normally be one overall entrance price covering all the activities inside. The term theme park is often used very loosely to cover a wide range of attractions from urban funfairs like Blackpool Pleasure Beach to the Elizabethan entertainments which were to be staged in the grounds and house of Avebury Manor. However, there is a world of difference in size and atmosphere between such places and the purpose-designed theme parks like Alton Towers, Thorpe Park and the American Adventure Theme Park. True theme parks are leisure parks within which all the activities are linked by a common theme: Disneyworld and Disneyland are the prime examples. Few leisure parks in the UK are true theme parks, although Granada (owners of the Camelot and American Adventure theme parks) is attempting to turn nominal themes into real ones at its properties. In the Disney Empire theming is carried through to the last pat of butter in the restaurant which has Mickey Mouse's ears moulded onto it.

There is nothing new about outdoor leisure parks. In 1661 pleasure gardens were laid out at Vauxhall (now in Lambeth) and became enormously popular with Londoners, including Pepys and Evelyn who recorded visits in their diary. The Ranelagh Gardens in Chelsea, which were laid out in 1690, were opened to the public in 1742 and soon boasted a rotunda for summer concerts. Vauxhall and Ranelagh were fashionable places for people to spend their leisure time in the 18th century; the pavilions in Vauxhall were painted by Hogarth and there was a Roubiliac statue of Handel in the centre. However, the gardens had critics who thought they encouraged lax public morality. By 1805 the buildings at Ranelagh had been demolished and the Gardens absorbed into the grounds of the Royal Hospital. In 1859 as increased urbanisation led to pressure on land the Vauxhall Gardens, too, were closed.

The American Theme Parks

It was in the United States, which has few alternative historical attractions, that the theme park idea really took off. Just as the British pleasure beaches were like prototype leisure parks, so the amusement complexes on Coney Island, near New

York, and at Atlantic City and Santa Cruz could be seen as forerunners of the modern theme parks. Disneyland, based on an original idea by Walt Disney but possibly inspired by De Efteling, a fantasy recreation of European fairy tales, opened in California in 1955, while Disneyworld in Florida opened in 1971. The Experimental Prototype Community of Tomorrow Centre, or EPCOT, was added in 1982. There are now more than 15 theme parks attracting more than 2 million visitors in the USA and 30 attracting one million visitors a year, with particular

FIG.11/1: FLORIDA'S MOST VISITED THEME PARKS IN 1995

Park	No. of visitors (millions)
Magic Kingdom at Walt Disney World	12.9
EPCOT at Walt Disney World	10.7
MGM Studios at Walt Disney World	9.5
Universal Studios	8.0
Sea World	5.0

concentrations of parks in the holiday areas of Florida and California. Disneyland alone attracts about 12 million tourists each year (more than the entire population of London), many of them accommodated in its own hotels. With one major theme park attracting between one and 2.5 million people within two hours' drive of every large North American city, it's estimated that half the US population makes between 1.4 and 1.6 visits to a park every year. However, this leaves little scope for further expansion and the Disney Empire has now turned its attentions to Europe. Disneyland Europe opened on the outskirts of Paris in 1992.

THE WALT DISNEY WORLD RESORT, FLORIDA

Covering 69 square kilometres, the resort has at its heart the real Disneyworld, The Magic Kingdom, presided over by Mickey Mouse. Individual attractions within The Magic Kingdom include a jungle cruise, Tomorrowland (with the spectacular Space Mountain), Fantasyland and the shops of Main Street. The Epcot Centre offers Spaceship Earth and a World Showcase with exhibitions and themed restaurants from around the world (many of the exhibits in the EPCOT Centre are sponsored by big companies, including General Electric, Sperry and Exxon). Visitors can also tour the Disney/MGM Studios on the site. The Resort is on a scale to dwarf anything in England; there are seven large hotels, a campsite, five smaller hotels and a conference centre right on the site. Cameras and pushchairs can be hired.

Apart from the Disney Empire there are several other theme parks with branches all over the States, including the 'Six Flags' and 'Boardwalk and Baseball' parks. Ownership of the largest theme parks is concentrated in the hands of a few big companies. In 1989 Anheuser, the company which brews Budweiser beer and already owned Busch Gardens, bought four of the Sea World sites together with

Cypress Gardens in Winterhaven and the new Boardwalk and Baseball Park in Orlando, making it the second largest leisure attractions operator in the USA after Disney.

DISNEYLAND PARIS

The first Disneyland outside the USA opened in Tokyo in 1983. The first in Europe opened in Marne la Vallée, 40 kilometres from Paris, in 1992 but was not the immediate success that had been anticipated. By the time it opened estimated development costs had doubled to £3.4 billion but France and Britain were in recession so that takers for its expensive admission fees were relatively few. The site's finances had to be restructured, with a 'holiday' on interest payments and a dollop of capital investment by the Saudi royal family. Ambitious plans to develop the rest of the 4,800-acre site had to be put on hold. It wasn't until 1995 that Disneyland Paris moved into profit.

The opening of the Channel Tunnel has made it easier for British visitors to get to Disneyland Paris which has its own TGV station. In 1995 1.2 million British visitors went to the park, making up 12% of the total 10.7 million visitors, despite the relative strength of the French franc. Forty per cent of visitors were French, after an initial period of resistance to the infliction of undiluted American culture on Paris. The Disney Corporation has been forced to reduce prices and acknowledge that there is no such thing as the 'European' customer, hence the change of name from the original Euro Disney. These days marketing is much more closely targeted, with much of it aimed at Britain.

Unlike Mirapolis and Asterix Park, Disneyland Paris stays open all year round (the Disneyworld in Tokyo has proved that there is a market even in winter).

The European Theme Park

Europe's theme parks are concentrated in the north where there is the highest level of disposable income and car ownership. There are at least four major leisure parks within two hours' drive of all the big towns. They probably evolved out of the idea

FIG.11/2: ATTENDANCE AT MAJOR EUROPEAN THEME PARKS IN 1994

Theme Park	Opened	No. of Visitors
Disneyland Paris (France)	1992	8,800,000
Alton Towers (Britain)	1973	3,000,000
De Efteling (Netherlands)	1951	2,600,000
Phantasialand (Germany)		2,000,000
Parc Asterix (France)	1989	1,550,000
Bellewaerde (Belgium)	1969	800,000

of providing public leisure amenities for urban populations and are not necessarily in traditional holiday areas. While US theme parks attract many repeat visits, European leisure parks are often visited in sequence and end up competing with each other for the same tourists. Between 70 and 95% of their visitors are day trippers but Disneyland Paris has six hotels ranging from three to five stars within half a mile of the park, offering more than 18,000 beds.

PORT AVENTURA

Europe's latest theme park opened at Port Aventura near Barcelona in 1995 and takes as its theme 'the discovery of exotic lands' (including Mexico, China and Polynesia). Development of the 115-hectare site cost £300 million and ownership is shared between the Tussaud's Group (40%), Anheuser-Busch (20%) and two other companies. The park is expected to attract 2.5 million visitors a year, 1.2 million of them from outside Spain, and about 340,000 from Britain. It will only open from April to October and will employ 170 permanent staff and 2000 seasonal workers.

The UK Theme Parks

In the UK leisure parks are a relatively recent development, perhaps because the seaside piers, pleasure beaches and many parks and gardens fulfilled some of the same functions; Thorpe Park only opened in 1979 and is usually regarded as England's first theme park. Unlike on the continent there was no tradition of building leisure amenities on the outskirts of large towns; in general Britons were used to travelling for their leisure entertainment, a fact which may have helped somewhere like Alton Towers which was not particularly easily accessible when it first opened.

More and more leisure parks have opened in the last 15 years, but evidence suggests that competition may actually increase the potential market for this type of attraction rather than dilute it as might have been expected. Several leisure parks have opened in France since the announcement that Disneyland Paris was on its way. In southern England a huge increase in the number of visitors to Windsor Safari Park and Chessington World of Adventures between 1985 and 1988 didn't significantly damage Thorpe Park's visitor figures even though all three attractions were increasing their entrance fees faster than the rate of inflation.

The Market for Theme Parks

Theme parks aim straight at the family market. They also draw more visitors from the C1/C2 socio-economic groups than stately homes and countryside attractions. Their greatest appeal is probably to children under 15, who can make up upto 40% of visitors. As a result although theme parks are entertainment centres first and foremost, some now pride themselves on providing educational opportunities as well. Thorpe Park receives 200,000 visits from school children every year and sees school visits as very important, partly because they take place in the quieter mid-week and because children who enjoy themselves often come back with their parents at a later date. Both Thorpe Park and Alton Towers produce special packs for students and their teachers with exercises on subjects as diverse as maths and biology to be carried out during their visit.

What makes a leisure park successful?

A new park is by no means guaranteed success. For example, Britannia Park in Derbyshire, which was intended to celebrate the theme of 'British Genius', opened to the public in June 1985 and closed again in September 1985. That the problem didn't lie with the site itself has been proved by the success of the American Adventure Theme Park which Granada later developed on it; this received 600,000 visitors in 1995. Disneyland Paris also got off to a notoriously shaky start, only moving into profit in its fifth year of operating.

FIG.11/3: ENGLAND'S MOST VISITED THEME PARKS IN 1995

Blackpool Pleasure Beach (free entry)	7,300,000
Alton Towers	2,707,000
Funland & Laserbowl, Trocadero, London	2,500,000
Pleasureland, Southport/Pleasure Beach, Great Yarmouth	2,000,000
Chessington World of Adventures	1,770,000
Thorpe Park	1,166,000
Frontierland, Morecambe	1,300,000
Drayton Manor Park, Staffs.	1,000,000
American Adventure Theme Park	600,000
Pleasure Island, Liverpool/Flambards/Camelot Theme Park	500,000

To be successful a park needs something to appeal to everyone. Alton Towers has a beautiful, peaceful garden for those guests not in search of white-knuckle thrills, and a selection of gentler rides for younger children. Thorpe Park also has a home farm. Ideally the parks should be within two hours' drive of 12 million residents, or within one hour's drive of a major holiday destination and two hours' drive of 5 to 6 million people. Many British theme parks are concentrated in the Midlands where they are within easy reach of the bulk of the population and where the collapse of heavy industry in the 1980s meant alternative sources of employment were eagerly sought. Dobwalls Theme Park at Liskeard in Cornwall might seem off the beaten track but is in one of Britain's most popular holiday areas and attracted 125,000 people in 1994. Ideally the park should also be within 15 minutes of a main road for easy access and signposting.

Up to 95% of visitors may arrive by car or coach so a large site will be crucial. Roughly 180 cars can be accommodated on an acre of land but to cope with peak periods enough space for 5-8,000 cars and 250 coaches at any one time will be needed. Of course with that volume of traffic theme park owners may need to invest in improvements to local traffic arrangements as well. Parking will need to be free if traffic jams aren't to form as people queue to pay. Sites with water are particularly appealing. Both Alton Towers and the American Adventure Theme Park have extensive lakes offering boat rides. Thorpe Park was built around a series of flooded ex-gravel pits.

The site will also need impressive rides. Unfortunately these are expensive to create and new ones must be added regularly to attract repeat visits. In 1995 Chessington World of Adventures invested £6 million in new rides, etc and rose from being Britain's sixth most popular charging attraction to being the fourth most popular, with 1,770,000 visitors. Enthusiastic and suitable staff must be recruited; Thorpe Park has a rigorous code of conduct for staff which even lays down which shades of eye make-up are acceptable. Scrupulous cleanliness on site is also essential and visitors to Alton Towers can hardly fail to spot the cleaning buggies that constantly tour the grounds clearing up litter. In the UK the 'theme' itself doesn't seem particularly important; Thorpe Park's theme is England's maritime heritage but it's neither the most important nor the most memorable feature of the site; Alton Towers has retired Henry Hound whose image used to appear on everything down to the restaurant sugar sachets. There are Camelot and Gulliver's Kingdom theme parks, but by far the most popular British 'theme' is the American West which has inspired three parks: American Adventure at Ilkeston, Pleasurewood Hills at Lowestoft and Frontierland at Morecambe.

Problems for Leisure Parks

One of the biggest problems facing someone planning a new theme park in the UK is getting planning permission for large-scale development of potentially noisy facilities; it took Thorpe Park six years and more than 150 planning applications before the site could open to the public. Britannia Park's problems were at least partly due to difficulty in obtaining planning permission. Even when a park is well-established permission is still needed for new rides and this too can be problematic as local people often fear the noise and traffic that will be generated. In 1989 Alton Towers built its new 'Beast' rollercoaster after planning permission had expired; the 'Mouse' had no permission at all. Local people objected to the extra noise and to the fact that both were visible above the trees, so the Council initially said they must be taken down again. Eventually it relented and granted retrospective planning permission on the understanding that both would be replaced eventually.

Cost is the next problem. A new theme park will require internal roads, sewage pipes and pumps, perimeter fencing, electricity, water, gas, telephone lines and landscaping, in addition to the costly attractions themselves, restaurants, shops, etc. When Legoland Windsor opened on the site of the old Windsor Safari Park in

1996 it had cost £85 million to develop. Such costs mean that most theme parks most be corporately opened, although Drayton Manor is still in private hands.

With most visitors arriving at theme parks before 1 pm and the average person staying for about six hours parks must be able to provide for requirements as diverse as plastic macs, sun-glasses, film and food. They must also offer ready access to first aid and medical facilities in case of accident or sickness. Inevitably children become separated from parents so 'lost children' posts are also essential.

Safety is also vitally important. In the UK rides must be inspected daily, with independent experts examining them at least once a year. Since 1986 the Health and Safety Executive and British Association of Leisure Parks, Piers and Attractions have had codes of good practice for theme park owners. At Alton Towers each ride has a radio link to the main control centre so any problems can be quickly notified. Most parks have attractively designed signs warning of rides which may not be suitable for those with heart and other health problems and stipulating height requirements for children. Water attractions have been responsible for the most accidents.

LEGOLAND WINDSOR

Britain's newest major theme park is the second Legoland which opened in 1996 on the site of the old Windsor Safari Park. Unlike the other parks it doesn't go for thrill rides, preferring a 'child-centred' approach which displays model villages created out of Lego and Duplo. The 150-acre site had cost Interlogo Europe £85 million to develop and is expected to attract 1.5 million visitors a year, 15% of them from overseas, despite a hefty £15 entrance fee. Its position, just 40 kilometres from central London and near Windsor Castle, is likely to be a benefit.

Queuing for popular rides is a difficulty which parks try to get round by providing wandering entertainers to prevent people getting bored. Notices are also posted telling visitors how long they can expect to wait from a particular point in the queue. As far as practicable rides must be designed to carry large numbers at one time to keep queuing time to a minimum.

Entrances for most UK leisure parks are inclusive and cost up to £16.50, with only small discounts for children. Although this sounds expensive it doesn't seem to deter visitors, perhaps because a site like Thorpe Park has more than 50 separate attractions. Most parks provide free transport, often by monorail or train, around the site so people can visit as much as possible in one trip. Unusually Drayton Manor charges a £2.50 entry fee and then a separate amount for each ride.

Access can also be problematic. Most British theme parks are in the countryside where they can be difficult for non-car owners to reach. However, many coach operators organise reasonably-priced day trips to the parks.

The UK's parks are not helped by the cheap price of holidays in Florida in the 1990s. In 1995 500,000 Britons visited Florida and witnessed the high standards of the great US theme parks, often in glorious sunshine. In general, standards at British theme parks have been improving. However, some of the smaller parks may eventually go out of business because of the competition.

Theme park proposals in the pipeline include a new Warner Brothers Studio site near Hillingdon in London, a development on the Battersea Power Station site and a proposed Tussaud's Group venture at Greenwich.

BRITAIN'S SEASIDE RESORTS AND PIERS

Despite the unpredictable climate domestic tourism in the UK has been linked to seaside resorts since the late 18th century. Amongst the earliest popular resorts were Weymouth (favoured by George III), Scarborough, Ryde (which became fashionable because of Queen Victoria's interest), Brighton (popularised by the Prince Regent at the start of the 19th century), Margate and Southend. However, most resorts only became really popular after the railways brought them within reach of the working classes. This popularity continued even after the railways declined and in 1969 75% of British holidays were still taken in seaside resorts. There were then about 70 widely recognised resorts in England and Wales. Seaside tourism has never been very popular in Scotland or Northern Ireland.

In the 1970s and 1980s a change took place in British holidaymaking habits as cheap packages lured people to guaranteed sun, more modern hotels and the glamour of holidays abroad. Even within the domestic tourism market seaside resorts fell in popularity as more people visited inland destinations and self-catering developments away from the traditional resorts. Too many of the seaside resorts looked just like other towns and were characterised by a mish-mash of architectural styles, garish neon signs and the tacky paraphernalia of a gradual slide downmarket. Central government restrictions on local government spending also made it difficult for councils to make the investments in infrastructure needed to upgrade the resorts. Damage was also done to their reputation by bad publicity about beach and sea pollution. However, by 1995 89% of the UK's bathing beaches met the EU's minimum standards. In 1992 the Tidy Britain Group launched the Seaside Awards to encourage local authorities to provide litter bins, toilets and other beach amenities. In 1996 their survey of 100 resorts found that 90% met basic standards, with 40, mainly in the South West and East Angia, achieving top marks for cleanliness. Most of the beaches which failed their tests were in the North West, Wales and Scotland.

By 1995 Blackpool was the most popular seaside resort and Blackpool Pleasure Beach was Britain's most visited free attraction, drawing an estimated 7,300,000 people to its 42-acre site which boasts a good 80 rides (unusually the Pleasure Beach is still privately owned). Other popular resorts were Scarborough, Great Yarmouth, Brighton, Bournemouth, Eastbourne, Torbay, Newquay, Tenby, Llandudno, Rhyl and the Isle of Wight. However, the new all-weather inland resorts like the Center Parcs developments at Sherwood Forest, Elveden Forest and Longleat presented a new threat. Brighton is the only British seaside resort which attracts a sizeable number of overseas as well as domestic visitors. This is partly because of its easy access from London but also because the Royal Pavilion is, in itself, a considerable attraction, drawing 399,791 people in 1995. Perhaps because it's home to Sussex University, Brighton also has a livelier, less 'buckets and spades' image than some other resorts, a fact reflected in the upmarket 'Lanes' development where fishermen's shops have been turned into attractive novelty shops.

Between 1991 and 1994 40 odd English resorts joined in an ETB Discover the English Seaside Campaign which aimed to reverse the decline in visitors and improve the resorts' image with the crucial C1/C2 families with children. Seven Local Area Initiatives, at Weston-super-Mare, Weymouth, Brighton, Eastbourne and Hemsby and along the North West and Lincolnshire coasts, also tried to improve the situation through better beach cleanliness, traffic management and overall resort appearance. In particular Weston-super-Mare's Promenade Project saw the restoration of much of its Victorian-style seafront.

Seaside resorts offer a full range of tourist attractions. Many have theatres, waxwork displays and local museums. Occasionally lighthouses are also open to visitors. The fate of many local attractions may also hinge on the success of the local resort which acts as a focus for day trips into the surrounding area. However, the attractions most closely associated with the resorts are their piers (see Fig.11/4).

The Piers

Although a few piers were built on the continent (at Blankenburghe in Belgium, Trouville in France and Scheveningen in the Netherlands), they were always particularly British in their appeal. Between 1814 and 1910, 89 piers were built in the UK resorts, 78 of them between 1860 and 1910; the only new pier built since 1910 was the one constructed at Deal in 1957 to replace an older model. They were originally built as landing stages for steamboats but quickly became popular as places where people could promenade and take the sea air. Gradually entertainments were added to the piers, including bandstands, theatres, amusement arcades, concert halls, fortune-telling booths, dance-halls, pier railways, 'what the butler saw' machines and deckchairs. Anglers also adopted piers as good places from which to hang their rods.

An Act of Parliament was required to open each new pier. The pier companies made their money by charging steamers for tying up at them and by charging promenaders an entrance fee. Businessmen were therefore happy to invest in piers. Railway and steamboat companies also bought shares in pier companies. By the end of the 19th century the steamboat companies were also making money by offering excursions from the piers to look at the coastal scenery.

Unfortunately piers have proved susceptible to fire, storms and collision damage. During the Second World War many of those on the south and east coasts were dismantled to prevent them being used by the enemy; they were never reerected. Many others have vanished since then. After serious storms in 1978 Margate Pier had to be demolished, Skegness Pier was damaged beyond repair and

FIG.11/4: BRITISH PIERS

Name of Pier		Date of construction	Ownership
Aberystwyth		1865	Privately owned
Bangor		1896	Bangor City Council
Beaumaris		1843	Beaumaris Town Council
Blackpool	North Pier	1863	First Leisure Corporation
	Central Pier	1868	First Leisure Corporation
	South Pier	1893	First Leisure Corporation
Bognor Regis		1865	Privately owned
Boscombe		1889	Bournemouth Council
Bournemouth		1861	Bournemouth Corporation
Brighton	West Pier	1866	Brighton Pier Trust
	Central Pier	1901	Noble Organisation Ltd.
Clacton		1871	Anglo-Austrian Automatics Ltd.
Cleethorpes		1875	Cleethorpes Borough Council
Clevedon		1868	Clevedon Pier Preservation Trust
Colwyn Bay		1899	Privately owned
Cromer		1901	North Norfolk Council
Deal		1957	Dover District Council
Eastbourne		1872	First Leisure Corporation
Felixstowe		1905	Owen Amusements Ltd.
Fleetwood		1910	Fleetwood Amusements
Great Yarmouth	Wellington	1854	Great Yarmouth Council
	Britannia	1902	First Leisure Corporation
Hastings		1872	Hastings Pier Co/Hamberglow Ltd
Herne Bay		1899	Canterbury District Council
Llandudno		1877	First Leisure Corporation
Lowestoft	South Pier	1882	Grand Hotels Ltd.
	Claremont	1903	Scott Bros.
Mumbles		1898	Amuseument Entertainment (Ameco) Co Ltd.
Paignton		1879	Paignton Pier Co.
Penarth		1898	Vale of Glamorgan Borough Council
Ryde		1814	Stena Line
Saltburn		1863	Borough of Longborough Council
Sandown		1878	Local council
St. Anne's-on-Sea		1885	Webb Group
Shanklin		1891	Privately owned
Southend		1888	Pier Action Group
Southport		1860	Sefton Metropolitan Borough Council
Southsea		1878	Portsmouth Corporation
Southwold		1900	Tomogan Ltd.
Teignmouth		1867	Grand Pier (Teignmouth) Ltd.
Totland Bay		1870	Totland Bay Hotel & Pier Co.
Ventnor		1872	Local council
Walton-on-the-Naze		1895	New Walton Pier Co.
Weston-super-Mare	Birnbeck	1867	Privately owned
	Grand	1904	Privately owned
Worthing		1862	Worthing Corporation
Yarmouth		1876	Yarmouth Harbour Commissioners

£100,000 had to be spent to make Clacton Pier safe again. In 1985 Scarborough Pier was flooded and had to be demolished; although it was a listed building repairs would have cost £1 million which was not forthcoming. A probable arson attack, also in 1985, caused £500,000 of damage to Ventnor Pier on the Isle of Wight. In 1986 a coaster sliced through Southend Pier just after £1.5 million had been spent on restoring it. Another million was required to make good the damage.

However, interest in piers is reviving slowly and more money is being spent on restoration. Bangor City Council bought its pier and restored it to its Victorian splendour; today it's lined with small shops and acts as a base for ferry trips to Anglesey. Clevedon Pier is a Grade II listed building which partially collapsed in 1970, whereupon the Clevedon Pier Trust acquired a lease to restore it. English Heritage and the National Heritage Memorial Fund gave £500,000 each towards its restoration, and a fund-raising Trust was set up to find the rest of the money. Work on the pier continues and visitors can help by 'adopting' a plank which will be inscribed with their name. Already River Severn cruisers are able to use it as a boarding point once again.

Many piers, including those at Cleethorpes, Bournemouth, Herne Bay and Saltburn, are now owned by local councils. Some, like those at St. Anne's-on-Sea and Ryde, are listed buildings. Others, like those at Clacton and Blackpool, are now in private ownership; the First Leisure Corporation in particular owns five of the piers. Southport pier is now the focal point for a £200 million marina and leisure complex development.

TOWNS AS TOURIST ATTRACTIONS

While much domestic tourism in Britain has centred on seaside resorts or countryside attractions, overseas tourism is often town and city-based. The most popular towns with overseas visitors are London, Edinburgh, Chester, York, Canterbury, Windsor, Cambridge, Stratford-upon-Avon, Bath, Oxford, Wells and Carlisle. Many London-based overseas visitors also embark on the traditional 'milk-run' tour of Britain, calling in at Oxford, Stratford-upon-Avon, Chester, Edinburgh, York and Cambridge, with a stop in the Lake District to experience the countryside as well. Coach tour operators provide day trips to Oxford, Cambridge and Stratford, and longer trips taking in the more northerly destinations as well. Day trips are also offered to towns popular with tourists that don't fit neatly into this circuit, including Bath and Canterbury.

The towns traditionally linked up in this way are so full of historical attractions that they can be viewed as attractions in their own right.

Although the milk-run towns offer mainly traditional tourist attractions, several have also opened new ventures, perhaps with an eye to the domestic market and its potential for repeat visits. Probably the best known is the Jorvik Viking Centre in York (see Chapter Five). The success of this development led to the creation of 'The Oxford Story' in Oxford which relates the city's history as visitors are taken round a series of tableaux on something like a moving lectern, and to the Pilgrim's Way in Canterbury. Edinburgh also has a Scotch Whisky Heritage Centre while Stratford has the World of Shakespeare, the brainchild of the American company White Oak Design who had already worked on attractions in Charleston and Salem. It features an audio-visual recreation of 16th-century England using the voices of Royal Shakespeare Company actors. Its development was helped by grants from the English Tourist Board and the Heart of England Tourist Board.

FIG.11/5: THE 'MILK-RUN' TOWNS AND THEIR TRADITIONAL ATTRACTIONS

Oxford	The colleges, some of them dating back to the Middle Ages (Brasenose, Christ Church, Magdalen, Merton, Trinity, University, Wadham and Worcester). Ashmolean Museum. The Bodleian Library. St. Mary the Virgin Church. The Sheldonian Theatre. Pitt-Rivers Museum. The Radcliffe Camera. The Botanic Gardens. River Cherwell.
Stratford-on-Avon	Shakespeare's Birthplace. Shakespeare's School. Holy Trinity Church. Hall's Croft. Anne Hathaway's cottage at Shottery. Royal Shakespeare Theatre.
Chester	Roman and medieval city walls. 'The Rows' shops. Cathedral.
Edinburgh	Edinburgh Castle. Holyroodhouse. The Royal Mile. Edinburgh Tattoo. Holyrood Abbey. Greyfriars Church. Edinburgh Festival. National Gallery of Scotland. National Portrait Gallery. Royal Scottish Museum. Arthur's Seat. Cathedral. Camera Obscura. Royal Botanic Gardens.
York	York Minster. National Railway Museum. Castle Museum. Yorkshire Museum. Bar Convent. Clifford's Tower.
Cambridge	The colleges, some of them dating back to the Middle Ages (Clare, King's, Magdalene, Peterhouse, Queen's, St. John's, Trinity). Fitzwilliam Museum. Great St. Mary's Church. Round Church. Botanic Gardens. River Cam and The Backs.

However, these 'honeypot' cities can be seen as suffering from too many tourists concentrated into relatively small areas of the centre. Even in 1975 Cambridge was receiving upto 3 million visitors (26 times the resident population) each year and they tended to limit themselves to exploring the area between The Backs and Silver Street and Magdalene Street. Congestion became so bad that flow control measures had to be introduced at King's College, by far the most popular attraction, with more than 350,000 people a year now cramming into the Chapel.

Towns can be made more attractive to tourists (as well as residents) by improving street furniture and lighting, and by pedestrianising central areas. By 1994 37% of British towns were partly pedestrianised, with the most heavily pedestrianised including York, Liverpool and Chester. Recently the area immediately in front of Buckingham Palace was pedestrianised, making it easier for tourists to view it.

The Spa Towns

Spa towns grew up round naturally occurring sources of water with curative qualities. The UK's best known spa towns are Bath, Cheltenham, Leamington, Harrogate, Tunbridge Wells and Buxton. Welsh spa towns include Llandridnod Wells, Llanwrtyd Wells, Llangammarch Wells and Builth Wells. The waters at Bath were already frequented by the Romans, but it wasn't until the 16th century that the health-giving possibilities of spa baths were once again appreciated. By the 18th century towns like Bath had become fashionable destinations for the wealthy. Modern tourists can visit the remains of the Roman and 18th-century baths and the Pump Rooms and old Cross Bath. Bath has also applied to the Lottery for £6.3 million to reopen the Beau Street and Hot baths which closed in 1978. Visitors to Harrogate can swim in the Turkish Bath as well as visiting a spa museum. 'A Day at the Wells', the Heritage Projects venture at Tunbridge Wells, focuses on its spa-town heyday in the 1740s. In Cheltenham tourists can sample spa water at the restored Pittville Pump Rooms.

In continental Europe spas are still very popular holiday destinations, particularly in Germany and the Czech and Slovak Republics; more than 16 million people a year visit European spas. However, in Britain the word 'spa' is often used to refer to a health farm or hydro club, places which are more popular with the health-conscious.

Tourism and Urban Revival

During the 1980s and '90s attracting tourists to a town was seen as one way to revive the fortunes of places which had lost their heavy industry, bringing new jobs and generally improving the environment. In 1984 a group of 13 English towns not traditionally seen as attractive to tourists joined up to change their image. The cities involved were Newcastle, Leeds, Bradford, Manchester, Liverpool, Stoke-on-Trent, Nottingham, Leicester, Coventry, Birmingham, Portsmouth, Plymouth and Southampton (see Fig.6/11). Each city put £10,000 into a joint marketing budget which was matched pound for pound by the English Tourist Board. The target of their 'Great English Cities' brochure was primarily the growing domestic short breaks market which was particularly useful for filling spare capacity in business hotels at weekends. In 1987 Hull joined the consortium, followed by Glasgow,

Dundee, Cardiff and Swansea in 1988 when the brochure was relaunched under the 'Great British Cities' strapline.

FIG.11/6: THE 'NEW' TOURIST TOWNS OF THE UK

The Great British Cities brochure was just one part of each city's strategy for attracting tourists. Liverpool was helped enormously by the money pumped into the Albert Dock by the Merseyside Development Corporation. Bradford, Portsmouth, Nottingham and Leicester also benefited from Tourist Development Action Programmes (TDAPs, see Chapter One). But perhaps the most striking success stories have been Glasgow and Bradford.

For decades Glasgow had been saddled with its Gorbals and gang-warfare image and overshadowed by its more immediately attractive neighbour, Edinburgh. However, a concerted marketing effort building up to the Garden Festival of 1988 and epitomised in the slogan 'Glasgow is Miles Better' eventually led to the city being declared European City of Culture in 1990. In 1982 only 700,000 tourists went to Glasgow. The Greater Glasgow Tourist Board set to work to increase the number of visitors, to extend the average length of stay in the city and to find ways to get people to part with more money during their stay. The Scottish Development Agency and Glasgow District Council both provided financial backing for projects to make the city more appealing; for example, pedestrianising Sauchiehall Street, regenerating the Forth/Clyde Canal and developing a programme of festivals. Investment in the attractions infrastructure included £30 million spent on a new gallery for the Burrell Collection which attracted 294,408 visitors in 1995. In 1995 three of Scotland's top ten most visited free attractions were in Glasgow, a city which now has a far more positive image amongst potential visitors.

Bradford's progress has not been so dramatic and much remains to be done. However, particular success stories have been the National Museum of Photography, Film and Television which attracted 620,000 visitors in 1995, and the restored Alhambra Theatre which has played to 98% capacity audiences. The Economic Development Unit created themed packages to promote the city. Themes included television series, the Brontes, industrial heritage, mill shopping, Bradford's Yorkshire, steam railways, flavours of Asia and art-lovers Bradford and were particularly successful in attracting media attention. Work still continues in the Little Germany conservation area where 54 of the 80 buildings, mainly dating from the 1860s, are listed.

Saltaire near Bradford was planned in 1851 by Titus Salt and provided housing for his workers on 25 acres around Salt's Mill on the Leeds/Liverpool Canal. Later a church, hospital, baths and school were added to the 700 houses to create a model town. Ten years ago, Saltaire was thoroughly run down, its industry departed, its homes redundant. Now, however, it has been turned into a thriving 'urban village' with assistance from Bradford City Council, English Heritage and Salts Estates Ltd. Focal point is Salt's Mill itself which now contains the David Hockney Gallery, but the surrounding streets have all been restored and turned into desirable places to live. In 1996 Saltaire won a Civic Trust Vision Award as a 'remarkable example of conservation-led economic regeneration'.

SHOPS

While shopping is often high on the average tourist's list of planned activities, shops are not normally thought of as tourist attractions per se. However, there are some exceptions, amongst which Harrods in London is the best example. Flagship of the House of Fraser chain of stores, Harrods opened its doors in Knightsbridge in 1905. It quickly established a reputation as a shop which sold everything and is visited by overseas visitors and non-Londoners in their thousands every year.

London has other shopping areas which are particularly popular with visitors. Oxford Street and Regent Street are favourites, especially in the six weeks leading up to Christmas when illuminations are strung across the streets. Both contain world-famous stores. The flagship Marks and Spencer Store where new product ranges are launched is at the Marble Arch end of Oxford Street and very popular with Arab visitors. Selfridge's is also in Oxford Street, while Liberty's and Hamley's are in Regent Street. King's Road in Chelsea also draws thousands of visitors.

The continuing popularity of Carnaby Street is harder to explain and illustrates the tendency of tourism to turn attractions into parodies of themselves. In the 1960s and early 1970s Carnaby Street was where fashionable Londoners went to buy their hippy clothes. It became so famous that overseas visitors still include it in their itineraries even though it's now little more than a drab annex to Regent Street.

In contrast Covent Garden is somewhere where the provision of shops with an eye to tourists has brought new life to a run-down area. Covent Garden market was established as London's fruit, vegetable and flower market in 1671. However, in 1974 the stalls were moved out to Nine Elms, leaving only empty warehouses and halls, many of them dating back to the 19th century. The site had obvious tourist potential because of its situation, squeezed in between the Royal Opera House, The Strand and Leicester Square. The Greater London Council (GLC) therefore invested £2.5 million in restoring the buildings and turning them into small shops. In 1981 Covent Garden won a Civic Trust award for sensitive restoration.

Covent Garden now offers a series of novelty shops on three levels interspersed with mainly outdoor cafes and restaurants. A crafts market takes place on stalls in one of the shopping alleys, and there are licensed buskers and street entertainers. Similar shops and restaurants have since opened in the surrounding streets as well. The London Transport Museum and the Theatre Museum (a branch of the Victoria and Albert) occupy one corner of the Piazza, and the Jubilee Hall, a Grade II listed building, now houses a conventional clothing market alternating with an antiques fair. But despite its success Covent Garden could still be vulnerable to insensitive development. In 1990 the Royal Opera House was narrowly prevented from turning the listed Floral Hall into a virtual theme park.

The Covent Garden revival was built on ideas developed in the United States where Faneuil Hall, a Boston market-hall, had become the focus of a $30 million project organised by the Boston Redevelopment Authority (BRA). The original Hall on the site was built in 1742 beside Boston Dock. When the Dock itself was filled in a new Hall was built to house the market. However, by the 1950s the market too was in decline. The BRA then persuaded the banks to put up the money to revive the market. The emphasis was put on quality, with original wood and stone used instead of reproductions. New England artists were encouraged to move their workshops into the new complex which reopened in 1976 and became extremely popular. A similar development also took place in San Francisco where the early 20th-century Ghirardelli Chocolate Factory was converted into retail shops, eating places and a theatre, generating 800 new jobs.

Outside London few shops are tourist attractions in their own right although the new Metro Centre in Gateshead has proved a big pull for domestic tourists in the north-east, attracting an estimated 640,000 shoppers in 1995. Nevertheless in popular tourist areas individual town-centre shops better reflect the needs of visitors than local people. Towns like Bath, York and Canterbury have lots of novelty shops similar to those found in Covent Garden, particularly in the streets round the abbey, minster and cathedral. In York the main tourist shopping streets are The Shambles and Stonegate, both of them picturesque in their own right.

Combined Shop and Attraction Complexes

Another concept which was developed in North America and spread to England was the vast mall incorporating shops, restaurants and conventional tourist attractions, often on the outskirts of town where providing adequate parking is easiest. In the USA the first such mall was the County Club Plaza which opened in Kansas City in 1926. By the mid-1980s the USA had more than 25,000 out-of-town shopping malls. The one at West Edmonton in Alberta has 817 shops, a zoo, a palm beach with wave machine, an amusement park and a Fantasyland Hotel developed round the theme of an Arabian harem.

On a smaller scale, London's Trocadero Centre builds on similar ideas. Unlike Covent Garden it's an all-weather, undercover development and the building itself is of no interest, although its position, on the road linking Leicester Square to Piccadilly, is perfect for attracting passing tourists. The Trocadero Centre looks like a standard shopping centre but houses several specific attractions, including a 3D Imax cinema, Funland, Virtual World, Virtual Glider, The Emaginator and a Haunted House. The £45 million Segaworld is the world's largest interactive indoor theme park, modelled on Japan's Joypolis Park. Spread over seven floors, it includes high-tech rides like Ghost Hunt which make use of interactive computer graphics. Redevelopment plans will add another £2 million ride on which visitors will plunge 38m. The expanded Trocadero Centre has absorbed the London Pavilion on the corner of Shaftesbury Avenue and Piccadilly which houses the Rock Circus.

The Gateshead Metro also has its Metroland, a sort of funfair-cum-theme park, a multiplex cinema and a GX superbowl bowling centre. The lakeside shopping centre at Thurrock also has a Fantasia and a multiplex cinema, while Swansea's new shopping centre houses Plantasia, an indoor garden and aviary which drew 46,000 visitors in 1995.

FILM AND TELEVISION STUDIOS

Although the Hollywood film sets and the MGM Studios in Florida had long been open to those who wanted to see the sets of famous films, when Granada Studios opened in 1988 it was unique in showing the sets of popular television programmes like *Coronation Street* which is still filmed there. 'That's Entertainment' cost £9 million to develop, and the English Tourist Board helped with a grant of £750,000.

Tourists can visit television sets of Downing Street, Checkpoint Charlie and Baker Street. There is also a 400-seater theatre, a New York Madison's store, a

Rover's Return pub and a selection of themed eating places. The reproduction House of Commons is even available as a novel conference venue when it's not being used for simulated political debates. In 1995 the Granada Studios attracted 750,000 visitors.

CHAPTER 12 : EVENT ATTRACTIONS

Tourists may be drawn to a place not by its fixed natural or man-made attractions but by special events, some of them one-off, but many of them regular or at least annual occasions. Some such events, like the Changing of the Guard in London, have long histories. Others are recent innovations which, it is hoped, will gradually attract more attention. Yet others, like the Millennium Exhibition, are expensive one-offs.

REQUIREMENTS FOR SUCCESSFUL EVENT ATTRACTIONS

Like other attractions, events won't attract visitors unless they're readily accessible by public transport or private car. Drivers will need adequate, reasonably priced and secure parking near the site. If groups are to be attracted there will also need to be plenty of coach parking space. The AA and RAC play an important role by providing temporary signposts to direct people to event sites.

There will also need to be suitable amenities at the site: plenty of clean public lavatories, a range of food and drink to suit all budgets, promotional materials like programmes and postcards, and clear signposting so people can find their way round the site. The needs of particular groups must also be taken into account, so the site will have to be safe for children, with suitable play areas. Preferably it will also have been selected with the requirements of disabled visitors taken into account.

In addition, if event attractions are to attract a non-local clientele there will need to be adequate accommodation to suit all budgets in the immediate vicinity. This is one of the trickiest problems facing those organising event attractions. Since by their very nature events are shortlived, they lead to sudden peaks in demand for accommodation which may be underoccupied for the rest of the year. This may not be a problem in capital cities like London and Paris where there are many other year-round attractions to take up slack capacity. However, for somewhere like Pamplona in Spain which sees an annual surge in the number of visitors to coincide with the Running of the Bulls, it's a source of frustration to watch potential tourist revenue lost to neighbouring towns, villages and campsites because it wouldn't be possible to provide enough hotel rooms for everyone. A similar problem faces those in charge of public transport; while extra long-distance coaches and trains can be laid on to coincide with the rush, local bus companies may find it much harder to cope with sudden extra numbers, leading to long queues and overcrowding. In 1996 the organisers of the Atlanta Olympics were criticised for failing to cater for the number of people moving between the different stadia.

These days many event attractions require massive investment in infrastructure, exhibition halls, etc. When it hosted EXPO '92, Seville built a new TGV railway station and several new hotels as well as completely redeveloping the island of La Cartuja. However, once the event had passed it proved impossible to find profitable new uses for all the pavilions and attractions or visitors to fill all the new hotel beds. This was particularly ironic given that Seville was already dotted with many empty buildings erected for the Ibero-American exposition of 1932 for which new uses had never been found.

Event attractions, especially new ones, are particularly dependent on well-placed and well-timed publicity; it's not much use people hearing about the Lord Mayor's Show the weekend after it takes place. For this reason it helps if the event can be held at the same time each year so that it becomes part of the social calendar, like the Wimbledon Lawn Tennis Championships. To generate publicity it also helps if the event is unique (like the Oberammergau Passion Play) or especially colourful and exciting (like the Running of the Bulls).

PROBLEMS FACING ORGANISERS OF EVENT ATTRACTIONS

While attendances at all attractions are influenced to some extent by the weather, event attractions, particularly those that take place outdoors, are uniquely vulnerable to bad weather. Even if people still attend because they have already paid and made their travel arrangements they are less likely to linger and spend money when it's pouring with rain. This means that countries like Britain with poor climates are at a disadvantage when it comes to organising events. Consequently they tend to be crowded into the short summer period with an above average chance of sun. In such circumstances events can end up competing with each other for visitors.

Security at event attractions can also be a problem since large numbers of people will be crowding into relatively small areas. Because they can be a magnet for pickpockets, drug dealers and other crooks, extra policing often has to be organised. Where alcohol is available there's also a risk of fights, making policing even more crucial; people are regularly killed during the Rio Carnival in Brazil, and even at London's much smaller Notting Hill Carnival there has been pickpocketing and at least one murder.

With the emphasis on excitement some events are intrinsically dangerous even without the crowding. People have been seriously hurt and even killed at Pamploma. In such circumstances organisers have to struggle to ensure that they're providing the safest conditions possible. They are also likely to face challenges to their right to continue with the event.

TIMING OF EVENT ATTRACTIONS

Many event attractions are linked, however tenuously, with religion, so there are particular times of year when more of them are likely to be taking place. The many ceremonies and events associated with Christmas in all Christian countries attract thousands of visitors every year. For example, some people make a special trip to London to see the Christmas Lights strung across Oxford Street and Regent Street.

Shrovetide, the period immediately preceding Lent in the Christian calendar, is also marked by many event attractions, with colourful carnivals taking place not just in Europe (Maastricht, Venice, etc.) but as far afield as Trinidad and Rio de Janeiro. Easter also has its ceremonies, some of them very dramatic, like the parades that take place in Seville, Valladolid and Malaga in southern Spain.

The coming of spring is celebrated throughout England with Maypoles, May Parades and ceremonies involving the crowning of a May Queen. On the continent Labour day celebrations are more popular; the parade in Moscow, with flags draping Red Square and fireworks over the Moskva river, used to be the high spot, but has now been eclipsed by the changed political climate.

FIG.12/1: IMPORTANT DATES IN BRITAIN'S EVENTS CALENDAR

JANUARY	New Year's Day
	Burns Night (25th)
FEBRUARY	Ash Wednesday
MARCH	St. David's Day (14th)
	St. Patrick's Day (17th)
	Spring Equinox (21st)
MARCH/APRIL	Good Friday
	Easter Sunday
	Easter Monday
	St. George's Day (23rd)
MAY	May Day Bank Holiday
	Whit Sunday
	Spring Bank Holiday
JUNE	Queen's Offical Birthday (10th)
	Summer Solstice (21st)
JULY	Orangeman's Day (12th)
AUGUST	August Bank Holiday
OCTOBER	Hallowe'en (31st)
NOVEMBER	All Souls Day (31st)
	Guy Fawkes Day (15th)
	Remembrance Sunday (Armistice of 1918)
	St. Andrew's Day (30th)
DECEMBER	Winter Solstice (21st)
	Christmas Day (25th)
	Boxing Day (26th)

Events in non-Christian countries also tend to be influenced by religious calendars. Thus in Muslim countries there are special ceremonies to celebrate the end of Ramadan, the month of fasting, the date of which moves each year in accordance with the lunar calendar. Chinatowns worldwide burst into colour each January/February as the New Year is celebrated with colourful Lion Dances. The Hindu festivals of Holi and Divali are also celebrated with lively festivities in Indian communities worldwide.

Since the dates of these events often vary from year to year, depending on the calendar being used, national tourist offices are the best source of information on what to see when and where. Increasingly they produce special annual festival guides with the tourist market in mind.

TYPES OF EVENT ATTRACTION

Traditional Ceremonies

Some of the biggest crowd-pullers are long established traditional ceremonies. In Britain, particularly in London, these are often associated with royalty. In summer the Changing of the Guards takes place outside Buckingham Palace every day and is so popular with tourists, particularly overseas visitors, that there have been suggestions that the ceremony should be carried out more often to enable more people to see it. (This is not such an outrageous suggestion as it might sound; the timing of the Changing of the Guards on Gibraltar was moved from 10.20 to 11am to allow day trippers from the Costa del Sol longer to get there.) Nearly as popular are the ceremonies of Mounting the Guard which takes place daily in Horse Guards Parade, Whitehall, and the Trooping of the Colour, which has been taking place on the second Saturday in June since 1805, when the Queen inspects her troops as part of the celebration of her official birthday. What these events have in common is that they take place in the open air in easily accessible places where large numbers of tourists normally congregate and that they are full of colour and therefore very photogenic.

Traditional ceremonies also take place all over the country, often in small villages which would otherwise attract few visitors, like Tissington and Youlgreave in Derbyshire which draw extra visitors each year to admire wells which have been decorated with flowers. However, such ceremonies tend to attract domestic rather than overseas visitors. Information about traditional events usually appears in standard guidebooks, but the English Tourist Board also produces an annual festival calendar and regional tourist offices keep lists of dates and events.

Sports Events

While many regular sporting events, like Saturday football matches, are primarily local leisure attractions, others like the four-yearly World Cup and the Summer and Winter Olympics, attract worldwide audiences and have to be planned years in advance. Special stadia may have to built, together with extra accommodation, and the bill for staging such events will run into millions. Despite the cost, most countries see them as great showcases and there's considerable competition to play host.

The **Olympics** are the longest established sporting event. The first Games were held in Olympia in Greece in 776 BC and records exist of four-yearly events there until 217AD. For the first 200 years athletes seem to have gathered from roughly 12 cities. Then they seem to have been drawn from one hundred European cities. The Olympics continued until 394 AD when they were abolished by Emperor Theodosius I. During the last hundred years athletes seem to have gathered from Antioch, Alexandria and Sidon as well as Europe.

FIG 12/2: SITES FOR THE OLYMPIC GAMES

	SUMMER OLYMPICS	WINTER OLYMPICS
1896	Athens	
1900	Paris	
1904	St. Louis	
1908	London	
1912	Stockholm	
1920	Antwerp	
1924	Paris	Chamonix
1928	Amsterdam	St. Moritz
1932	Los Angeles	Lake Placid
1936	Berlin	Garmisch-Partenkirchen
1948	London	St. Moritz
1952	Helsinki	Oslo
1956	Melbourne	Cortina d'Ampezzo
1960	Rome	Squaw Valley
1964	Tokyo	Innsbruck
1968	Mexico	Grenoble
1972	Munich	Sapporo
1976	Montreal	Innsbruck
1980	Moscow	Lake Placid
1984	Los Angeles	Sarajevo
1988	Seoul	Calgary
1992	Barcelona	Albertville
1996	Atlanta	Lillehammer
2000	Sydney	Nagano, Japan (1998)

(There were no Summer or Winter Games during the two world wars.)

In 1887 Baron Pierre de Courbetin suggested reviving the games. The idea was accepted in 1894 and an International Olympics Committee was established. The first modern Olympics were held in Athens in 1896 and 300 athletes representing 13 countries competed in 42 events from ten different sports. Following these games National Olympics Committees were set up around the world to promote the Olympics movement and amateur sport.

The international Olympic Committee is now a permanent committee of about 70 members who decide where the Games shall be held. The modern Games last for 15 days and are supposed to be seen as contests between individuals rather than between countries. However, since 1972 when there was a Palestinian attack on the Olympic Village in Munich, politics have obtruded more and more, with athletes withdrawing from the Games in protest at the presence of South African and Russian competitors.

Only amateur athletes can compete in the Olympics. At least 15 sports must be represented and there will also be two demonstration sports and exhibitions of art. Since 1932 each Games has had an Olympic Village to ensure the competing athletes can find adequate, reasonably priced bed and board. The Village also makes security easier to arrange and helps the organisers police the event.

The **Winter Olympics**, which give winter sports experts their chance to compete, were first held at Chamonix in France as recently as 1924 and now last for ten days.

The **World Cup** competition was first organised by FIFA (the Federation Internationale de Football Association) in 1930 and has been held every four years since then except during the Second World War. International section tournaments culminate in a final elimination event involving 16 national teams. In 1986 the finals were held in Mexico City, in 1990 in Naples and in 1994 in Pasadena.

One of the most popular sporting event attractions in the UK is the **All-England Lawn Tennis Championship**. The first championship was held at the All-England Croquet and Lawn Tennis Club at Wimbledon in 1877. In 1884 the first women's championship was held and the men's doubles competition moved to Wimbledon from Oxford. In 1913 the first mixed and women's doubles were added to the tournament. Although the championships were originally only open to amateur tennis players professionals have been competing since 1968. Now around 400,000 people crowd into Wimbledon every June, and the event is particularly popular with American visitors. However, this is an example of a tourism product with a fixed and limited capacity. There are only so many Centre Court seats for the finals available. The result is a black market in tickets which often change hands for much more than their face value. Their scarcity has been exacerbated in recent years by an increase in the number of companies using Wimbledon for corporate entertainment and prepared to pay over the odds for tickets.

Racing is a particularly favoured sport in Britain and involves many popular annual events. The **Derby** At Epsom has been taking place since 1789 and has a festive atmosphere with funfairs alongside the racing. **Royal Ascot** has been held at Ascot since 1711 and is more upmarket. Races take place over four days and are preceded by a daily royal carriage parade. Thursday is Ladies' Day which is like a huge open-air fashion parade, with outrageous hats the rule. Ascot is probably the biggest outdoor catering event in the whole of the UK. The **Grand National** takes place at Aintree, near Liverpool, every April and is Britain's most exciting steeplechase event. The **Goodwood Races** take place from mid-May to mid-September each year, with the main meet in late July when the Goodwood Cup is awarded. The **Badminton Horse Trials** is another four-day event which takes place in the grounds of a stately home each June. The **St. Leger** is run at Doncaster every year. The **National Hunt Festival** takes place in Cheltenham every March near Cleeve Hill. Racing is also very important in Ireland where there are meets on 250 days in the year; the Killarney, Galway, Laytown Strand and Irish Oaks Races in July are particularly popular. Every year about 150,000 people also attend the Dublin Horse Show in August. Racing is also particularly popular at Deauville in northern France.

Some sporting events in the UK are almost as traditional as the Changing of the Guard. The **Oxford and Cambridge Boat Race** which takes place on the Thames between Putney and Mortlake in late March/early April has been happening since 1845 and became an annual event in 1856. The **Royal Regatta** (a meeting for boat races) has been taking place at Henley-on-Thames since 1839 and still attracts the rich and fashionable. The **Veteran Car Race** from London to Brighton first started in 1896 when the Red Flag Act, which insisted that every car must have a man with a red flag walking in front of it, was scrapped. It has been officially organised since 1933, and only cars built between 1895 and 1905 can take part. The **Scottish Highland Games**, which take place in July, August and September and which feature such picturesque sports as tossing the caber and throwing the hammer, may date from the 11th century. There are Games at Inverary, Mull, South Uist, Dornoch, Newtonmore, Fort William, Nairn, Portree, Edinburgh, Dunoon, Bute, Lonach, Lanark, Aberdeen and Oban. Probably the best known is the Royal Highland Gathering at Braemar each September.

Most sporting events other than the big international competitions attract a mainly domestic market. However, those which offer something unique to a particular country will also attract foreign tourists. Thus the Scottish Highland Games are popular with overseas tourists as well as local visitors. Tourism has even been blamed for the continued survival of bullfighting which is so closely identified with Spain in people's minds that it attracts the sort of visitors who wouldn't normally have anything to do with such barbaric activity.

Festivals of Music, Drama and Film

European festivals of Classical music are often held in places associated with famous composers. So there is a Wagner festival in Bayreuth, a Chopin festival in Poland, a Haydn festival in Vienna and a Classical music concert in Salzburg, bithplace of Mozart, every year. There are also annual festival s of jazz (New Orleans, Copenhagen, Nice, the Hague, Viersen, Cork), country music (Stuttgart) and rock (Glastonbury). Montego Bay hosts an annual reggae festival (Sunsplash Jamaica), Falun in Sweden a large folk festival, Chicago a blues festival and Warsaw a modern music festival. Music festivals are labour intensive and expensive to organise, so all such festvials tend to take place in summer, Europe's peak tourist season, when capacity audiences are most likely.

England's major music festivals include the Glyndebourne Opera season, Aldeburgh Festival, the Henry Wood Promenade Concerts (the "Proms"), and the international Musical Eisteddfod at Llangollen in Wales. Opera is staged at

Glyndebourne in Sussex from late May to early August in a converted Tudor manor-house. The **Aldeburgh Festival** takes place in June in churches in Orford, Blythburgh and Framlingham and in the Maltings at Snape in Suffolk. The **Proms** are held from July to September in the Royal Albert Hall, London.

"Eisteddfods" (Welsh for 'sitting together') are Welsh gatherings of musicians for musical competitions, many of them held in March to coincide with St. David's Day. They started in the Middle Ages as assemblies of harpists, poets, etc.; the first recorded eisteddfod was held in Cardigan Castle in 1176. In the 17th century they declined in popularity, only to revive in the 18th century. The real revival came after the First World War and the Depression. In the late 20th century the most important are the Royal National Eisteddfod, and the International Musical Eisteddfod, a competition for folk dancing, singing and choirs from all round the world which has been taking place at Llangollen in North Wales since 1947. About 150,000 people a year attend the Llangollen Eisteddfod at its site on the banks of the River Dee. The Royal National Eisteddfod, attended by about 20-30,000 people a year, alternates between sites in north and south Wales, and aims to encourage indigenous Welsh culture. The presence of the Archdruid and Bards in ceremonial robes makes it very colourful. During the week the chair is award to the writer of the best poem on a set theme in a Welsh verse form, while the crown is awarded for the best free verse poem.

FIG.12/3: THE EUROPEAN CITIES OF CULTURE

Athens	1985
Florence	1986
Amsterdam	1987
Berlin	1988
Paris	1989
Glasgow	1990
Dublin	1991
Madrid	1992
Antwerp	1993
Lisbon	1994
Luxembourg	1995
Copenhagen	1996
Salonika/Thessaloniki	1997

European drama festivals also tend to take place in summer; in some cases outdoor sites like the ancient Greek theatre at Epidaurus are used. Theatres like the Chichester and Malvern put on special summer seasons of plays. Drama is also a major part of the Bath Festival in June and the Edinburgh Festival in August. Every four years in mid-June medieval mystery plays are reenacted in York in the grounds of the ruined St. Mary's Abbey. A professional actor plays Jesus; the other parts are taken by local people.

There are annual film festivals in Cannes and Venice, and mixed arts festivals in Prague, Kiev, St. Petersburg and Granada. The World of Music and Dance organisation (WOMAD), which is dedicated to bringing world music and dance to a wider audience, also arranges mixed music and dance events in the UK, Europe and North America, usually in the summer.

Since 1985 the European Community has nominated **a European City of Culture** for a year at a time. This is not strictly a festival but is promoted in much the same way and has much the same effect in terms of attracting extra visitors. What's more festivals themselves play a big part in the activities planned by the reigning city.

Athens, Florence and Amsterdam mainly used the accolade as an opportunity to stage art festivals focusing on their cultural assets. However, the West German government and West Berlin Senate developed a programme of special events to promote Berlin in general, starting a trend followed by Paris and Glasgow. In 1991 a new Writers Museum opened in Dublin as a permanent reminder of the city's year of fame.

Unfortunately although attractions in the designated city tend to receive more visitors during the year, it's not easy to keep up the momentum. In 1991, visitors to Glasgow Art Gallery fell by 11.4% from the 1990 figure, and those to the Museum of Transport fell by 8%.

Food and Drink Festivals

Inevitably food and drink play a major part in most events. However, they are also the raison d'être of some festivals like the **Munich Beer Festival** and the Wine Festival in Limassol, Cyprus, which take place in September every year. The Munich event is so popular that tour operators even offer package deals to it. Jersey in the Channel Islands also hosts a Good Food Fair every June.

Flower and Garden Festivals

The flower festivals organised in English churches have already been mentioned (Chapter Four). Flowers are also a major lure for tourists who flock to the Netherlands and parts of Lincolnshire to see the spring bulbfields in flower; in fact the Dutch bulbfields are so popular that tour operators include visits to them in package deals. Tulips have been growing in the Netherlands since the 16th century when they were introduced from Turkey. One of the best places to see them is the 30-acre Keukenhof Gardens site where there have been special displays since 1949. Twelve thousand varieties of tulip, hyacinth, narcissus and muscari are on show, with 6.5 million bulbs hand-planted every year. About 850,000 people a year visit the Keukenhof Gardens. London's most popular flower show (and the world's largest) is the **Chelsea Flower Show** which has been staged by the Royal Horticultural society in the grounds of the Royal Hospital every May since 1913.

Europe's biggest floral carnival has been taking place in St. Helier on Jersey since 1902 when it started life as part of the celebrations for King Edward VII's coronation. Millions of flowers are grown to decorate floats which are watched by more than 50,000 people a year. At the end of the festival a 'battle of the flowers' takes place, with spectators and exhibitors pelting each other with blossoms.

Although it's not strictly speaking a festival the annual 'England in Bloom' competition encourages towns, cities and villages to improve the environment by providing attractive floral displays. Traders and local authorities pick up the costs. In 1988 there were 650 entries in the competition and Port Sunlight, Oxford and Market Bosworth all won prizes. The winners can then enter the countrywide 'Britain in Bloom' competition. 'Best Kept Station' awards also encourage the planting of flowers at stations.

After the Second World War many European cities were left with expanses of derelict land. Germany was first to think of Garden Festivals as a way to renew the cities; the first such site was laid out in Hanover in 1951. Since then there have been 19 Garden Festivals in Germany, some of them hugely successful; the 1983 Munich festival alone attracted 13 million visitors. The idea was quickly picked up in Switzerland, the Netherlands, Austria and Canada; the United States hosted its first Garden Festival in 1992.

SUCCESS AT STOKE-ON-TRENT

According to the Stoke-on-Trent City Council Tourism Division, the 1986 Garden Festival was 'undoubtedly the key factor in the stimulation of Stoke-on-Trent as a major tourist attraction'. During the 179 days of the Festival, 2,184,052 people visited in 367,249 cars and 11,451 coaches. The Festival had cost £17.45 million to organise but £8.08 million of that was recouped in admission charges, payments from exhibitors and sales of assets. Visitors spent a further £7.2 million in the Stoke area, and £12.5 million-worth of contracts were awarded to local companies. During the course of the Festival 1,280 people were employed. Stoke-on-Trent has also been successful in making continued use of the Festival site which now boasts a four star hotel, leisure complex, retail park, marina, dry ski slope and offices; these enterprises have created an estimated 2,300 permanent jobs. During 1997 a Canal regeneration Project will revive the canal running alongside Festival Park.

Britain's first National Garden Festival was held in Liverpool in 1984 and others followed in Stoke-on-Trent (1986) Glasgow (1988) and Gateshead (1990). The fifth festival was held in Ebbw Vale in Wales in 1992 as part of a 'greening of the valleys' campaign to bring tourism jobs to an area badly affected by the collapse of the coal industry. As in Germany the sites chosen to host Britain's garden festivals were all in areas suffering from industrial decline and decaying infrastructure. Consequently, with the exception of Ebbw Vale, they were concentrated in the north of the country and in areas not traditionally thought of as attractive to tourists.

These festivals were successful in their short-term aim of boosting local tourism; the Ebbw Vale Garden Festival attracted around 2 million visitors, 69% of them from outside South Wales. However, while the German festivals resulted in a permanent legacy in the form of urban parks like Hanover's Stadtpark, much less of the festival landscape has survived in Britain. In 1992 the Pleasure Island leisure complex opened on the site of the Liverpool Garden Festival; in 1995 it attracted around 420,000 visitors. At Ebbw Vale the Festival Park Visitor Centre and parkland survive. A continuing programme of events attracted 237,000 in 1995.

In 1997 no new Garden Festivals were planned.

Religious Events

Apart from events and ceremonies associated with the big dates in the religious calendars there are other festivities associated with religion. For example, festivities in European towns and villages are frequently associated with saints' days. So visitors to Santiago de Compostela who arrive on 25th July, feast day of the city's patron saint St. James, will be able to watch fireworks displays and the burning of a cardboard model of the Cordoba mosque.

The **carnivals** which traditionally took place in Catholic countries before the rigours of Lent are some of the most exciting and colourful festivals. Many take place in February, including the Venice carnival which dates back to the Middle Ages. It was abolished by Napoleon in 1797 but revived in 1979. Its focal points are St. Mark's Square and the Rialto Bridge where people gather in fantastic costumes and masks. Other carnivals. like those in Rio de Janeiro and Trinidad, involve huge floats with fantastic decorations. Carnivals divorced from even nominal religious context take place during the summer in Havana and in Notting Hill, London and St. Paul's, Bristol.

Oberammergau Passion Play is in a class of its own. Once every ten years a small Bavarian village organises a Passion Play in which all the parts are played by villagers. The first play was held in 1654 to give thanks for the end of an outbreak of plague. Since 1680 it has been performed once a decade (in the intervening years the villagers keep in practise with plays on other Biblical subjects). The text used dates back to 1850. Actors for the 18 main parts are selected by a secret committee of 26 men who pray for divine inspiration. All 1,500 residents who take part share in the takings. Until 1990 only single women below the age of 30 could be selected. Without the Play there would be little to attract outsiders to the village, but this event is so popular that all tickets for the 1990 play, many of them handled through major tour operators, were sold out by 1989. In 1990 tickets for the seven performances cost. at least £30 each. A special open-air theatre had been built specifically for the plays. Altogether 500,000 people attended the 75 performances, 30,000 of them from the UK.

Outside Europe religious celebrations can be even more exciting. India has particularly spectacular festivities including the one at Puri when giant chariots are driven around the town during the Festival of the Cars in June The Amarnath Pilgrimage, with thousands of pilgrims making their way to a remote Kashmiri cave, is another popular attraction. During Loi Krathong in Thailand candles are placed inside banana leaf boats and floated down the river. In Mexico on the Day of the Dead in November people dress up in skeleton costumes and there are all-night parties in graveyards.

Political Events

Important dates in a country's history are often the focus for festivities. Bastille Day (14th July) is an exciting day to be in Paris, with red, white and blue balloons floating over the city and music everywhere. Ex-colonial countries tend to celebrate the dates of their independence in a big way. In India the anniversary of the founding of the republic in 1950 is celebrated in New Delhi with processions of elephants decked out in finery.

Markets

Some markets, like the Sunday flea-market of 'Rastro' in Madrid, take place on a weekly basis, but others, like the Pushkar Camel Fair in India which attracts thousands of people to Rajasthan at the end of October, are annual events. Market towns sometimes depend almost entirely on their markets for their visitors; Chichicastenango, a small hill town in Guatemala with one of the world's most colourful markets, only really comes alive on Thursdays and Sundays when the market is in full swing.

Illuminations

Tourists can also be attracted by special lighting arrangements, especially in winter. 'Son et lumière' performances are popular at historic houses both in the UK and on the continent; the building's history is related to a background of sound and lighting effects. The Christmas lights in London's West End also attract extra evening visitors in the six weeks leading up to Christmas. In 1995 275,000 people visited the illuminations at Walsall Arboretum.

Several British seaside resorts also put on special illuminations to attract visitors. Best known are the **Blackpool Illuminations** which line the seafront from late September to November each year. The first street lights were introduced to Blackpool in 1879, but in 1897, electric trams and coloured, flashing advertisments were added and turned into prototype illuminations. In 1912 when Princess Louise visited the town to open the new promenade the first real illuminations were created to celebrate. By 1990 the illuminations were costing £1.38 million per year and 1500 designs for 50 different themes used 500,000 separate light bulbs. Preparations offer employment for 100 people all year round. It is calculated that tourists spend £200 million in Blackpool during the period of the illuminations. There are also illuminations in Eastbourne, Southsea, Torquay, Brighton, Douglas, Bournemouth, Morecambe, Southend-on-Sea and Skegness.

Circuses

The work 'circus' refers to the circular shape of the site where circus performances take place but also suggests an entertainment of spectacle consisting of animal acts or feats of human daring. The 1981 Zoo Licensing Act defined circuses as 'places where animals are kept or introduced wholly or mainly for the purpose of performing tricks or manoeuvres'.

The Ancient Egyptians trained baboons to play musical instruments and to pick out the letters of the alphabet, but the first real circus was probably the Circus Maximus in Rome where chariot races took place. More unpleasant were the gladiatorial contests between men and beasts that took place in Rome regularly until 325 AD and which can be seen as the forerunners of modern circuses. These games were often bloodbaths; 11,000 animals were slaughtered during Trajan's games in the 2nd century AD. Although Constantine officially abolished the contests in 325 AD they continued unofficially and were actually revived by Justinian in the 6th century. It wasn't until the 12th century that such events disappeared altogether.

During the Middle Ages jugglers and other artistes we now associate with circuses wandered Europe's trade fairs. Then in 1768 an Englishman, Philip Astley, discovered that centrifugal forces made it possible to stand upright on a horse's back and ride in a circle on it. He erected a roof over a ring and provided seats to show off his new-found skill. In 1782 one of his riders set up a 'Royal Circus', the first modern use of the word.

From Europe the circus spread to India and Iran, while touring companies visited Africa, South America and Australia. Then in the early 19th century Isaac Van Amburgh introduced wild animals to the performances; he was probably the first man to put his head in a lion's mouth. In the USA animals were shown as wild and ferocious with much shooting and cracking of whips; in Europe they were more often shown as tame and obedient.

In 1859 Jules Leotard introduced the flying trapeze. When Blondin crossed Niagara Falls on a tightrope that idea was also taken up by circuses. In the United States, where circuses usually had three rings rather than one as in Europe, Barnum was soon adding sideshows, often exhibiting freaks like giants and dwarves in fairs attached to the entertainment. In 1874 the first group of performing elephants seems to have appeared in a London circus.

After the First World War circuses went into decline. Those that traditionally toured the continent ran up against difficulties in obtaining passports and clearing quarantine. In England it was Bertram Mills who revived circuses, using Olympia in London as a showcase and taking his troupe on tour by train. Elsewhere troupes tended to merge; in the United States the Ringling brothers joined forces with Barnum and Bailey to form one enormous circus. However, inflation meant that expenses were often rising faster than income. Nowadays circuses are thought of as outdoor attractions. However, there were some permanent purpose-built indooor circuses (or 'Hippodromes') where companies could perform all year round, as in London, Liverpool, Brighton and Great Yarmouth. There was even a circus inside Blackpool Tower. Since the war the public has lost much of its enthusiasm for performing animals. In the 1960s even the famous Bertram Mills circus was forced to close.

FIG.12/4: EVENTS CALENDAR

MONTH	INTERNATIONAL	NATIONAL
January		First Footing Burns Night

February	Carnivals: Rio, Trinidad,
	    Maarstricht,
	    New Orleans
	Berlin Film Festival
		Shrovetide Festivals
		Cruft's Dog Show

March	Santa Semana…Seville, Valladolid, etc. Holi (India)	St. David's Day Universities' Boat Race
April	Puram (India)	Well-dressing Battersea Easter Parade Pilgrimage to Walsingham Grand National, Aintree
May	Cannes Film Festival Venice Biennale Corpus Christi Parade, Toledo Monaco Grand Prix Le Mans race	Spalding Tulip Parade Minehead Hobby-Horse Founder's Day for Chelsea Pensioners
June	Athens Festival White Nights, St, Petersburg Puri (India)	Trooping of the Colour Bath Festival Highland Games Good Food Fair, Jersey Garter Ceremony, Windsor Solstice ceremonies at Stonehenge Derby Royal Ascot TT Races, Isle of Man
July	Palio, Siena Calgary Stampede Running of the Bulls Pamplona Bayreuth Wagner Festival North Sea Jazz Festival Havana Carnival Saltzburg Festival	Royal Tournament Llangollen International Eisteddfod Swan upping on Thames Battle of the Flowers, Jersey Royal National Eisteddfod Wimbledon Finals

MONTH	INTERNATIONAL	NATIONAL
July (cont)	Tour de France Sunsplash Jamaica	Royal International Agricultural Show, Stoneleigh Henley Regatta Dressing of Buxton Wells Racing at Silverstone Goodwood Races
August	Amarnath Cave Pilgrimage Chopin Festival (Poland) Wine Fair, Limassol	Notting Hill Carnival Sidmouth Folk Festival Cowes Week, Isle of Wight Grouse Shooting starts 12th August
September	Hadyn Festival Venice Regatta 'Rhine in Flame' Munich Beer Festival	Braemar Gathering Kite Festival, Bristol Edinburgh Festival St. Giles' Fair, Oxford St. Leger Races, Doncaster Farnborough Air Show
October	Mooncake Festivals Divali (India) Pushkar Camel Fair	Blackpool Illuminations Horse of the Year Show Nottingham Goose Fair
November	Day of the Dead (Mexico) Loi Krathong (Thailand)	State Opening of Parliament Lord Mayor's Show Bridgewater Carnival London to Brighton Veteran Car Run Remembrance Sunday
December	Whirling Dervishes (Turkey) Feast of Virgin of Guadeloupe (Mexico)	King's College Carols Hogmanay Royal Smithfield Show Trafalgar Square Christmas lights

Local authorities must give consent for circuses (or fairs) to take place, and they are controlled by the terms of the 1961 Public Health Act and the 1976 Local Government (Miscellaneous Provisions) Act. The 1971 Animals Act made site owners liable for any harm caused by dangerous animals. By the 1980s most British circuses were seasonal events which take place on commonland, and those without animals were at least as popular as those with them. Only in Russia was circus still truly fashionable. Moscow State Circus is one of the world's best and still occasionally tours.

About 24 different circuses attend the annual international Circus Festival in Monte Carlo.

Millennium

All around the world people are gearing up to celebrate the new millennium and all sorts of events are being planned. Focus of the celebrations in Britain will be the vast **Millennium Exhibition** at Greenwich where the world's largest dome is planned.

Miscellaneous Events

A few event attractions are more difficult to categorise. Some are as big and well-known as the Calgary Stampede, a Canadian rodeo, and the Palio in Siena where riders in colourful medieval costumes charge through the city centre (both in July). Others are as obscure as the Matrimonial Tea Party at Ecaussines in Belgium when bachelors parade the town and organise a ball. Nevertheless, all can make a tremendous difference to how many people visit a particular town and when they choose to do so.

Fig.12/4 above lists some of the most important event attractions both in the UK and worldwide. Neither of these lists is comprehensive.

Every country in the world has responsibility for the conservation of its own heritage, but this can be hugely expensive; it's much easier for wealthy developed countries to find the necessary resources than it is for impoverished developing countries with more pressing calls on their limited funds. In any case the world as a whole has a vested interest in preserving the most important cultural and natural features of each country, particularly now that international tourism is one of the world's largest industries. If tourist-receiving countries are too poor to protect their own heritage, the tourist-generating countries may have to take on some of the responsibility, if only to ensure that visitors will have something to look at when they reach their destinations.

With so many possible sites to protect some kind of qualitative selection is necessary. As long ago as the 2nd century BC the Greeks designated the Pyramids at Giza, the Colossus of Rhodes, the Pharos at Alexandria, the Hanging Gardens of Babylon, the Mausoleum at Halicarnassus, the Temple of Artemis at Ephesus and the Statue of Zeus at Olympia the Seven Wonders of the World. In the 20th century the task of drawing up an equivalent list fell to UNESCO, the United Nations Educational, Scientific and Cultural Organisation.

UNESCO AND THE WORLD HERITAGE

UNESCO was founded in 1946 and took as its emblem the 5th-century BC facade of the Parthenon in Athens (see Fig.13/1). Some of its aims were:

- to help return cultural properties to their country of origin

- to designate and protect world heritage sites

- to help renovate older museums and set up new ones, especially in developing countries

- to set up an International Centre for the Study of the Preservation and Restoration of Cultural Properties, to be based in Rome

In addition in 1970 UNESCO drew up a convention against the illicit import, export or transfer of ownership of cultural property, a problem which had worsened as the international art market boomed.

In 1965 a UNESCO conference called for 'a trust for the world heritage to be responsible to the world community for... efforts to identify, establish, develop and manage the world's important natural and scenic areas and historic sites for the present and future benefit of the international citizenry'. In the same year UNESCO underwrote the massive task of moving the great temples of Rameses II and his queen Nefertari which were to be flooded by the creation of Lake Nasser behind the

FIG.13/1: BRITAIN'S WORLD HERITAGE SITES IN 1997

Aswan Dam on the River Nile. However, it wasn't until 1972 that an International Convention for the Protection of the World Cultural and Natural Heritage was created to provide the legal, administrative and financial framework for protecting worldwide sites of 'outstanding universal value'.

The Convention had two underlying principles: that each country must recognise its own duty to preserve its heritage, and that it must acknowledge the need to co-operate with other countries to conserve the world's heritage.

The result was the creation of a World Heritage Committee with representatives from 21 different states elected from the 100 countries that had signed the original document. Representatives meet once a year to update a World Heritage List of cultural or natural sites of outstanding universal value (see Appendix III). These lists are republished every two years. By 1996 469 sites in 136 different countries had been designated. Some were chosen for historic or aesthetic reasons, while others were picked for their scientific merits or because of their great natural beauty; some fit into both categories. In every case the site was assessed on its intrinsic value rather than on whether it was in particular need of help. In deciding which sites to designate the Committee takes advice from the International Union for Conservation of Nature and Natural Resources (IUCN), the International Centre for the Study of the Preservation and Restoration of Cultural Properties, and the International Council on Monuments and Sites (ICOMOS).

FIG.13/2: SYMBOL OF A WORLD HERITAGE SITE.

The Committee is also responsible for a World Heritage in Danger List of sites in need of immediate help and works out the rough cost of emergency conservation work. If necessary it also organises technical help or training for those doing the work. Finally it has an important role in educating the public about the significance of the chosen World Heritage Sites.

Once somewhere has been added to the World Heritage List the site owner can display a special logo with a square representing the man-made heritage set inside a circle to represent the natural heritage, with the two linked to represent the world heritage transcending time and borders (see Fig.13/2). The country in which the site is found is then morally obliged to undertake its care and conservation. To that end India and Bhutan cancelled a planned hydroelectric dam to protect the Manas Sanctuary, home of the Bengal tiger. In contrast the set-up at Stonehenge, with a tunnel leading from singularly tacky visitor facilities to a site fenced off from its visitors and with a main road roaring past, has been widely condemned as inadequate (new arrangements are currently under discussion). Sir Jocelyn Stevens,

Chair of English Heritage, has also slated the surroundings to the Tower of London as a disgrace.

The World Heritage Fund (for the protection of the World Cultural and Natural Heritage of Outstanding Universal Value) administers mandatory and voluntary contributions from those countries which are signatories to the Convention and can make loans or even grants to help with important conservation work. For example it provided $75,000 to encourage reafforestation, the use of alternative fuels for cooking and heating, and the restoration of Buddhist temples in the Sagarmatha National Park in Nepal.

THE ABU SIMBEL TEMPLES

In 1960 the Egyptian government began work on the Aswan High Dam which was to create a 480 kilometre-long lake on the River Nile. The temple at Philae had been drowned nine months previously when the Old Dam was created, Now many Ancient Nubian sites, including the great temples to Rameses II and his queen Nefertari dug out of the sands by Giovanni Belzoni in 1819, were to be drowned by this new lake.

In 1960, the Director-General of UNESCO, launched an appeal for money to save the monuments. The estimated cost of lifting the temples whole would have been $90 million so that idea was abandoned, along with proposals to build a second dam round Abu Simbel or to build a filter dam to let visitors view them underwater. Finally the Swedes devised a scheme for rebuilding the temples at a cost of $36 million. Work began in May 1965.

Firstly a coffer dam was built to hold the waters back. Then the facade was covered with sand while the rear parts were removed. The ceilings were removed in blocks. Synthetic resin was injected into the four colossal heads of the statues of Rameses in case they crumbled while being moved. Then the statue bodies were fixed to cranes with epoxy resin and lifted in pieces. Finally in January 1966 builders started to re-erect the temples, setting them into artificial hills with protective concrete cores on higher ground. They were carefully realigned so the sun should penetrate the interiors on the solstices as it had done on the original site. However, no attempt was made to make good damage that had already been done to the temples; one of the statues was left as it had fallen in front of the building. Marks of removal were also left in place to avoid any later confusion over what had been done. In all the project cost in excess of $80 million.

Abu Simbel is now a popular add-on excursion to many Egyptian holiday itineraries and can be reached by boat, plane or four-wheel drive vehicle.

As it exists the list of World Heritage Sites is biased towards European, Christian and historic monuments. In future it's hoped that more non-European sites and sites of archaeological or technological importance will be listed.

INTERNATIONAL RESCUE EFFORTS

Just as British archaeologists have been involved in an increasing number of rescue digs in the 20th century, so the international community (often with UNESCO as the co-ordinator) has been involved in ever more efforts to protect historical and cultural sites of world significance. In the 1950s the 7th-century Buddhist temples at Borobudur on Java were collapsing because their foundations weren't strong enough

---

THE ACROPOLIS

The Acropolis is a complex of beautiful temples on a rock in the centre of Athens. These were constructed between 520 and 480 BC on the initiative of the great Athenian leader Pericles as a shrine to the city's patron goddess Athena and a showcase for Greek art. The biggest and best known of the temples is the Parthenon, from which the majority of the Elgin Marbles were removed. The Erechtheum is most famous for its caryatids (female figures used as pillars). The smallest temple is to Nike, the goddess of Victory, and overlooks the Propylaea, or monumental entrance. The fame of the Parthenon is so great that it has been used as a symbol for UNESCO. An estimated 4 million people a year visit the Acropolis.

In 1687 the Acropolis was extensively damaged by an explosion when a Venetian shell hit the Parthenon, then being used by the Turks as a powder store. In 1894 more damage was caused by an earthquake and by 1976 the temples were also suffering from wear and tear caused by the passage of time and the number of visitors to the site. Pollution was proving particularly damaging to the Pentelic marble used to build the temples.

In 1971 UNESCO's calls for an urgent programme of conservation led to the setting up of a planning committee to determine what could be done. The international community agreed to add $10 million to the $5 million the Greek government had earmarked for restoration work. As a result the pediment of the Parthenon and the caryatids on the Erechtheum were replaced with fibreglass and cement copies; the originals were moved into a site museum where they could be protected from weathering, pollution and souvenir-seekers. A ten-year project to restore the entire complex is currently underway. This will involve replacing thousands of iron clamps and one thousand marble blocks. It's also intended to preserve the evidence of later Greek, Byzantine and Turkish occupation of the site.

---

and the monuments had been built without mortar. The cost of restoration was estimated at $8 million, and the Indonesian government appealed to UNESCO for help. Aid came from Australia, Burma, Belgium, Cyprus, Italy, Iran, Germany, Ghana, Japan and Thailand. Over ten years the foundations were rebuilt, drains were added, 1,300,000 stones were taken down, treated chemically and replaced, and a computer record of the stonework was created. In 1966 the Venice in Peril fund was established to find ways to save the marvellous Renaissance palaces and churches which were threatened as the Venetian island gradually sank into the surrounding lagoon. In 1974 an appeal was launched to raise $7.5 million to build flood defences to protect the ruins of Mohenjo Daro in Pakistan from the rising water table. In 1976 money was sought to rescue the Gate of Diocletian before it disappeared beneath Lake Nasser.

As soon as the embargo on international aid to Cambodia was lifted in 1991, UNESCO stepped in to advise the new government on methods of protecting their ancient monuments and preventing a trade in stolen antiquities. As a result some objects were actually recovered via Interpol. A group of experts are now working with local people to define the boundaries of the spectacular Angkor Wat temple complex and to devise a management plan for it.

WHO OWNS WHAT?... THE PROBLEM OF HERITAGE OWNERSHIP

While there's little argument over the ownership of world heritage sites, even when much international money has been invested in their preservation, the same cannot be said of the contents of many museums and art galleries. In the 18th and 19th century individuals began to travel, first in Europe and then further afield. As they were followed by the administrators of the European colonial regimes, priceless items found their way out of their countries of origin and into private collections and state museums in Europe.

In some cases items were stolen. In others they were removed in situations of dubious legality. Developing countries might also dispute any 'right' colonial powers could claim to have had to dispose of their heritage.

Britain has already returned the following foreign items to their original owners:

- Ethiopian manuscripts (1872).

- the shrine, sceptre and orb of the King of Kandy, Sri Lanka (1930s).

- the Mandalay regalia from Burma (1964).

- the belongings of the Kabaka of Buganda in Uganda (1964).

However, requests that the British Museum should return the Benin bronzes, stolen from the king and his chiefs in 1897 when a British Company seized Benin City and overthrew the ruler, have been refused by citing the 1963 Museums Act. When Nigeria asked to borrow an ivory head from Benin for a festival the British Museum demanded £2 million worth of insurance, claiming the head would be damaged if it was moved. Until recently this head was on show in the Museum of Mankind. However, 2,000 of the bronzes are kept in storage.

Other countries have returned foreign items that have found their way into their keeping. In 1977 the United States government returned the 11th-century jewelled crown of King Stephen, first king of Hungary, to the National Museum of

Hungary in Budapest. The crown was seen as a symbol of the Hungarian state and had been displayed in the Palace of Buda since 1916. During the Soviet invasion of Hungary in 1945 it vanished. Its whereabouts remained unknown until August 1965 when the US government revealed that it was in Fort Knox. In June 1977 when Janos Kadar backed the Helsinki Accord on human rights President Carter agreed to the crown's return. It was taken back to Budapest by Cyrus Vance, ostensibly during a holiday.

Picasso's *Guernica*, a vivid depiction of aerial bombing during World War Two, was also taken to the United States where it hung in the New York Museum of Modern Art. Picasso himself stipulated that the painting should not be displayed in Spain while General Franco was in power. On Franco's death in 1975 *Guernica* was returned to Madrid where it now hangs in a special annexe to the Prado together with the artist's preliminary sketches and studies.

To circumvent problems of ownership countries like Greece and Turkey now have draconian legislation prohibiting the export of antiquities. The difficulty comes in weighing up the relative importance of showing items in their original context against the value of museums being able to show a wide range of objects from many different places. Those who have seen *Guernica* since its return to Spain would probably agree that it gains from having a context again, particularly since it was such a political painting. But only a limited number of masterpieces are so completely place-identified. Nor are all items unique. There are, for example, innumerable surviving Greek vases from the 4th century BC and Ancient Egyptian mummy cases. Education might suffer if all people could see in museums was the produce of their own country. It is even possible that multiculturalism in education, while theoretically more sympathetic to the claims of emerging nations, will in practice make it harder to return items which might help widen people's viewpoints; as long as the emphasis was all on national culture it might have been easier to agree to give up undervalued items. It might help if each country compiled a list of those moveable items it regarded as crucial to an understanding of its history or appreciation of its culture. These could then be designated inalienable parts of their heritage.

However, it isn't always easy to define 'national culture'. A chair carved in 18th-century England by an English carver is clearly part of our heritage. But what if the carver had been an Italian living in England? And what if the carver had been English but working in Italy? What about a masterpiece of the Italian Renaissance which has hung in England since the 16th century? Some national groups have also technically ceased to exist and there might be room for debate about who should inherit their treasures. Do the Iraqis automatically have sole rights to the heritage of the Babylonians, for example?

It's also true that some countries are still unable to provide the protection that might be needed, especially in poorer developing countries. However, even in some parts of Europe irreplaceable monuments are sometimes left to crumble because the money to repair them is hard to find. In 1996 in an interesting gesture the Stone of Scone, the Scottish coronation stone, was returned from England to Scotland. Since it was stolen by Edward I in 1297 it had resided under the Coronation Chair in

Westminster Abbey except for a brief period in 1950 when a group of Scottish nationalists managed to remove it. It's now in the museum at Edinburgh Castle.

THE ELGIN MARBLES

Typical of items removed under dubious circumstances are the Elgin Marbles which have been housed in the British Museum since 1816. The Marbles were sculpted by the 5th-century BC Greek architect Phidias to adorn the facades of the Parthenon and formed an integral part of the building. The pediments showed the birth of Athena and the contest with Poseidon, while the friezes showed Greek myths with particularly Athenian content, and the great processions to the temple during the Panathenian Festivals.

The Parthenon suffered various vicissitudes over the years, becoming a Christian church and then the garrison mosque of a Turkish fortress. The worst damage was probably done to the Marbles by the 1687 explosion and by Venetian efforts to remove them from the building during their brief occupation of Athens afterwards. In 1689 the Turks recovered the city and the Parthenon once again served as a mosque. In 1799 Thomas Bruce, the Seventh Earl of Elgin, became British Ambassador to the Ottomans. By then renewed interest in Classical culture was at its height and he spent his spare time drawing and modelling the Parthenon sculptures. The Ottoman Sultan wanted British protection against the French and was therefore willing to give Elgin a *firman* or permit to remove pieces of the sculpture. As a result 50 whole and two half slabs of the frieze and 15 of the metopes were hacked off the temple and sent to England where they were put on public display first in Park Lane and then in Burlington House. Pressed for cash, Elgin considered turning them into a private museum and charging people to see them. When the British Museum expressed an interest in the Marbles he claimed they had cost him £62,440 to collect. Finally in 1816 the government bought them for £35,000 and put them on show in the British Museum.

Meanwhile the Parthenon was further damaged during fighting between the Greeks and Turks in the 1820s. Between 1824 and 1826 it also served as a school. Finally in 1835 the Greek Archaeological Service took over the site, and started removing most of the medieval and later additions. Sadly some of their repairs, including using iron securing clamps, further damaged the marble.

Almost from the beginning there were those who questioned Lord Elgin's right to have removed the Marbles. In 1812 Byron wrote scathingly of Elgin in Childe Harold:

"The last, the worst, dull spider, who was he?
Blush, Caledonia, such thy son could be."

In a debate in the House of Commons in 1816 Hugh Hammersley suggested that the British Museum should simply store the Marbles until the Athenians wanted them back. By the end of the 19th century the question of their ownership was being raised by the Greek poet Constantine Cavafy, by Nathanial Curzon and by Sir Roger Casement. In 1924 Thomas Hardy wrote a poem on the theme and in 1924 Harold Nicolson suggested that the caryatid should be returned to Athens to celebrate the centenary of Byron's death; he argued that a *firman* to remove bits and pieces of stone hardly amounted to carte blanche to remove an entire figure. In 1941 Thelma Cazalet, MP, even suggested that the Marbles should be returned to Greece as recognition of their war-time struggles. Despite the fact that many of the issues of principle involved were conceded nothing happened and in 1963 the Museums Act decreed that the British Museum could not part with its property. After a military junta took control of Greece in 1967 the subject was quietly dropped.

In 1974 democracy was reestablished and Greece joined the EEC in 1981. In 1982 the Greek Minister of Culture asked a UNESCO meeting to arrange for the return of the Marbles so they could be shown in their proper context again. In 1986 she announced that a museum would be built on the Acropolis so that the Marbles could be shown on site without being exposed to Athens' notorious atmospheric pollution.

Nevertheless in 1996 the Elgin Marbles are still on display in the Duveen Gallery of the British Museum which had opened in 1962 as the first part of the Museum with a purpose-designed air filtration system. While it was once possible to argue that they were safer and likely to be better cared for in the British Museum, it is harder to justify that position now that Greece is part of the EU and has high quality museums of its own. In fact the Marbles have suffered while in English hands; in 1938 the minutes of a meeting record that damage had been done to them during cleaning; in 1940 the Marbles were only just moved into a vault and to Aldwych Station before a bomb damaged the Duveen Gallery, their intended home.

There are not only problems over past acquisitions. A thriving international market in art and antiquities exists and not all of its activities are legitimate. The British Museum will no longer buy any items which don't have a clear and provable provenance, but not everyone is so scrupulous. Some of the worst problems occur when items in private collections come on the market. The American Getty Museum is unique in having a £100 million a year purchase grant; most museums must make do with a fraction of this sum. Consequently items are sometimes sold to overseas buyers that should probably stay in the UK.

With the collapse of communism in 1991, a flood of treasures from Eastern Europe and the ex-Soviet Union, including many church icons, found their way abroad, sometimes legitimately, sometimes illegitimately.

do with a fraction of this sum. Consequently items are sometimes sold to overseas buyers that should probably stay in the UK.

With the collapse of communism in 1991, a flood of treasures from Eastern Europe and the ex-Soviet Union, including many church icons, found their way abroad, sometimes legitimately, sometimes illegitimately.

Marketing of tourist attractions is about identifying the key selling points of each site and then promoting it to its potential markets in such a way as to cover its running costs and make a profit. For new attractions marketing may be primarily about alerting the public to its existence. For long established attractions it may be about encouraging repeat and off-peak visits.

The UK tourist attraction industry mainly consists of small units which may have small marketing budgets and little expertise in the subject. In the case of long-established attractions like the national museums and art galleries they may also have product- rather than market-orientated attitudes, although governmental pressure for greater self-sufficiency in the 1990s has slowly changed that; the Museum of London, the Imperial War Museum and the Natural History Museum all employ professionals to help with their marketing.

Nevertheless some tourist attractions like Alton Towers, Thorpe Park and Madame Tussaud's are big businesses and are operated as such, with as much as 10% of their admissions takings going to the marketing budget. Owners of multiple attractions like the National Trust and English Heritage are also big business. Most new purpose-built attractions are developed on commercial lines from the start, with marketing playing a vital part in their development and promotion.

MARKET RESEARCH

Most large tourist attraction in the UK organise their own market research, sometimes by means of one-off surveys, sometimes through exit questionnaires given to all visitors and designed for easy computer analysis. Questionnaires are likely to cover such questions as:

- the day, date and time of the visit. There may also be a question about the weather aimed at finding out whether particular tupes of weather encourage or detract from the likelihood of visits.

- whether the visitor is holidaying, visiting friends or relatives, or on a business trip. Tourists may also be asked whether they are on a day trip or staying visit.

- where they are staying. This may influence decisions about the distribution of advertising materials.

- whether they are UK residents (and if so, from where) or overseas visitors. This may also help in deciding how widely to distribute advertising materials.

- how they reached the attraction. This may also help identify advertising possibilities.

- whether this is a first or a repeat visit.

- how they heard about the attraction. Visitors may also be asked which newspapers they read and which TV and radio channels they favour. This is vital for measuring the effectiveness of advertising.

- where else they have visited, both in the immediate area and in the country. This information may suggest places to supply with promotional leaflets.

- whether they though the attraction offered value for money. If the answer to this question is negative then further advertising expenditure may be pointless until something has been done to improve the attraction itself.

- whether they were impressed with the service they received in shops and restaurants and from the staff they met. An attraction is unlikely to draw repeat business unless it receives positive responses to these questions. If they are negative it will probably be cheaper to invest in staff training in customer care than in new facilities.

- how many people there were in the group of visitors.

There will also be questions about sex, age, occupation and interests of the respondent, aimed at identifying the particular segments of the market the attraction appeals to.

Some research is carried out by the statutory tourist boards to identify regional and national trends. The English, Scottish, Wales and Northern Ireland Tourist Boards send annual questionnaires to attractions in their area to find out how many visitors they received in the previous year. At the same time they ask attraction owners what factors they though responsible for increases and decreases. Professional groups also carry out research on behalf of their members; the Society of London Theatre collects statistics on West End theatre attendance to detect overall trends.

Some research is carried out by observing visitor's behaviour inside the attraction. The findings can cause alterations in presentation (see Chapter 10). At Madame Tussaud's visitors were found to interact more positively with the exhibits than had been assumed previously. People were most interested in models of figures with which they identified in some way. Once they had picked out these figures they proceeded to engage with them in a variety of ways, from putting an arm round them to sticking out their tongues. As a result the remaining barriers were removed so people could mingle more intimately with the exhibits. Now cameras are also hired out so visitors can be snapped with their particular heroes and villains.

After spending £3.75 million on a new exhibition, Tower Bridge carried out a quick survey to see what people liked best. When 45% of people said the views were the main attraction, they developed a 'quick tour' to bypass the exhibition.

DEVELOPING A MARKETING STRATEGY

All attraction owners need to develop a marketing strategy both for the year ahead and for the longer term. This can be worked out in the quieter, off-peak periods, perhaps in October and November.

The strategy will be determined in part by whether the attraction only needs to cover its current running costs or to recoup its capital costs as well. Sometimes it may only need to make a contribution to its running costs as a result of grants from central or local government. However, even grant-aided attractions are expected to be as self-supporting as possible these days. Market research should have suggested which segments of the market the attraction particularly appeals to. These different segments might include:

- local residents within one hour's drive
- day visitors, usually from within two hours' drive
- people visiting friends who live within one hour's drive
- holidaymakers staying within one hour's drive
- foreign tourists
- coach tour groups
- school parties

Smaller sites may not be able to do much to broaden the segments they appeal to, although the narrower their base the harder they will probably find it to operate at a profit. Larger attractions, however, may have scope to add features to appeal to different groups. Many of the open-air museums are gradually adding to what they offer: Beamish now has a farm, steam railway and fairground as well as the industrial heritage attractions it started with.

Ideally the marketing strategy should be evolved in the light of the attraction's perceived strengths. weaknesses, threats and opportunities (SWOT). It should be expressed in terms of specific objectives whose success or failure can be quantified; for example, 'to increase off-peak business between January and March by 5% by developing a programme of events which will be advertised by means of special leaflets distributed to local tourist information centres, coach companies and hoteliers.' It will also be important to identify precisely what experiences visitors anticipate getting from their trip so that appropriate facilities and materials can be developed. The strategy should take into account local developments which may be useful; for example, in 1996, Lyme Park hosted an exhibition of costumes from *Pride and Prejudice* to cash in on the popularity of a television programme partly made in its grounds.

In most areas of tourism attracting repeat business is important. But not all visitor attractions find it easy to bring people back for a second bite and the problem may be getting worse as more competing ventures open. Large sites can sometimes lure people back by adding new attractions; theme parks can build new rides and some of the open-air museums are still being developing anyway. Museums and galleries can advertise new acquisitions or put on temporary exhibitions. Zoos can publicise new births. English Heritage and National Trust properties host special events in their grounds. Theatres offer new productions. However, most of these possibilities are either capital - or labour -intensive and therefore costly. It's usually cheaper to invest in offering better standards of customer care. This can be done by ensuring that all interviewing, induction courses and staff training, even at management level, emphasise the importance of the customer. Job descriptions can be written to focus on the customer. Specific standards of dress and manners can be laid down for all staff, while targets, perhaps sweetened with incentives, can be set.

A time scale for marketing efforts should be established. For a large-scale attraction, like a new theme park, advertising may need to begin long before it is even completed; Disneyland Paris was already being promoted in 1988, and the campaign to promote the Welsh Valleys for tourism began four years before the Ebbw Vale Garden Festival which was to be its centrepoint. Planning for 1991's Year of the Maze had to start in 1981 because new mazes need ten years to mature.

PRICING STRATEGIES

While some tourist attractions have evolved out of buildings that already existed (cathedrals, stately homes), others have been purpose-built at enormous cost which needs to be recovered. Even where the basic product already existed the mere fact of opening to the public brings expenses: for guides, security, installing lavatories and other facilities, and insurance. There will also be the inevitable increased cost of wear and tear to take into account.

Unlike some other tourist products, visitor attractions have a high percentage of fixed costs, for things like rent, business rates, maintenance, feeding livestock and insurance. These remain the same regardless of how many or how few visitors are received. Where use is made of temporary summer staff there may be some variable costs as well. However, these are often offset by the increased cost of heating and lighting in winter. Consequently pricing strategies have to be aimed at covering all operational costs for the year and cannot reflect the cost of each individual visit.

Traditionally many British tourist attractions, including the national museums and art galleries, many countryside attractions and the churches and cathedrals, were free. In the countryside it's often difficult to levy a charge since this requires a single entry point where it can be collected. Instead people are sometimes charged for car parking or for admission to the Visitor Centre. The picturesque Devon village of Clovelly now has a £1.60 charge for admission to the village and its Visitor Centre. The possibility of charging for admission to the National Parks has also been considered; popular Cotswold villages like Bourton-on-the-Water have also contemplated charges. For churches and cathedrals a moral issue is involved. Despite the high cost of maintaining the buildings many people think it inappropriate to introduce commerce into what are essentially religious buildings. It's also essential to ensure that no one wishing to use them for prayer is deterred from doing so by charges.

The national museums have adopted a range of strategies, from 'voluntary' charges at the Victoria and Albert (now replaced with fixed fees), to set fees at the Natural History and National Maritime Museums. Others continue a policy of free admittance. In his book *The British Museum: Purpose and Politics* the ex-Director David Wilson highlights the costs involved in starting to charge. He calculated that it would cost the British Museum about £260,000 just to install the turnstiles and make other alterations. Once an admission fee had been introduced he assumed the money received in donations would disappear and that it would no longer be possible to charge for admission to temporary exhibitions. The estimated cost per visitor to the British Museum was £5.65, but such a high charge would lead to an enormous drop in the number of visitors. At Bradford entry to the National Museum of Film, Photography and Television is free, but there are charges to watch films on the giant IMAX screen which, at five storeys high, is the biggest in the UK. These charges match those at commercial cinemas, with higher prices for double bills.

Depending on the market segment they appeal to attractions usually offer a range of prices aimed at enabling as many people as possible to visit. Pricing can become quite complex, with discounts for students, senior citizens, children and groups. Child discounts are usually largest at gardens and historic properties and smallest at leisure parks and country parks.

Some attractions, like the Bronte Parsonage, offer low season price reductions. There may also be pre-season discounts, as at the American Adventure Theme Park which offers reduced prices for a few days before the main season starts. In contrast attractions like Leeds Castle in Kent which offer special guided tours at times when they would normally be closed charge a premium for the privilege. Ironbridge Gorge Museum offers an unusual 'passport' ticket which allows people to visit each of the attraction once, although not necessarily during the same visit. In general pleasure beaches don't charge admission fees but visitors must pay for each individual ride, whereas theme parks off all-inclusive tickets.

Sometimes attractions which charge an entry fee waive it for local residents. In Europe, some attractions admit passport-carrying members of other EU countries free while charging everybody else to come in.

Attractions sometimes offer other discounts asa well. For example, tourists can sometimes pick up booklets of leaflets offering discounts at attractions as diverse as Madame Tussaud's and the London Dungeon, Tower Bridge, London Zoo, the London Transport Museum, Kensington Palace, the London Diamond Centre and the Criterion Theatre. In 1996 visitors to any one of the Treasure Houses of England were given a leaflet offering them a discount at the other nine properties, especially sensible marketing since the properties are too widely spread round the country to compete directly with each other.

London theatres often offer cheap stand-by tickets because any seat left unfilled when the curtain rises is a 'dead' seat and it's better to generate a small sum from it than nothing at all. Other tourist attractions are not usually seen as suitable for this type of discounting. It's often argued that it would be too difficult to notify the relevant temporary price changes. In reality, visitors might simply time their trips to take advantage of price cuts. In any case research at National Trust properties suggest that provided the price is not completely out of line with what is charged elsewhere people aren't much bothered by it. In particular foreign tourists seem unconcerned about prices, probably because as a percentage of what they have had

FIG.14/1: ADMISSION FEES AT THORPE PARK 1996

THE GREAT THORPE PARK 1996 TARIFF

	EARLY £	SUMMER £
GROWN UPS (adults and children over 1.4 metres)	13.25	14.75
COOL CATS (children between 0.9 metres and 1.4 metres)	11.25	11.75
LITTLE ONES (children under 0.9 metres)	FREE	FREE
CONCESSIONS (senior citizen, disabled and disabled attendant each)	7.00	7.00
PLAN AHEAD SUPERSAVER (pay in advance only, minimum 4 tickets. Valid for 1 day visit any day of the season except day of issue)	10.00	10.00
PRICEBUSTERS PREPAID GROUP RATE (groups 12 plus visitors, pay 14 days in advance)	8.00	8.00
PRICEBUSTERS PAY-ON-THE-DAY GROUP RATE (groups 12 plus visitors)	9.00	9.00
PRICEBUSTERS PREPAID SCHOOLS RATE (schoolchildren 16 & under, organised school visit pay 14 days in advance)	5.25	6.25
PRICEBUSTERS PAY-ON-THE-DAY SCHOOLS RATE (schoolchildren 16 & under, organised school visit)	6.25	7.25
COME BACK SOON TICKET (for return visit later in the season. Valid for all admission categories. Limit 10 or number of tickets plus 25%, whichever is less.)	6.50	6.50
PARENT & TODDLER PASS (pay full individual price on first visit apply for pass for discount return visit)	5.00	5.00

to pay to come here these will seem small. Nor would they want to miss what might be a once-in-a-lifetime opportunity to see something specific.

In England in 1995 the average admission charge was £2.42 (£1.82 at museums, £2.17 at gardens, £2.44 at historic buildings, £3.52 at wildlife attractions and £2.34 at visitor centres). Between 1989 and 1995 the average adult price had risen 68% compared with a rise in the retail price index of 29%. In Scotland in 1995 41% of attractions charged between £1 and £2.99.

OTHER METHODS OF RAISING MONEY

Membership and 'Friends' Schemes

The National Trust/NTS, English Heritage/Historic Scotland/Cadw, the Zoological Society of London, the Royal Society for the Protection of Birds, and the Wildfowl and Wetlands Trust all run membership schemes which operate in a similar way. Members receive free admission to sites and regular magazines in return for their fees. They are also offered discounted admission to special events. They are encouraged to pay by direct debit which reduces administrative costs and makes membership more likely to continue after the first year. Alternatively they are asked to sign a deed of covenant which allows the recipient to regain the tax paid on the subscription.

Membership can be a vital source of funding. In 1995 the National Trust had 2,284,708 members and their subscriptions brought in 38% of their annual revenue.

The 'Friends' schemes operated by many museums and galleries are effectively membership schemes attached to single properties. Usually they offer supporters the opportunity to visit outside normal opening hours or to attend previews of new exhibitions in return for their financial support. Some 'Friends' schemes are more activity-centred than other; the 'Magpies', the friends of Bristol Museum and Art Gallery, run a Victorian sweetshop in the museum in the weeks leading up to Christmas, while the Friends of the Victoria and Albert Museum act as guides and look after the information desks. The Friends of York Archaeological Trust scheme provides members with free admission to Jorvik, ARC and the newly-opened York Barley Hall, as well as granting them 10% discounts at the ARC shop in the city.

Gardens like Penshurst Place also sell season tickets so people can come back and see the different displays throughout the year.

'Adoption' Schemes

The Zoological Society of London and the Wildfowl and Wetlands Trust (see Chapter 10) operate animal and bird adoption schemes. Apart from the money these schemes generate they also offer potential for publicity, particularly when celebrities can be persuaded to become 'parents'. London Zoo's 'Adopt an Animal' scheme has featured on TV-AM and ITV's 'This Morning' programme. A joint promotion with Harrods brought in £5,000 worth of sponsorship. The actor Anthony Hopkins has sponsored a penguin and the comedian Rolf Harris a koala bear.

The success of these schemes led the British Library to introduce a similar 'Adopt a Book' scheme, publicised through the British Museum. The Library has a backlog of books in urgent need of conservation. Sponsors are asked to contribute £200 to restore individual named books. Wherever possible sponsors are matched with 'appropriate' books to help generate publicity; so Paul McCartney, whose own song lyrics are on display in the British Museum, has adopted a collection of 18th century ballads.

Shops

With most attraction now boasting on-site shops, it wasn't long before off-site retail outlets developed as well. The National Trust led the way, and by 1996 it had more than 200 site shops and another 26 in towns which didn't necessarily feature one of their properties. High quality goods on sale in these shops reflect the Trust's own interests and often visitors can buy replicas of items in the Trust's care. The shops are managed by National Trust Enterprises which had a turnover from all its outlets (including catering) of £42.7 million in 1995; £7 million of this was donated to the National Trust. The Trust also has garden centres at some of its properties, including Blickling Hall and Bodnant.

The vast Disney empire has also spawned Disney stores in most British towns.

Museums from all over the country sell merchandise through the Museums Store in London's prestigious Covent Garden, set up in 1989 by the Museums Development Unit of the Charities Advisory Trust. An annual Museums and Galleries Book and Trade Fair also takes place at the Royal Festival Hall.

ADVERTISING

Advertising is very important to all attractions, if for rather different reasons; new attractions may simply want to get their name and location known, while long-established ones may want to promote something recently added or encourage visits at a different time of the year.

Most attractions produce folded leaflets which are distributed to tourist information centres, coach companies and local hotels. They may also be placed in libraries although surprisingly rarely in travel agencies. An increasing number of attractions also operate tourist information points (TIPs) where a range of information about local tourism will be found. Sometimes attraction owners arrange their own leaflet distribution but often this is contracted out to specialists. Ideally such leaflets give details of how to reach the site, its opening hours, the facilities available and what can be seen. There may also be locational and site maps. Prices are not always given, insuring that the same leaflets can be used year after year. Sometimes prices appear on a separate sheet tucked inside but often they aren't given at all, especially when they would look relatively high. All such literature must conform to the terms of the 1968 Trades Descriptions Act which provides for fines of up to £2,000 for recklessly making a false statement. To protect themselves attraction owners may include the phrases 'all information correct at the time of going to print' or 'it may be necessary to change exhibits at certain times'.

The cost of this sort of advertising can be reduced where a number of attractions join together like the Treasure Houses of England. Clifford's Tower in

York attributed increased visitor numbers to its appearing in a joint leaflet with other York attractions. In 1996 Trebah, Heligan, Trewithen, Tresco and Mount Edgcumbe gardens joined together to produce a 'Great Gardens of Cornwall' leaflet which also publicised five National Trust gardens.

Countryside areas which may be owned by many different people are sometimes advertised by local authorities. In 1996 Cornwall County Council produced a foldout map showing all the Cornish gardens open to the public with their opening hours and entrance fees regardless of who owned them. Sometimes business sponsorship enables production of a glossier, more professional brochure.

The most attractive and therefore the most effective leaflets are in full colour. However, some attractions produce two-tone leaflets for restricted circulation. Leaflets must also be sensibly slanted towards their chosen audiences. So the Frontierland theme park in Morecambe attributed increased visitor numbers to better targeting of its advertising towards family groups. Advertising aimed at overseas visitors needs to be in a variety of languages; the leaflet advertising Jorvik is printed in eight different languages. The British Tourist Authority helps attractions promote their products overseas.

Television offers the most powerful form of advertising but as it's expensive only the largest attractions usually make use of it. However, when they do the results can be satisfying. Of 27 attractions spending more than £80,000 on television advertising in 1995, ten were leisure parks which spent £4,934,000 between them, six were wildlife attractions which spent £690,000 and seven were museums or galleries which spent £916,000. These big-spending attraction ploughed 71% of their advertising expenditure into television compared to 12% to radio. Alton Towers spent £2,123,000, Chessington £657,000, and Sea LifeCentres £120,000

Some attractions including Portland Castle and Dungeness Power Station, also find radio advertising effective. In 1995 the Natural History Museum also spent £271,000 on radio ads. The London and York Dungeons have turned the sides of buses into mobile advertisements. Other attractions have concentrated on poster advertising; London Underground stations are popular places to site them, either alongside the escalators where people can read them as they go up and down, or in the carriages themselves where the Museum of the Moving Image and the Imperial War Museum have run conspicuous campaigns. London Zoo has also placed advertisements inside London taxi cabs. When the National Railway Museum in York reopened after a refit it was advertised at motorway service stations with the help of toured exhibits. Theatres usually concentrate posters for current attractions outside the building and in the foyer, with publicity for future productions lining the corridors on the way out of the building.

The design of such advertising can be controversial. A furore greeted Saatchi and Saatchi's advert for the Victoria and Albert Museum which aimed to give it a zappier image by describing an 'ace café with a rather nice museum attached'. This was not how many people felt one of the world's great art collections should be promoted.

Most attractions also offer a range of merchandise, from pencils, biros and badges to mugs, posters and tee-shirts carrying advertising slogans, often put into carrier bags which in themselves bear advertising logos. In 1990 a survey suggested that perhaps 21% of expenditure at attractions went on gifts and souvenirs. Another in 1992 showed that 80% of the 1200 attractions reviewed sold postcards and souvenirs, 40% sold crafts and 20% sold clothes.

Indirect Advertising

It can be at least as useful for attractions to appear in actual television programmes, particularly the BBC1 and ITV holiday programmes. Lyme Park saw its visitor figures more than double after television audiences swooned at the sight of Mr. Darcy in the grounds of 'Pemberley'. Others have seem visitor numbers boosted as a result of features in home and garden programmes. Even cinema and television films which feature attractions incidentally can boost their visitor figures; in 1995 visitor numbers at the National Wallace Monument in Stirling rose from 55,264 to 84,062 on the strength of the Mel Gibson blockbuster *Braveheart*. Similarly the Trossachs Visitor Centre attracted 210,713 visitors after the release of *Rob Roy*.

FIG.14/2: WINNERS OF ENGLAND FOR EXCELLENCE AWARDS IN 1995	
Visitor Attraction of the Year	Hampton Court Palace, with Alton Towers and Blackpool Pleasure Beach as runners-up
Tourism Town of the Year	Manchester, with Stoke-on-Trent as runner-up
Tourism for All	Shrewsbury Quest
Outstanding Contribution to English Tourism	*Pride and Prejudice*

Since some people are suspicious of direct advertising, many attractions also earmark part of their publicity budget to offer familiarisation trips for domestic and overseas journalists whose features may be regarded as more objective by the public. This was certainly the case at Ironbridge Gorge Museum, but may have been counter-productive at the short-lived Britannia Park where journalists saw only an incomplete building site.

Wining awards is another good way to attract extra publicity (see Fig.14/2). After the National Museum of Photography in Bradford won the Museum of the Year award in 1988 visitor numbers rocketed to 824,811. National Heritage offers a range of other annual awards, some of them individually sponsored. In 1996 Unilever sponsored its award for the best museum of industrial or social history,

IBM sponsored the Multimedia Award and Museums Casts sponsored the award for the museum which had achieved the best results with limited resources. From 1993 to 1995 IBM also sponsored the main Museum of the Year Award. In 1988 when the prestigious ETB England for Excelllence Awards were first introduced Peat Marwick McLintock sponsored the best visitor attraction development award which was won by the Museum of the Moving Image, Hilton International sponsored the visitor attraction (marketing) award which went to the Granada Studios Tour. Alton Towers were themselves sponsors of the tourism transportation award.

However, well-established attractions can find that it gets harder to generate new publicity. Ironbridge Gorge Museum achieved a great deal on a very small publicity budget (£100,000 in 1996) and still catches the media's attention with events like 'Duck Races' (10,000 plastic ducks floated down a river) and 'Name Days' when people with the same surname as historic figures associated with the site are invited to visit, but it has now won most of the possible awards and been featured in most sections of the media. Generating new publicity is becoming an uphill struggle.

The World Wide Web

In the 1990s a new source of providing information and so advertising an attraction appeared in the form of the Internet and, in particular the World Wide Web. An increasing number of attractions now have their own website where they can provide any information they want. Not surprisingly, a technological attraction like the Science Museum has made full use of this opportunity and currently has 66 pages of information covering everything from what's on to its finances on its site at http://www.nmsi.ac.uk.

In the short term the drawback to using the World Wide Web is that not everyone has access to it. Nor does everyone know how to use it. However, as technology makes it accessible via ordinary television sets and as schools, colleges and libraries go on-line so this difficulty should fade away, making the Internet one of the most important potential channels of communication for attractions.

ANNIVERSARY PROMOTIONS

Anniversaries offer excellent opportunities for attractions to get extra visitors and publicity. The centenary of the National Trust took place in 1994. Fifty-five per cent of the historic properties and 52% of the gardens thought they had gained extra visitors as a result; overall, National Trust properties may have attracted 9% more visitors from the publicity. The fiftieth anniversaries of VE and VJ Days took place in 1995, and the Imperial War Museum and assorted other military museums attracted more visitors as a result of commemorative exhibitions. It was also the 350th anniversary of the Battle of Naseby, and Ashby-de-la-Zouch Castle attracted 80% more visitors as a result of a reenactment of the battle.

Interest in some anniversary events is limited to English visitors. In contrast exhibitions to celebrate the 250th anniversary of John Wesley's conversion in 1988 were able to tap into a market of 54 million Methodists worldwide. In his lifetime Wesley travelled 250,000 miles on horseback, passing through Kirklees and Calderdale, South Humberside, Sheffield, Stoke-on-Trent, the Black Country, Dover and Canterbury. There were therefore innumerable sites which could link into the promotion.

It's not always easy to maintain such sudden increases in popularity. The National Maritime Museum staged a very successful exhibition to commemorate the Armada in 1988. However, it took another three years to attract the same number of visitors again.

TRADE FAIRS

The World Travel Market held at Olympia in London every winter is the single biggest shop window for the UK travel trade. Individual attractions may not be able to afford the cost of a private stand but can buy into a regional or local tourist office stand to get their message across. Nevertheless there are some stands specifically featuring attractions; Heritage Projects, the Treasure Houses of England, the National Trust and English Heritage have all had stands in the UK area of the arena.

The World Travel Market is mainly a forum for different parts of the travel industry to meet and exchange ideas; owners of attractions can, for example, discuss potential joint packages with coach tour operators and hoteliers. The public are no longer admitted to the Market. Instead they visit the Holiday Show at Earl's Court in January where fewer attractions are represented. There are similar Holiday shows in big cities all round the country, including the Northern Holiday and Travel Show in Manchester.

The biggest industry showcase in Europe is the ITB in Berlin every year. The British Tourist Authority is sometimes able to help would-be British exhibitors, but few attractions find this the best use of their marketing budget.

THEMES

In the 1990s finding linking themes is seem as an effective way of publicising different attractions. Sometimes owners work out their own themes, but often the development work is carried out by local tourist boards. For example, Bradford Council identified the following themes around which tourism could be developed: TV serials *(James Heriot, Emmerdale* and *Last of the Summer Wine* Country), the Brontes, industrial heritage, mill shopping, Bradford's Yorkshire, steam railways and the flavours of Asia. The English Tourist Board also spearheaded a campaign to promote South Tyneside as 'Catherine Cookson Country', with a special mini-guide and trail linking up sites associated with the authors life. With help from Cleveland County Council the Captain Cook Tourism Association developed a heritage trail stretching from the Captain Cook Birthplace Museum in Middlesborough along the

Cleveland and North Yorkshire coast to Whitby and Staithes, again linking up sites associated with the famous explorer.

FIG.14/3: THE 'COUNTRIES' OF ENGLAND IN 1996

Television Themes

Heriot Country (*All Creatures Great and Small*), round Thirsk, in North Yorkshire.
Emmerdale Farm Country, round Esholt, North Yorkshire
Last of the Summer Wine Country, round Holmfirth, West Yorkshire
Howard's Way Country, Southampton

Literary Themes

Jane Austen Country, Hampshire
Poldark Country, Devon
Catherine Cookson Country, South Tyneside
Woman of Substance (Barbara Taylor Bradford) Country, West Yorkshire
Bronte Country, Haworth, West Yorkshire
Shakespeare Country, Stratford-Upon-Avon, Warwickshire
Lorna Doone Country, Somerset
Thomas Hardy Country, Dorset
Dylan Thomas Country, Laugharne, South Wales
Kilvert Country, Welsh borders

Historical Themes

Robin Hood Country, Nottinghamshire
Hereward the Wake Country, Lincolnshire
Nelson Country, North Norfolk
King Arthur Country, Somerset
Captain Cook Country, Cleveland
1066 Country, Kent
England's Border Country, Northumbria

Miscellaneous Themes

Constable Country, Essex and South Suffolk
Glenn Miller Country, Bedfordshire

In 1979 several attractions in and around Stratford-Upon-Avon joined together to form the Shakespeare's Country Association of Tourist Attractions. Since then England has been divided into an increasing number of 'countries' (see Fig.14/3). These are extremely useful as marketing tools, for creating heritage trails and for giving an image to otherwise anonymous or downright unattractive areas like

South Tyneside. Not all have been equally successful. For example, 'Brideshead Revisited Country' based on Castle Howard and 'Woman of Substance Country' based in Leeds have not attracted much attention. Haworth always received plenty of visitors even before it was dubbed Bronte Country. In contrast there were virtually no tourists in South Shields until South Tyneside Borough Council persuaded Catherine Cookson, whose books have been translated into 17 languages, to agree to its being labelled 'Catherine Cookson Country'.

LOGOS

In the 1990s logos are another important marketing tool for attractions, especially those with shops where the logo can be stamped onto merchandise and carrier bags. The best logos are clear, simple and preferably relate to the attraction. For example, the National Trust has a bunch of acorns reflecting its countryside concerns, the Wildfowl and Wetlands Trust a pair of Bewick's swans, the RSPB an avocet, the Oxford Story a don riding a bicycle and the Jorvik Viking Centre a stylised Viking helmet. The Ironbridge Gorge Museum uses the iron bridge itself as a logo (see Fig.14/4).

Some of the national museums with traditionally staid images have had snappy logos designed as part of an effort to alter the public's perception of them. The Victoria and Albert Museum, long known affectionately as the V&A, is a case in point.

Similar to logos are the straplines used by some attractions to summarise what they have to offer. Thus London's Zoo's publicity materials bear the phrase 'conservation in action', while Madame Tussaud's reads 'where the people meet the people'.

OFF-PEAK MARKETING POSSIBILITIES

For tourist attractions 'off-peak' can refer to quieter times of the year (usually November to March, with a short 'peak' period over Christmas and the New Year), or to days of the week (perhaps Wednesday) or times of the day (perhaps before eleven in the morning). Some attractions close at off-peak times or have shorter opening hours, but because of the high proportion of fixed costs, any money that can be generated in these quieter periods will make a worthwhile contribution to running costs. What's more some attractions are so crowded at peak periods that diverting some visits to quieter times helps protect the fabric of the attraction and insure that people actually enjoy their visit.

Before starting a special marketing campaign it's important to define particular off-peak selling points: the possibility of enjoying the attraction in peace and quiet, the autumnal colours of the trees, any special events that have been organised, the value for money if there are lower off-season prices. Then it's important to ensure that advertising and promotional materials make it clear that the

FIG.14/4: MOST TOURIST ATTRACTION LOGOS GIVE AN IDEA ABOUT THE NATURE OF THE ATTRACTION

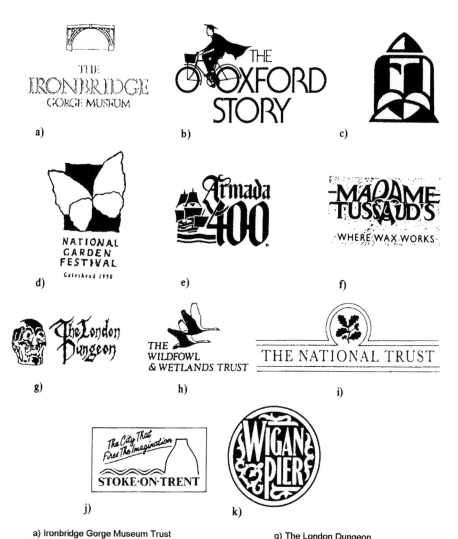

a) Ironbridge Gorge Museum Trust
b) The Oxford Story
c) Jorvik Viking Centre
d) Gateshead Garden Festival, 1990
e) 400th Anniversary of the Sailing of the Armada, 1988
f) Madame Tussaud's

g) The London Dungeon
h) The Wildfowl & Wetlands Trust
I) The National Trust
j) Stoke-on-Trent city
k) Wigan Pier Heritage Centre

attractions is open all year round. Where mailing lists of past clients have been kept they can act as the basis for advertising special events and promotions.

Leeds Castle in Kent has increased winter visits by almost 50% by offering traditional Sunday lunches, fireworks displays for 5th November, private guided tours, banquets and Kentish evenings with a five-course meal following a tour of the castle. While the fireworks displays require expensive television advertising, the Sunday lunches and Kentish evenings often sell out on the basis of press publicity and word-of-mouth recommendation. Christmas Kentish evenings are booked up six months in advance.

The Mid-Hants Watercress Line organises a programme of events to attract extra off-peak visitors. These include 'Mothers' Day Specials' when mother are presented with flowers paid for by advertisers, 'Easter Bunny Runs' when children are given Easter eggs, and 'Steam Trains to Santaland'. The West Somerset Railway also organises Thomas the Tank Engine events to attract families.

Some attractions opt to focus on different markets in off-peak periods. A few make unusual conference venues or training centres. Tour operators offering 'hobby holidays' may also rent attractions as venues. Other owners allow their properties to be used for filming. London Zoo has been used for filming, particularly of adverts, as has Castle Howard.

APPENDIX I

Registered battefields of England	Year
Maldon, Essex	991
Stamford Bridge, North Yorkshire	1066
Hastings, East Sussex	1066
Northallerton, North Yorkshire	1138
Lewes, East Sussex	1264
Evesham, Hereford & Worcester	1265
Myton, North Yorkshire	1319
Boroughbridge, North Yorkshire	1322
Halidon Hill, Northumberland	1333
Neville's Cross, County Durham	1346
Otterburn, Northumberland	1388
Homildon Hill, Northumberland	1402
Blore Heath, Staffordshire	1459
Northampton, Northamptonshire	1460
Towton, North Yorkshire	1461
Barnet, Greater London/Hertfordshire	1471
Tewkesbury, Gloucestershire	1471
Bosworth, Leicestershire	1485
Stoke Field, Nottinghamshire	1487
Flodden Field, Northumberland	1513
Solway Moss, Cumbria	1542
Newburn Ford, Tyne & Wear	1640
Edgehill, Warwickshire	1642
Braddock Down, Cornwall	1642
Stratton, Cornwall	1643
Hopton Heath, Staffordshire	1643
Adwalton Moor, West Yorkshire	1643
Lansdown Hill, nr Bath	1643
Roundway Down, Wiltshire	1643
Newbury, Berkshire	1643
Winceby, Lincolnshire	1643
Cheriton, Hampshire	1644
Cropredy Bridge, Oxfordshire	1644
Marston Moor, North Yorkshire	1644
Nantwich, Cheshire	1644
Naseby, Northamptonshire	1645
Langport, Somerset	1645
Rowton Heath (South), Cheshire	1645
Stow-on-the-Wold, Gloucestershire	1646
Worcester, Hereford & Worcester	1651
Sedgemoor, Somerset	1685

ENGLAND'S PRESERVED RAILWAYS, 1996

SOUTH WEST ENGLAND	ROUTE
Dart Valley Railway	Buckfastleigh to Totnes
West Somerset Railway	Minehead to Taunton
East Somerset Railway	Cranmore
Bicton Woodland Railway	Bicton House
Torbay and Dartmouth Railway	Paignton to Kingswear
Forest of Dean Railway	Lydney Town to Lakeside

SOUTH EAST ENGLAND

Mid-Hampshire Railway	Alresford to Ropley
Hollycombe Woodland Railway	Hollycombe House
Bluebell Railway	Horsted Keynes to Sheffield Park
Kent and East Sussex Railway	Tenterden to Bodiam
Sittingbourne and Kelmsley Railway	Kelmsley Down to Sittingbourne
Romney, Hythe and Dymchurch Railway	Hythe to Dungeness
Isle of Wight Steam Railway	Wootton to Haven Street

HOME COUNTIES

Leighton Buzzard Narrow Gauge Railway	Leighton Buzzard to Stonehenge (Beds)
Whipsnade and Umfolozi Railway	Whipsnade Park
Knebworth Park and Winter Green Railway	Grounds of Knebworth House
Quainton Railway Society	Quainton Road Station (Bucks)

EASTERN COUNTIES

Stour Valley Railway	Chappel and Wakes Colne Station
Bressington Steam Museum	Bressingham Hall
North Norfolk Railway	Weybourne to Sheringham
Nene Valley Railway	Wansford to Orford Mere
Lincolnshire Coast Light Railway	Humberston
Bure Valley Railway	Norfolk Broads

MIDLANDS

Great Central Railway	Loughborough to Rothley
Cadeby Light Railway	Cadeby to Sutton Lane
Shacklestone and Bosworth Railway	Shacklestone to Market Bosworth

Bulmer Railway Centre	Bulmer
Severn Valley Railway	Bewdley to Bridgnorth
Chasewater Light Railway	Chasewater Pleasure Park
Foxfield Light Railway	Foxfield to Blythe Bridge
Dinting Railway Centre	

NORTH WEST ENGLAND

East Lancashire Railway Preservation Society	Bury
Steamport Museum	Southport Derby Rd station
Lytham Motive Power Museum/Creek Railway	Museum to Fylde coast
Steamtown Railway Museum	Carnforth
Lakeside and Haverthwaite Railway	Lakeside to Haverthwaite
Ravenglass and Eskdale Railway	Ravenglass to Boot
Isle of Man Railway	Douglas to Port Erin

NORTH EAST ENGLAND

Middleton Railway	near Leeds
Keighley and Worth Valley Railway	Keighley to Oxethorpe
Yorkshire Dales Railway	Embsay
Derwent Valley Railway	York to Dummington
North Yorkshire Moors Railway	Pickering to Grosmont
Tanfield Railway	Bowes Bridge to Marley Hill

THE WORLD HERITAGE SITES DESIGNATED BY DECEMBER 1995

NP = National Park   HP = Historic Park

Albania:	Butrinti
Algeria:	Al Qal'a of Ben Hammad; Tassili-n-Ajjer; M'Zab Valley; Djemila; Tipasa; Timgad; Kasbah of Algiers
Argentina:	Los Glaciares NP; Iguazu NP
Argentina & Brazil:	Jesuit Missions of the Guaranis
Australia:	Kakadu NP; Great Barrier Reef; Willandra Lakes Region; Western Tasmania Wilderness NP; Lord Howe Island Group; Central Eastern Australian Rainforest; Uluru-Kata Tjuta NP; Wet Tropics of Queensland; Shark Bay, Western Australia; Fraser Island; Australian Fossil Mammal Sites
Bangladesh:	Historic Mosque City of Bagerhat; Ruins of the Buddhist Vihara at Paharpur
Belarus and Poland:	Bialowieza Forest
Benin:	Royal Palaces of Abomey
Bolivia:	City of Potosi; Jesuit Missions of the Chiquitos; Historic City of Sucre
Brazil:	Historic Town of Ouro Preto; Historic Centre of Olinda; Historic Centre of Salvador (Bahia); Sanctuary of Bom Jesus in Congonhas; Iguazu NP; Brasilia; Serra da Capivara NP
Bulgaria:	Boyana Church; Madara Rider; Thracian Tomb of Kazanlak; Rock-hewn Churches of Ivanovo; Ancient City of Nessebar; Rila Monastery; Srebarna Nature Reserve; Pirin NP; Thracian Tomb of Sveshtari
Cambodia:	Angkor
Canada:	L'Anse aux Meadows National HP; Nahanni NP; Dinosaur Provincial Park; Anthony Island; Head-Smashed-In Bison Jump Complex; Wood Buffalo NP; Canadian Rocky Mountain Parks including the Burgess Shale; Historic Area of Quebec; Gros Morne NP; Lunenburg Old Town
Canada & the USA:	Kluane and Wrangell-St. Elias NPs; Waterton Glacier International Peace Park
Central African Republic:	Manovo-Gounda St. Floris NP
Chile:	Rapa Nui NP
China:	Mount Taishan; The Great Wall; Imperial Palaces of the Ming and Qing Dynasties; Mogao Caves; Mausoleum of

First Qin Emperor; Peking Man Site at Zhoukoudian; Mount Huangshan; Jiuzhaigou Valley Scenic and Historic Interest Area; Huanglong Scenic and Historic Interest Area; Wulingyuan Scenic and Historic Interest Area; Mountain Resort and its Outlying Temples, Chengde; Temple and Cemetery of Confucius, and the Kong Family Mansion in Qufu; Ancient Building Complex in Wudang Mountains; Potala Palace, Lhasa

Colombia: Port, Fortress and Group of Monuments, Carthagena; Los Katios NP; Historic Centre of Santa Cruz de Mompox; National Archaeological Park of Tierradentro; San Agustin Archaeological Park

Costa Rica/Panama: La Amistad NP

Croatia: Old City of Dubrovnik; Historical Complex of Split with the Palace of Diocletian; Plitvice Lakes NP

Cuba: Old Havana and its Fortifications; Trinidad and the Valley de los Ingenios

Cyprus: Paphos; Painted Churches in the Troodos region

Czech Republic: Historic Centre of Prague; Historic Centre of Cesky Krumlov; Historic Centre de Telc; Pilgrimage Church of St John of Nepomuk at Zelena Hora; Historic Centre of Kutna Hora with the Church of St Barbara and the Cathedral of Our Lady at Sedlec

Denmark: Jelling Mounds, Runic Stones and Church; Roskilde Cathedral

Dominican Republic: Colonial City of Santo Domingo

Ecuador: Galapagos Islands; Historic Centre of Quito; Sangay NP

Egypt: Memphis and its Necropolis and the Pyramid Fields from Giza to Dashur; Ancient Thebes with its Necropolis; Nubian Monuments from Abu Simbel to Philae; Islamic Cairo; Abu Mena

El Salvador: Joya de Ceren Archaeological Site

Ethiopia: Simien NP; Rock-hewn Churches of Lalibela; Fasil Ghebbi in the Gondar Region; Lower Valley of the Awash; Tiya; Aksum; Lower Valley of the Omo

Finland: Old Rauma; Fortress of Suomenlinna; Petajavesi Old Church

France: Mont St. Michel and its Bay; Chartres Cathedral; Palace and Park of Versailles; Basilica and Hill at Vézelay; Decorated Grottoes of the Vézère Valley, including Lascaux Caves; Palace and Park of Fontainebleau; Chateau and Estate of Chambord; Amiens Cathedral; the Roman Theatre and its surroundings and the Triumphal Arch of Orange; Roman and Romanesque Monuments of Arles; Cistercian Abbey of Fontenay; Royal Saltworks of

	Arc-et-Senans; Place Stanislas, Place de la Carrière and Place d'Alliance in Nancy; Church of St.Savin-sur-Gartempe; Cape Girolata, Cape Porto and Scandola Nature Reserve in Corsica; Pont du Gard Roman Aqueduct; Strasbourg- Grande-Île; Paris, Banks of the Seine; Cathedral of Notre-Dame, former Abbey of Saint-Remi and Palace of Tau, Rheims; Bourges Cathedral; Historic Centre of Avignon
Georgia:	City-Museum Reserve of Mtskheta; Bagrati Cathedral and Gelati Monastery
Germany:	Aachen Cathedral; Speyer Cathedral; Wurzburg Residence with the Court Gardens and Residence Square; Pilgrimage Church of Wies; Castles of Augustburg and Falkenlust at Bruhl; St. Mary's Cathedral and St. Michael's Church at Hildesheim; Monuments of Trier.
Ghana:	Forts and Castles of Ghana; Ashanti Traditional Buildings.
Greece:	Temple of Apollo Epicurius at Bassae; Archaeological Site of Delphi; Acropolis, Athens; Mount Athos; Meteora; Paleochristian and Byzantine Monuments of Thessalonika; Archaeological Site of Epidaurus; Medieval City of Rhodes; Mistra; Archaeological Site of Olympia; Delos; Monasteries of Daphni, Hossios Luckas and Nea Moni of Chios; Pythagoreion and Heraion of Samos
Guatemala:	Tikal NP; Antigua Guatemala; Archaeological Park & Ruins of Quirigua
Guinea & Ivory Coast:	Mount Nimba Strict Nature Reserve
Haiti:	National HP - Citadel, Sans Souci, Ramiers
Honduras:	Maya Site of Copan; Rio Platano Biosphere Reserve
Hungary:	Budapest, the Banks of the Danube and the Buda Castle Quarter; Hollokö
Hungary and Slovak Republic:	Caves of the Aggtelek Karst and Slovak Karst
India:	Ajanta Caves; Ellora Caves; Agra Fort; Taj Mahal; Sun Temple at Konarak; Group of Monuments at Mahabalipuram; Kaziranga NP; Manas Wildlife Sanctuary; Keoladeo NP; Churches and Convents of Goa; Group of Monuments at Khajuraho; Group of Monuments at Hampi; Fatehpur Sikri; Group of Monuments at Pattadakal; Elephanta Caves; Brihadisvara Temple, Thanjavur; Sundarbans NP; Nanda Devi NP; Buddhist Monuments at Sanchi; Humayun's Tomb, Delhi; Qutb Minar and its Monuments, Delhi
Indonesia:	Borobudur Temple Compounds; Ujung Kulon NP; Komodo NP; Prambanan Temple Compounds

Iran:	Tchogha Zanbil; Persepolis; Meidan-e-Shah of Esfahan
Iraq:	Hatra
Ireland:	Archaeological Ensemble of the Bend of the Boyne
Italy:	Rock Drawings in Valcamonica; Historic Centre of Rome; Church and Dominican Convent of Santa Maria delle Grazie in Milan with *The Last Supper* by Leonardo da Vinci; Historic Centre of Florence; Venice and its Lagoon; Piazza del Duomo, Pisa; Historic Centre of San Gimignano; I Sassi di Matera; Vicenza, City of Palladio; Historic Centre of Siena; Historic Centre of Naples; Crespi d'Adda; Ferrara, City of the Renaissance
Ivory Coast:	Taï NP; Comoé NP
Japan:	Buddhist Monuments in the Horyu-ji Area; Himeji-jo; Yakushima; Shirakami-Sanchi; Historic Monuments of Kyoto; Historic Villages of Shirakawa-go and Gokayama
Jerusalem:	Old City of Jerusalem and its Walls
Jordan:	Petra; Quseir Amra
Korea:	Sokkuram Buddhist Grotto; Haeinsa Temple Changgyong P'Ango, the Depositories of the Tripitaka Koreana Woodblocks; Chongmyo Shrine
Laos:	Town of Luang Prabang
Lebanon:	Anjar; Baalbek; Byblos; Tyre
Libya:	Archaeological Site of Leptis Magna; Archaeological Site of Sabratha; Archaeological Site of Cyrene; Rock-art Sites of Tadrart Acacus; Old Town of Ghadames
Lithuania:	Vilnius Historic Centre
Luxembourg:	City of Luxembourg Old Quarters and Fortifications
Macedonia:	Ohrid Region
Madagascar:	Tsingy de Bemaraha Strict Nature Reserve
Malawi:	Lake Malawi NP.
Mali:	Old Towns of Djenne; Timbuktu; Cliff of Bandiagara (Land of the Dogons)
Malta:	Hal Saflieni Hypogeum; City of Valletta; Ggantija Temples
Mexico:	Sian Ka'an; Pre-Hispanic City and NP of Palenque; Historic Centre of Mexico City and Xochimilco; Pre-Hispanic City of Teotihuacan; Historic Centre of Oaxaca and Archaeological Site of Monte Alban; Historic Centre of Puebla; Historic Town of Guanjuato and Adjacent Mines; Pre-Hispanic City of Chichen-Itza; Historic Centre of Morelia; Pre-Historic City of El Tajin; Whale Sanctuary of El Vizcaino; Historic Centre of Zacatecas; Rock Paintings of the Sierra de San Francisco; Earliest 16th-Century Monasteries on the Slopes of Popocatepetl

Morocco:	Medina of Fez; Medina of Marrakesh; Ksar of Aït-Ben-Haddou
Mozambique:	Island of Mozambique
Nepal:	Sagarmatha NP; Kathmandu Valley; Royal Chitwan NP
Netherlands:	Schokland and Surroundings
New Zealand:	Te Watipounamu-South West New Zealand; Tongariro NP
Niger:	Air and Tenéré Natural Reserves
Norway:	Urnes Stave Church; Bryggen Area in Bergen; Roros; Rock Drawings of Alta
Oman:	Bahla Fort; Archaeological Sites of Bat, Al-Khutm and Al-Ayn; Arabian Oryx Sanctuary
Pakistan:	Archaeological Ruins at Mohenjo Daro; Taxila; Buddhist Ruins of Takht-i-Bahi and Neighbouring City Remains at Sahr-i-Bahlol; Historical Monuments of Thatta; Fort and Shalimar Gardens in Lahore
Panama:	Fortifications on the Caribbean Side at Portobelo-San Lorenzo; Darien NP
Paraguay:	Jesuit Missions of La Santisma Trinidad de Parana and Jesus de Tavarangue
Peru:	City of Cuzco; Historic Sanctuary of Machu Picchu; Archaeological Site of Chavin; Huascaran NP; Archaeological Site of Chan Chan; Manu NP; Historic Centre of Lima; Rio Abiseo NP; Lines and Geoglyphs of Nasca and Pampas de Jumana
Philippines:	Tubbataha Reef Marine Park; Baroque Churches of Philippines; Rice Terraces of the Philippine Cordilleras
Poland:	Historic Centre of Krakow; Wieliczka Salt Mine; Auschwitz-Birkenau Concentration Camps; Bialowieze NP; Historic Centre of Warsaw; Old City of Zamosc
Portugal:	Central Zone of the Town of Angra do Heroismo in the Azores; Monastery of the Hieronymites and Tower of Belem in Lisbon; Monastery of Batalha; Convent of Christ in Tomar; Historic Centre of Evora; Monastery of Alcobaca; Cultural Landscape of Sintra
Romania:	Danube Delta; Biertan and its Fortified Church; Monastery of Horezu; Churches of Moldavia
Russian Federation:	Historic Centre of St Petersburg and Related Group of Monuments; Kizhi Pogost; Kremlin and Red Square, Moscow; Historic Monuments of Novgorod and Surroundings; Cultural and Historic Ensemble of the Solovetsky Islands; Architectural Ensemble of the Trinity Sergius Lavre in Sergiev Posad; Church of the Ascension, Kolomenskoye; the Virgin Komi Forests
Senegal:	Gorée Island; Niokolo-Koba NP; Djoudj National Bird Sanctuary

Seychelles:	Aldabra Atoll; Vallée de Mai Nature Reserve
Slovakia:	Vlkolinec; Banska Stiavnica; Spissky Hrad and its Associated Cultural Monuments
Slovenia	Skocjan Caves
Spain:	Mosque of Cordoba; the Alhambra and the Generalife in Granada; Burgos Cathedral; Monastery and Site of the Escorial in Madrid; Gaudi's Park Guell, Guell Palace and Casa Mila in Barcelona; Altamira Cave; Old Town of Segovia and its Aqueduct; Churches of the Kingdom of Asturias; Old Town of Santiago de Compostela; Old Town of Avila with its Extramuros Churches; Mudejar Architecture of Teruel; Historic City of Toledo; Garajonay NP; Old Town of Caceres; Cathedral, Alcazar and Archivo de Indias in Seville; Old City of Salamanca; Poblet Monastery; Archaeological Ensemble of Merida; Royal Monastery of Santa Maria de Guadalupe; Route of Santiago de Compostela; Doñana NP
Sri Lanka:	Sacred City of Anuradhapura; Ancient City of Polonnaruva; Ancient City of Sigiriya; Sinharaja Forest Reserve; Sacred City of Kandy; Old Town of Galle and its Fortifications; Golden Temple of Dambulla
Sweden:	Royal Domain of Drottningholm; Birka and Hovgarden Engelsberg Ironworks; Rock Carvings in Tanum; Skogskyrkogarden; Hanseatic Town of Visby
Switzerland:	Convent of St. Gall; Benedictine Convent of St. John at Müstair; Old City of Berne
Syria:	Ancient City of Damascus; Ancient City of Bosra; Site of Palmyra; Ancient City of Aleppo
Tanzania:	Ngorongoro Conservation Area; Ruins of Kilwa Kisiwani and Ruins of Songo Mnara; Serengeti NP; Selous Game Reserve; Kilimanjaro NP
Thailand:	Historic Town of Sukhothai and Associated Historic Towns; Historic City of Ayutthaya and Associated Historic Towns; Thungyai-Huai Kha Khaeng Wildlife Sanctuaries; Ban Chiang Archaeological Site
Tunisia:	Medina of Tunis; Archaeological Site of Carthage; Amphitheatre of El Djem; Ichkeul NP; Punic Town of Kerkouane and its Necropolis; Medina of Sousse; Kairouan
Turkey:	Historic Areas of Istanbul; Goreme NP and the Rock Sites of Cappadocia; Great Mosque and Hospital of Divrigi; Hattusas; Nemrut Dagi; Xanthos-Letoon; Hierapolis-Pamukkale; Town of Safranbolu
Ukraine:	Kiev, Santa-Sophia Cathedral and Related Monastic Buildings, Kiev-Pechersk Lavra

United Kingdom:	Giant's Causeway and Causeway Coast; Durham Castle and Cathedral; Ironbridge Gorge; Studley Royal Park including the Ruins of Fountains Abbey; Stonehenge, Avebury and Associated Sites; Castles and Town Walls of King Edward in Gwynedd; St Kilda; City of Bath; Old and New Towns of Edinburgh; Canterbury Cathedral, St Augustine's Abbey and St Martin's Church; Hadrian's Wall; Blenheim Palace; Westminster Abbey & Palace; the Tower of London; Henderson Island; Gough Island Wildlife Reserve
Uruguay:	Historic Quarter of City of Colonia del Sacramento
USA:	Redwood NP; Mesa Verde NP; Yellowstone NP; Grand Canyon NP; Everglades NP; Independence Hall National HP; Mammoth Cave NP; Olympic NP; Cahokia Mounds Statue Historic Site; Great Smoky Mountains NP; La Fortaleza and San Juan National Historic Site in Puerto Rico; Statue of Liberty National Monument; Yosemite NP; Chaco Culture National Historical Park; Monticello and university of Virginia in Charlottesville; Hawaii Volcanoes NP; Pueblo de Taos; Carlsbad Caverns NP
Uzbekistan:	Itchan Kala; Historic Centre of Bukhara
Vatican City/Italy:	Historic Centre of Rome, the Properties of the Holy See in that City Enjoying Extraterritorial Rights and San Paolo Fuori le Mura
Venezuela:	Coro and its Port; Canaima NP
Vietnam:	Complex of Hue Monuments; Ha Long Bay
Yemen:	Old City of San'a; Old Walled City of Shibam; Historic Town of Zabid
Yugoslavia:	Stari Ras and Sopocani; Kotor Region; Durmitor NP; Studenica Monastery
Zaire:	Virunga NP; Garamba NP; Kahuzi-Biega NP; Salonga NP
Zambia/Zimbabwe:	Victoria Falls
Zimbabwe:	Mana Pools NP; Sapi and Chewore Safari Areas; Great Zimbabwe National Monument; Khami Ruins National Monument

Much of the information for this book has come from field research at the sites themselves or from guidebooks and other publications produced by the various attractions and amenity groups associated with them. I have also found the ETB's *Insights* marketing publication especially helpful. Information on new attractions has often come from newspaper cuttings or from travel and tourism industry magazines. The same texts have often provided information for several chapters.

Chapter 1 : From Tourist Attractions to Heritage Tourism

Treasures for the Nation: Conserving Our Heritage, BM Publications, 1989
Sightseeing in 1995, ETB/BTA
English Heritage Monitor, ETB, 1996
Visitor Attractions Survey: 1995, STB
Visitors to Tourist Attractions in Wales 1995, WTB
Visitor Attraction Report 1995, WTB
Visitor Attraction Report: 1995, NITB
Foreign Language Provision in the UK Tourism Industry, J. Hillage, ETB Insights, 1993
Tourism Law, Second Edition, J. Corke, Elm Publications, 1993
School Visits Market, P. Keeley, ETB Insights, 1993
Primary School Visits Market, P. Keeley, ETB Insights, 1993
Visitor Attractions and the Tourism Industry... Helping Each Other, P, Colton, ETB Insights, 1995
The Disability Discrimination Act and the Tourism Industry, C. Gooding, ETB Insights, 1995
Visitor Attractions and the Commercial Sector, Dr. J. Heeley, ETB Insights, 1989
The Impact of Recession on Attendances at Major Visitor Attractions, J. Brown, ETB Insights, 1992
What Makes a Successful Attraction?, B. Martin and S. Mason, ETB Insights, 1990
The National Lottery... Can Tourism Win the Jackpot?, S. Beioley, ETB Insights, 1996
The Heritage Industry, R. Hewison, Methuen, 1987
Britain's Heritage: The Creation of the National Heritage Memorial Fund, A. Jones, Weidenfeld &Nicolson, 1985
Benefiting from the Heritage, Y. French, ETB Insights, 1992
Heritage Tourism, New Leisure Markets, 1993
Loot... The Heritage of Plunder, E.R. Chamberlin, Thames & Hudson, 1983
Preservation Pays, M. Hanna and M. Binney, SAVE Britain's Heritage
The Future of Heritage Attractions, J. Swarbrooke, ETB Insights, 1993

Chapter 2 : The Museums

The British Museum...Purpose and Politics, David M. Wilson, BM Publications, 1989
That Noble Cabinet: A History of the British Museum, Edward Miller, Deutsch 1973

The Museum Time Machine, R. Lumley (ed.), Routledge, 1988

A Social History of Museums, K. Hudson, Macmillan, 1975

Palaces of Discovery: The Changing World of Britain's Museums, S. Tait, Quiller, 1989

What's Happening to our Museums? Holiday Which?, 1990

National Heritage Museum of the Year Award Judges' Report, 1996

Preserving the Past, E.R. Chamberlin, Dent, 1979

Priceless Heritage...The Future of Museums, I. Finlay, Faber and Faber, 1977

Alfred Waterhouse and the Natural History Museum, M. Girouard, Yale University Press, 1981

National Museum of Science & Industry Annual Review, 1995/6

Museum and Gallery Security, Museums & Galleries Commission, 1996

The Museums Association Annual Report, 1989-90

Neil Cossons, in Leisure Management, Vol. 10, No.1, 1990

Museums and Galleries in Great Britain and Ireland, British Leisure Publications

The North of England Open Air Museum at Beamish, K. Harrop in 'Travel and Tourism', Business Education Publishers Ltd, 1989

Chapter 3 : Stately Homes, Castles, Palaces and Gardens

Royal Parks, D. Edgar, W. H. Allen, 1986

Ruins: Their Preservation and Display, M. W. Thompson, Colonnade, 1981

English Castles, R. Humble, ETB/Weidenfeld & Nicolson, 1984

A History of Country House Visiting, A. Tinniswood, Nt/Blackwell, 1989

National Trust Handbook 1996

Uppark, National Trust guidebook, 1995

The Treasure Houses of England, Travel Trade Manual, 1996

Historic Houses Directory, Historic Houses Association

Caring for Country Houses, National Trust, 1990

Royal Botanic Gardens Kew Three Year Report, 1993-96

Gardens of England and Wales Open to the Public 1996, National Gardens Scheme

Chapter 4 : Religious Heritage

Change and Decay: The future of Our Churches, M. Binney and P. Burman, Studio Vista, 1977

Churches' Salvation...the Work of the Redundant Churches Fund, C. Dalton Country Life, 1986

Historic Churches Preservation Trust Annual Report, 1995

Highgate Cemetery: Victorian Valhalla, V. Gay & F. Barker. John Murray, 1984

Chapter 5 : Other Historical Attractions

The Continuing Heritage: The Story of the Civic Trust Awards, Lionel Esher, Franey, 1982

The Rape of Britain, Avery & Cruidshand, Paul Elek, 1975

Our Vanishing Heritage, M. Binney, Arlington Press, 1984

Underneath English Towns: Interpreting Urban Archaeology, M. Carver, Batsford, 1987

Past Imperfect: The Story of Rescue Archaeology, B. Jones, Heinemann, 1984

Working in Partnership: English Heritage Annual Report, 1994/5

Historic Scotland Annual Report, 1995/6

Cadw Annual Report, 1995/6

Introduction to the Ancient Monuments and Archaeological Areas Act 1979, DOE, 1985

Listed Buildings: The Law and Practice, R. Suddards, Sweet & Maxwell, 1982

Future of the Past, J. Fawcett (ed.), Thames & Hudson, 1976

Great Britain, H. Cleere in Approaches to the Archaeological Heritage, H. Cleere (ed.)

Archaeology and Planning... a Consultative Document, DOE, 1990

Visitors Welcome, HMSO (for English Heritage), 1988

The Jorvik Viking Centre: An Experiment in Archaeological Site Interpretation, P. Addyman & A. Gaynor, International Journal of Museum Management and Curatorship, 1984

York Archaeological Trust Annual Report 1995/6

Remnants, Journal of the English Heritage Education Service

Landmark Trust Handbook, 1996

Chapter 6 : The Arts

Arts Council of England Report 1995/6

Culture or Commodity?...the Economics of the Arts and the Built Environment in the UK, B. Casey, R. Dunlop and S. Selwood, PSI, 1996

Cultural Trends Quarterly, 1994, Policy Studies Institute

Victoria and Albert Museum Annual Report, 1995/6

The National Gallery, M. Wilson, Orbis, 1982

The Arts and the People, R. Shaw, Cape, 1987

The Great Exhibition of 1851, HMSO, 1981

SOLT Box Office Data Report 1993, Dr. C. Gardiner

Theatre Administration, F. Reid, A & C Black, 1983

Chapter 7 : Industrial Heritage

BP Book of Industrial Archaeology, N. Cossons, David and Charles, 1987

The National Trust Guide to Our Industrial Past, A. Burton, 1983

John Broome's Fawlty Towers, M. Tomkinson, The Independent, 1990

Ironbridge Gorge... an Extraordinary Museum, K. Foster, ETB Insights, 1990

Visitor Survey Report for the Ironbridge Gorge Museum Trust, 1985

Ironbridge Gorge Museum Trust Annual Report, 1995

The Regeneration of Bristol City Docks, Bristol City Council Planning Dept., 1987

Industrial Tourism, A. Menzies, ETB Insights, 1989

Portsmouth Harbour, Tourist Development Action Programme Background Document, 1986

Stoke-on-Trent Tourism Information Pack, Stoke-on-Trent City Council, 1996

Stoke-on-Trent City Council Tourism Strategy 1996-97, Stoke-on-Trent City Council, 1996

Visitor's Guide to the Potteries, 1989

Chapter 8 : Transport Heritage

BP Book of Industrial Archaeology, N. Cossons, David and Charles, 1987

The National Trust Guide to Our Industrial Past, A. Burton, 1983

Chapter 9 : Countryside Attractions

A Future for Our Countryside, J. Blunden & N. Curry, Blackwell, 1988

Protected Landscapes: The UK Experience, D. & J. Poore, ISCN, 1987

Visitors to National Parks... Summary of the 1994 Survey Findings, Countryside Commission, 1996

English Nature: The First Five Years, English Nature, 1996

A National Park in the Balance?, Lake District National Park Authority, GCSE Resource Guide

A Vision for Cumbria, Cumbria Tourist Board, 1990

Putting Tourism into Perspective: A Case Study of the Norfolk Broads, P. Mason in 'Tourism', WWF, 1990

Broads Authority Annual Report 1995-96

Designed for Recreation: a Practical Handbook for All Concerned with Providing Leisure Facilities in the Countryside, E. Beazley, Faber & Faber, 1969

The Future for Rural Tourism, B. Lane, ETB Insights, 1989

Farm Tourism, J. Clarke, ETB Insights, 1995

The National Trust Annual Report 1995/6

National Trust for Scotland Annual Trust, 1990

In Search of Neptune, C. Pye-Smith, National Trust, 1990

Forests for the Community, Countryside Commission, 1989

Chapter 10 : Wildlife Attractions

Great Zoos of the World: Their Origins and Significance, Lord Zuckermann (ed.), Weidenfield & Nicolson, 1977

Zoo 2000, J. Cherfas, BBC, 1984

International Zoo Handbook, 1988

The Zoological Society of London Annual Report, 1989-90

The Good Zoo Guide, J. Ironmonger, HarperCollins, 1992

Chapter 11 : Miscellaneous Attractions

Madame Tussaud: Waxworker Extraordinare, A. Leslie & P. Chapman, Hutchinson, 1978

Madame Tussaud's; Chamber of Horrors, P. Chapman, Grafton, 1985

Pearson Annual Report and Accounts, 1989
Travel and Tourism, Third Edition, P. Lavery. Elm Publications, 1996
The Future for Theme Parks, B. Richards, ETB Insights, 1995
Theme Parks, New Leisure Markets, 1996
Managing Inland Water for Leisure and Recreation... an Example for Southern England, D. Oliver, The Environmentalist, 1985
Seaside Resorts, V. Middleton, ETB Insights, 1992
The Seaside Fights Back, P. Travis, ETB Insights, 1992
Tourism and the Environment: The Role of the Seaside, G. Turner, ETB Insights, 1993
Pavilions on the Sea, C. Bainbridge, Robert Hale, 1986
Investing and Living in Bradford, Bradford Economic Development Unit
'Miles Better', J. Henderson in Travel and Tourism, Business Education Publishers Ltd
The Inner City Challenge: Tourism Development in Inner City Regeneration, ETB, 1988

Chapter 12 : Event Attractions

A Seasoned Traveller, C. Wright, Christopher Helm, 1989
Festivals and Special Events, New Leisure Markets, 1995
Garden Festival Wales, C. Thomas, ETB Insights, 1993

Chapter 13 : World Heritage

A Legacy for All, UNESCO, 1982
Our World's Heritage, National Geographic Society, 1987
Properties Included in the World Heritage List, UNESCO, 1995
The World Heritage Newsletter, UNESCO, 1996
The Elgin Marbles; Should They be Returned to Greece?, C. Hitchens, Chatto and Windus, 1987

Chapter 14 : Heritage Marketing

Marketing Tourist Attractions, in 'Marketing in Travel and Tourism', V. Middleton, Heinemann, 1988
Using Exit Surveys at Visitor Attractions, S. Brigg, ETB Insights, 1995
How to Succeed in Off-pead Marketing: Case Studies for British Tourism, BTA
Retailing and Tourism, A. Menzies, ETB Insights, 1989
Marketing for Tourism, C. Holloway & R. Plant, Pitman, 1989

—**M**—

—**N**—

—O—

—P—

—R—

—S—

other books from ELM

Tourism and Leisure Studies

MUSIC INDUSTRY MANAGEMENT AND PROMOTION - Chris Kemp
Music industry management & promotion, plus useful tips if you enter the
business. Using industry terminology, the author's enthusiasm is infectious.
Selecting a band; the agent; managing publicity; marketing; managing the
venue; staffing, crew & security; the perfect promotion; finance &
administration; managing the band; setting up a tour; music events outdoors;
record companies; studio production.
Book 288pp + Single User Program on PC disks, 1 85450 149 6
Network Version on PC disk + Tutor's Manual, 1 85450 142 9

EUROPEAN LEISURE BUSINESSES: strategies for the future
Brian Eaton
Topical, well-researched organisation studies on major companies in the
European Leisure Industry–Stakis, First Leisure, Eurocamp, David Lloyd
Leisure, Rank, Allied Leisure, Ladbrokes and VCI, plus the history, strategy
and competitive environment of European leisure.
Illustrations/maps/charts/tables.
Book 288 pp., 1 85450 230 1   Tutor's Manual 185450 430 4

TOURISM & LEISURE IN THE COUNTRYSIDE second edition
Richard Sharpley
Material for a full year's course with nine stand-alone chapters on countryside
recreation, management, planning and the law. Level HND and above.
Book, 336pp, 185450 245 X, £11.95
Tutor's Manual - one year's course materials, 185450 440 1, £59.00

TRAVEL AND TOURISM, third edition - Patrick Lavery
Introduction to the main sectors of the tourism industry, defining and outlining
the development in the UK, Europe, USA. Enlarged and updated with a new
chapter on sustainable tourism. Level HND and upwards, GNVQ suitable.
An adopted and recommended text in many colleges and universities.
Book, 288pp, 1 85450 199 2
Tutor's Manual, exercises/OHPs, 1 85450 024 4

TRAVEL AND TOURISM: A North-American-European perspective
Patrick Lavery and Carlton Van Doren
An overview of the industry and the role of private and public sectors in the
UK, USA and Europe. Level introductory and upwards for higher education.
Book, 224pp, 1 85450 125 9

TOURISM IN THE U.K. - Pat Yale
The business and management of tourism. With commentary on UK tourist
attractions. Adopted by many colleges and schools as a set text for those new
to the business of tourism. Clearly written, well researched and presented in an
accessible style. Level BTEC National., A level and upwards.
Book - maps, charts and diagrams, 320 pp, 1 85450 017 1
Tutor's Manual - exercises/notes/OHPs, 1 85450 094 5

TOURISM LAW, second edition - Jim Corke
Updated and revised edition of the first text specially written on the law relating
to tourism and travel. New material on EC regulations.
Level HND and upwards.
Book, 480pp, 1 85450 028 7   Tutor's Manual, 1 85450 140 2

TOURISM, TOURISTS AND SOCIETY - Richard Sharpley
An in-depth study of the relationship between tourism and the societies that
both generate and host tourism and tourists. Includes: the effects of social
change on the pattern of tourism consumption; motivation for tourism; impact
of tourism on host societies; and commoditisation and authenticity.
Book, 288pp, 1 85450 159 3
Tutor's Manual - exercises/notes/OHPs, 1 85450 233 6

WATER BASED RECREATION: managing resources for leisure
Fiona McCormack
Comprehensive treatment of the scope and development of water based
resources for leisure. Aspects of management, marketing, environmental issues,
conservation, conflicting uses, access and future trends. The first encapsulation
and full coverage of this important and growing area of leisure management.
The author is a qualified and experienced sailor and instructor.
Book, 320pp, 1 85450 154 2 Tutor's Manual, exercises/OHPs, 1 85450 152 6

Computer Software - PC disks

TRAVEL COMPANY BUSINESS - Ray Garnett
Interactive group exercise in business decisions for a Travel Company.
Can be networked. Demo disk available. Level HND and upwards.
Disk and Tutor's Manual, 1 85450 035 X

INTERACTIVE MANAGEMENT SIMULATIONS (DOS)- Humphrey Shaw
To improve decision making and presentation skills. Students work competitively
in groups managing a simulated business. Emphasis on the business and
management aspects rather than the subject or industry context. Disk and Tutor's
Manual. Level BTEC, HND and upwards. Demo disks available.
ISSN 0954-030X. **Football Manager**, 0 946139 24 5;
Property Manager, 0 946139 29 6; **Restaurant Manager**, 0 946139 34 2

Business and Management

EUROPEAN BUSINESS STRATEGY, sixth edition - Terry Garrison
An updated and expanded edition of a popular textbook for business students.
27 well-researched & presented topical case studies from EMU to
Barings Bank, from the BSE crisis to Cable & Wireless.
Level DMS/PG Diploma, MBA. Book, 576pp, 1 85450 169 0
Tutor's Manual, answers/notes 1 85450 415 0

PEOPLE IN ORGANISATIONS, fifth edition – Pat Armstrong & Chris Dawson
A popular introduction to managing people at work. Includes theory and
application, underlying psychology & personnel aspects. Suitable for HND
level upwards. Adopted at many colleges for full time and part time courses
and especially for post-experience short courses for managers and professionals.
Book, 472pp, 1 85450 240 9   Tutor's Manual, 1 85450 407 X

ELM Publications, Seaton House, Kings Ripton, Huntingdon PE17 2NJ.
Telephone **01487**–773254 or –773238, fax –773359